SPECIAL BRANCH WAR

SPECIAL BRANCH WAR

Slaughter in the Rhodesian Bush
Southern Matabeleland, 1976-1980

Ed Bird

Helion & Company Ltd

Helion & Company Limited
26 Willow Road
Solihull
West Midlands
B91 1UE
England
Tel. 0121 705 3393
Fax 0121 711 4075
Email: info@helion.co.uk
Website: www.helion.co.uk
Twitter: @helionbooks
Visit our blog http://blog.helion.co.uk/

This edition published by Helion & Company 2014

Designed and typeset by SA Publishing Services, South Africa (kerrincocks@gmail.com)
Cover designed by SA Publishing Services, South Africa (kerrincocks@gmail.com)
Printed by Henry Ling Limited, Dorchester, Dorset

Text © E.A. Bird 2013
Images © as individually credited

Front cover: The inimitable Sergeant Theo Nel BCR of 1 Indep Company en route to a Fire Force action. Photo courtesy of Theo Nel.

ISBN 978 1 909982 34 5

British Library Cataloguing-in-Publication Data.
A catalogue record for this book is available from the British Library.

All rights reserved. No part of this publication may be reproduced, stored in a retrieval system, or transmitted, in any form, or by any means, electronic, mechanical, photocopying, recording or otherwise, without the express written consent of Helion & Company Limited.

For details of other military history titles published by Helion & Company Limited contact the above address, or visit our website: http://www.helion.co.uk.

We always welcome receiving book proposals from prospective authors.

To each and every member of the security forces and civil administration who served so valiantly during hostilities in the Beitbridge area, particularly those who were maimed or who paid the supreme sacrifice:
I salute you.

To the members of the BSAP either stationed at or seconded to Beitbridge who, although greatly outnumbered by the enemy and in spite of being poorly equipped, did not hesitate in taking the fight to the enemy, especially the brave young policemen of the Ground Coverage teams who fought and died for a cause they believed in:
I salute you.

To the community of Beitbridge who, in spite of enemy artillery and heavy mortar attacks, stood together with heads held high during this difficult period:
I salute you.

Contents

Illustrations	8
Maps	15
Glossary	28
Foreword *by Winston Hart*	32
Introduction *by Don Price*	33
Special Branch Beitbridge incident log *by Brian Perkins*	37
Author's note	38
About Rhodesia	40
Prologue	44

Chapter One:	Selous Scouts attachment, 1974–1976	50
Chapter Two:	Beitbridge: first blood to ZANLA, May 1967	65
Chapter Three:	Insidious intensification, late 1976	69
Chapter Four:	Overt intensification, January 1977–June 1977	73
Chapter Five:	Landmines, ambushes and poison, July–December 1977	89
Chapter Six:	Protected villages and the litany of terror continues, January–June 1978	108
Chapter Seven:	Dirty tricks	132
Chapter Eight:	A busy two months, July–August 1978	140
Chapter Nine:	Deployment of 1 (Indep) Company Rhodesian African Rifles, September–December 1978	150
Chapter Ten:	Routine slaughter, January–June 1979	180
Chapter Eleven:	*Sweet Banana* and a Q bus, July–November 1979	218
Chapter Twelve:	Transfer to Gwanda, November 1979	239
Chapter Thirteen:	A case of political expedience	242

Afterword		246
Appendix I:	The *Povo* system: Beitbridge area	251
Appendix II:	Samples of the incident log	258
Appendix III:	Weapons used in the Beitbridge area of conflict	277
Appendix IV:	Letter from Lt-Gen G.P. Walls to Margaret Thatcher	282
Appendix V:	Foreign and Commonwealth Office responds	285

Illustrations

Section 1

Growing up on my parents' farm in the Bembesi area of Matabeleland, 1951. My sister Pat is flanked by my brother Ken (left) and me (right); my youngest brother Martin was only born the following year.

Recruit Squad 4/64 dismounted pass-out parade, December 1964. Back row from left: Constables Stead, Bird, Mackenzie, Scott-Roger, Harrison; third row: Constables Deamer, Musson, Gerber, Thornley, Taylor, Bagley; second row: Constables Rosser, Tunney, Nevitt, Little, Wood; seated: STAFF Senior Inspector Winchcombe (squad instructor), Mr D.W. Wright (Deputy Commandant), Mr G.M. Harries (Acting Commissioner), Mr A.R. Godwin (Commandant Depot), Mr Downham, Depot Chief Inspector Trangmar.

The initial PATU Section Leaders' course held over a two-week period in the Mavuradona Mountains in the Centenary/Sipolilo area in 1967. I am standing fifth from right in the middle row and my brother Ken is third from right in the same row. The instructors on this course were, among others, Chief Superintendent Bill Bailey who had fought with the Long Range Desert Group during the Second World War and Reserve Patrol Officer Reg Seekings DCM MM (seated ninth from the left) who was a founding member of the SAS with Colonel David Stirling. I took the training and deployments very seriously which stood me in good stead during the coming years.

Preparing for the mounted pass-out parade at the BSAP Depot, Salisbury, December 1964.

Patrolling the Zambezi Valley in the early days of the newly-formed Police Anti-Terrorist Unit (PATU). Back from left: unknown, Constable Fambarayi and Constable Bernard (with Greener shotgun); front: Patrol Officer Dave Lee, Section Officer Dave Parry (with Sterling sub-machine gun) and me. We had only recently been issued with Belgian-manufactured FN rifles, replacing the pre-First World War .303 Lee Enfields (SMLEs).

The famous BSAP Jam Jar Inn at Kariba – so named because of the lack of glasses when it first opened, forcing the lads to use alternative drinking vessels, the most popular being empty jam jars – on the occasion of the transfers of myself (at left), Brain Croasdale, Tim Yeoman and Mark Berger in June 1969.

Visiting the Concession police station in my modified Land Rover in early 1973 with the suave George Mitchell in the passenger seat. Looking on are Section Officer Ted Crawford and Inspector Robin Johnson, respectively the 2 i/c and i/c of the station.

Me posing inside of the Selous Scout fort at Mount Darwin. The photo was taken from my bedroom door with the operations and radio rooms directly behind me. The pale concrete in the background is the helipad.

With Winston Hart (right) in the Mount Darwin area, 1974. *Photo Winston Hart*

In 1974 I revisited the site of the vehicle ambush in the Mukumbura area where I had been wounded the year before. *Photo Winston Hart*

Maya sitting between old friends Reg and Veronica Anderson while on holiday on Paradise Island, Mozambique in 1975. Reg's two boys Gerald and Alec are also in the photo.

Gray Branfield at Katima Mulilo, South West Africa, after a fishing competition on the Zambezi River in 1988. Gray was to die under tragic circumstances in Iraq in 2004.

Some of my hunting trophies obtained during 1976 in the Beitbridge area. I hunted and shot the leopard on Lesanth Ranch at Les Mitchell's request after it had started killing livestock in spite of the abundance of game on the ranch.

Servicemen enjoying the Four Jacks and a concert at Mount Darwin, 3 February 1976. Fred Schmitt, i/c Chesa Ground Coverage base, is on the left in the white shirt and I am back centre with the big grin. *Photo Bulawayo Chronicle*

Patrol Officer Dave Ward in 1977. *Photo Dave Ward*

Engineers examining the TMH-46 landmine crater after the mine was 'found' by Ian 'Perkie" Perkins on the Tshiturapadzi road. The damaged mine-protected Land Rover can be clearly seen and although extensively damaged, it was repaired and returned for service. Apart from earache Perkie and his passenger escaped unscathed. *Photo Dave Ward*

A plucky Ian Perkins and his faithful Bloggs only moments after the Land Rover he was driving detonated a boosted landmine. Geoff Blyth – to be involved in four landmine detonations but who on this occasion was travelling in the escort vehicle – looks on. *Photo Ian Perkins*

Ian Perkins at the Beitbridge police single quarters with his faithful dog which survived a landmine detonation on the Tshiturapadzi road in 1977. *Photo Ian Perkins*

The placid Limpopo River at the gorge during the dry season. The trees on the southern bank were under water during the floods of 1976.

Another view of the Limpopo during the dry season.

Floodwaters subside on the Umzingwani River at the access drift to River Ranch and Tuli. In 1977 I was involved in a contact with terrorists about two hundred metres downstream from the drift before the terrorists fled into the thick riverine vegetation.

Ian Perkins in a dried riverbed in the Mtetengwe TTL, 1977. *Photo Ian Perkins*

Tshiturapadzi police base, 1977. *Photo Ian Perkins*

Substantial defences at Tshiturapadzi police base, 1977. *Photo Ian Perkins*

In 1977, the SAP CID in Messina requested assistance from the BSAP as there had been a spate of break-ins on their side of the border with all indications that Rhodesian criminals were involved. A Beitbrige police team under Patrol Officer Ian Perkins crossed the Limpopo River from South Africa one night and the following morning located the gang's spoor, resulting in two of the criminals being shot and the recovery of all the stolen goods. Here the team poses with the recovered goods in front of SAP CID vehicles. From left are NS Patrol Officers Steve Thomas, Tom Vafeus, Mike Harvey, Remo Gardini and Constable Sibanda. *Photo Ian Perkins*

3 March 1977. I and a very brave man – my only staff member not wounded in action during the previous two days – pose with weapons recovered from these engagements: an RPD machine gun, an RPG-7 rocket launcher plus two projectiles and boosters, AKM/AK-47 rifles, stick grenades, a 60mm mortar bomb, a tin of AK/RPD ammunition and blood-soaked AK-47 magazine webbing. *Photo Dave Ward*

A PATU stick with captured weapons after a contact in the Tshiturapadzi area, 1977.

The high-level security bridge over the Bubye River in the Chikwarakwara area in 1977. The left bank is the Chipise TTL and the right the Sengwe TTL. Days after this photograph was taken, one span of the newly-constructed bridge was washed away by floodwaters and was never to be repaired during hostilities. *Photo Dave Ward*

Tshiturapadzi police base, 1977. *Photo Dave Ward*

A Hyena mine-protected vehicle.

Section 2 (Colour section)

Shortly after my arrival in Beitbridge with my newly-issued mine-protected Land Rover.

Tshiturapadzi police base, Christmas Eve 1976. Patrol Officer Dave Ward's mine-protected Land Rover which rear-ended a Hyena MPV that had been towing the Land Rover when the patrol was ambushed and the Hyena was hit by RPG-7 rocket fire, causing it stop abruptly. *Photo Dave Ward*

Tshiturapadzi police base, Christmas Eve 1976. Unidentified security force members who had been ambushed only hours earlier pose with the damaged Land Rover and Hyena MPV. *Photos Dave Ward*

One of the dozens of fuel tankers ambushed and destroyed by terrorists on the main Bulawayo–Beitbridge road. This tanker was empty and stopped while travelling to South Africa to replenish stocks in 1977. The terrorists pulled the vehicle off the road – the Mtetengwe TTL, their escape route, is on that side of the road – before destroying it; smarter groups destroyed the vehicles on the road itself, causing damage to the tarmacadam and blocking the road for hours.. *Photo Geoff Blyth*

Geoff Blyth posing with the Hyena MPV shortly after being blown up on the Tshiturapadzi Road in 1977. His dog Jock was also in the vehicle. *Photo Geoff Blyth*

A police patrol on the Tshiturapadzi road locates another landmine, the hard way, 1977. *Photo Geoff Blyth*

A policeman at the Tshiturapadzi police base in 1977. *Photo Dave Ward*

Panhard armoured cars parked outside the Beitbridge police mess in 1977. *Photo Dave Ward*

Scouter X-Ray, a temporary Police Ground Coverage patrol base on Robin Watson's Mikado Ranch in 1977 prior to the establishment of more permanent facilities. Dave Ward relaxes on his stretcher. *Photo Dave Ward*

Dave Ward's Scouter X-Ray team at the entrance to the more permanent base on Mikado Ranch. They are armed with an assortment of weapons including G3 and FN rifles, an MAG machine gun and a 60mm mortar, Dave with an AK-47. The mountain in the background is in the Siyoka TTL, the site where on the 13 October 1978 the Beitbridge Fire Force attacked a terrorist base and killed six ZANLA terrorists, the entire command structure of the Siyoka Detatchment. *Photo Dave Ward*

A Rhodesian Air Force DC-3 Dakota preparing to land at the Tshiturapadzi airstrip in 1977. The sparsely populated scrub-mopane terrain is typical of the Beitbridge area. *Photo Dave Ward*

A typical police Land Rover: open-doored, vulnerable and they went everywhere.

Two of the outstanding Shangaan trackers based at the Tshiturapadzi police base in 1977. Members of the African Field Reserve, the Shangaans were outstanding men of the bush, blessed with phenomenal bushcraft and tracking skills. *Photo Dave Ward*

Fire Force Delta prepares to deploy from the Mazunga airfield, October 1978. Stop 1 emplanes in the foreground. Second Lieutenant Arthur Kegel is standing at left, I am sitting in the door of the helicopter checking my RPD and Sergeant Theo Nel approaches on the right. Within the hour we were in action against a large ZANLA force in the Mtetengwe TTL. *Photo Theo Nel*

The inimitable Sergeant Theo Nel BCR (left) of 1 Indep Company en route to a Fire Force action. Nel, along with several 1 Indep officers, followed Major Price to the RLI on his transfer as OC 3 Commando. *Photo Theo Nel*

The Pookie landmine-detection vehicle, a marvel of Rhodesian engineering. *Photo Theo Nel*

The Zulu Base camp guard.

At the Limpopo Gorge the day before I left Beitbridge on transfer to Gwanda, November 1979.

Map: Rhodesian Security Forces operational boundaries.

Section 3

The wedding of Alice Cook and John Bryan at Beitbridge in mid-1977. Alice, Bruce's daughter, ran the police communication centre before resigning to get married. Others in the photo are from left: Don Munroe, the Liebigs Ranch Mazunga Section HQ manager, District Commissioner's wife Phyllis Watson obscuring her husband Lew, Mrs Roth and my neighbour Monty van Vuuren of the Parker Hale .30/06 rifle saga.

Another wedding shot of Alice and John. In the foreground is Tom Crawford, the Liebigs Ranch Shobi Section manager and ex-member of the BSAP. Mimi Cawood is at the back (with spectacles) with her sister Norma on her left. Mimi took over the communication centre from Alice and played an anchor role at the station where she stayed until after the end of the 1979 ceasefire.

Cleaning up at the Beitbridge foot and mouth quarantine camp after the Shu Shine bus was commandeered for the round trip to Tshiturapadzi in early 1977. We had dressed as locals in an attempt to lure the terrorists into contact. I am smiling on the left, with Bruce Cook directly behind me.

Another shot of the clean-up. Piet van der Merwe of River Ranch is washing his hands in the centre.

Major Don Price BCR.

Pete Burgoyne's bachelor party in the Bulawayo SB mess, 1978. Standing are Ken Bird and Hamish Scott-Barnes; in front Les Milne, Pete Burgoyne and Willie van der Merwe.

Captain André van Rooyen, the SADF Liaison Officer and his wife Carmen on their wedding day in November 1979. Gail White and Brian Perkins look on.

'Les Girls' – Patsy Smith, Sharron Bailey and Gail White – prepare to strut their stuff at the Beitbridge Club, late 1979. Due to the town's isolation the local community had to band together to provide their own entertainment.

'Beauty and the Beast' – Sharron Bailey briefs Keith Lowe of the BSAP on his duties as a bunny boy at the Beitbridge Club, late 1979.

Patsy posing on my 3.5 Chevrolet, November 1979. This was an ex-SAP vehicle that had been issued to Lieutenant Johan Taute of the Security Branch and which I purchased at an SAP auction held at the Messina police station in 1977 after it had been boarded. The auctioneer was under strict instruction to ensure that I purchased the car for precisely R100. To this end all the tyres were deflated, the spare tyre and battery were removed and tatty electrical wiring placed strategically in the engine and dashboard. After the auction the tyres were inflated, the battery and spare wheel replaced and the wiring removed and I drove happily out of the Messina police station.

Notification that the BSAP Commissioner had instructed that a 'Note of Good Work' be brought to my attention. This was awarded for my work while attached to Special Branch in 1972–73 and for my actions during the vehicle ambush of 1973.

The Commissioner's Commendation (Bronze Baton) was awarded for leading a successful rescue operation to save the lives of four African children who were stranded on a fast-disappearing island in the middle of the flooded crocodile-infested Lundi River. Patrol Officer Jim Higham and Constable Gwala were also awarded the Bronze Baton for their brave efforts in the rescue, undertaken in 1972 when I was stationed at Chibi.

The Commissioner's Special Commendation (Silver Baton) was awarded to me during September 1977 in recognition of actions against the enemy in the Beitbridge area.

BSAP Gwanda District OC, Officers in Charge and Members in Charge, December 1979. Standing from left: Ed Bird, P.J. Cloete, G.J. Oberholzer, C.T. Crage, R.A. Munro, P. Frankleyne; seated: R.G. Francis, T.A. Deacon, D.W. Kerr, H.G. Marshall, D.C. Waddon, D.C. Blake, Brian Perkins.

The court summons for Don Price, Neill Jackson and me to appear in the Bulawayo Regional Court on 5 May 1980. Detective Chief Superintendent Dave Blacker was really going for the jugular by splitting the charges against the three of us.

The Limpopo River in full flood, looking south and upstream from the Limpopo Gorge and Beitbridge, late 1976.

The Beitbridge PATU stick at the Tshiturapadzi police base, 1977. Standing from left: the late Tom Crawford, stick leader, Doug Dugmore Eddie King and Herman Neimeyer; Aleck Croik is sitting. *Photo Ian Perkins*

Steve Acornley guides a typical SB vehicle patrol across a swollen stream in the Gwanda TTL sometime during 1978. Due to the shortage of troops, we were forced to operate without escorts in the operational areas.

Fire Force Delta positioned at Mazunga airfield, October 1978. The four helicopters are identified from left as Stop 1, Stop 2, Stop 3 and, next to the armoured Crocodile troop-carriers at the back, the command K-Car with the 20mm Matra cannon. In the foreground is the air force Lynx strike aircraft armed underwing with 250-pound frantan bombs and SNEB rocket pods, with the machine guns mounted centrally on top of the wing. *Photo Theo Nel*

Sensationalized coverage of the fourth day of the trial as reported in the *Bulawayo Chronicle*.

The final outcome of the trial as reported in the *Bulawayo Chronicle*. Blacker must have fumed when he had to report the not-guilty verdict to the Commissioner of Police.

Prospecting in the Gwanda area, May 1980.

Construction of the 30-ton leaching tanks at the Emerald Isle Mine in Gwanda, June 1980.

Assisting in the filling of the leaching tanks on the Emerald Isle, June 1980.

Emerald Isle, June 1980.

The first 'button' of gold recovered from the Emerald Isle, July 1980. The button weighed seventeen ounces. After refining by the Bullion Department, ten ounces of 99.9% of pure gold was realized – not bad for a beginner. The price of gold at that time was US$650 per fine ounce, a fortune in those days.

Patsy, Diane and Tracey, Durban, October 2011.

The Bird family – Ed, Diane Tracey and Patsy – October 2011.

Maps

Rhodesia	16
Beitbridge area of operations	17
Siyoka	18
Bubye River	20
Nuanetsi	22
Tuli	23
Beitbridge	24
Tshiturapadzi	26
Rhodesian Security Forces operational boundaries	p. 8 colour section

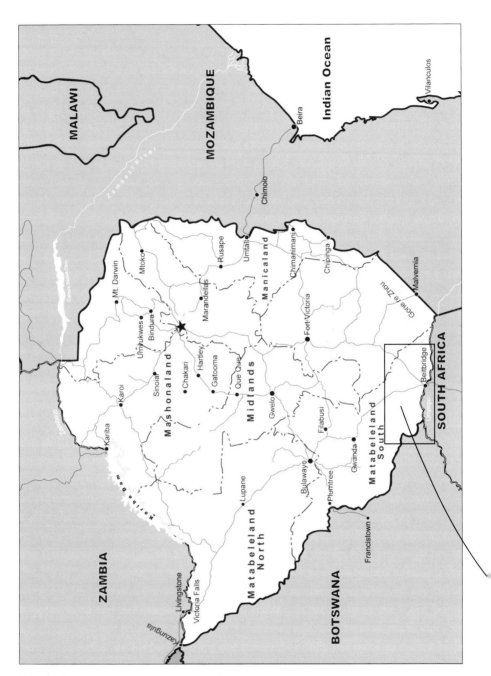

Rhodesia

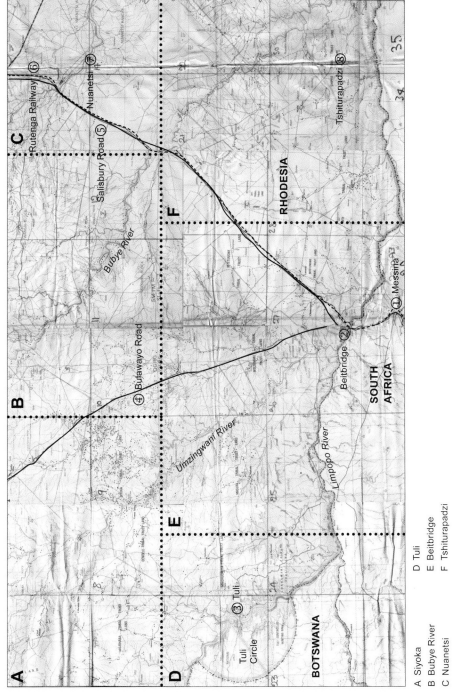

Beitbridge area of operations

A Siyoka
B Bubye River
C Nuanetsi
D Tuli
E Beitbridge
F Tshiturapadzi

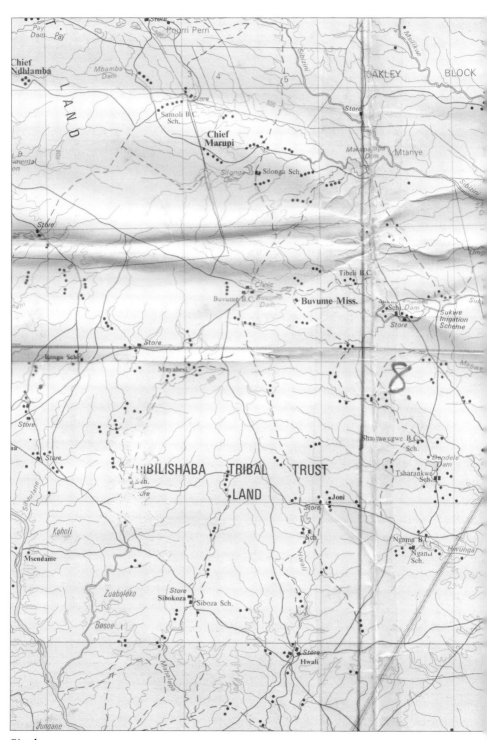

Siyoka

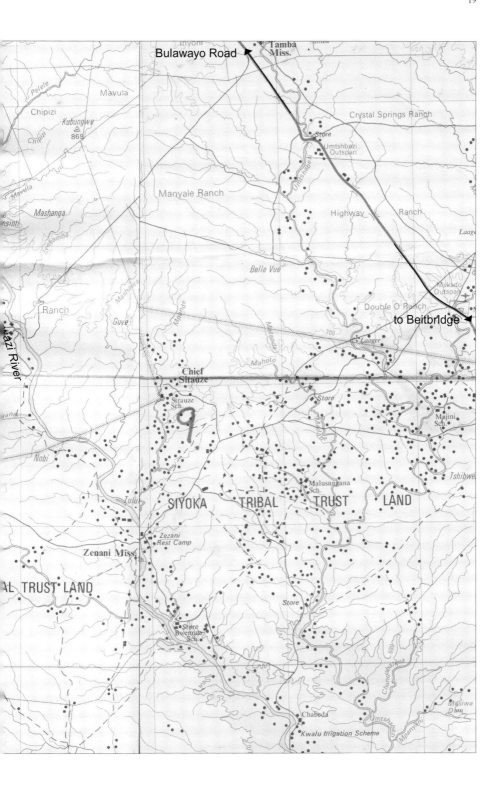

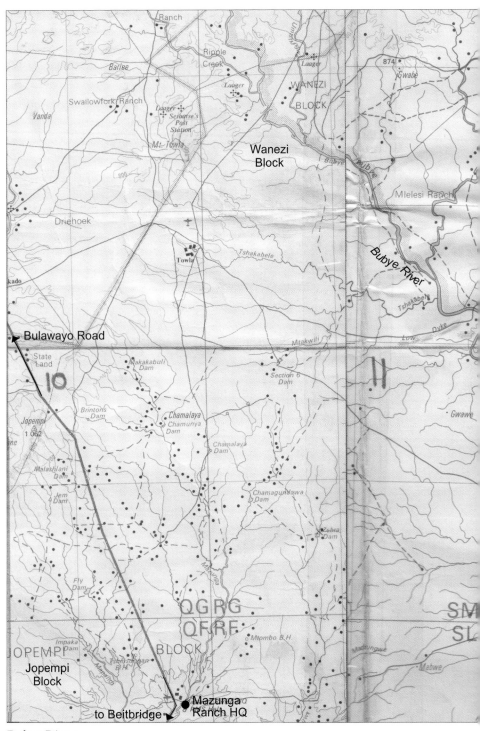

Bubye River

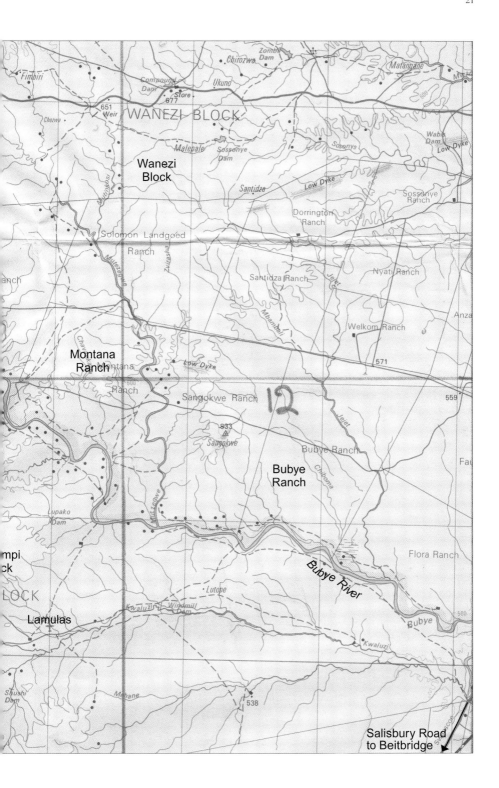

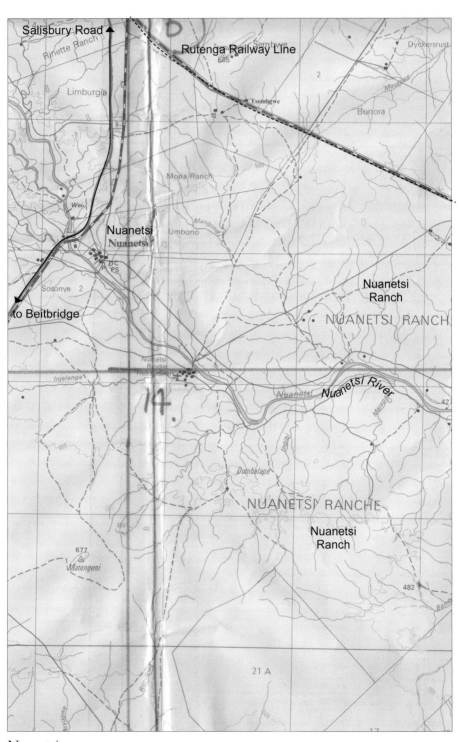

Nuanetsi

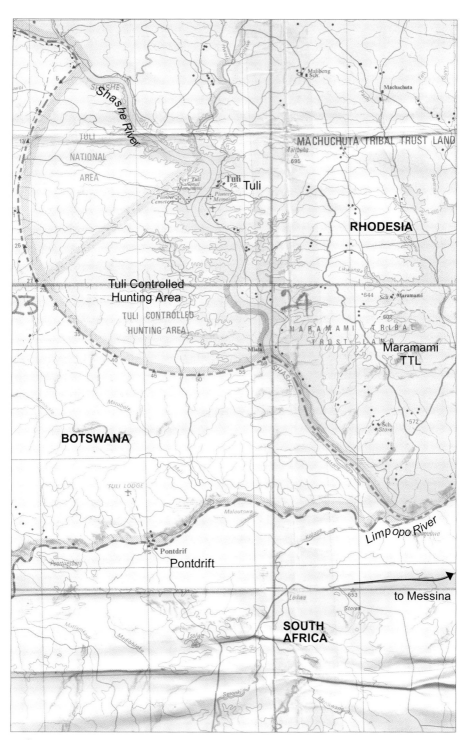

Tuli

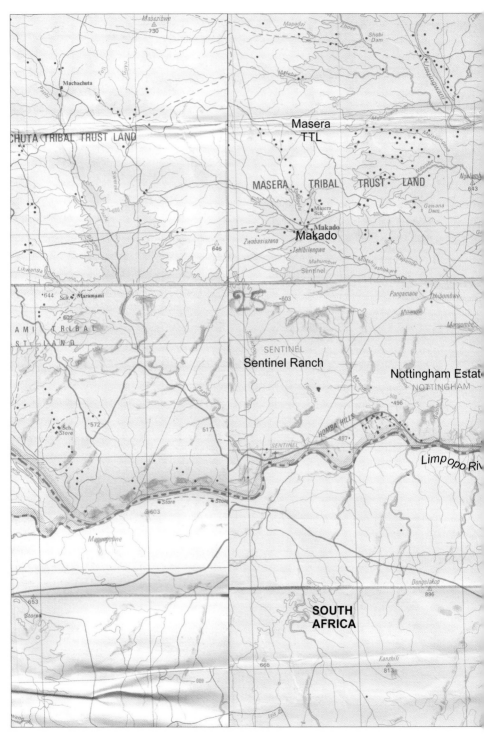

Beitbridge

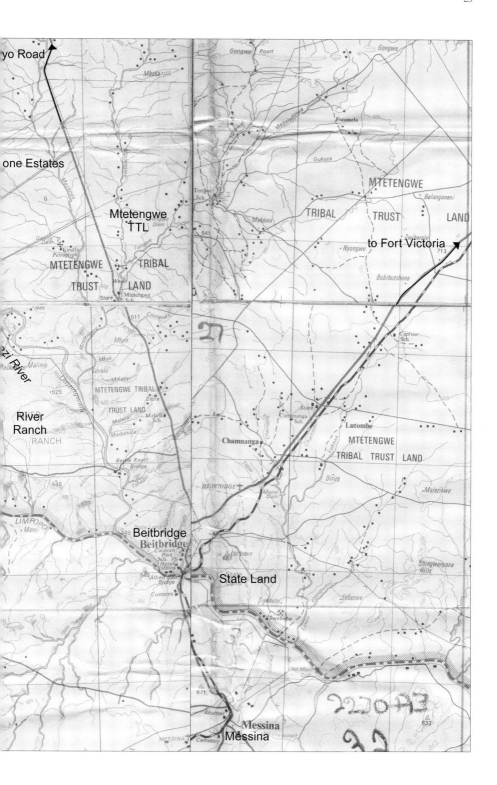

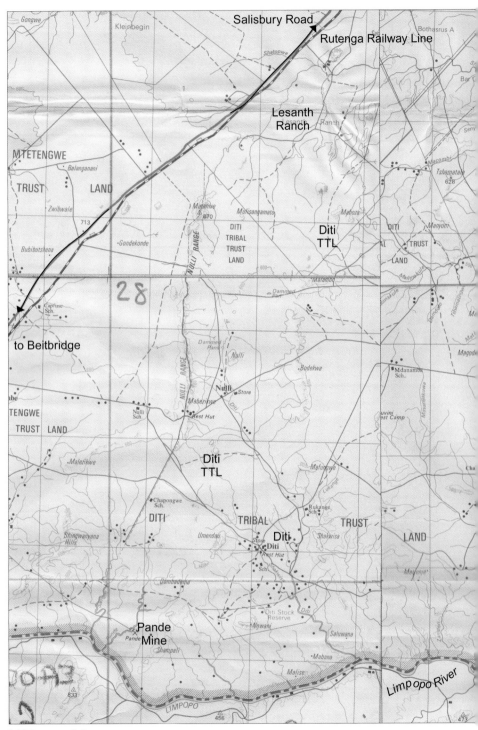

Tshiturapadzi

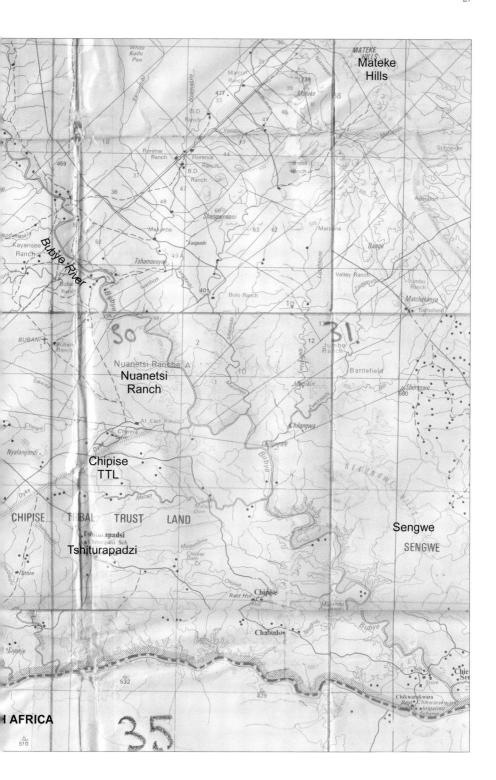

Glossary

AP:	anti-personnel
AP:	assembly point
APA:	African Purchase Area (Rhodesian Land Tenure Act)
BCR:	Bronze Cross of Rhodesia (equivalent to the Military Cross)
	(The) Black Boots: nickname for the BSAP's Support Unit
bombshell:	to flee or scatter in all directions (insurgent dispersal tactic on contact)
Bright Lights:	BSAP reservists, used primarily as farm protection
Brown Job:	soldier (slang)
BSAP:	British South Africa Police (the Rhodesian Police Force)
cadre:	insurgent rank and file
casevac:	casualty evacuation
Chimurenga:	Shona term for the Rhodesian bush/civil war. ZANLA's 'Second War of Liberation', first used in the Mashona Rebellion of 1896, or 'The First War of Liberation'
CIO:	Central Intelligence Organization
CMED:	Central Mechanical and Equipment Department
CO:	Commanding Officer
COIN:	counter-insurgency
ComOps:	Combined Operations Headquarters
CQMS:	company quartermaster sergeant
CSM:	company sergeant-major
CT:	communist terrorist
DC:	District Commissioner
DSBO:	District Special Branch Officer
FAF:	forward airfield
Fire Force:	airborne/airmobile assault group
(The) Force:	nickname for the BSAP
frantan:	Rhodesian euphemism for napalm (der. frangible tank)
FRELIMO:	Mozambique Liberation Movement (*Frente de Libertação de Moçambique*)

G-Car:	troop-ferrying helicopter, normally an Alouette III, armed with twin .303 Brownings or 7.62 MAGs
GC:	ground coverage (of the BSAP)
gook:	insurgent (American military slang from the Korean War)
HE:	high explosive
HEAT:	high-explosive anti-tank
HMG:	heavy machine gun
Intaf:	Department of Internal Affairs (abbreviation)
JOC:	Joint Operations Centre
K-Car:	helicopter command gunship, normally an Alouette III, equipped with a 20mm cannon (col. 'Killer car')
KIA:	killed in action
kraal:	African village (South African corruption of the Portuguese
curral	meaning a cattle pen or enclosure)
LO:	liaison officer
MAG:	*matireurs à gas*—gas-operated, belt-fed section machine gun, manufactured by Fabrique Nationale (FN, Belgium) and used by Rhodesian security forces
Mantle:	appointments code for BSAP Support Unit
mealie meal:	maize meal
MFC:	Military Forces Commendation
MMG:	medium machine gun
MPV:	mine-protected vehicle
NCO:	non-commissioned officer
NS:	national service/man
NSPO:	national service patrol officer
OAU:	Organization of African Unity
OC:	officer commanding
OP:	observation post

PATU:	Police Anti-Terrorist Unit (BSAP paramilitary COIN specialist unit)
PF:	Patriotic Front (ZANU/ZAPU alliance)
PGHQ:	Police General Head Quarters
POU:	Psychological Operations Unit (*also* Psyops)
povo:	people (Portuguese, and now commonly Shona)
PRAW:	Police Reserve Air Wing
PSBO:	Provincial Special Branch Officer
Psyops:	*see* POU
PV:	protected village
RAF:	Royal Air Force
RAR	Rhodesian African Rifles
RBC:	Rhodesian Broadcasting Corporation
RDR:	Rhodesian Defence Regiment
RDU:	Rhodesian Defence Unit
RHU:	Rhodesian Holding Unit
RIC:	Rhodesian Intelligence Corps
RLI:	Rhodesian Light Infantry
RMS:	Railway Motor Service, the vehicle-transport arm of Rhodesia Railways
RPD:	Soviet *Ruchnoy Pulemyot Degtyaryova* 7.62mm light machine gun
RR:	Rhodesia Regiment (white territorial battalions numbered 1 to 10)
RSM:	regimental sergeant-major
SAAF:	South African Air Force
SAANC:	South African African National Congress
SADF:	South African Defence Force
SAP:	South African Police
SAS:	Special Air Service
SB:	Special Branch (of the BSAP)
scene:	a contact, firefight (slang)
SCR:	Silver Cross of Rhodesia
sellout:	guerrilla term for a traitor
SF:	Security Forces (Rhodesian)
sitrep:	situation report
snaai:	to cheat (Afrikaans)
SNEB:	air-to-ground attack rocket

snivel:	to sneak off (slang)
stick:	four-man battle group, from an Alouette helicopter troop-load, originally five men until fifth man replaced by machine guns
TA:	Territorial Army (*see also* TF)
Tac HQ:	tactical headquarters
TF:	Territorial Force (*see also* TA)
TT:	turned terrorist
TTL:	Tribal Trust Land/s (Rhodesian Land Tenure Act). Along with the National Parks these areas made up the bulk of the country. These areas were reserved exclusively as the traditional habitable domain of indigenous tribal people.
UANC:	United African National Council, headed by Bishop Abel Muzorewa
UDI:	Unilateral Declaration of Independence
WO:	warrant officer
WP:	white phosphorus
ZANLA:	Zimbabwe African National Liberation Army, ZANU's military wing
ZANU:	Zimbabwe African National Union, externally headed by Robert Mugabe
ZAPU:	Zimbabwe African People's Union, headed by Joshua Nkomo
ZIPRA:	Zimbabwe People's Revolutionary Army, ZAPU's military wing
ZNA:	Zimbabwe National Army
ZRP:	Zimbabwe Republic Police

Foreword

I am honoured to be able to write this foreword as the author, Ed Bird, is a good friend and respected former member of the British South Africa Police, who served with distinction in the Rhodesian conflict. He worked with me particularly during the formation of the Selous Scouts and in other areas of intelligence gathering, in which he was never found wanting. He worked tirelessly in the operational area without any consideration for his own safety, his endeavours often carried out in isolation and under extreme circumstances.

What is hardly ever recognized is that the BSAP, in all aspects of defence, was integrated in the fabric of Rhodesia and at the forefront of a wrestle – not in a 'racist war' – with the onslaught of communist terrorism. This took the form of terrorists trained and armed by Russia and China, and their infiltration into Rhodesia from Zambia and Mozambique, which eventuated in a prolonged 'bush war'. The infiltrators perpetrated acts of terrorism which were extremely vicious, the main objective being to intimidate and subjugate the masses in the rural districts. It was in these areas where the author worked. The war was never won but, as history has shown, ended in a political solution which, over three decades later, the country is still having difficulty with.

—*Winston Hart*

Introduction

I first met Ed Bird when I was based as OC Tracking Wing at Kariba. The Selous Scouts had just been formed and Tracking Wing became Training Troop of the Scouts. Ed was on a visit to Kariba as part of a Special Branch team and, after work the one evening, we all went off to one of the local watering holes for a few drinks. I must say right off the bat that I enjoyed this quiet man and we seemed to 'click'. When he left the next day little did I know that, in 1978, we were destined to become much closer allies when I would find myself in Beitbridge as OC 1 (Independent) Company where Ed was the SB man on the ground.

Ed was a quiet but very efficient operator, more a hands-on, field-type guy than a paper-pusher admin type: a gladiator as opposed to a bumph pusher. I could relate to this and empathized greatly as I was much the same. He was a pleasure to work with and, unlike the average SB guy, did not make his army counterparts feel inferior or less intelligent. Many SB operatives were arrogant and acted as if they knew far more than a mere soldier knew or had the right to know and gave little or no credence to army rank. In many instances, SB officers were Brits and as the war progressed the loyalty and honesty of a few became questionable. But Ed Bird was different: a Rhodesian through and through and a man totally committed to fighting and winning the war.

When we were posted to Beitbridge in 1978 the area was 'hot', almost overrun by terrorists. The two main roads leading out of 'the Bridge' – one to Salisbury and the other to Bulawayo – were hit daily: the area was a boiling pot of ZANLA and ZIPRA aggression. The army sub-units before us had done little to remedy the problem: over a two-year period their only success was one wounded capture! They had expended millions of rounds of ammunition and eaten thousands of army rations but little else had been achieved.

The brigade commander briefed me: "Makumbi, taking over at Beitbridge is a huge responsibility, but I know that you and 1 Indep Company are up to the tremendous job ahead of you. The terrs have the upper hand down there, and ambushes on the roads from Beitbridge to Bulawayo and Salisbury are a daily occurrence. I am counting on you to turn things around, so don't let me down."

Tan-tan-ta raah! But believe me, this was no joke: the place was crawling with terrs and we had our hands full. My mission statement was as follows:

1. The security and safety of the town;
2. To protect and maintain the integrity of the large fuel depot on the outskirts of the town (this fuel dump was of vital importance as it was the

main fuel artery into the country from South Africa);
3. To keep the two main roads to Salisbury and Bulawayo open and safe;
4. To keep the international bridge over the Limpopo River open and secure;
5. To uphold the general state of morale in the entire area and to protect civilians, black and white;
6. To maintain communication at all times and to liaise at the highest level with our South African Army neighbours.

My task was indeed daunting. As we had experienced at Victoria Falls, the locals were initially very unfriendly but I guess we really couldn't blame them. The previous army sub-unit in the area, a regular company from one of the African battalions, achieved nothing in the months it was based there. The terrorists ambushed the roads to Bulawayo and Salisbury on an almost daily basis so it was only safe to travel as part of an armed convoy; the terrorists were attacking the local farmers' homesteads and laying mines on the farm roads and the community, rightly so, wanted to know what the army was doing to rectify things. Come on, not even one kill? Morale was rock bottom and it was up to us to show the locals just what 1 (Indep) Company was made of.

When I attended my first daily sub-JOC meeting held at the council offices I was shocked to learn how my erstwhile counterpart had handled the meeting just prior to his departure. Complete with monocle in place, he told the assembled townsfolk: "Ladies and gentlemen, let me explain something. Your situation here is still one of mind over matter: I don't mind and you certainly don't matter." What a pompous prick! No wonder they were angry with the army.

And so we began our stint at Beitbridge and my time working alongside Ed 'Wol' Bird. Before our arrival, Ed was the only white operative present and took gooks on almost single-handedly, often with a stick of black constables as his only support. In my opinion, he was extremely lucky not to have been either badly wounded or killed in many of these actions. Using the previously unseen SB operations log as his reference, Ed's book is filled with accurately reported contacts and incidents; his matter-of-fact style and manner are typical of the man's character and humble nature.

Anyway back to our time together …

An independent company was not a regular outfit like the RLI, RAR, the SAS or the Selous Scouts and as a result was often understaffed and poorly equipped. This could not have been more apparent when we found ourselves tasked with manning and operating a Fire Force. In this backs-to-the-wall situation Ed Bird immediately volunteered his services as a machine-gunner and became a valuable member of Stop 1. He quashed any rebuttal from his boss by arguing, "But it will be a first and really good for SB to have a man on the ground right there where the action is. Just think of all the field intelligence we will be able to gain, plus it will stop the army *snaaing* us on weapons, kit and equipment. Come on Wol?" (You see, Ed referred to everyone as 'Wol', I suspect from 'Wally', a generic Australian term of familiarity.)

So Ed operated with us on Fire Force Delta. On our first deployment, as an inexperienced, untrained Fire Force, we succeeded in breaking the JOC Repulse record for the most gooks killed in one day: fourteen I recall. Ed was right in the thick of this action in Stop 1 and went on to become a magnificent machine-gunner, always an example to the men with him. He was fearless and in my book definitely a far better soldier than a policeman.

As an independent company we were often forced into doing things out of the ordinary, things that had not been done before. When there was no air support other than PRAW, or Police Reserve Air Wing (civilian pilots with their personal aircraft), we were forced to adapt … hugely. We removed the two back doors from a Cessna 206 and replaced the rear seats with a 7.62 standard infantry machine gun, an MAG or GPMG, mounted on a tripod and set in place on the floor of the aircraft with sandbags. We also gave the 'gunner' an assortment of homemade bombs: cut-off dumpie beer bottles loaded with either high-explosive or white phosphorus grenades. When the lads were in action and we did not have the luxury of a regular Fire Force to help us, this was our *only* means of support. More often than not Ed volunteered to man the MAG in the rear of the aircraft. I directed operations from the front seat next to the civilian pilot while old Ed in the back blazed away, sniggering each time he tossed a 'bomb' out of the door. How we laughed! He jumped at any opportunity to fight the enemy and was always available, day or night.

On other occasions, when we deployed as part of our own local pseudo team, Ed was again in the middle of things. Ed Bird was totally committed to the war: it did not matter what it took, he was always the first to put his hand up. This was noticed by his superiors and I recently learned – he'd kept all this very much under wraps – that while serving in the BSAP, he was the recipient of three awards for bravery: the Commissioner's 'Note of Good Work', the Commissioner's Commendation (Bronze Baton) and the Commissioner's Special Commendation (Silver Baton). The Bronze Baton was roughly on a par with the army's Military Forces Commendation (MFC). As far as I am aware, Ed was the only member of the BSAP to hold the distinction of being awarded all three: indeed, a unique combination.

In all wars there are always those, who for one reason or the other, do not receive just recognition for their efforts and actions. Ed Bird is definitely one of these people and although he was recognized for certain services, this was not reflected in his work place. He passed all his promotion exams but was generally overlooked when promotions came around. He was not one of the elite blue-eyed boys treated with kid gloves and given the best of everything. He was a detective section officer and, after being found not guilty of some spurious poaching charges levelled against him, he was promoted to detective inspector in retrospect after threatening the commissioner with civil action, but he was out of the police by then. In the end, that is why he resigned.

We became great friends and enjoyed fishing, hunting and, at times, chasing chicks! The army had their smooth dudes and charmers; I am talking about the masters of the game like John Dawson, Huge Rowley and the late Bruce Snelgar to name a few. But on the police side, there were few smoother than our man Ed: a legendary ladies' man.

In closing, it was a great privilege to work and socialize with Ed Bird. We remain distant, good friends and if I was to once again, by some weird stroke of fortune, find myself in battle, I would want to have old Wol standing next to me. I salute you, my friend.

—*Don Price*

Special Branch Beitbridge incident log

The Special Branch Beitbridge incident log, initiated by Ed Bird at the commencement of the terrorist infiltration of the district toward the end of 1976, was maintained for the duration of the conflict until the advent of Zimbabwe in April 1980. With the passage of time, the log was not merely used to chronicle terrorist incidents in the designated Beitbridge operational area but was to become a fundamental aid in the collation and correlation of intelligence to assist in the pursuit of the enemy which, in the latter years, not only included resident groups but also large transit infiltrations of ZANLA heading west into the Gwanda, Kezi, Belingwe and Essexvale areas of Operation *Tangent*.

Its contents, updated on a daily basis, detailed specific information and cross-referencing, including ballistics results, which in turn were meticulously transferred with the assistance of the local Rhodesian Intelligence Corps (RIC) to a detailed operational map maintained at the Special Branch office. This information assisted in the monitoring of the movement of both individual and groups of terrorists and, coupled to intelligence gleaned from captured terrorists and recovered documents, was to play a significant role, in conjunction with the local JOC, in the deployment of security personnel and ultimately their success rate in the latter years under command of Major Don Price and his 1 Indep Company.

The incident log, in concert with the intelligence map, was used on a regular basis by Special Branch Beitbridge in the briefing of JOC *Tangent* and neighbouring JOC *Repulse* representatives, as well as other security force components in the area. These regular briefs were also given to the SADF and South African Police Security Branch members stationed on the South African side of the Beitbridge border with Rhodesia. With the advent of regime change in April 1980, a directive was received by Special Branch offices throughout the country from Special Branch headquarters in Salisbury to destroy listed documents/files including all operational documents. In addition to the destruction of the files, a large quantity of classified files and documents was trunked by Special Branch offices, including Special Branch HQ, and transported over a twenty-four-hour period to Beitbridge for safe keeping by myself before releasing them, by prior arrangement, to representatives of the South African Police Security Branch from Pietersburg. It was during this process that I decided to preserve the Special Branch Beitbridge incident log which today plays a significant part in and authenticates Ed Bird's memoirs.
—*Brian Perkins*

Author's note

My memoirs are centred on the Special Branch incident log, or war diary, which was maintained throughout the Rhodesian bush war in the Beitbridge area and which covers the period 1976–80. I have expounded on those incidents that I can clearly recall; incidents that I recall, but which are unrecorded in the Incident log, I have omitted for reasons of verification and authenticity.

During the writing of this book I contacted many people who had been involved in the bush war and received many good accounts of their experiences but, due to the passing of time, many cannot remember the year, let alone the month, when a particular incident took place. Again, for complete authenticity I have not included these wonderful accounts. For the same reason I have been unable to draw from the accounts of specific people who worked under adverse and extremely dangerous conditions for long periods of time – men like Ken Gault and Les Milne automatically spring to mind.

Some names in the book have either been omitted, or changed, particularly for some of the black operators who fought for the Rhodesians, and who are today living in Zimbabwe.

I would like to thank Brian Perkins, who on leaving the Force in May of 1980, had the foresight to 'liberate' the Special Branch Incident log, kindly furnishing me a copy and encouraging me to expand upon the historical document for prosperity.

To Don Price, a valued brother in arms, I would like to express my sincere thanks for being the catalyst that culminated in the writing of this book. Don asked me to jot down some of my experiences in the Beitbridge area for inclusion in his as yet unpublished book on the exploits of 1 (Independent Company) the Rhodesia African Rifles, which he commanded with distinction for a number of years. I agreed to his request and obtained the Special Branch Incident log from Brian Perkins for this specific reason.

On paging through the log, memories came flooding back and it was then, I realized, that a valuable historical account of the Rhodesian bush war would be lost if the log was not fleshed out into a proper historical account. I had started the log at the end of 1976 and was at Beitbridge for the final three-year duration of the war, having spent more time in that area than any other member of the security forces. If anyone was going to record the details then it would have to be me. So, with no previous experience in writing a book I took the plunge.

After writing three or four chapters, I gave what I had to the renowned Rhodesian historian Dr Richard Wood, author of *The War Diaries of André*

Dennison and many other fine historical works, to peruse and give me an honest opinion. His report back was positive, so I continued writing. From time to time I was to contact him for some form of inspiration to carry on, which I am pleased to say I did. Apart from this, I would also like to thank Dr Wood for providing particulars of security force members who paid the ultimate sacrifice in the Beitbridge area, drawn from his meticulously maintained Rhodesian roll of honour.

I must also thank Barry Woan, an illustrious former member of the BSAP Support Unit – 'The Black Boots' – for his assistance in identifying members of that fine unit who were involved in actions against terrorist forces in the Beitbridge area. Barry also supplied the original 1:250,000 map which proved so crucial in the compilation of this book. He is currently writing a book on the history of the Support Unit and I wish him everything of the best for this mammoth undertaking.

A brief word on terminology: I have tried to retain the language and terminology of the times in order to provide an authentic account as possible. Words such as 'gook' or 'terrorist', freely interchangeable with 'insurgent' or 'guerrilla' in this book, are used as they were used and spoken by the Rhodesian security forces at the time, and are without any derogatory, racist, negative or disrespectful connotation.

Finally, I would like to thank my wife Patsy for the invaluable assistance and encouragement she has given me, not only in the writing of this book, but by standing by me in all my endeavours over the past thirty-odd years that we have been together and for giving me Tracey and Diane, the best daughters a father could wish for.

—*Ed Bird*
Amanzimtoti, March 2013

About Rhodesia

The country today known as Zimbabwe lies in southern-central Africa between the Zambezi River to the north and the Limpopo to the south. Toward the end of the first millennium AD, Bantu peoples migrated southward from the Congo basin into central-southern Africa, displacing the indigenous Bushmen. Between AD 1300 and 1450, the empire of Great Zimbabwe was at its zenith, flourishing from trade with Arab and Chinese merchants on the east coast of Africa. Inexplicably, but probably as a result of a series of droughts, the empire disintegrated and split into two distinct groupings: the Torwa who migrated west to Khami in today's Matabeleland and the Mwenemutapa who settled in the north along the Zambezi escarpment to establish what became commonly known as the Kingdom of Monomatapa, consisting of a loose affiliation of clans.

The five main sub-groups, or tribes, of what was later referred to by the white colonizers as the 'Mashona' nation were, and still are, the Zezuru, Korekore, Ndau, Manyika and Karanga (the latter the original inhabitants of Great Zimbabwe), the term 'Shona' deriving from the common language of *chiShona*, that was and is used in its various dialects by these five tribes. Other offshoots and 'non-Shona' tribes that inhabit the region are the Tonga in the Zambezi valley, the Shangaan in the southeast and, of course, the martial Matabele in the west of the country.

Apart from limited Portuguese intervention, the region enjoyed a period of relative peace and prosperity until the renegade Zulu general, Mzilikazi, established the Ndebele kingdom in Bulawayo in the late 1830s, having fled north across the Limpopo to escape the ravages of alternately Shaka's Zulu impis and the Boers. Under Mzilikazi, and latterly his son, King Lobengula, the warlike amaNdebele – more commonly known as the Matabele – subjugated the Mashona tribes; Matabele impis roamed the country with impunity, pillaging and capturing and assimilating Mashona women and children into the Ndebele tribe. (Over a century later tribal friction would again erupt when the Mashona turned the tables on their old Matabele foes in a post-independent Zimbabwe.)

This all came to an end when Cecil John Rhodes's British South Africa Company (BSAC), under charter from Queen Victoria, occupied the region in 1890 and raised the Union Flag at Fort Salisbury, now Harare. The colony, or more correctly, the territory, became known as Rhodesia.

In 1893, the Matabele under Lobengula rebelled, taking the white occupiers by surprise. After some initial successes – such as destroying Major Allan Wilson's 'Shangani Patrol' to a man – the Matabele were ultimately defeated by the white men and their Maxim guns at the Battle of Bembesi. Three years later the Mashona revolted in what became known as the first *Chimurenga*, the 'war of liberation'. In spite of inflicting some notable casualties on the settler population, the Mashona were defeated and their leaders, the spirit mediums Kaguvi and Nehanda, a woman, were hanged for their troubles.

Rhodesia grew and flourished. In 1923, with the BSAC making way for formal colonial administration, a referendum was held, a whites-only franchise, with the electorate voting by a narrow margin to become a self-governing Crown colony rather than incorporation into the Union of South Africa. With the new colony of Northern Rhodesia across the Zambezi River, Rhodesia became Southern Rhodesia. During both World Wars, 'the Rhodesias' contributed considerable numbers of personnel, both black and white, to the Allied war effort.

After the Second World War, the two Rhodesias experienced a phenomenal period of growth and prosperity, mainly thanks to the copper boom in the north and tobacco in the south and with a large white immigration from a dreary Britain. During this period, to consolidate political and economic control, the white colonial politicians led by one-time boxer and railwayman Sir Roy Welensky formed The Federation of Rhodesia and Nyasaland. It was during this period of the 1950s that Black Nationalism began raising its head. An economically crippled post-war Britain, in unseemly haste to divest herself of her African colonies, began granting independence to her African colonies, starting with Ghana in 1957. This signalled the demise of the Federation which collapsed in 1963, with Nyasaland being granted independence as Malawi the same year and Northern Rhodesia as Zambia the following.

Southern Rhodesia dropped its prefix and the conservative white Rhodesian Front party (RF) came to power in 1964 under Winston Field, followed shortly thereafter by farmer and ex-Spitfire pilot Ian Smith. Joshua Nkomo became the leading Black Nationalist and, with his Soviet-sponsored Zimbabwe African People's Union (ZAPU), fomented a national campaign of violent civil unrest. The ZAPU Shona faction broke away under Ndabaningi Sithole and formed the Chinese-sponsored Zimbabwe African National Union (ZANU). Both Nationalist parties began dispatching cadres overseas to the Eastern bloc and China for military training in order to commence the so-called second *Chimurenga*.

In the meantime, prime minister Ian Smith and the equally intransigent British Labour prime minister Harold Wilson were deadlocked in talks, with the British insisting upon immediate majority rule – 'one man one vote' – and Smith demanding a gradual phasing-in of the black franchise. In frustration, on 11 November 1965, Smith unilaterally declared the country independent (UDI). Britain, and the UN, immediately imposed international sanctions as the Nationalists seized their opportunity and began infiltrating guerrillas into the country. Robert Mugabe had by now wrested the ZANU leadership from Sithole.

So began a fifteen-year-period of stand-off and conflict with ZANLA (Zimbabwe African National Liberation Army, ZANU's military wing) operating out of Mozambique's Tete Province, supported by the Mozambican liberation movement Frelimo and ZIPRA (Zimbabwe People's Revolutionary Army, ZAPU's military wing) operating out of Zambia. The 'bush war', as it became known, consisted of three distinct phases. Phase 1, 1966 to 1971, saw armed incursions from across the Zambezi by both ZAPU and ZANU. These incursions were dealt with easily enough by the Rhodesian security forces in the harsh, sparsely populated terrain of the Zambezi valley; Phase 2, 1972 to 1975, saw the guerrillas, particularly ZANLA, changing tactics, using subversion and terror against the local tribespeople to gain local supremacy. The Rhodesians, caught by surprise, opened Operation *Hurricane* in the northeast of the country, and gradually gained the ascendancy with the introduction of some novel military tactics such as the Fire Force concept. It was during this phase that two events, which were to signal the ultimate demise of the Rhodesians, occurred. In 1974, South African prime minister, John Vorster, using his economic trump card – South Africa kept the Rhodesian economy and war effort afloat with fuel and arms supplies – forced Smith to accept his policy of African *détente* (effectively, compliant independent black states north of the Limpopo, including Rhodesia), which entailed a general ceasefire and release of all detained Nationalists. ZANLA, in particular, used the opportunity to lick its wounds and regrouped on the borders. 1975 saw the overnight withdrawal of the Portuguese from Mozambique, handing power to an astonished former male nurse Samora Machel and Frelimo. In one fell swoop the Rhodesians now found themselves defending a further 1,000 kilometres of hostile border, from the Zambezi to the Limpopo. Phase 3, 1976 to independence in 1980, saw ZANLA and to a lesser degree ZIPRA flooding the country with guerrillas.

In mid-1979, after a general election boycotted by both Mugabe and Nkomo, an 'internal settlement' was mapped out between Smith and his black-moderate allies, with Bishop Abel Muzorewa and his United African National Council (UANC) assuming power in the short-lived and largely irrelevant state of Zimbabwe–Rhodesia. With South African support dwindling and the country in dire economic straits, Smith, Muzorewa, Chirau and Sithole were forced to the negotiation table at Lancaster House. Mugabe and Nkomo, with both ZANLA and ZIPRA staring military defeat in the face, were likewise forced to attend the talks as the 'Patriotic Front' (PF), an unholy alliance between the two tribal arch-enemies. To rid himself of the troublesome colony, the British mediator, Lord Carrington, bulldozed through a constitutional agreement clearly biased in favour of Mugabe. A ceasefire was declared in December 1979 and a general election was held in early 1980, which Mugabe's ZANU (PF) won overwhelmingly, with the vast majority voting for Mugabe, either popularly or simply as a means to end the war, depending on one's view. On 18 April 1980, Mugabe became the first prime minister of Zimbabwe.

Prologue

I was born in Belfast, Northern Ireland on the 3 May 1946. My birth was a direct result of the Second World War as my father, who had been in Rhodesia for a number of years, had joined up at the outbreak of war and served with the Royal Air Force. He was posted to 44 (Rhodesia) Squadron as air crew on Lancaster bombers where he was Mentioned in Dispatches. The squadron was posted to Belfast which was where he met and married my mother.

So it was, as a baby that I arrived in Rhodesia with my elder sister Pat.

My first recollections as a child were growing up on my parents' farm in the Bembesi area of Matabeleland. Bembesi was typical of Matabeleland: arid and open and only suitable, at that stage, for breeding cattle. As a result of numerous droughts, my father was eventually forced to sell the place and the family, which had grown by the birth of my younger brothers Ken and Martin, moved to Bulawayo.

A month after my eighteenth birthday I joined the British South Africa Police. After a six-month recruit course at the police depot in Salisbury, I passed out as a brand-new constable. I opted for the District Branch and was posted to Mashonaland. Before being allocated a station, I had to report to the officer commanding Mashonaland Province, Senior Assistant Commissioner Eric van Sittert. He was a tough, no-nonsense man who, on completion of the interview, gave me the following advice: "Never trust a man who doesn't drink or smoke as he has hidden vices." To some extent, over the years, I found this to be true.

My first station was Bindura, followed by a brief stint at Mount Darwin, then to Shamva and finally to Umvukwes. These stations all fell under Mazoe Valley District with the headquarters situated at Bindura.

Around May 1968, while stationed at Umvukwes, an incident occurred which resulted in my transfer to Kariba on twenty-four hours' notice. The second-in-command of the station, Section Officer Pat Drayton, had gone on long leave and before departing asked me if I would be interested in taking over the Tattersalls horse-racing agency in his absence. This simply entailed receiving a pile of betting forms on the Tuesday for the Saturday races, putting the official BSAP Umvukwes stamp on each form and leaving them at the post office where anyone interested could take a form. The remuneration was not very great – I could expect roughly £2 a week in commission – however, I snapped up the offer. But before I could benefit from the business, fate intervened in the form of the officer commanding Mazoe Valley.

Chief Superintendent Bert Fremantle was a strict disciplinarian who had jumped at Arnhem with the British Parachute Regiment during the Second World War. He was taken prisoner by the Germans and spent the rest of the war in captivity. He now arrived to conduct the annual station inspection. During the course of the inspection he was using my desk to go through various documents and for some unknown reason opened one of my drawers and there looking up at him was a buff envelope with the Tattersalls logo on it; the envelope was addressed to me with the word 'agent' in brackets after my name. He turned purple and said, "We have a bloody bookie on the station!" On opening the letter he read confirmation from Tattersalls that I had been accepted as their agent. I was ordered to explain myself. I couldn't and all I could say was that I had no excuse.

The following day, after completing his inspection, he returned to Bindura. That same evening he telephoned my member in charge and advised him that I was to get out of his district and report on transfer to the member in charge at Kariba within the next forty-eight hours. As instructed, I reported to Inspector Chris Carver on my arrival at Kariba. I never heard another word regarding the horse-racing incident and Pat Drayton thanked me later for not implicating him.

Kariba was regarded as a punishment station and for the first six months of my posting I undertook continuous foot patrols of the Kariba Gorge in the Zambezi Valley, a very inhospitable place indeed. The routine consisted of a seven-day patrol with two days off and then back for another seven days, with the exception of the odd six-week Bumi Hills patrol to break the monotony. This was in line with the BSAP's contribution to border-control operations.

I was a bit peeved at having to leave Umvukwes as I had made some good friends, was having a wonderful social life and was dating one of the local farmer's daughters. However, I soon got into the swing of things at Kariba and started enjoying myself, becoming exceptionally fit in the process. After six months of foot patrols, I was put on a coxswain's course and, on passing, commenced boat patrols on the lake for periods of two weeks at a time. On one occasion, I was dispatched with one of the Kariba police boats to Chirundu from where I undertook a month-long patrol of the Zambezi River from the Kariba Dam wall as far downriver as Mana Pools. These were magical times and I was really very privileged.

I carried out three 'Bumi Hills patrols', known as such because the police patrol base was situated at Bumi Hills at the top end of the lake. Apart from the police post, Bumi Hills boasted a fine hotel, the District Commissioner's upmarket house and a government harbour. However, the patrol area covered the vast Omay Tribal Trust Land, home to the primitive Batonka tribe. For some obscure reason the Ministry of Internal Affairs, or Intaf, had no intention of developing the area and providing the basic amenities to improve the lot of these people. The Omay covered thousands of square miles and, although sparsely populated, no bus companies were issued with road permits to operate in the area. The roads were maintained by the District Commissioner's Internal Affairs staff and because they were only used by government employees – the main roads, at least – they were fine roads indeed. There were no clinics, schools were few and far between and there were no local stores or butcheries. Because of the presence of tsetse fly, cattle could not survive but the locals did keep a few goats and donkeys. Dogs were also practically absent because of the 'fly'. The Batonka survived by netting fish and growing subsistence crops. The area teemed with wildlife.

A land-based police patrol consisted of a white patrol officer and two black constables, with one constable remaining at the police post while the patrol officer and the other constable patrolled the area, either by Land Rover or by foot. The patrol generally left Bumi on a Sunday afternoon or early Monday morning and returned to base the following Saturday. On return, after servicing the Land Rover and cleaning his kit, the patrol officer adjourned to the hotel for a few beers and a good meal.

A few months before my transfer from Kariba I was assigned observation post duties at the Sengwa Sound on Lake Kariba. The OP was to observe movement on the Zambian bank and report suspicious movement. I was stuck on the OP for two weeks and after my two-week spell, was immediately relocated to Bumi Hills for a six-week patrol.

I carried out the normal patrolling and on about the fourth week I shot a young kudu bull for the pot. This was highly illegal but being deprived of fresh meat for six weeks was beginning to take its toll. None of the meat was wasted as I gave the surplus to a nearby village.

I must here relate what had transpired a week or two earlier. At about midday on one particular day the constable and I decided to brew a cup of tea on the bank of a small stream. Making a fire, we waited for the kettle to boil and were dozing in the shade of some large trees when all of a sudden we heard a commotion in the bush with warthogs squealing in distress. My immediate thought was that a lion was at large. The warthogs broke cover only metres from us and charged across the track followed by several hunting spears thrown at them. One spear hit a warthog boar in the shoulder, instantly bowling him over. The hunting party, consisting of young men, broke cover and so intent were they on dispatching the boar that they were oblivious to our presence. I couldn't help myself and burst out laughing because in literally thousands of square miles of tribal trust land, the hunting party had found the only two policemen. By rights I should have arrested the entire hunting party, confiscated their weapons – and the now dead warthog – and transported them back to Bumi for onward transfer to Kariba for prosecution. All I could think of was that if it wasn't for bad luck they would have no luck at all. However, I gave them a stern warning and after 'confiscating' one or two of their best hunting spears, let them proceed on their way – and with the spoils of the hunt to boot. No doubt they would continue hunting illegally but as long as snares were not used I would continue to turn a blind eye as hunting on foot with spears and without the aid of dogs is a very difficult task – not to mention providing sorely needed fresh meat for the locals.

But back to my story of the kudu bull. I never gave the matter another thought and returned to Kariba late one Friday afternoon on completion of my patrol. I had been away for two months and was looking forward to a few beers with my mates in the renowned Jam Jar Inn, the local police pub. At that stage, I must have been about the only person in Kariba who was not aware that the Game Department had lodged poaching charges against me for shooting the kudu. As was customary, I reported to Inspector Raymond Weare, the member in charge. He was non-committal and told me to report to Section Officer Roger Liebish, the second-in-command. Roger was a good friend and explained the situation, outlining the evidence against me. I had had the same luck as the warthog hunting party – I had shot the kudu within earshot of a Game Department game scout who, on hearing the shot, investigated. He found my vehicle tracks and expended cartridge case and followed the tracks to the village where he had found the meat and head which I had donated to the villagers. On being questioned, the villagers gave out that a *majonny*, a white policeman, had given them the meat. I decided that the evidence was overwhelming and in the warned and cautioned statement admitted my guilt on the two charges: hunting without a permit and hunting without the landowner's permission, in this case the Kariba District Commissioner. As I was to be transferred to Sinoia in the near future, it was decided that I would appear in court in Sinoia when my transfer became effective.

In early September 1969 I was transferred to Sinoia where, shortly after my arrival, I appeared before the local magistrate on the poaching charges. I duly pleaded guilty but, in mitigation, explained that I had been continuously on patrol for over six weeks and was thus deprived of any type of fresh meat, with the exception of fish which I caught on a regular basis. I had encountered a herd of kudu and shot one for the pot. I explained that there were no African stores or butcheries in the area and that after shooting the animal, I had ensured that none of the meat went to waste. I was then sentenced to a fine of £5, or five days' imprisonment with hard labour, on each count and my warrant of committal (to prison) was suspended until two o'clock that afternoon in order to give me time to draw the money from the bank and pay the clerk of the court, which I did.

Before appearing in court the officer commanding Lomagundi District (Sinoia), Chief Superintendent Ray Stenner, had called me into his office to discuss the pending case. He was concerned, in view of the penalties recently having been dramatically increased for offences under the Wild Life Conservation Act, that I would not be able to pay the fine and explained that there were various options available to me within the BSAP to raise a loan. This worried me as I was only earning around £50 a month but as it turned out I did not need the loan.

Although I had also contravened the Police Act, inasmuch as I had used my service rifle to shoot the kudu and then transported it in the back of a police Land Rover, no mention was ever made of my 'misuse of government property' and I was never charged for these offences. However, the following year, the poaching charge was held against me when I failed the promotion board interview in spite of passing the written examinations and the two-week police depot promotion course. But this was standard procedure and I accepted it.

However, it was a completely different matter ten years later when my promotion to detective inspector was withheld by Commissioner of Police P.K. Allum when he attempted to have me convicted, on a technicality, under the Wild Life Conservation Act for shooting a bull elephant in the Beitbridge area where I was stationed at the time. I was found not guilty of all the charges in the Bulawayo regional court. The charges related to me having not been in possession of permits to hunt elephants although I had the landowner's – again the District Commissioner's – permission. In his attempt to have me convicted, the commissioner had instructed a detective chief superintendent in the Criminal Investigation Department and one of the leading investigators in the BSAP at that time, to head the investigation. I never disputed shooting the elephant and assisted the investigation team as much as possible, so the mind boggles as to the real reason for a senior officer, particularly in the CID, being appointed to oversee the investigation. I was later told that the commissioner – to many a spineless individual lacking the leadership skills required of such a high level – was desperate to secure a conviction against me for his own professional and political motives, which he realized in mid-1980 when he was appointed commissioner of the newly formed Zimbabwe Republic Police. After the court case and after resigning from the BSAP, I had to threaten him with civil action before he would promote me, in retrospect, with full monetary benefits, a task I should imagine he found highly distasteful but nonetheless that he was forced to do under threat of civil action.

Toward the end of 1970, I became restless and decided to resign from the BSAP to travel overseas on a working holiday for a year or so. If I liked the experience then I would stay, but if did not work out I would return to Rhodesia. So, in early 1971, I left the BSAP and departed on my new adventure. I travelled by train from Bulawayo to Cape Town where I boarded the *Edinburgh Castle* destined for Southampton and returned via the same route nearly a year later. I travelled all over Europe, only returning to the UK to work on a variety of odd jobs to finance my European trips. The best part of the experience was when Rhodesia Railways took over the train from their South African counterpart at Mafeking for the final leg of the journey through Botswana to Bulawayo.

On my return to Rhodesia, I was undecided what to do but I knew I had to get a job quickly. After contemplating various options, I decided to rejoin the BSAP and after travelling to Salisbury to sign on again, was posted to Chibi in the Victoria Province. However, I was only there for several months before I was attached to Special Branch for a three-month deployment to the northeast of the country, my old stomping ground. There had been an alarming rise in terrorist activity and Special Branch was mounting an intensive intelligence-gathering operation to monitor enemy infiltrations from the Tete province in Mozambique. As October 1972 was drawing to a close, I was issued with a Land Rover in Salisbury with instructions to report to the Special Branch officer at Centenary. On arrival, I was briefed and, with a constable as company, commenced operations in the Zambezi Valley.

After about six weeks, I was urgently recalled to Centenary where I was informed that a terrorist presence had been confirmed in the Mazarabani Tribal Trust Land and that I was to assist with interrogations. This was the start of my Special Branch career. After an absence of eight months from Victoria, I returned to Chibi to collect the kit I had left behind before immediately returning to the northeast. I remained in the Operation *Hurricane* area, opened in December 1972, until I commenced a shortened probation period with the Criminal Investigation Department in Salisbury prior to being recruited by Superintendent 'Mac' McGuinness for duties with the Selous Scouts in early 1974.

CHAPTER ONE
Selous Scouts attachment
1974–1976

Sunday, 21 March 1976 will forever be etched in my memory. I can recall that day as if it was yesterday. I was travelling from Bulawayo to the sleepy Rhodesian border town of Beitbridge, some three hundred and thirty kilometres distant. The town is situated on the banks of the Limpopo River which forms the border with South Africa. I was to take over command of the BSAP Special Branch station from the outgoing member in charge, Pete Gatland, who was leaving the Force at the end of the month. I was really looking forward to the posting and the challenges it would bring over the next few years. Being a Sunday, there was little traffic on the road which made driving very easy indeed and my thoughts wandered. I can remember vividly thinking what fate had in store for me as I crossed the Umzingwani River outside West Nicholson on that beautiful, sunny, cloudless day. I am a confirmed fatalist who believes everything happens for a reason. My thoughts turned to the reason for this trip and the posting, which had been at my request.

I was a detective section officer with the Special Branch. The week before I had been attached to the Selous Scouts where I had served the previous two years as one of the Special Branch liaison officers under the command of the colourful and charismatic Superintendent Mac McGuinness, alongside Major Ron Reid-Daly, commander of the Selous Scouts. During the early stages of 1974, Mac had recruited me for one of the two positions which had been created to assist detective inspectors Winston Hart and Harry Keffort; my good friend Detective Section Officer George Mitchell filled the other position. At the interview and in typical Mac fashion, a popular Police Reserve drinking establishment set within the confines of the police depot in Salisbury was selected for the interview. Obviously Mac was unable to disclose too much in the way of duties and responsibilities due to the Scouts' top-secret classification and all I really knew was that I would be posted to the Office of the Prime Minister at Special Branch headquarters in Salisbury. Although I was given a few days to consider my decision, I waived this option and accepted the transfer there and then. I had just been transferred to Salisbury Special Branch so the transfer to headquarters did not take long. On the appointed day, George Mitchell and I reported to Mac in his offices at the mysterious Special Branch headquarters in Salisbury, commonly referred to as 'Red Bricks' for the obvious reason that the building had been built entirely from red brick.

Mac then briefed George and me on the responsibilities and duties of an SB liaison officer, or LO, which, among others, were that we would be solely responsible for all captured terrorists, that is, the assessment and suitability of these individuals for inclusion within the Selous Scouts' ranks for use in the pseudo teams; in other words, we as SB LOs would make the final decision on the future use of the captures. As experienced interrogators this did not pose too much of a problem and in the vast majority of cases the captured terrorist would readily change sides and many fought and died with distinction during the war. Mac emphasized the fact that people's lives would be at risk and that future pseudo operations would be jeopardized in the event of a wrong decision being made. Pseudo operations involved 'turning' a captured guerrilla, i.e. getting him to change sides, and then sending him back into the bush with a Selous Scout 'pseudo' team posing as ZANLA or ZIPRA guerrillas in an effort to identify and eliminate bona fide guerrillas. The obvious danger was that a turned guerrilla might easily turn on his new masters, though this was an extremely rare occurrence but nevertheless a reality.

After the briefing, I was deployed to the Mount Darwin operational theatre and George to Mtoko. At Mount Darwin a fort had been built by the Selous Scouts with a ten-foot-high corrugated-iron wall forming the perimeter. The fort included a barrack block, ablution block, operations room, bedrooms for the permanent staff as well as for visiting Selous Scouts personnel, a single cell with a large iron ring cemented in the floor, a sick bay and the essential helicopter landing pad in a centre courtyard. At that stage, George operated out of a farmhouse on the outskirts of Mtoko as the fort there had yet to be built.

I settled in well and liked working under Winston Hart. We soon became firm friends. I enjoyed working with the Scouts and for the first six months was involved more or less exclusively with 1 Troop, commanded by Lieutenant Dale Collett SCR, with the non-commissioned officers, or NCOs, being Colour Sergeant Alan 'Stretch' Franklin SCR (later killed in a motorcycle accident at Kariba Heights), and corporals Chris Robins BCR and 'Chunky' Graham (later killed in a training accident). With the exception of Dale, all were originally from the Special Air Service, Dale having served as a platoon commander with the Rhodesian African Rifles, the RAR. They were all excellent men and it was a real pleasure working with them. I found them to be extremely professional with no elevated egos or attitudes.

However, as the size of the Selous Scouts rapidly grew, I began to notice that some of the newer white operators had over-inflated egos and regarded themselves as God's gift to the Rhodesian army. The vast majority was now being recruited from the Rhodesian Light Infantry, an outstanding regiment recognized as one of the finest bush-fighting units in the world. As far as I was concerned, the newcomers had already proved themselves on the field of battle, many being recipients of bravery awards prior to successfully passing the selection course.

The root of this issue, in my mind, stemmed directly from the commander, Major Ron Reid-Daly, who had been an extremely tough NCO, having fought with the Malayan Scouts, later to become C Squadron SAS, in Malaya in the early 1950s, and rising through the ranks to become the regimental sergeant-major of the Rhodesian Light Infantry. He was then commissioned and commanded Training Troop and finally Support Group 1RLI. He retired as a captain in 1972 but was persuaded by the army commander, Lieutenant-General Peter Walls, to come out of retirement to run the embryonic Selous Scouts. I first met him shortly before his retirement when I was operating in the Mount Darwin area. His men idolized him and he was a legend in the Rhodesian army.

As he had spent the majority of his service in the ranks, he seemed to have an affinity with his men who, because of this familiarity, thought they were a law unto themselves. To illustrate the point, I can remember being present at the Mount Darwin club one evening and the Selous Scout colour sergeant I was with started an argument with an air force helicopter pilot with the rank of flight lieutenant. The argument became very heated with the colour sergeant swearing at the pilot and jabbing his finger into the pilot's chest, a case of gross insubordination and a court martial offence in any man's army. We managed to get the colour sergeant out of the club before the situation deteriorated further. The next morning the colour sergeant telephoned Major Reid-Daly and explained his clearly biased side of the affair and nothing more was heard on the matter.

On another occasion, I was at Wafa Wafa, the Selous Scout selection camp on the shores of Lake Kariba, when Major Reid-Daly pitched up. At that stage, the instructors were all permanently based at Kariba with their HQ being located within the grounds of 2 (Independent) Company HQ and known as the Tracking Wing. The instructors ran tracking selection courses for members of the Territorial Army as well as the Selous Scout selection courses. There was not much going on at the time so, after greeting Major Reid-Daly, I sat down in the shade of a mopane tree with the major and Colour Sergeant Ant White sitting on the trunk of a collapsed tree within earshot of me. From the gist of the conversation, it was apparent that Major Reid-Daly had travelled to Kariba at the behest of White who had a long-standing association with him. White, or

'Worms' as he was affectionately called by Reid-Daly, began berating the officer commanding of the Tracking Wing, Captain Don Price, who, by design, was absent on duty from the Kariba area and who knew nothing of this meeting. The main complaint made by White against Price was that he (White) had recently taken leave with his family and had set out on a hunting safari to travel around the lakeshore by personal Land Rover to the hunting grounds. However, before they reached their destination, the Land Rover broke down in a remote area. All attempts to repair the vehicle were in vain and the family was forced to camp next to the vehicle. Before leaving Kariba, White had made it known that he would be away for four days and that if he had not returned by the fifth, a search for him should be undertaken. According to him, no one – in particular, Don Price – had lifted a finger to rescue him until the sixth day when their position had become perilous through lack of water. He was quick to point out to Reid-Daly that he would have been able to survive on his own but that his family was at its limits. (In fairness to White, he was an outstanding tracker, survival expert and a very brave soldier.)

Other points regarding Price's command capabilities were also mentioned. From the reaction of Reid-Daly it was apparent that the outcome would not favour Price. A week or two later, Price was posted out of the unit, White was promoted to warrant office class II and took over command of the Tracking Wing. However, he was shortly thereafter transferred to Inkomo, the Selous Scout barracks near Salisbury, on handing over to Captain Dave Scott-Donelan, ex-RLI. Years later, I spoke to Don Price about this incident and he confirmed that he had been given no opportunity to respond and, in fact, did not know the reason for his posting.

Sometime later, I was working with Ant White who was having issues with a Selous Scout army liaison officer holding the rank of captain. White made a remark to the effect that he had "fucked up" one army officer's career and that he would do the same again. He was obviously referring to Don Price, little realizing that Don was to make a name for himself, not only in the army but with the air force and police force as well.

So these were the problems I faced, inasmuch that any disagreeable decision I made would be overturned with a simple telephone call to Reid-Daly who would then, in turn, bring the dispute to the attention of Mac who would order me, without exception, to reverse my decision. Obviously I was unhappy with this state of affairs, becoming more and more disenchanted as time went by.

• • •

Late March 1975 saw me involved in pseudo operations in the Mount Darwin area. Three pseudo teams were operating under the command of Colour Sergeant Bruce Fitzsimmons in the Chesa African Purchase Area (APA) and were achieving phenomenal results. Fitzsimmons, another blue-eyed boy of Reid-Daly, was an outstanding soldier but it was apparent to me that his past and recent successes had gone to his head. I had spent several days in the field with Fitzsimmons during this deployment, interrogating and turning terrorists who were being captured on a daily basis by the pseudo teams. He seemed to resent the interference and made it clear that he could undertake this side of the operation as well. I have no doubt that he was capable but this was a responsibility which I took very seriously and I did not fully trust Fitzsimmons's judgment on the matter. In any event, I turned, without reservation, all the terrorists who had been captured on this deployment and they were reintroduced into the pseudo teams.

On my return to the fort at Mount Darwin, Captain Neil Kriel, the Selous Scout army liaison officer, informed me that a decision had been taken to withdraw Fitzsimmons and the pseudo teams for a twenty-four hour period to enable them to regroup and reorganize the pseudo teams which, by this stage, were operating in unacceptable ratios of turned terrorists to Selous Scouts, in some cases the former outnumbering the latter. The order was given that afternoon for all the pseudo teams to regroup at Fitzsimmons's position for helicopter uplift to Mount Darwin the following evening, a Saturday.

On Saturday morning, Fitzsimmons reported by radio the capture of a further terrorist by one of the teams. In view of the fact that they were to return later that day, there was no need for me to deploy to his position to carry out the interrogation as I need simply wait for the latest capture to arrive at the fort in a few hours' time. That evening, the whole team was extracted by helicopter, arriving safely at the fort. On their arrival, and after greeting and congratulating Fitzsimmons and his men on their success, I got hold of the terrorist who had been captured that morning for the purpose of interrogating him. Fitzsimmons immediately objected and advised me that he had already interrogated and turned the capture. I informed him that he was out of line and led the capture to my office-cum-bedroom where I intended interrogating him.

As normal, after any extraction of teams, the party was soon in full swing with the beer flowing, big steaks grilling over coals and the men thoroughly enjoying themselves. As the teams were to redeploy the following evening, all forms of personal hygiene were disregarded as a neat, fresh, clean look would most certainly have compromised them.

This was then the scene taking place as I was attempting to interrogate the capture but it was abundantly clear that Fitzsimmons had promised him a party as his attention was continually drawn toward the noise of the celebrations outside. However, I had established that the capture was a ZANLA section commander by the name of Habakuku Gumbo serving in the Chesa detachment and who had been recruited in 1972, trained in Tanzania and had been operating inside Rhodesia for about two years. About fifteen minutes after I had started the questioning, Fitzsimmons and Kriel came into my office and demanded that Gumbo be permitted to attend the party so that he could socialize with the other members to enable them to get to know one another prior to their deployment the following night. I refused and they left.

In those short few minutes of talking to Gumbo I could see that he was an extremely dangerous individual. He was cocky, over-confident and bragged about his exploits. He displayed none of the traits of any other captured terrorist I had had experience of. The terrorist hierarchy, through propaganda, brainwashed their cadres into believing that surrender to the Rhodesian security forces (SF) was not an option as they would face torture and a slow death, so the terrorists were always fearful and apprehensive when first captured. In Gumbo's case, it can be argued that at the time of his capture he had witnessed his erstwhile comrades willingly working with the security forces and being well treated which, coupled with Fitzsimmons's offer, may have given him cause to realize that no harm would come to him as long as he cooperated. I considered this possibility while interrogating him: his whole demeanour was wrong and my gut was telling me that he was no ordinary capture but a dangerous, hardcore terrorist who would use this opportunity to his own advantage. He readily volunteered information that he had planted two landmines – Soviet TM46 types – on the main Chesa road earlier that morning and had heard both detonate after his capture. I later established that a security force vehicle had detonated one and a local black farmer in his pick-up van the other. Security force members sustained injuries in their detonation but the black farmer and his entire family had been killed in the other blast. Although he was only aware of the detonations and not the results, he thought the whole incident was a joke.

I decided, after an hour or two, that Gumbo was a serious security threat and that I could not allow him to be integrated into the pseudo teams. My recommendation would be that he first needed to be fully interrogated and debriefed by Detective Inspector Pete Stanton of Special Branch, the foremost authority on terrorist interrogation and ZANLA operations both inside and outside the borders of Rhodesia. Pete had a phenomenal memory for names, identities, incidents and seemingly insignificant detail and was the perfect man for the job. He had helped tremendously in the past and was a great character and a good friend.

After I had made my decision, I informed Fitzsimmons and Kriel. I was met with open hostility and, at one stage, I feared that Gumbo would be taken from me by force but I remained steadfast in my resolve. After shackling and placing Gumbo in leg irons, I secured him to the iron ring in the cell, locked the door and retired to my room. Not half an hour later, the signaller on duty informed me that there was a telephone call for me in the operations room. On the other end, Mac wanted to know what the hell was going on because a fuming Reid-Daly had disturbed him, complaining that I was jeopardizing a successful operation. I explained my side of the story and remained resolute in my decision, but I was ordered to hand over Gumbo. I took a stance and refused to release Gumbo, again, giving my reasons. I realized that I was playing with fire but suggested I transport Gumbo to Bindura the following morning where Mac would have an opportunity to meet and assess the prisoner. This was agreed to but in my heart I knew full well what the final decision would be. But at least my conscience would be clear.

Early the next morning I loaded a still-shackled and -leg-ironed Gumbo into the back of my Land Rover and after securing a hood over his head to protect his identity, departed on my one hundred and sixty-kilometre round trip to Bindura. I found Mac in his office awaiting my arrival. Leaving Gumbo in the back of the vehicle, I addressed Mac on my findings and recommendation, emphasizing the fact that I regarded him as a hardcore terrorist. Mac then spoke to Gumbo in my presence and, after a few minutes, decided that Gumbo should be released for deployment that afternoon. To say that I was angry with this decision is an understatement – I was fuming. I returned to Mount Darwin and after driving into the fort, handed over the shackle and leg-iron keys to the gloating Fitzsimmons and Kriel who had been advised of my orders prior to my arrival at Mount Darwin. I was not going to be the one who liberated Gumbo by removing his constraints.

Gumbo was deployed as part of the pseudo teams late that afternoon. I was never to see him again. No further success was achieved by Fitzsimmons and his teams on this particular deployment and they were all, including Gumbo, withdrawn from the field and returned to the Selous Scouts barracks at Inkomo where Gumbo was welcomed with open arms.

A few short weeks later, Colour Sergeant Charlie Krause, a fine soldier, expert tracker and good friend, was deployed into the Kandeya Tribal Trust Land with his pseudo teams. Winston Hart had undertaken the predeployment briefings so I had little to do with the actual operation at the outset but became aware of their progress from my presence at the Mount Darwin fort. They had not been deployed for more than a few days when, on the morning of 29 April 1975, one of Charlie's pseudo teams failed to make their scheduled morning radio contact with him. He passed this information back to the Selous Scouts operations room at Mount Darwin.

Pseudo teams, in line with Rhodesian army standard operating procedure, were required to make radio contact twice a day – in the early morning and in the evening – when they would transmit their situation report, or 'sitrep'. Among other information, the teams were required to supply map coordinates of the location where they would base for the night. In the morning they would report any incidents that had taken place during the night and their intended destination that day. They could, however, at any time, make radio contact with their field commander, especially in an emergency. It was not unusual for a team to miss one radio schedule which might be for security reasons, such as when locals were visiting their base which would make any form of radio communication impossible. The terrorists did not carry radios so if the locals detected the presence of this type of equipment it would most certainly result in a compromise. However, once the threat had passed, the team was required to make immediate contact with their commander and pass the morning situation report.

Nothing was heard from this particular team for the rest of the day which was causing concern and so when they failed to make their evening radio schedule, Major Reid-Daly sprang into action. He ordered that a helicopter be made available the next morning and Charlie Krause and his team be uplifted and flown to the last reported location as passed by the team on the evening of 28 April.

Early the next morning, Charlie and his team were uplifted by helicopter from his mountain base and flown to the last reported map coordinates. His orders were to follow the tracks of the missing team until he located them. On landing, he did not have to look far. He found them all dead in their sleeping bags, gunned down while they had slept. There were six bodies comprising two BSA Police constables, three Selous Scout soldiers and a turned terrorist. The team had been seven strong when they deployed so one was missing. It was none other than Habakuku Gumbo.

Some days later, Charlie related his findings to me. The team, as per normal procedure, had slept in a defensive circle with one detail on rotational guard throughout the night. The moon was still fullish with the full moon having occurred on the 25th, so that after ten o'clock that night the blackness would have been transformed into near daylight. The assassin, Habakuku Gumbo, must have been performing guard duty sometime during the night and when the opportunity presented itself, put his well-prepared plan into action, dashing from one sleeping body to the next and firing a short burst into each. He had controlled his rate of fire, restricting the bursts to no more than three rounds per hapless victim, clearly realizing that he only had thirty rounds in the magazine of his AK-47 assault rifle and would have had no time to change his magazine if he had prematurely emptied the one on his weapon. It was apparent that as he had opened fire, the sleeping men had begun to stir with some reaching for their weapons before being cut down.

Once he had finished his dastardly deed, he disappeared into the bright moonlit night and made a bee line for the Mozambican border which was not too distant. He had a thirty-six-hour start on Charlie, he was travelling alone and he was implementing anti-tracking measures, so Charlie stood no chance of undertaking a successful follow-up. Thus Gumbo crossed the border into the safety of Mozambique.

Reid-Daly and McGuinness initiated an immediate cover-up. Reid-Daly issued orders that, under threat of dismissal or worse, no one who knew any details of the incident was to discuss or mention it, even among themselves. He arranged with the commander of Combined Operations (ComOps), Lieutenant-General Peter Walls, to have the names of the murdered policemen and soldiers withheld so that there would be no mention of their deaths on the daily security force headquarters communiqué which was released to the media and broadcast by the Rhodesian Broadcasting Corporation on the midday news bulletin. I am unclear how long this information was withheld before being released. Other details were altered which I was not privy to, one being that the date of death of the policemen differed from those of the soldiers, as well as the causes of death. This incident was never mentioned by either McGuinness or Reid-Daly in my presence nor did either one acknowledge the fact that my recommendation and decision should have been considered. At any rate, six young lives ended needlessly. History records:

Muchechwa, Constable: Special Branch BSA Police/Selous Scouts, killed in action at Mount Darwin, 28 April 1975
Zaranyika Constable: Special Branch BSA Police/Selous Scouts, killed in action at Mount Darwin, 28 April 1975

Muchenje, Lance-Corporal: Selous Scouts, killed by gunshot wound, 29 April 1975

Musafare, Private: Selous Scouts, killed by gunshot wound, 29 April 1975

Pakayi, Private: Selous Scouts, killed by gunshot wound, 29 April 1975

(The turned terrorist was not mentioned.)

As for Habakuku Gumbo, he made a successful escape to Mozambique where he was regarded as a war hero and treated as a celebrity. He survived the war but never returned to Rhodesia during hostilities. The information he passed on with regard to pseudo operations being undertaken by the Selous Scouts was invaluable to ZANLA. He also lectured on the subject at terrorist bases in Mozambique and Tanzania.

After writing this chapter, and most of the book for that matter, a friend of mine sent me several pages of Colonel Ron Reid-Daly's book *Pamwe Chete: The Legend of the Selous Scouts* which covers the capture and escape of Habakuku Gumbo. After reading this account, I have decided to set the record straight.

After Gumbo's capture Reid-Daly reported the facts as follows: "Gumbo was decidedly and very clearly put out by the turn of events, and although he eventually agreed to join up with us, there was something about his manner that worried the black Selous Scouts." This is a fabrication. A captured terrorist was never given time to decide if he wanted to work for the Selous Scouts or not. After interrogating the capture, the Special Branch LO would recommend whether he was suitable or not. In the event of his unsuitability – which I have mentioned rarely happened – the terrorist, as in my findings with Gumbo, would certainly have 'gone mining', a term used for a capture who was deemed a security threat, as in the case of a hardcore or fanatical terrorist. He would be shot and his body dumped in one of the many disused mineshafts in the bush. There was simply no way that a captured terrorist who was deemed unsuitable for inclusion in the ranks of the Selous Scouts would ever be handed over for prosecution by the courts as the Scouts' operations were classified TOP SECRET and the extent of the Selous Scouts pseudo operations, denied until the end of the war, would have become public knowledge. I wonder what Reid-Daly's reaction was when, "He [Gumbo] eventually declined to join up with us"; perhaps he was given a packet of jub-jub sweets and sent on his way. But there was more to come.

As mentioned when Bruce Fitzsimmons and his men, including Gumbo, were withdrawn from the field and returned to their barracks at Nkomo, Gumbo was transferred to Charlie Krause's troop and thereafter deployed into the Kandeya TTL. Reid-Daly goes on to say, "Regrettably, the members of the relieving troop, understandably not having the same feel for the situation as Bruce's section, fell out with Gumbo … A short, sharp contact resulted between the Scouts and Gumbo's section, which remained loyal to him. No one was injured but the insurgents absconded and returned to Mozambique." Unfortunately this was not the case and five Selous Scouts and one loyal turned terrorist met their end. In any event turned terrorists never operated in their own sections but were proportionally included in Selous Scout sections as in this particular case of five Selous Scouts to two turned terrorists. I had been deeply involved in this operation from the outset, having spent several days with Bruce in his 'mountain hideout' but Special Branch was never acknowledged and certainly no mention was made of my involvement with Habakuku Gumbo.

Reid-Daly also mentions that Gumbo returned to Rhodesia to continue the fight. This too is an untruth. Having single-handedly killed five Selous Scouts and one traitor, he was greeted as a hero in Mozambique and Tanzania and was therefore too valuable an asset to ZANLA for them to risk his redeployment into Rhodesia as he was personally known to scores of Selous Scouts. I never stopped in my search for Gumbo and the dozens of ZANLA terrorists I spoke to or interrogated were always asked of his whereabouts. He was well-known and every reply was the same: "He is still in Mozambique," or "He was last seen in Tanzania."

And then, just when I thought I had had my say on the Habakuku Gumbo incident, the saga again reared its ugly head. In Jonathan Pittaway's recently published *Selous Scouts: The Men Speak*, an article by Charlie Krause entitled 'A TT turns again' immediately aroused my curiosity. It is clear that Charlie is relating the Habakuku Gumbo incident. The first two paragraphs are in line with my reportage of the incident with regards to sending twice-daily sitreps by the call sign and to the presence of Patrol Officer Mike Clayton, which would confirm the presence of two BSAP constables in the pseudo team as all three had recently qualified as Selous Scout operators; however, Krause makes no mention of the composition of the pseudo team in his narrative. From then on, though, the story makes no sense. Knowing Charlie and the person he is, in my mind he would not have concocted this story.

Krause writes that he was based at the Mukumbura police post from where he was controlling his team on the ground – this is questionable for security reasons – and that he had overheard radio conversations between the police post and an early-morning border-clearance patrol, the latter reporting that they had found an African sitting on the side of the road who claimed that he had been involved in a 'shoot-out' and that he had run away to save his life. For some unexplained reason Krause contacted Major Reid-Daly and requested that a helicopter be made available to him so that he could find out what was going on. The helicopter duly arrived with Neil Kriel on board and after uplifting Krause, the helicopter flew to the position of the patrol with the 'shoot-out' victim. Neil Kriel, posing as a Special Branch officer, then took control of the man, the apparent 'shoot-out' victim. Krause stayed on board but as Kriel and the man approached the aircraft, Charlie recognized him as a TT, a turned or tame terrorist, who was a member of his call sign, the same call sign that had failed to make the previous evening's radio schedule. The TT was then questioned and claimed that he could not remember anything from the previous night and, in Charlie's own words, "he was put on the right track". The TT then admitted that he had been on guard duty during the night and that on detecting movement he had opened fire before taking off in the direction of the border.

Krause and Kriel then decided to fly to the area where the pseudo team had been working and, on landing, discovered the bodies of seven members of the pseudo team in a thicket. The bodies and all equipment were subsequently recovered to the fort at Mount Darwin. Not satisfied with the TT's story, Krause continues, "I had him placed in a cell with another TT [presumably the cell the author has alluded to] … The cell was bugged and the full story came out." Krause, however, makes no mention of dates, names or any other pertinent detail in his narrative, let alone 'the full story as it came out', nor does not relate how Gumbo was treated after the cell tappings or what was his eventual fate. After thirty-seven years, it appears that this incident is still being covered up, for what reason I do not know. I can only surmise that this is but another attempt to sanitize the Selous Scouts as a squeaky-clean outfit, without flaws. Unfortunately, this brings into question the integrity of Pittaway's otherwise fine publication.

•••

This incident was the final straw that broke the camel's back and I was more resolved than ever to transfer out of the unit. George Mitchell was still extremely unhappy with his lot and he moved around the same time from his position as a Special Branch liaison officer to work directly under Mac as his special tasks officer, and in which position he remained until the disbandment of the Selous Scouts in early 1980. Winston Hart continued with the Selous Scouts until 1978 when he moved across to the Special Air Service as the regiment's Special Branch liaison officer, together with another very good friend of mine, Detective Section Officer Peter Dewe. Mac remained in his position until disbandment, being promoted to chief superintendent along the way. Reid-Daly rose to the rank of lieutenant-colonel and eventually resigned his commission in late 1979, in some disgrace.

Although I was planning on leaving the Selous Scouts, I did not realize at the time that I was to work with them again in the future. I would also have close contact with the Special Branch officers I had worked with in the Selous Scouts. However, I had to wait several months before I could realize my ambition. In November 1975 I heard that the Special Branch station at Beitbridge was falling vacant in early 1976 and decided to make a bid for the posting. I approached Mac because I knew that if anyone had the right connections at the highest level, he did.

In January 1976, I was informed that my transfer to Beitbridge had been authorized and that I would assume command of the station on 31 March 1976. The Matabeleland Provincial Special Branch Officer (PSBO) in Bulawayo requested that I spend a week at the Bulawayo SB offices, familiarizing and orientating myself with SB procedures as conducted in Matabeleland. I would then take over the Beitbridge station from Pete Gatland over a meet-and-greet week of orientation, getting acquainted with the officials I would be working closely with: the chief immigration officer, the controller of customs, the District Commissioner and my opposite number in the South African Police Security Branch whose office was located at the South African border post.

I began the transfer process, getting quotes for furniture removals and so on. My wife Maya resigned from her job in Salisbury as of 19 March, her birthday, and joined me in Bulawayo the day prior to my departure for Beitbridge. I eventually bade the Selous Scouts farewell.

These were some of the thoughts that passed through my mind on that uneventful drive to Beitbridge. We arrived in the late afternoon and booked into Peter's Motel where we were to stay for the next week.

•••

In late February 1973, I was a passenger in a Land Rover that was ambushed by terrorists approximately ten kilometres from the Mukumbura police post that was situated on the eastern bank of the eponymous river, adjacent to the Tete province of Portuguese East Africa, or Mozambique. The driver, Gray Branfield, received serious gunshot wounds and collapsed. I received a gunshot wound to the left knee with the bullet lodging behind my kneecap. I suppose, owing to the adrenaline pumping through my body, I did not feel any pain or discomfort for a while and managed to take control of the steering wheel. Fortunately, Gray's foot was jammed on the accelerator pedal so we did not slow down through the killing zone, carrying on for another kilometre or so before the engine died and the vehicle came to a standstill in the middle of the road. A detective sergeant and two detective constables had been travelling in the open back of the vehicle. The sergeant had suffered terrible wounds, being hit by five AK rounds in different parts of his body. On stopping and with the assistance of the two uninjured policemen, we dragged the wounded to cover as I expected an immediate follow-up by the terrorist force. I was fortunate that tied to a piece of string suspended around my neck I had two ampoules of morphine which I injected into each of the wounded. I then instructed the two constables to hurry through the bush to the police post to summon help as our only means of communication was the vehicle radio set which had been rendered unserviceable by enemy rifle fire. Luckily, a motorized police patrol, under the command of Andy MacNeil, was alerted to our plight by the constables who encountered the patrol a few kilometres from the ambush site.

My knee was now giving me trouble; I was in pain and could exert no pressure on the leg. Help in the form of an air force helicopter arrived from Mount Darwin. Gray, the sergeant and I were casevaced to the Bindura district hospital after stopping at Mount Darwin to refuel.

As I was the least critical of the three, the other two were attended to first. While waiting to see the doctor, a nursing sister began cleaning me up. I had been in the bush for over a month and we got chatting. She introduced herself as Mair Roberts, a nursing sister from north Wales who had been working in Rhodesia for the past six months. We seemed to click straight away and I was sorry when I was eventually seen by the doctor. The X-rays confirmed that a large fragment of the bullet was lodged behind my knee and, as the hospital was not equipped to operate and remove the foreign object, I was transferred to a bigger hospital where I was successfully operated on.

As luck would have it, once fully recovered, I was posted to Bindura where I started seeing Mair. After a few months, our relationship had developed into something serious. Her contract with the Rhodesian nursing service expired at the end of September that year when she intended returning to the United Kingdom. As September approached, we began talking about getting married and decided that once she left, I would take leave and join her in the UK where we would make the final decision regarding our future together. Shortly before the end of September, she left Rhodesia for the UK. I applied for leave and took the precaution of applying to Police General Head Quarters for permission to get married. The application was submitted to Detective Inspector Vic Opperman, the member in charge of Special Branch, Bindura and whom I had sworn to secrecy as I did not know if I was to marry or not. In the event of a marriage not transpiring, then I could, on my return to Rhodesia, merely cancel the application.

Early in October, I flew to London where Mair met me at Heathrow airport and where we stayed with her cousin Beryl for a few days before travelling to her parents' home in Carno, north Wales. Toward the end of October, we were married and returned to Rhodesia at the end of that month. We set up home in a flat in the Avenues of Salisbury, and Mair started work at Andrew Fleming hospital, previously known as Salisbury Central hospital. I reported to the Criminal Investigation Department at Salisbury Central police station where I was to remain until my transfer to the Selous Scouts.

The name Mair is Welsh for Mary but I had difficulty in pronouncing it correctly, so I started calling her Maya by which name she was known from thereon.

Growing up on my parents' farm in the Bembesi area of Matabeleland, 1950. My sister Pat is flanked by my brother Ken (left) and me (right); my youngest brother Martin was only born the following year.

Recruit Squad 4/64 dismounted pass-out parade, December 1964. Back row from left: Constables Stead, Bird, Mackenzie, Scott-Roger, Harrison; third row: Constables Deamer, Musson, Gerber, Thornley, Taylor, Bagley; second row: Constables Rosser, Tunney, Nevitt, Little, Wood; seated: Staff Inspector Winchcombe (squad instructor), Mr D.W. Wright (Deputy Commandant), Mr G.M. Harries (Acting Commissioner), Mr A.R. Godwin (Commandant Depot), Mr Downham, Depot Chief Inspector Trangmar.

The initial PATU Section Leaders' course held over a two-week period in the Mavuradona Mountains in the Centenary/Sipolilo area in 1967. I am standing fifth from right in the middle row and my brother Ken is third from right in the same row. The instructors on this course were, among others, Chief Superintendent Bill Bailey who had fought with the Long Range Desert Group during the Second World War and Reserve Patrol Officer Reg Seekings DCM MM (seated ninth from the left) who was a founding member of the SAS with Colonel David Stirling. I took the training and deployments very seriously which stood me in good stead during the coming years.

Preparing for the mounted pass-out parade at the BSAP Depot, Salisbury, December 1964.

Patrolling the Zambezi Valley in the early days of the newly-formed Police Anti-Terrorist Unit (PATU). Back from left: unknown, Constable Fambarayi and Constable Bernard (with Greener shotgun); front: Patrol Officer Dave Lee, Section Officer Dave Parry (with Sterling sub-machine gun) and me. We had only recently been issued with Belgian-manufactured FN rifles, replacing the pre-First World War .303 Lee Enfields (SMLEs).

Above: The famous BSAP Jam Jar Inn at Kariba – so named because of the lack of glasses when it first opened, forcing the lads to use alternative drinking vessels, the most popular being empty jam jars – on the occasion of the transfers of myself (at left), Brain Croasdale, Tim Yeoman and Mark Berger in June 1969.

Centre: Visiting the Concession police station in my modified Land Rover in early 1973 with the suave George Mitchell in the passenger seat. Looking on are Section Officer Ted Crawford and Inspector Robin Johnson, respectively the 2 i/c and i/c of the station.

Bottom: Me posing inside of the Selous Scout fort at Mount Darwin. The photo was taken from my bedroom door with the operations and radio rooms directly behind me. The pale concrete in the background is the helipad.

With Winston Hart (right) in the Mount Darwin area, 1974.
Photo Winston Hart

In 1974 I revisited the site of the vehicle ambush in the Mukumbura area where I had been wounded the year before.
Photo Winston Hart

Maya sitting between old friends Reg and Veronica Anderson while on holiday on Paradise Island, Mozambique in 1975. Reg's two boys Gerald and Alec are also in the photo.

Gray Branfield at Katima Mulilo, South West Africa, after a fishing competition on the Zambezi River in 1988. Gray was to die under tragic circumstances in Iraq in 2004.

Some of my hunting trophies obtained during 1976 in the Beitbridge area. I hunted and shot the leopard on Lesanth Ranch at Les Mitchell's request after it had started killing livestock in spite of the abundance of game on the ranch.

Servicemen enjoying the Four Jacks and a Jill concert in Bulawayo, 3 February 1976. Fred Schmitt, i/c Chesa Ground Coverage base, is on the left in the white shirt and I am back centre with the big grin. *Photo Bulawayo Chronicle*

Patrol Officer Dave Ward in 1977.
Photo Dave Ward

Engineers examining the TMH-46 landmine crater after the mine was 'found' by Ian 'Perkie" Perkins on the Tshiturapadzi road. The damaged mine-protected Land Rover can be clearly seen and although extensively damaged, it was repaired and returned for service. Apart from earache Perkie and his passenger escaped unscathed. *Photo Dave Ward*

A plucky Ian Perkins and his faithful Bloggs only moments after the Land Rover he was driving detonated a boosted landmine. Geoff Blyth – involved in four landmine detonations but who on this occasion was travelling in the escort vehicle – looks on. *Photo Ian Perkins*

Ian Perkins at the Beitbridge police single quarters with his faithful dog which survived a landmine detonation on the Tshiturapadzi road in 1977. *Photo Ian Perkins*

The placid Limpopo River at the gorge during the dry season. The trees on the southern bank were under water during the floods of 1976.

Another view of the Limpopo during the dry season.

Floodwaters subside on the Umzingwani River at the access drift to River Ranch and Tuli. In 1977 I was involved in a contact with terrorists about two hundred metres downstream from the drift before the terrorists fled into the thick riverine vegetation.

Ian Perkins in a dried riverbed in the Mtetengwe TTL, 1977.
Photo Ian Perkins

Tshiturapadzi police base, 1977.
Photo Ian Perkins

Substantial defences at Tshiturapadzi police base, 1977. *Photo Ian Perkins*

In 1977, the SAP CID in Messina requested assistance from the BSAP as there had been a spate of break-ins on their side of the border with all indications that Rhodesian criminals were involved. A Beitbrige police team under Patrol Officer Ian Perkins crossed the Limpopo River from South Africa one night and the following morning located the gang's spoor, resulting in two of the criminals being shot and the recovery of all the stolen goods. Here the team poses with the recovered goods in front of SAP CID vehicles. From left are NS Patrol Officers Steve Thomas, Tom Vafeus, Mike Harvey, Remo Gardini and Constable Sibanda. *Photo Ian Perkins*

Left: 3 March 1977. I and a very brave man – my only staff member not wounded in action during the previous two days – pose with weapons recovered from these engagements: an RPD machine gun, an RPG-7 rocket launcher plus two projectiles and boosters, AKM/AK-47 rifles, stick grenades, a 60mm mortar bomb, a tin of AK/RPD ammunition and blood-soaked AK-47 magazine webbing.
Photo Dave Ward

Below: A PATU stick with captured weapons after a contact in the Tshiturapadzi area, 1977.

The high-level security bridge over the Bubye River in the Chikwarakwara area in 1977. The left bank is the Chipise TTL and the right the Sengwe TTL. Days after this photograph was taken, one span of the newly-constructed bridge was washed away by floodwaters and was never to be repaired during hostilities. *Photo Dave Ward*

Tshiturapadzi police base, 1977. *Photo Dave Ward*

A Hyena mine-protected vehicle.

CHAPTER TWO
Beitbridge: First blood to ZANLA
May 1967

On the morning of 22 March 1976, I reported to the Special Branch offices at the main Beitbridge police station and commenced the take-over procedure from Pete Gatland. The role of the Special Branch officer, up until that stage, was a fairly cushy one, limited to liaison, on matters of mutual interest, with the heads of various government departments, as well as the South African Police Security Branch on the opposite bank of the Limpopo River.

On 25 March 1976, I officially assumed command of the Special Branch station. I had a staff of one detective sergeant and two detective constables who were mainly engaged in routine security matters within the confines of the Beitbridge townships as well as screening migrant mineworkers returning to Rhodesia from the South African goldmines. Two patrol officers on attachment to Special Branch would boost my staff in the near future.

However, one did not have to be a rocket scientist to realize that the peaceful existence enjoyed at that time would not last much longer as, with the Marxist FRELIMO government assuming power in Mozambique only a few months beforehand, ZANLA would soon be opening up new fronts in the southern and eastern parts of the country.

On taking over, my area of responsibility consisted of a five-kilometre radius around Beitbridge, whereas the actual police area covered a massive piece of real estate incorporating thousands of square kilometres, stretching from the Botswanan border in the west to the Bubye (now Bubi) River in the east, with the northern boundary of the Siyoka Tribal Trust Land forming part of the northern border. The Limpopo River demarcated the official border with the Republic of South Africa with Beitbridge being the only port of exit. I set about taking steps to resolve this area imbalance and became proactive with the uniformed member in charge and his Ground Coverage (GC) section.

The member in charge was an old friend, Inspector Mobie van Wyk, who had recently arrived on transfer from Mount Darwin of all places, where he had also been in charge. Mobie, when his transfer from Mount Darwin was due, was offered the station of his choice and selected Beitbridge as it was situated on a friendly border – the only one – and was not threatened by terrorist incursions. I have no doubt that the good game hunting in the area also played a part in his decision. In any event, a more suitable and experienced person would have been hard to find and his Mount Darwin service would certainly be beneficial in the years to come. He was a good, solid man. Mobie's staff consisted of two section officers, five or six patrol officers, four or five African NCOs and about twenty constables. They were all good men and the white patrol officers, black NCOs and black constables who were engaged on security duties, would prove themselves time and time again during the years to come.

To the west of Beitbridge and from where the Umzingwani River joins the Limpopo, three huge game ranches existed. Between them, they covered over one hundred and eighty thousand acres. In the 1950s, the Rhodesian government, at the behest of their South African counterpart, sold this land at ten shillings, the equivalent of one 1970s Rhodesian dollar, an acre. This was to combat the spread of cattle disease, in particular, foot and mouth, from Rhodesia into South Africa, as it was the practice of the locals to drive their cattle into South Africa to trade. From east to west the ranches were River Ranch, Nottingham Estates and Sentinel Ranch. To the east of Beitbridge lay the Mtetengwe and Diti tribal trust lands and to the north the massive Liebigs Ranch which covered an area of over a million acres, split across the Beitbridge and West Nicholson police districts. The western sections of Liebigs Ranch were bordered by the Siyoka Tribal Trust Land. The extreme southeastern corner of the Diti Tribal Trust Land lies within miles of the famous Crooks' Corner where Mozambique, Rhodesia and South Africa meet. Crooks' Corner was used as a hideout in the old days by ivory poachers and other unsavory characters to escape the clutches of the law of the various countries by either moving the boundary beacons or by hopping from one country to another.

Two main roads, one from Bulawayo and the other from the capital Salisbury, converged on Beitbridge. The vast majority of the country's imports and exports went through this border, either by road or rail, including the vital fuel need to keep the country going. During school holidays, the border was always congested with human traffic on holiday to and from South Africa keeping the immigration and customs officials busy.

The area was sparsely populated, comprising desert-type sandy mopane scrub to the west and mopane, mahogany, teak and fever tree forests farther east. The monster baobab trees grew in abundance throughout the area. Water, or rather lack of water, was the biggest problem affecting the whole area. All the main rivers stopped flowing or ran dry in winter, including the Limpopo which held pools of water fed by subterranean streams under the sand. Keith Knott of Nottingham Estates made use of deep sand pumps to irrigate his citrus orchards from the Limpopo. It is said that, on a yearly average, more water flows under the riverbed than above it. As the entire area consisted of lowveld terrain, summer temperatures hovered in the mid-forties (Celsius) but in winter the days were lovely, cloudless and warm and the nights chilly.

The Beitbridge club, built and financed by Keith Knott's father and donated to the residents, was the social hub of the town, boasting a cricket pitch, squash courts, a swimming pool, tennis courts and a bar. Other draw cards were the Beitbridge Hotel, run by the likeable Dick O'Callaghan and which served the coldest beers in town and Peter's Motel which served excellent meals at reasonable prices. There was no television reception. If so inclined, hunting and fishing offered the sportsman plenty of opportunity and excitement. The area was teeming with game, with bull elephant hunting licences costing Rh$100 (100 Rhodesian dollars), the equivalent of £50. Lion and buffalo cost Rh$5 apiece and impala Rh$2. Licences were issued by the District Commissioner's office and were only valid for hunting in the tribal trust lands. On the private ranches the landowner could allow any amount of controlled hunting. All in all, Beitbridge was a very lively place, the ranchers and the farmers were of hardy stock and I was to make friends with some wonderful people.

Shortly after arriving, I attended a district security meeting with Section Officer Alan Ross-Smith at the District Commissioner's office in Beitbridge. Inspector Dan Werth, the member in charge of Nuanetsi, bordering the eastern side of the Beitbridge area and demarcated by the Bubye River, gave a comprehensive security briefing. I was astounded by the extent of terrorist activity taking place in his area and felt sure that the Beitbridge district, if not already infiltrated, would see terrorist activity in the very near future.

Although not occurring in the Beitbridge area, one incident would have an impact on our area. During the evening of 18 April 1976, terrorists attacked and killed two South African motorcyclists and badly wounded two others as they were returning to the border after attending a motorcycle rally in Fort Victoria. The terrorists then attacked a northbound freight train travelling from Beitbridge to Rutenga in the same vicinity. The incidents occurred approximately twelve kilometres south of the village of Nuanetsi on the main road. This led to the immediate introduction of the convoy system which was to be operated for the duration of the war. Two convoys ran daily between Beitbridge and Fort Victoria and vice versa.

Shortly thereafter, a convoy system was introduced, initially running from Beitbridge to West Nicholson, but as the war intensified, the distance was increased to run as far as Essexvale, some thirty kilometres from Bulawayo. Like the Fort Victoria road, this convoy operated twice a day from both centres. The convoy system was not compulsory but it was strongly recommended that drivers take advantage of it for their and their passengers' safety. Some who refused to heed this advice were to regret their decision.

The first terrorist incident in the Beitbridge area took place on 12 May 1976 when a 9th Battalion Rhodesia Regiment (9RR) vehicle was ambushed by terrorists on the road from Tshiturapadzi to Chikwarakwara. The ambush resulted in the deaths of Corporal T.J. van Tonder, Rifleman F.W.E. Bint and Rifleman P.W. Blignaut. Two soldiers were also seriously wounded in this engagement.

At the time of the ambush, I was engaged in a security patrol in the Chikwarakwara area where I had been for several days. I was unaware of the incident or the deployment of the 9RR company for that matter. Radio communications were virtually non-existent due to the topographical nature of the terrain which only permitted limited early-morning communications with Beitbridge. However, on the day of the ambush, I decided to return to Beitbridge and late that afternoon drove through the ambush position, glibly ignorant of the earlier ambush. At Tshiturapadzi, I became aware of the army deployment and stopped at the 9RR base only to be advised of the incident. No one, including me, had had an inkling that an aggressive terrorist incursion would have taken place so soon. To boot, I was travelling without an escort, with only my detective sergeant armed with a .38 Smith and Wesson revolver and twelve rounds of ammunition, as company.

A general round-up of locals living in the immediate area of the ambush ensued and I spent the night questioning them. From the interrogations, it was apparent that the terrorist group responsible had recently arrived in the area from the Sengwe Tribal Trust Land situated east of the Bubye River in the Nuanetsi area. From ongoing SF follow-up operations, it was apparent that the group had returned to the Sengwe after the ambush where it was engaged in a reconnaissance mission.

The area returned to some form of normality and was quiet for the next four months but it was apparent that the terrorists had infiltrated the area and were busy 'mobilizing the masses' in accordance with their Maoist doctrine.

In the meantime, Maya had started working at the South African government hospital in Messina, a mining town some eighteen kilometres south of Beitbridge and was commuting on a daily basis.

CHAPTER THREE
Insidious intensification
Late 1976

Rhodesia was for administrative purposes divided into various provinces. Each province had been declared an operational area and designated an operational name: Operation *Hurricane* covered Mashonaland, Operation *Thrasher* Manicaland, Operation *Grapple* Midlands, Operation *Repulse* Victoria and Operation *Tangent* covered Matabeleland. With the intensification of the conflict, other, smaller operational areas later came into being, the likes of operations *Splinter* and *Salops* covering Kariba and Salisbury respectively.

Beitbridge fell under Matabeleland, so one would assume that once hostilities commenced, Beitbridge would come under Bulawayo, the headquarters of Operation *Tangent*. However, this was not as simple as it would seem. Matabeleland was facing the full might of Joshua Nkomo's Zimbabwe African People's Union's (ZAPU's) military wing, the Zimbabwe People's Revolutionary Army, or ZIPRA, that was infiltrating the country from Zambia and Botswana in an attempt to secure their traditional Ndebele stronghold of Matabeleland. ZAPU/ZIPRA was primarily Soviet Bloc-sponsored.

On the other hand, Beitbridge was being infiltrated by ZANLA, the Zimbabwe African National Liberation Army, the armed wing of ZANU, the Zimbabwe African National Union under Robert Mugabe, which was supported, in the main, by Red China. Being bitter rivals, ZANLA was attempting to usurp ZIPRA's claim to Matabeleland by infiltrating through the 'back door' from Mozambique, which would eventually see both factions embroiled in a desperate struggle for supremacy, particularly in the Gwanda area.

Because of this, the high command decided that, for operational purposes, the Beitbridge area would become part and parcel of Operation *Repulse* and fall under Fort Victoria. This was to have a marked influence on Beitbridge as far as troop deployments were concerned. Both Matabeleland and Victoria provinces were stretched to the limit as far as their troop allocations were concerned with Beitbridge viewed as a burden, an unwanted orphan that no one wanted to assume responsibility for. We were left to fend for ourselves, as best we could, with minimal army support. The British South Africa Police would have to show that fighting spirit of old.

During the latter part of 1976, it was apparent from intelligence obtained by policemen on the ground that a substantial number of terrorists had infiltrated the area but who were maintaining a low profile. The first overt sign of such activity occurred on 30 September when five terrorists robbed the Tshiturapadzi store of clothing, foodstuff, and cash.

Police GC bases had been opened at the District Commissioner's sub-station at Tshiturapadzi and at Pande Mine from where selected patrol officers ran intelligence-gathering networks, or Ground Coverage operations, in their areas of responsibility. The teams would soon increase to operate out of bases at Latumba and in the Siyoka and the Masera TTLs. The GC teams operated under the protection of either police or military personnel for escort and base-security purposes. Due to the shortage of manpower and vehicles, GC bases operated with the bare minimum of protection. For section radio identification purposes the GC teams were allocated the codename 'Scouter', followed by the base identification reference, a letter of the alphabet, which in the case of Tshiturapadzi was Scouter Romeo, for 'R'.

Toward the latter part of 1976, there was a marked increase in terrorist incidents, with soft targets such as Internal Affairs bearing the brunt. On 24 November, Izak Nel of the Department of Internal Affairs (DC's office) was ambushed by five terrorists on the Tshiturapadzi road. No injuries were sustained but his vehicle was damaged by rifle fire.

On 8 December, Johan Campbell, also of Internal Affairs, was ambushed by an estimated eight terrorists on the Tshiturapadzi road, resulting in three district assistants receiving minor wounds. The vehicle was also damaged.

On 13 December, an Internal Affairs bulldozer was gutted by ten terrorists who instructed the driver to report the matter to the police patrol base at Tshiturapadzi. Fearing an ambush, the policemen did not react immediately but when they did, found the burned-out bulldozer.

On 19 December, Kayancee Ranch on the Bubye River, south of the Lion and Elephant Motel, was attacked by eight terrorists. The ranch owner was absent and the group broke into the homestead, stole weapons and ammunition and destroyed property. Interestingly, five or six ranches on the western bank of the Bubye River were all owned by South Africans. The same applied to the ranches on the eastern bank, stretching to the Mateke Hills in the Nuanetsi area, with the area being referred to locally as an extension of the Northern Transvaal.

At this time, more to reassure the Bubye ranchers with a presence than anything else, I was conducting a Special Branch patrol in the area, assisted by Roger Brittland and four detectives. Basing ourselves on the ranches, we would also be able to access the Diti Tribal Trust Land. Starting on Martin Grobler's ranch for a few days, we then leapfrogged from one occupied ranch to the next (several ranches were owned by absentee landlords, often South African). The patrol was uneventful but the presence of security forces in the area had a morale-boosting effect. The most frustrating part of any patrol was coming to grips with the enemy who fought only on their terms and, even then, did not hang around for long.

Also, at this time, the 'Bright Lights' system was introduced to the area. If the owner of an occupied ranch requested protection, then two police reservists, normally older men over forty, would be allocated for a two-week tour of duty to protect the homestead, particularly at night when the terrorists normally launched their attacks. Few ranchers accepted this service, preferring to organize their own security.

On Christmas Eve a patrol of Rhodesian Engineers operating in the Tshiturapadzi area called on some locals running away from the patrol to stop. The locals failed to heed the warning and the engineers opened fire, killing two of them. The police base at Tshituapadzi was informed of the incident and as in all such cases the circumstances had to be investigated and an inquest conducted by a magistrate, so Patrol Officer Dave Ward, in charge of the GC team at Romeo Base – the police patrol base at Tshiturapadzi – reacted and proceeded under police and army escort to the scene of the incident. The Land Rover that Dave was travelling in broke down and had to be towed back to base by his police escort travelling in a Hyena, a South African-developed mine-protected vehicle (MPV) based on a Ford F250 pick-up chassis and engine. While returning to base, the convoy was ambushed by approximately eight terrorists. The Hyena was struck by an RPG-7 projectile, injuring national service patrol officers Weaks and Folks and causing the Hyena to stall, resulting in Dave Ward tail-ending it with his Land Rover. During the subsequent firefight, Dave Ward and his partner, Constable Mudau, received wounds but, fortunately, none was serious and the patrol was able to fight off their attackers, causing them to flee. All four injured policemen returned to duty after receiving medical treatment. This was the last recorded incident for the year.

During 1976, the South African Defence Force took over control of their northern border from the South African Police. A company of Citizen Force territorial troops was based on a three-month rotational basis at Messina from where they patrolled the river. A regular Permanent Force detachment under Major Louw de Beer and his second-in-command, Lieutenant André van Rooyen, opened up the Soutpansberg military area headquarters in Messina at the same time. Van Rooyen was appointed liaison officer to the Rhodesian security forces and a close friendship developed between him and me which lasted until well after the end of the war. I was sorry when we eventually lost contact altogether. I also became good friends with some of the commanders of the Citizen Force units posted to Messina and was to benefit a great deal from their largesse, being 'donated' a 60mm mortar tube, plus base plate, sights and thirty bombs from one major who organized a shortened mortar course for me on a farm on the outskirts of Messina.

I positioned the mortar at the Tshiturapadzi base and gave the resident policemen instructions on its use. During the ceasefire in early 1980, when stationed at Gwanda, I was reunited with the mortar and loaned it, complete with a dozen bombs, to a lieutenant from the Royal Regiment of Wales who was in charge of the Commonwealth monitoring forces at the Juliet guerrilla assembly point at Siyoka, and who feared an uprising by the occupants. The mortar was duly returned to me and I made my intentions known that I aimed to return the weapon to the South African Defence Force but, on hearing of this, a senior officer ordered me, under threat of being charged, to hand it in to the national armoury, which I reluctantly did.

CHAPTER FOUR
Overt intensification
January 1977–June 1977

Another GC team, commanded by Patrol Officer Bruce Yates, a very keen young policeman, was based near Pande Mine, situated approximately twenty kilometres east of Beitbridge, Yates's area had been reasonably quiet until 1 and 4 January 1977 respectively when he discovered two landmines, both TMB-3A anti-tank mines of British manufacture, on the main Diti TTL road. Both mines were successfully lifted by army engineers.

At approximately 8.30 p.m. on 5 January, the homestead on Bar G Ranch came under small-arms and mortar attack from an estimated eight terrorists. The owner, Martin Grobler, and his wife, assisted by two Police Reserve Bright Lights, fought off the attack without sustaining injuries. The following morning, an army unit, assisted by trackers, followed the attackers' tracks into the Diti TTL where they had a long-range fleeting contact with the group and, although there were no injuries on either side, an RPG-7 rocket launcher and three rockets were recovered.

During the morning of 8 January, Martin Grobler, his wife and the same two Bright Lights who had helped resist the homestead attack three days earlier were travelling in Grobler's mine-protected Land Rover on the main access road to the ranch. A kilometre or so from the homestead the vehicle detonated a landmine, instantly killing the two police reservists in the back. Grobler was seriously injured and was to lose both his legs. His wife, however, escaped injury. The trackers who attended the scene estimated that the mine had been planted the previous night. The two reservists who died were both school teachers on call-up over the school holidays: Field Reservist Basil Calder and Field Reservist Raymond F. Gough. The Groblers, who were South African, returned to their home country after the incident and never again came back to Rhodesia.

•••

On 8 January, Dave Ward and his team located a TMB-3A anti-tank mine on the main Tshiturapadzi road near the police base.

On 11 January, Patrol Officer Bruce Yates and his team had a fleeting contact with a group of terrorists in the Pande Mine area. There were no casualties on either side.

On 15 January, an army patrol had a contact with an unknown number of terrorists, resulting in the death of one terrorist and the recovery of one AK-47, one RPG rocket and a Soviet stick grenade.

• • •

On 17 January, an army call sign apprehended a local who was acting suspiciously in the Diti TTL. This individual was handed over to me for interrogation. It was apparent that he was not from the area and could give no feasible explanation what he was doing here. When pressed, he admitted to being a trained terrorist who had become separated from his group during a beer drink and at the time of his arrest was searching for his comrades. He volunteered to indicate where he had hidden his weapon when he had become aware of the army patrol. I then drove him, under escort, to the area where he had been arrested and recovered an AK-47 assault rifle, an AK magazine pouch containing three fully charged magazines and a pack. After recovering this equipment, the captured terrorist, with whom I had established a kind of rapport, volunteered that he knew the locations of another four arms caches. From three of the caches, under his direction, we recovered two RPG-7 projectiles, nine 60mm mortar bombs intact, two TMH-46 landmines and fives sealed tins of AK-47 ammunition containing five thousand rounds of ammunition. The fourth cache had earlier been removed by the gang. I now had a problem on my hands with regards to the capture. The terrorist groups operating in that area would realize that he had been captured and had indicated the caches, thereby compromising him for use by the Selous Scouts. He could be handed over to the CID for prosecution before the courts on terrorism charges – an alternative which I quickly dispensed with – or he could work for me. He therefore became the first of five ZANLA terrorists who would work directly under my command during the coming years. He received a monthly salary paid out of Special Branch funds, was given accommodation in the African police camp and I looked after his general wellbeing. He reported for work every morning with my African staff, initially cleaning the offices and vehicles but was later armed and deployed with the Special Branch team. He became a very loyal and valuable member of the team over the coming years but was to face a very gruesome death at the hands of his former comrades during the ceasefire period in 1980 – a very tragic episode indeed and one which I will relate in due course. I also had his weapon tested by the BSAP ballistics section which reported that the cartridge cases from his weapon did not match those from any other incident.

∙∙∙

On 22 and 26 January, army mobile patrols detonated anti-tank mines in the Tshiturapadzi area, fortunately without casualties.

On the night of 29 January, Les and Fran Mitchell's homestead at Lesanth Ranch was attacked by a group of approximately ten terrorists with AK-47s and RPG-7s. Les and Fran were at home at the time and both returned fire, holding the group at bay. As Lesanth Ranch was on the main Fort Victoria road, a good tarred road, a police patrol was able to react immediately and, on nearing the scene of the attack, observed a green flare in the sky in the vicinity of Lesanth Ranch, obviously the terrorist signal to break off the attack. With the terrorists having withdrawn, the patrol remained at the scene until the next morning when army trackers commenced their follow-up. The tracks headed in the direction of the Diti Tribal Trust Land where they were soon lost. Fran was a terrific lady who observed the old farming tradition of preparing an extra place at the table and cooking an additional meal for any unexpected traveller, catering for breakfast, lunch and supper. I experienced her hospitality on several occasions and must say that I enjoyed a hearty meal every time, especially so if I had been on patrol for several days.

∙∙∙

Toward the end of the previous year, Superintendent Mac McGuinness had contacted me, inquiring if I was in need of any assistance in the Beitbridge area, as he had a team available to deploy in a pseudo role if required. I immediately accepted his offer and a few days later, Detective Inspector Henry Wolhuter arrived at Beitbridge to discuss and plan the pseudo deployment with me. Henry was a good man, who at one stage had been the police heavyweight boxing champion. We decided that the best chance of success for a pseudo team would be in an 'infiltration' to take place in the Chikwarakwara area, because of its close proximity to the Mozambican border. As a cover, the team would give out that they were a new group entering the area from Mozambique. In the meantime, I would prepare a full briefing of the area.

Henry and his team duly arrived at Beitbridge toward the end of January. The pseudo team was headed by Keith Cloete who had served in both the SAS and the BSAP. The African members of the team, for security reasons, were accommodated prior to deployment by Bruce Cook at Mazunga Ranch. After briefing both Henry and Keith, we travelled to Rutenga where a Joint

Operations Centre (JOC) was situated. The JOC was in a position to deploy air force aircraft; however, this would be limited to a fixed-wing aircraft for air support and a helicopter for casevac purposes only. It was arranged that Henry would keep the JOC informed of developments on a daily bases.

It was apparent that this deployment would not take the typical form of a Selous Scout operation, inasmuch as the Scouts planned longer term. The goal of the Selous Scouts was their successful infiltration of the target area as 'terrorists', being accepted as genuine terrorists by the locals and other terrorist groups operating in the area, with the view to capture terrorist groups intact, or for the deployment of Fire Force to attack these groups in such a way that the pseudo teams on the ground would not be compromised. This deployment would be the exact opposite inasmuch as the team would adopt a hunter-killer role. I don't know if Major Ron Reid-Daly was aware of these deployments, but I think not, because this was contrary to all the principles under which the Scouts operated.

I accompanied Henry and the team to Chikwarakwara where we based at the District Commissioner's rest house. The team was successfully deployed and I remained at Chikwarakwara for the next two days. On 29 January, I decided to return to Beitbridge and Henry relocated his headquarters to the police base at Tshiturapadzi while the team was making its way northward. I made an early start and headed home in a lone Land Rover, with only a police reservist as company. Approximately twenty kilometres from Chikwarakwara and on rounding a bend in the road, we observed a group of about eight males, apparently unaware of our approach, on the road at a distance of about fifty metres. We obviously saw each other simultaneously and shots were fired at the vehicle. Not wanting to drive into their position, I stopped the Land Rover and we immediately took up defensive positions on the roadside and returned fire, but by this time the group had disappeared into the bush on the side of the road. Feeling brave, we decided that we would conduct a two-man sweep of the area ahead, get back to the vehicle and hightail it out of there. Fortunately, the terrorists had fled the scene and we returned to Beitbridge without further mishap, stopping at the Tshiturapadzi police base for a cup of tea on the way.

On 8 February, Henry advised me by radio that Keith and his team had had a contact with four terrorists in the Tshiturapadzi area. Three terrorists had been killed, with the fourth being wounded but making good his escape. Three AK-47 rifles had been recovered, together with kit and equipment. The three dead were identified by locals as being the group's section commander, security officer and political commissar, all big fish indeed. Obviously, the pseudo team was now compromised and returned to Beitbridge before heading back to their base in

Bindura. This was a successful but short-lived deployment with no chance of replication in the future, as the terrorists were now more aware than ever of the pseudo-terrorist peril.

∙ ∙ ∙

After my experience of the 29 January when I had bumped into the terrorist group on my return from Chikwarakwara, and another close call toward the end of February when my convoy of two Land Rovers came under long-range terrorist fire in the Diti TTL, I decided to operate with a permanent escort and spoke to Mobie van Wyk in this regard. He suggested that the Beitbridge Police Anti-Terrorist Unit (PATU) be activated on an as-required basis with twenty-four hours' notice of intent, or a warning order, being issued. I agreed to his suggestion at once, immediately giving my intention to deploy on 1 March but without specifying where.

On 1 March, I departed Beitbridge in a convoy of three vehicles. My vehicle, a mine-protected Land Rover, was in the lead and I had as company an army major. The next vehicle comprised the Beitbridge PATU stick, made up of Doug Dugmore, the section leader, with Eddie King and Herman Neimeyer and accompanied by Detective Patrol Officer Hamish Barnes of Special Branch Bulawayo who was doing a stint assisting me. The third vehicle, another mine-protected Land Rover, was occupied by my staff in the form of one detective sergeant and two detective constables, one being a fine young man called Buranda. To add extra firepower I now carried an RPD machine gun of Soviet manufacture, complete with two hundred rounds of ammunition fitted to two belts housed in two drum magazines. We set off at the appointed hour but I found the RPD machine gun laid across my legs hampered my driving ability, particularly the awkward drum magazine, so it was agreed that the major, armed with an Uzi sub-machine gun, would drive. The doors of all mine-protected Land Rovers had by that stage been removed.

It was my intention to proceed directly to Tshiturapadzi and work back toward Beitbridge, the objective of the patrol being to visit kraals in the area and to attempt to obtain information on the whereabouts and numbers of terrorists operating in that area. This was a near-impossible task as the terrorists exercised, through terror, complete control of the locals. At worst, the locals could expect a cuff round the ear from the security forces, but a painful death from the terrorists if they suspected that they were collaborating with the authorities. Several suspected collaborators had already been murdered by the terrorists as a warning to others. We turned off the main Fort Victoria road onto the Tshiturapadzi dirt road but, owing to the condition of the road, had to reduce our speed to a crawl. We had been travelling for about twenty minutes or so and had just negotiated a slight incline in the road before negotiating a blind bend which commenced our decline on the other side. All three vehicles were travelling down the slight decline when suddenly a terrorist ran out into the middle of the road at a distance of no more than forty metres and aimed his RPG-7 rocket launcher at my Land Rover. I had visualized this type of ambush on a number of occasions and was determined that I would not die in this manner, so I immediately threw myself bodily out of the vehicle and, still airborne, brought the RPD machine gun to bear on my assailant and opened fire. Things then happened very fast.

On hitting the ground, I saw the RPG operator flee into the bush when all hell broke loose from the side of the road as the terrorists opened fire while I was taking cover. I immediately returned fire on the terrorist ambush party which was no farther than three paces from where I was lying. The PATU stick and Hamish Barnes were returning fire from their armoured mine-protected vehicle which they had stopped behind my motionless Land Rover and the major was returning fire with his Uzi sub-machine gun. I could not see my detectives but could hear Detective Constable Buranda screaming in pain from an obvious bullet wound. The PATU stick, urged on by Doug Dugmore, then drove through the killing zone, debussed from their vehicle and opened with a heavy volume of fire on the enemy position. However, the terrorists soon gave up the fight and fled the scene.

I rushed to Buranda's assistance and found him lying just off the road with a bullet wound to the stomach. I instructed Doug to sweep the contact area with his men and take up defensive positions in case of a counter-attack while I attended to the wounded Buranda as best I could. My detective sergeant appeared with a bullet wound to the hand which had severed one or two fingers, so I also attended to him as best I could. In the meantime, Doug's sweep party had recovered the body of one terrorist, together with his AK-47 and a variety of other equipment abandoned by the group. Contact was established with Beitbridge via a radio relay station and Mobie, after receiving our situation report, organized a casevac helicopter from Rutenga which seemed to arrive in next to no time. The injured were casevaced to Messina hospital just across the border.

The terrorist with the RPG-7 never fired the rocket and I was quite pleased with myself thinking that my fire had driven him off, but some months later I met up with Detective Section Officer John Davey, in charge of the Special Branch station at Chiredzi, who told me, from documents captured after a contact in the Sengwe Tribal Trust Land that one entry referred to our ambush where it was reported that the RPG-7 operator had experienced a misfire when aiming at the Land Rover and had been forced to take cover. Oh well, you can't win them all.

Bruce Cook, from Mazunga Ranch, who happened to be in Beitbridge at the time, arrived with his Shangaan trackers an hour or two later and we commenced a follow-up on the spoor. Thirty firing positions were located by the trackers who were able to track spoor for about three kilometres before it was lost as a result of bomb-shelling and anti-tracking methods, and so the follow-up was called off. Being late, it was decided that everyone would withdraw to Beitbridge where the Beitbridge Hotel was invaded by a bunch of dirty, scruffy and extremely thirsty individuals.

However, I was resolved to pursue the terrorist gang the following morning. Unfortunately, the PATU stick was unable to deploy but the army major who had accompanied me during the ambush came to my rescue by organizing elements of the army to accompany me. I was given fifteen territorial soldiers for the day, as well as one heavy army vehicle; I was also able to make use of the armoured mine-protected vehicle that we had used the day before. To my mind, we were deploying in force.

The following morning, 2 March, with the reliable Hamish Barnes and me leading the convoy in our trusty Land Rover, we once again drove down the Tshiturapadzi road and through the ambush site of the previous day. My intention was to travel halfway to Tshiturapadzi and then head north into the Diti Tribal Trust Land where the local population was extremely sparse. The tracks we had followed the previous day headed in the general direction of Chitongoni, specifically borehole 39 where there was a kraal situated. The road was in a terrible state and progress was slow but around midday we arrived at the kraal. I noticed a baobab tree on the near slope of a ridge feature to the south of the kraal, the only prominent high ground for miles around. From experience, I knew that we would find a terrorist base in the vicinity of the baobab. However, I did not expect it to be occupied as our patrol would have been observed approaching from a long way off. Nevertheless, I organized a line of troops to sweep the ridge, beginning the sweep from the baobab.

I had just started to question the kraal head when a runner from the sweep line reported that there were numerous plates of food under the baobab. The food was untouched but was still warm. Jackpot! A group of terrorists was in our immediate vicinity. I ordered that the sweep line be reinforced and continue sweeping eastward along the ridge.

The bush was thick, consisting of mopane scrub about five or six feet high. I had just positioned myself on the left flank of the sweep line when the terrorists opened fire. However, it was inaccurate with most of the rounds going over our heads. Although no terrorists had been seen as yet, our patrol immediately replied, by directing a heavy volume of fire into the terrorist position. All of a sudden, panic appeared to erupt in the terrorist ranks as they took to their heels away from the sweep line. With their weapons and packs, they were literally clearing the mopane scrub in leaps and bounds. They were very fast and, although I loosed a terrific amount of fire into the fleeing bunch with my RPD machine gun, I was unsuccessful as they had vanished over the ridge in a flash. There was a general lull in the firing but, as I was making my way to the vehicles to report the contact on the vehicle radio, a terrorist suddenly broke from cover, running frantically across my front at about forty paces. Without hesitation, I took deliberate aim at the target, gave him a lead of two or three paces and squeezed the trigger. He ran straight into my burst of fire and dropped dead.

I was then summoned to the centre of the sweep line where heavy blood spoor had been found indicating that one of the terrorists had been severely wounded: the signs showed that he was dragging himself along the ground, his blood dark red. We did not have to follow far and found him dead in a thicket where he had concealed himself. He had waited for the sweep line to pass him before crawling in the opposite direction to his final hiding place.

On the vehicle radio I was able to contact Beitbridge via the radio relay station and report the contact. Once again, Mobie van Wyk came to the fore and organized an air force Lynx, a Cessna 337 'push-pull' fixed-wing aircraft, armed with two 250-pound frantan (napalm) bombs, SNEB rockets and machine guns. However, when the aircraft arrived overhead there was not much for the pilot to do except sweep the area in the direction the terrorists' flight on the off-chance of detecting a target.

It was now late in the afternoon and we decided to make tracks for Beitbridge and asked the pilot it he could provide air cover for our return journey, a long shot but worth asking nonetheless. Without hesitation, he replied in the affirmative and recommended that we look sharp as it would be dark in an hour or two when he would have to abandon us and return to Rutenga.

Among ourselves we discussed the possibility of leaving an ambush party behind but as the terrorist base was next to a kraal it would be impossible for any ambush to succeed without compromise, and so the idea was dropped. All the food in the base was destroyed and thirty tin plates confiscated. The kraal head was to be taken back to Beitbridge for interrogation. The action resulted in two terrorists killed and the capture of one RPD machine gun and a tin of ammunition, one AKM rifle (a modified version of the AK-47), one AK-47, one RPG-7 rocket launcher and two rockets, three packs and various other odds and ends. From the interrogation of the kraal head, as well as captured documents subsequently recovered, this group, numbering fifteen, had been part of the group who had ambushed us the previous day and had arrived at the scene of the action only a few hours before us.

We returned without incident to Beitbridge with the Lynx providing top cover for most of the journey which included the site of the previous day's ambush. Once again a scruffy, dirty and extremely thirsty bunch of individuals invaded the Beitbridge Hotel. I decided to catch up with office work the following day.

•••

On 1 March, Jan Louw of Internal Affairs was ambushed by what appeared to be a lone terrorist at Fulton's Drift over the Mazunga River. Louw was unhurt but his vehicle was hit by five rounds. Several expended AK-47 cartridge cases were recovered from the ambush site. This incident was puzzling at the time as ZANLA were operating far to the east and had not extended their operational area north of the main Fort Victoria road, let alone across the main Bulawayo Road.

On 7 March, Detective Constable Julias Nyoni Buranda died of the wound he received in the action against the terrorist group on 1 March. He was a good man and was posthumously promoted to the rank of detective sergeant.

On 9 March, twelve terrorist recruits were arrested at Baboon store in the Nuli area of the Diti TTL. They were part of a group of thirty-nine who had congregated in that area awaiting the arrival of a terrorist group to escort them to Mozambique. The terrorist group was due to arrive at the store on 10 March. Elements of 2RR reacted but without success. It was apparent that the terrorists had been alerted to the arrest of the twelve recruits and had taken alternative action.

•••

On 14 March, a report was received from locals that four terrorists had been killed by one of their comrades near Mazebele kraal in the Diti TTL. On investigation, four bodies were discovered, together with four AK-47 assault rifles. There was no doubt that the four had been shot to death. This was significant as it was the first reported case of faction fighting between ZANLA and ZIPRA in the area.

Both ZANLA and ZIPRA were under pressure from the Organization of African Unity and its surrogate liberated states to project a united front and fight alongside one another for the common goal: the liberation of Zimbabwe. However, the enmity between them went back to the early 1800s when Mzilikazi's, and latterly Lobegula's, Matabele impis rampaged across Mashonaland, slaughtering the men and enslaving the women and children. It was only the white occupation of Mashonaland in 1890 that put an end to the perennial violence, but the historical tribal antagonism again manifested itself in the 1950s and 1960s with the formation of ZAPU and ZANU, based predominantly on the Ndebele- and Shona-speaking tribes respectively. (Mugabe, of course, would have the final say on the matter with the ensuing Matabele genocide in the early 1980s.)

The military wings of both parties thus made an attempt to comply with the OAU's demands to present a united front. ZIPRA recruits were sent for training to the ZANLA camps in the Morogoro Crater area of Tanzania. The camps were run by ZANLA who controlled every aspect of life: training, welfare and rations and no integration took place. ZIPRA recruits were kept separated from their ZANLA counterparts with their own mess halls and barrack blocks. Things finally erupted into a full-scale revolt by ZIPRA cadres over the issue of food which they claimed was substandard and nowhere near the quality given to the ZANLA recruits. Lethal force was used to crush the uprising and many ZIPRA recruits were killed.

When it came time for the trained recruits to be amalgamated, which took place in Mozambique prior to infiltration into Rhodesia, the ZANLA military commanders would ensure that the ratio favoured ZANLA with no more than two ZIPRA cadres in a section of eight. None of the ZIPRA cadres, no matter how competent, was ever given a position of responsibility. In nearly all cases, it was the intention of the ZIPRA cadres, that when infiltration into Rhodesia had been made and when the opportunity presented itself, to desert and make their way to either Botswana or Bulawayo to rejoin their comrades.

Acting suspiciously, one such terrorist was arrested by my detectives in the beerhall at Beitbridge during February 1977. He put up no opposition when arrested. I spoke to him the following morning and asked him, on no basis whatsoever, where he had been trained. After some hesitation, he eventually replied, "Tanzania." I nearly fell off my chair. He was quite open after that, admitting to being a ZIPRA fighter who had been trained at Morogoro. He had been involved in the food revolt. He had been shipped from Dar es Salaam to the Mozambican port of Beira before being transported to ZANLA camps near the

Rhodesian border and had entered Rhodesia in the area of Mapai, near Crooks' Corner, just after Christmas 1976.

On entering Rhodesia, his sole intention was to desert and attempt to make his way to Botswana to join his ZIPRA comrades. Near Pande Mine, three days prior to his arrest, his opportunity to escape came when his ZANLA colleagues drank themselves into a stupor, On deserting and before reaching Beitbridge, he had cached his weapon and spent the next day or two looking for ZIPRA operators who were in a similar situation. I think his hatred of ZANLA was greater than mine. After speaking to him for an hour or so, he directed me to where he had hidden his weapon where I recovered an SKS rifle, a weapon far inferior to the AK-47 assault rifle and normally issued to lowly militia, not to front-line soldiers. I mocked him about this and he was very angry indeed.

As he had not been compromised to any great extent, I deemed that his services to the Selous Scouts – who had just opened up a fort in Bulawayo and were concentrating on the ZIPRA incursions into Matabeleland – would be vital. I accordingly apprised Mac McGuinness who organized his immediate collection by a team from Bulawayo.

My detective sergeant and one of my detective constables received the Commissioner's Commendation for carrying out this arrest and for other outstanding work they had performed. Several months later, the Selous Scouts deployed into the Beitbridge area and I was visiting them at their camp on the Limpopo River when a beaming pseudo member approached me. He was none other than my deserter friend. He proudly displayed his AKM assault rifle, together with bayonet; additionally, he was carrying a Tokarev pistol in a leather holster, a far cry from the antiquated SKS rifle that ZANLA had issued him.

•••

On 16 March, Scouter Romeo, operating from Tshiturapadzi in a mine-protected Land Rover, detonated a landmine with the left front wheel. No injuries were sustained; however, three locals travelling in the back of the vehicle fled the scene after the explosion but ran into a PATU stick which took them for terrorists and opened fire, killing one and wounding the other two.

On 24 March, a vehicle travelling between Pande Mine and Beitbridge was ambushed by approximately eight terrorists. The sole occupant, the driver, was uninjured, but the vehicle was hit several times. The attack took place late in the evening so the follow-up commenced just after first light. Spoor was followed in a northeasterly direction for four kilometres before being lost.

On 29 March, young Patrol Officer Bruce Yates, the GC operator from Pande Mine, was travelling in a two-vehicle convoy. He was in the lead in a mine-protected vehicle, with a detective constable as company, followed by an escort of police national servicemen in a Hyena armoured vehicle. He was negotiating a small rise when, from the top of the rise, two RPD machine guns on either side of the road opened fire on him. Yates was killed almost instantly. Fire was returned by the escort and the group, estimated at twelve strong, fled the scene. This was a sad day indeed as Bruce was a fine brave lad. I was involved in the follow-up but spoor, heading in an easterly direction, was lost in difficult terrain a few kilometres from the site of the ambush.

At this stage, a BSAP Support Unit section, the 'Black Boots', had been detailed to continue the follow-up. The section was commanded by Patrol Officer George Hawkins. I again consulted my map while planning our next course of action, and Diti store stuck out like a sore thumb, being in the direct path the terrorists were taking before the spoor had been lost. I reckoned that the terrorist group would be in a state of elation after killing a white policeman and would be in a mood to celebrate. Everything pointed to Diti store as the likely place: beer was sold there.

I discussed this possibility with George Hawkins and it was agreed that he would ambush the store that night. He managed to move into position without being compromised but due to the lack of cover was not able to select the best site. At approximately nine o' clock, a terrorist group of around thirty descended on the store. The section commander initiated the ambush and the gang fled. The Support Unit section remained in ambush for the remainder of the night. At first light, a sweep of the contact area revealed one dead terrorist, one RPD machine gun and three AK-47 assault rifles. Several packs and documents were also recovered. Blood spoor was also found indicating other terrorists had been wounded. Once again, a follow-up of the spoor was initiated but was again lost after a few kilometres.

On 7 April, a section of Support Unit under the command of Patrol Officer Ron Rink had a further contact with an estimated twenty terrorists in the Diti area. No casualties were inflicted on the group but two AK-47 assault rifles were recovered from the contact area, as well as a 60mm mortar tube. The troop commander, Section Officer Tom Archer, handed the weapons over to me but asked that he retain the 60mm mortar as his troop had no support weapons. I readily agreed and therefore only declared the two AKs as having been recovered.

I even gave him all the captured 60mm mortar bombs in my possession. I must add that I really enjoyed working with the BSA Police Support Unit: we were all on the same wavelength, so to speak.

•••

On the 11 April, over one hundred head of cattle were stolen from Groenevelt Farm on the Bubye River and driven into the Diti TTL. During follow-up operations, contact was made with an estimated twelve terrorists. No casualties were inflicted on them but three AK assault rifles were recovered, together with most of the missing stock.

On 28 April, an Internal Affairs convoy travelling from Tshiturapadzi to Beitbridge was ambushed by an estimated twelve terrorists. One Internal Affairs district assistant received gunshot wounds and one went missing; whether he fled the scene or not is unknown but, on 1 May, reports were received that a group of three terrorists travelling in the area was accompanied by a male dressed in khaki cloth, similar to that worn by district assistants.

On 1 May, a group of six terrorists robbed a store in the Siyoka Tribal Trust Land. All were Ndebele speakers which indicated that they were ZIPRA. This was the first report of ZIPRA infiltrating the area. Troops from Gwanda conducted the follow-up and located an abandoned base.

On 2 May, an army section, call sign 86 Bravo, had a fleeting contact with an unknown number of terrorists in the Diti TTL. There were no security force casualties but blood spoor was found, indicating that one of the terrorists had been wounded. Tracks were eventually lost.

Also on 2 May, Dave Ward and his men from Tshiturapadzi had a contact with an unknown number of terrorists in the Diti TTL. No casualties were sustained on either side.

On 9 May, the police base at Tshiturapadzi came under terrorist attack at nine o' clock in the evening. Most occupants were in bed at the time but the camp guards reacted immediately and the 60mm mortar that I had sited in the base and zeroed in on the ridge to the north of the base, the obvious area of attack, was brought into action and was instrumental in driving off the assault. The terrorists, apart from AK and RPD fire, also fired several RPG-7 rockets into the base. Minor injuries were inflicted on several members in the base but the terrorists did not hang around for long and fled the scene. The follow-up, undertaken the following morning, indicated that at least twelve terrorists had taken part in the attack.

On 14 May, a civilian vehicle detonated a landmine on the Tshiturapadzi road, resulting in the death of the driver and causing serious injury to four passengers. The passengers were all casevaced by air force helicopter to Chiredzi hospital.

On 19 May, the police base at Pande Mine was attacked by an unknown number of terrorists. The attack was repelled, without injury to either side. However, the Pande Mine store was attacked by six terrorists simultaneously and a large quantity of goods stolen. During this attack, the mine compound police sergeant was shot and killed and another local injured. The next morning, a sweep of the area resulted in the recovery of two notebooks, one Soviet stick grenade and several AK-47 assault rifle magazines.

On 3 June, a Mr Thompson from Bubani Ranch was ambushed by an unknown number of terrorists on the Bubye River road. Thompson managed to drive through the ambush without sustaining injury. However, the follow-up patrol could not locate the ambush site as Thompson was reluctant to return to the scene.

On 4 June, elements of the police Support Unit had a fleeting contact with a group of seven terrorists in the Diti TTL. On the same day, another Support Unit section had a fleeting long-range contact with a group of ten terrorists. Again, there were no injuries sustained by either side. Both follow-up operations ended after spoor was lost owing to anti tracking methods implemented by the terrorists.

On 8 June, elements of Support Unit had a fleeting contact with a group of approximately nineteen terrorists; once again, no injuries were inflicted on the enemy and spoor was lost after a short follow-up.

•••

On 10 June, Patrol Officer Webb-Martin, who had taken over command from Dave Ward at the Tshiturapadzi police base, was ambushed by approximately eight terrorists on the Tshiturapadzi road. Webb-Martin was slightly wounded in the hand during the contact. By chance, I was conducting a patrol in the area with the intrepid Bruce Cook and his Shangaan trackers when we heard the report of the ambush on the police radio net. We immediately responded, arriving at the scene some thirty minutes later.

Bruce's trackers immediately cast for spoor and, although the terrorists had bomb-shelled, selected and decided on following one particular set of tracks. We were reinforced by an army stick and began the follow-up. After about a kilometre, the spoor indicated that the person we were following had reduced his run to a walk and was obviously starting to relax. We followed the tracks for a further three or four kilometres when the spoor was joined by another set of tracks which the trackers confirmed was present at the ambush site. We carried on until the trackers indicated some very heavy bush ahead and, using sign language, told us that the enemy, at least two of them, was holed up there. As I say, the bush was very thick and so, after a quick council of war, decided on a headlong charge through the suspect area. We formed up into an extended line and, on the count of three, charged. All suspected hiding places were subjected to prophylactic fire. The terrorists, about five of them, returned fire before fleeing. We continued our forward charge but in the thick bush lost contact with one another so we ceased fire, fearing one of us might be shot by friendly fire. The trackers, who had taken cover during the charge, came up and again began to cast for spoor, in the process discovering the body of a terrorist, his AK-47 assault rifle, two packs and some AK magazines. After a water- and smoke break, we decided to call it a day as it was now late in the afternoon. On our return to Beitbridge that evening, Bruce and I celebrated our small victory with some ice-cold Lion Lagers at the Beitbridge Hotel.

•••

On the night of 11 June, the police base at Pande Mine was attacked by a large group of terrorists with 82mm mortars, small arms, RPG-7 rockets and, of all things, a 75mm recoilless rifle. Pande Mine had recently closed due to the security situation and it was deserted, except for the police who had moved into some of the mining houses.

At first light the following morning, I proceeded to the mine and spoke to the patrol officer in charge, an American (he deserted shortly after the attack and returned to the US). He reported that just after nine o'clock the previous evening, the peace and tranquillity of the night had been shattered by several terrific explosions. Realizing that they were under attack and with the bunkers and trenches still under construction, they took cover as best they could. The attack was being launched from the top of a hill to the south of the base from a distance of about four kilometres. The occupants returned fire but knew that it was ineffective because of the distance. The enemy was also using small arms but this was also ineffectual. The barrage lasted for about half an hour before the terrorists broke off the engagement. It was only at daylight that the police realized what they had been up against when several 82mm mortar tail fins were recovered, all fortunately off target and ineffective; but it was a different matter with the 75mm recoilless rifle. One of the rooms, occupied by two civilians, had received a direct hit with the shell passing over the sleeping men and exiting the opposite wall. Not being an artillery man, it was later explained to me that the terrorists had used the wrong type of warhead. They were using HEAT (high-explosive anti-tank) rounds which were only effective against armour. I was also impressed with the accuracy of the fire; it was also explained to me that the sighting was normally carried out in conjunction with a mounted 12.7mm heavy machine gun, an HMG, which zeroed in on the target with tracer, and the elevation of the weapon adjusted accordingly. However, if the HMG was not available, as in this case, then the weapon would have to be bore-sighted on the target with good daylight needed for this which meant that the terrorists had set the weapon up during the afternoon prior to the attack: a sobering thought.

A clearance patrol had already deployed to the area from where the terrorists had launched their attack, returning with six empty 75mm shell cases and an unopened box of one thousand AK/RPD machine-gun rounds which pleased me no end as I now had plenty of ammunition and did not have to be reliant on ammunition stripped from AK magazines recovered from contacts. The follow-up lasted for eight kilometres before the tracks were lost.

It was not a pleasant thought knowing that the terrorists had a heavy weapon, nothing we could match, in the area.

•••

On 15 June, an Internal Affairs vehicle detonated a landmine on the Tshiturapadzi road. No injuries were sustained by the occupants.

CHAPTER FIVE
Landmines, ambushes and poison
July–December 1977

The terrorists had been very active during the first six months of the year and had extended their area of operation by crossing the main Fort Victoria road into the Mtetengwe Tribal Trust Land. Beitbridge, although experiencing an increase in terrorist numbers – it was now estimated that one hundred and fifty terrorists were operating in the area – and an expansion of their operational area, was not to benefit from increased security manpower: no extra troops were drafted into the area and we had to continue the fight as best we could.

Mobie van Wyk was compelled to open a further GC base at the Latumba shopping centre, only twenty kilometres from Beitbridge, on the main Fort Victoria road and opposite the turn-off to the dreaded Tshiturapadzi road. Patrol Officer Ian 'Perkie' Perkins was given command of the base, nominated as Yankee Base, with his protection consisting of either Support Unit or elements of the Rhodesia Regiment. His area of responsibility would encompass the whole of the Mtetengwe TTL north of the main Fort Victoria road.

•••

On 1 July, an Internal Affairs convoy was ambushed by an estimated ten terrorists on the Tshiturapadzi road. Fire was returned but no casualties were sustained by either side.

On 2 July, elements of D Company 6RR, call sign 241 Bravo, were patrolling in the Mtetengwe Tribal Trust Land when they were attacked by a group of terrorists using small-arms and 60mm mortar fire. The attack, in the main, was unsuccessful but a fluke 60mm bomb fell among three of the troops, killing one and seriously wounding the other two. The wounded were casevaced by helicopter to the Messina hospital. Rifleman Michael C. Bosch, D Company 6th Battalion Rhodesia Regiment was killed in action that day.

On 8 July, a civilian vehicle, travelling alone to Beitbridge on the main Bulawayo road and occupied by four African males, was ambushed by terrorists approximately twenty-seven kilometres from their destination. Two of the occupants were badly wounded and transferred to the Messina hospital, where one succumbed.

During the evening of 8 July, two terrorists, armed with pistols, entered the cocktail bar at the Beitbridge beer hall and gathered some of the locals together.

The reason for this was not known as they started firing their weapons in the air. One of my off-duty detectives was present. He was armed, drew his pistol and fired on the terrorists and a kind of Wild West shootout ensued. On the first shots being fired, absolute pandemonium erupted, with only one object in mind: the patrons set about exiting the premises as fast as possible; the security fence surrounding the beer hall was stampeded and, within minutes, the hall had emptied, with the two terrorists also making a hurried departure. One of the locals was wounded in the foot. When I arrived on site a short while later, there were hundreds of pairs of shoes abandoned at the fence, supposedly to enable the owners to grip the diamond mesh with their toes. I had a good laugh.

On 9 July, a Support Unit section contacted an unknown number of terrorists in the Mtetengwe TTL. No casualties were sustained by either side. One RPD machine gun was recovered from the contact area.

On 13 July, a section of D Company 6RR contacted a group of approximately six terrorists in the Mtetengwe TTL. No casualties were sustained by either side.

On 21 July, an Internal Affairs vehicle detonated a landmine in the Chipisi TTL. No injuries were sustained by the occupants. Elements of B Company 9RR reacted.

On 26 July, elements of D Company 6RR, travelling by vehicle, detonated a landmine in the Mtetengwe TTL. No casualties were sustained.

On 1 August, Scouter Bravo from Tshiturapadzi, travelling in convoy in a mine-protected Land Rover, detonated a landmine on the Tshiturapadzi road. Patrol officers Ward and Webb-Martin had been transferred by this stage and I was yet to meet the GC operator involved. There were no casualties. Scouter Bravo would soon change their identification name to Scouter Zulu and the police base at Tshiturapadzi would be known as Zulu Base.

On 3 August, elements of Support Unit, call sign Mantle India, had a long-range, fleeting contact with an estimated fifteen to twenty terrorists in the Mtetengwe TTL. No injuries were inflicted by either side and tracks were followed for approximately five kilometres before being lost owing to anti tracking methods employed by the terrorists.

On 8 August, a police vehicle patrol acting as escort for an Internal Affairs vehicle was ambushed by an unknown number of terrorists on the Tshiturapadzi road. Fire was returned, without effect, but causing the attackers to flee. No injuries were sustained by either side.

On 10 August, in the Tshiturapadzi area, three locals were shot dead by terrorists who accused them of collaborating with the security forces.

On 11 August, elements of B and F companies 9RR attacked a group of eight terrorists in the Tshiturapadzi TTL, resulting in the capture of one terrorist and the recovery of his AKM assault rifle.

On the same date and in the same area, elements of Internal Affairs had a contact with unknown number of terrorists in the Tshiturapadzi area at the Sinyoni cattle dip tank. There were no casualties on either side.

On 12 August, in the Diti TTL, elements of Support Unit, call sign Mantle India 1, contacted and killed one terrorist and recovered an AK-47 assault rifle. No casualties were sustained by Support Unit members.

On 13 August, elements of D Company 6RR, call sign 83 Charlie, made contact with an estimated five terrorists in the Mtetengwe TTL with one terrorist killed and one AK-47 assault rifle recovered.

...

During the early hours of 14 August, an employee of Raymond Roth, the local supermarket owner, staggered into the Beitbridge clinic where he was treated for bayonet wounds. Roth had reported him and four other employees as missing during the late afternoon of the previous day when they had failed to return from his store at Pande Mine, which they had visited that morning.

The full story behind this tragedy began about a month earlier. I was aware that Superintendent Mac McGuinness had access to poisons which could be introduced into foodstuffs, medicines and clothing. I gave this some thought and realized that I could arrange to have similar poisoned items delivered to the terrorists without suspicion. Raymond Roth's staff and, in particular, those members who visited Pande Mine every Saturday morning to replenish stocks and pay wages were strongly suspected of supplying the terrorists with food as a form of protection. I decided that they could be unwittingly used to deliver goods to the intended victims.

To this end, I contacted Mac and explained the situation, stressing the point on more than one occasion that I required slow-acting poison. He agreed to my request and subsequently dispatched Henry Wolhuter to assist me. Prior to his arrival at Beitbridge, Henry dropped off three turned terrorists, one of whom was his right-hand man, Sydney, with my old mate Bruce Cook at Mazunga who had once again agreed to look after them.

I explained my plan of action to Henry. Raymond Roth's vehicle normally departed from the supermarket every Saturday at eight in the morning and proceeded to Pande Mine, returning to Beitbridge by three in the afternoon. I suggested that his team stop the vehicle about ten kilometres east of Beitbridge on the Pande Mine road, inform the driver and his assistants that they, Henry's team, were part of a terrorist gang who had robbed a store in the area but, as they were required for operations elsewhere, instruct the driver to either deliver the goods to their comrades at Pande Mine or to ensure that the comrades received the goods intact and, finally, to threaten the vehicle occupants with death if the whole consignment wasn't handed over. This was a simple but effective plan and Henry agreed to it. Henry also confirmed that the poison was slow-acting.

The contaminated items included Dr Strong 500 capsules, a branded medicine that supposedly increased sexual prowess and which the terrorists craved. Tins of bully beef were also a favourite. Sachets of Eno's liver salts – which the terrorists believed cured hangovers – were also high on their list. Underpants and vests were contaminated with a mercury-based heavy metal solution which entered the body via the sweat glands in the groin and armpits. For obvious reasons, not all the capsules, Eno's sachets or tins of bully beef were contaminated and other innocent items, such as bottles of Coke, bread, cigarettes and the like were added to the consignment.

On Saturday 30 July, Henry and I did a dry run, but without the team. Henry positioned himself about five kilometres out on the Pande Mine road while I kept Roth's supermarket under surveillance. As soon as I observed the vehicle leaving the supermarket, I radioed the information to Henry and the vehicle passed him by shortly thereafter.

On the morning of 6 August, Henry collected the team from Mazunga and drove directly to the selected spot on the Pande Mine road and concealed the vehicle in thick bush just off the road. I contacted Henry once the vehicle had departed the supermarket. The team observed the approaching vehicle and stopped it. The driver and his assistants were pleased to see them, wanting to stop and chat. The consignment was duly handed over, along with instructions and warnings, and the vehicle proceeded on its way to Pande Mine. There was nothing else to do now but to wait for information to come through regarding any results, which might take months.

Henry and his team returned directly to Bindura without passing through Beitbridge, and I wasn't to see him again for several months.

No report was forthcoming from any of Raymond's staff involved in the incident or from Raymond himself, on the presumption that the staff might have reported the incident to him. Raymond and his two brothers had been born and bred in Beitbridge, and his father, from whom they had inherited the store, insisted that they spend time living among the locals as youngsters. All three were absolutely fluent in the Venda language, a Shona dialect, and over the years had developed a strong bond with the locals. Little went on in Beitbridge and the surrounding countryside that they did not know about.

A week later, on Saturday 13 August, Raymond's driver and four staff members departed for the store on schedule. Exactly what later transpired came to light as a result of a police investigation, from interrogations by my detectives of the locals who witnessed the incident and from statements made by the surviving employee.

When the vehicle was stopped and the 'goods' handed over to Raymond's staff on the morning of 6 August, they apparently went looking for the terrorists, as we had planned. It was unclear if they actually located them in the nearby kraal and personally handed over the goods or whether they simply left them with the kraal head for safekeeping until the terrorists made an appearance. What was established was that on the afternoon of 6 August, a group of twelve terrorists, including the detachment commander Metzi Rimwe, was present in the kraal celebrating their windfall of Cokes, cigarettes and food. They had not been celebrating for long when one became violently sick and died, then a second and then a third. By this stage, Rimwe and his gang were in a state of absolute panic, apparently scuttling around hysterically trying to escape from some unseen terror. When they eventually calmed down Rimwe had all the food and goods collected and moved the surviving gang members to their nearby base, for the rest of the afternoon purging themselves with saltwater to induce vomiting. That night two of the women who were sleeping with the terrorists died. They were from the village and their death incensed the inhabitants.

The following morning the death toll stood at four terrorists and the two local girls. Rimwe pledged to avenge their deaths.

On the morning of 13 August, Rimwe had a reception committee waiting for Raymond's vehicle which his men stopped on the Pande road, forcing the driver to drive to the kraal of the incident. At the kraal a large crowd had gathered, including people from neighbouring kraals. A kangaroo court was held and all five of Raymond's employees were sentenced to death. However, prior to sentence being carried out, Rimwe had all the 'goods' brought forward and the five condemned men were forced to eat the food, smoke the cigarettes, drink the Cokes and take the pills, while everyone stood back and waited. After an hour or so, the crowd became impatient and started baying for the condemned to be killed. Metzi Rimwe then gave the order for the public executions to commence.

The five were then brought forward, one at a time, and bayoneted to death to tumultuous cheers and applause from the spectators. After the sentence had been carried out, the deceased were placed in a common shallow grave and covered.

But one was still alive. Seriously injured, he regained consciousness sometime during the night and, realizing that the dead bodies of his colleagues were on top of him, managed to claw his way out of the grave. Under cover of darkness, he made good his escape and reached the safety of Beitbridge ten kilometres away: a very lucky man indeed as he was to make a complete recovery.

The four bodies were recovered from the grave by the police and released to the relatives for burial. Raymond and his staff suspected my involvement from the outset but Raymond never broached the subject with me personally. Instead, he had Dave Amos, a senior customs officer at Beitbridge, who was also a captain in the Rhodesia Regiment, approach me in confidence. I obviously denied any involvement.

Several months later, Henry Wolhuter had cause to visit me in Beitbridge, leaving his vehicle parked outside my office. After an hour or so, he went to collect something from the vehicle and found a letter containing a death threat, mentioning him by name and referring to the incident. After that, nothing more was ever heard on the matter.

After the incident, I contacted Mac McGuinness and reported what had occurred. Again I raised the matter of needing slow-acting poison as I knew that a lot more terrorists would have been killed if this type had been supplied.

I never intended for any civilians to be harmed but my main responsibility was the elimination of terrorists by any means possible. All those involved were either terrorists or terrorist sympathizers actively assisting the enemy. The age old adage of 'those who play with fire …' is indeed apt.

I was to use poison on one more occasion in the years to come. From terrorist documents captured later, it would appear that I achieved my objective and enjoyed considerable success, as outlined in chapter seven.

•••

On 13 August, elements of Support Unit, call sign Mantle India, located a landmine in the Mtetengwe TTL which was successfully lifted by army engineers.

On 13 August, an Internal Affairs convoy was ambushed on the Tshiturapadzi road by an estimated fifteen terrorists. Fire was returned and the terrorists fled. One district assistant was slightly wounded.

On 19 August, Piet van der Merwe's store on River Ranch was broken into by four suspected ZIPRA terrorists. ZAPU propaganda material was recovered from the scene.

On 21 August, Scouter Zulu from Tshiturapadzi had a fleeting contact with eight terrorists. There were no casualties on either side and elements of Support Unit conducted the follow-up.

On 26 August, ZANLA terrorists became active on the main Bulawayo road, stopping and robbing drivers of heavy commercial vehicles and buses of cash. Between this date and 1 September a total of three vehicles were stopped and robbed and two others that failed to stop were fired upon; fortunately, none of the occupants of these vehicles sustained injury. All the incidents occurred where the main road formed the western boundary of the Mtetengwe TTL. As a result of these attacks, an increased security force presence was established in the affected areas.

On 4 September, elements of D Company 2RR made contact with two terrorists in the Mtetengwe TTL, killing one and recovering an AK-47 assault rifle and two suitcases containing medical supplies.

On 6 September, elements of Support Unit contacted an estimated twenty terrorists in the Mtetengwe TTL. No casualties were inflicted on either side but during a sweep of the contact area an African male broke cover and ran. He was shot and killed. It was highly likely that he was a terrorist but as no weapon was recovered, he was recorded as being a local running with the terrorists.

On 7 September, a Special Branch patrol under the command of Ian 'Perkie' Perkins operating in the Mtetengwe TTL detonated a landmine in a mine-protected Land Rover. Ian was driving and apart from ringing ears he suffered no injury, nor did his passenger or the other occupants.

On 12 September, a Support Unit patrol contacted an estimated fifteen terrorists in the Mtetengwe TTL. One terrorist was killed and an AK-47 assault rifle and an American 3.5-inch rocket launcher, a bazooka, were recovered. No injuries were inflicted on the patrol.

On 15 September, an empty Wards Transport petrol tanker travelling to Beitbridge on the main road from Bulawayo was stopped. The driver, after being relieved of his cash, was chased away. The terrorist gang then fired upon the tanker before heading back to the Mtetengwe TTL.

•••

On the night of 18 September, four terrorists entered the Beitbridge beer hall and approached the cashier, demanding that he hand over the cashbox. To emphasize their point, they fired an AK-47 into the air, causing chaos as the panicked patrons fled for safety. Constable Godfrey Soka, off-duty and unarmed, and an

African police reservist immediately tackled the AK-47-toting terrorist. Soka knocked the terrorist to the ground but another terrorist opened fire, killing Soka instantly but missing the police reservist who remained unscathed.

Within minutes I was informed of the incident. Although the circumstances of the shooting were vague at that stage, Mobie van Wyk, who had arrived at the beer hall shortly before me, apprised me of the situation as known to him. I think it was the utter frustration of our inability to come to grips with the terrorist situation in the area, coupled with the sight of Constable Soka lying dead on the floor that caused me to erupt in a fit of anger, driven to exact instant revenge for the slaying of such a fine young policeman. I didn't appreciate it at the time but the conflict was affecting me personally, with an overriding desire to kill pervading my very being.

I gathered my detectives together and that night we embarked on a reign of terror in the African township. We raided the houses of known or suspected terrorist sympathizers or African nationalists, smashing down doors to gain entry and dragging the suspects out of their homes and interrogating them. After meting out some harsh punishment, the urge to kill passed and I called off the raid. Fortunately, no one died during the raids that night and we left the township empty-handed, no better off than when we had started. Constable Soka was posthumously awarded the Police Decoration for Gallantry, with the African police reservist receiving the same award.

After this incident and because of the uncharacteristic affect it had had on me, I took a long hard look at myself. I had been stationed at Beitbridge for eighteen months, the majority of the time being actively engaged on terrorist operations which had seen some good men die. All of a sudden, the war had become very personal. I knew that I needed a break but I was so firmly sucked into the habitual cycle of violence that the thought of taking leave and being away from the adrenaline-fuelled action was unthinkable. I had no one to really talk to. My marriage was taking enormous strain due to the nature of my duties and my continual absence from home. Maya wanted to start a family but I did not want the extra responsibility and so we argued constantly. I realize now that I was being extremely unreasonable and very selfish and that my attitude eventually led to the breakdown of the marriage. Mobie van Wyk was a close friend and I should have put my pride in my pocket and confided in him but I felt that this would have been a sign of weakness, so I consequently dispelled this idea and resolved to carry on regardless. I was never to take leave in all the time I was stationed at Beitbridge or for that matter during the rest of my service in the BSAP.

LANDMINES, AMBUSHES AND POISON, JULY–DECEMBER 1977 | 97

•••

The war against the terrorists in the Beitbridge area was not going well because of the lack of military support. The area was regarded as low priority by both JOC Repulse and JOC Tangent. From captured documents and interrogations of captured terrorists, it was estimated that a minimum of two hundred and fifty terrorists were now operational in the area. This number was increasing daily.

Apart from my operational responsibilities, I was still required to liaise closely with the South African Police Security Branch, a time-consuming business what with the amount of public relations required. I had built a tremendous rapport with Captain Johan Taute, Warrant Officer Hannes Maré, Warrant Officer Dirk Venter and Sergeant 'Fires' van Vuuren, my counterparts on the southern bank of the Limpopo. There was a direct telephone link between my office and theirs, making contact very simple indeed. Liaison normally consisted of roasting meat over a fire and drinking copious amounts of beer in the bush on their side of the border. I was also responsible for arranging regular hunting trips for Brigadier Johan Viktor and Colonel Sarel Strydom, both senior Security Branch personnel. Organizing a trip was simple enough, but I was expected to spend a few nights around the campfire with them when a hunt was in progress and although far from unpleasant, it kept me away from home unnecessarily.

My main point of contact in the South African Defence Force was the recently promoted Captain André van Rooyen. We spent some wonderful times together. He always referred to the Beitbridge Hotel as 'Tac HQ' (tactical headquarters) or simply 'Tac'. He would tell his boss, Kommandant Louw de Beer, that he was "urgently required at Tac HQ", where we would meet and have a few beers. He assisted me tremendously and on a number of occasions facilitated reconnaissance patrols along the South African border road to observe suspect areas on the Rhodesian side, arranging for me and security force personnel to deploy across the southern bank of the river.

I was also required to facilitate entry, with the assistance of the Security Branch, into South Africa of members of the various security services of the government and security forces travelling on official business, as well as assisting them on re-entry. All in all, these additional duties, which mainly took place after hours, added extra pressure on my already strained marriage.

On 22 September, I was advised that I had been awarded the Commissioner's Special Commendation (Silver Baton), complementing my Commissioner's Commendation (Bronze Baton) awarded in 1972 and the Commissioner's 'Note for Good Work' awarded in 1973. I was told that I was the first recipient of all three awards, a real honour indeed. As the Special Commendation (Silver Baton) had only been recently introduced, I am convinced that more deserving policemen would have received the 'hatrick' if this award had been available during their time. As far as I know, I am the only former member of the BSAP to have been awarded all three.

•••

On 20 September, a C Company 2RR vehicle detonated a landmine with a heavy vehicle in the Mtetengwe TTL. No injuries were sustained.

On 26 September, a Wards Transport vehicle was ambushed by between ten and fifteen terrorists approximately twenty kilometres from Beitbridge on the main Bulawayo road. Although the vehicle was hit by rifle- and machine-gun fire, no injuries were sustained by the occupants. Elements of C Company 2RR and D Company 6RR reacted.

On 27 September, elements of F Company 9RR detonated a landmine in the Mtetengwe TTL with a heavy vehicle. No injuries were sustained.

On 11 October, a large group of terrorists attacked a Roads Department gang working on the main Bulawayo road. Elements of the Rhodesian Defence Regiment (RDR) guarding the workforce repelled the attack without injury. The terrorists fled into the Mtetengwe TTL where spoor was lost in rocky terrain.

On the 12 October, a Police Reserve Air Wing aircraft came under heavy ground fire from an estimated ten terrorists while overflying the Mtetengwe TTL shortly after taking off from the Beitbridge airfield. Follow-up operations were conducted by elements of the Selous Scouts trackers.

On 13 October, a group of ten terrorists attacked and destroyed by fire the main homestead on Sentinal Ranch. Bristow, the owner, was absent from the ranch at the time.

On 21 October, Scouter X-Ray from X-Ray base in the Siyoka TTL was ambushed by an estimated fifteen terrorists, with no casualties on either side.

On 25 October, a civilian vehicle detonated a landmine in the Mtetengwe TTL. The driver, an African male, was killed and three African females were injured

On 26 October, elements of 2RR engaged approximately seven terrorists in the Mtetengwe TTL. Fortunately top cover in the form of an air force Lynx aircraft was available and managed to attack the terrorists with bombs and machine-gun fire. The result was one terrorist killed and one AK-47 assault rifle recovered. Three African females and one African juvenile who were running with the terrorists were also killed.

Toward the end of October, Sergeant-Major Pete McNeilage of the Selous Scouts arrived at Beitbridge with the intention of deploying a ZIPRA pseudo team into the Siyoka TTL. Pete was a long-standing friend of mine from his Rhodesian Light Infantry days and who, as a sergeant, had been awarded a well-deserved Silver Cross of Rhodesia. His objective was to assess the situation and determine the number of ZANLA and ZIPRA forces operating in the area. The Siyoka was a traditional ZIPRA stronghold but somehow ZANLA had managed to entrench themselves, through terror and intimidation, which had resulted in some vicious firefights between the two factions.

As no Special Branch liaison officer had accompanied him, I was more than willing to assist and to this end provided an in-depth intelligence overview of the target area, as well as a briefing on the overall security situation in the Beitbridge area. On 28 October, the pseudo team arrived and we all camped on the banks of the Limpopo River downstream from Beitbridge. It was decided that the pseudo team would be deployed on the night of 30 October. Due to Pete being short-staffed, I readily agreed to accompany the deployment. With local knowledge of the area, I might prove useful.

At approximately eight o'clock on the evening of the 30th we departed for the Siyoka TTL, some eighty kilometres distant on the Bulawayo road. We were travelling in a Mercedes Benz one-and-a-half-ton Unimog fitted with twin MAG machine guns in the back. During the journey I sat in the open cab next to Pete who was driving. The night was warm with a sky full of brilliant stars.

After successfully deploying the team, Pete and I started back on the return journey. As the only passenger, I moved to the back of the Unimog and stood to the mounted twin machine guns, each loaded with a one-hundred round belt of ammunition.

We had reached the halfway mark and I was deep in thought, feeling a little drowsy with the warm wind in my face. All of a sudden, I heard a tremendous noise. The side of the road seemed to light up. The truck swerved as Pete's thoughts were interrupted by the noise. I immediately disengaged the safety catches located near the pistol grips of the guns and opened fire at the muzzle flashes coming from the bush on the Mtetengwe TTL side of the road. At that moment, possibly due to the adrenaline, I felt invincible and began laughing. Every fifth round was a tracer which assisted my aim as I was able to adjust the guns accordingly. The whole engagement didn't last more than thirty seconds or so before we were out of the ambush area and clear of danger.

Pete drove directly to the camp where we examined the vehicle for bullet strikes and congratulated ourselves on our narrow escape. I informed Mobie van Wyk of the ambush and arranged for Bruce Cook, his Shangaan trackers and some of his security personnel to meet us on the main road early the following morning. Mazunga Ranch, where Bruce lived, was only twenty kilometres away from where the ambush had taken place. We managed to find a few cold beers which we consumed with relish around a blazing fire where we sat chatting until the early hours of the morning before crawling into our sleeping bags.

Pete and I, with two of his headquarters staff to guard the vehicles, met up with Bruce as arranged and then located the ambush site. We recovered three dead bodies but only one AK-47. All three were dressed in similar clothing but because only one weapon was recovered we could only confirm one terrorist killed and two African males, either recruits or running with the terrorists, killed. It was quite likely that their weapons had been removed by the ambush party. The Shangaan trackers located eleven firing positions as well as blood spoor heading into the Mtetengwe TTL. As a Selous Scouts tracker team was operating in the area, Pete organized for them to take over the spoor.

•••

On 31 October, Selous Scouts trackers operating in the Mtetengwe TTL had a fleeting, long-range contact with approximately ten terrorists. One terrorist was killed and an SKS rifle and documents were recovered. It was possible that this was the group which had ambushed Pete and me the night before.

On 4 November, elements of 2RR, call sign 95, had a fleeting contact with an unknown number of terrorists while on follow-up operations in the area of the Selous Scouts contact of 31 October.

On 6 November, in the Mtetengwe TTL, elements of 2RR fired on two curfew breakers who failed to stop when called upon to do so. One was killed and the other who sustained minor injuries was treated at the Beitbridge clinic.

On 7 November, elements of 1 Rhodesian Holding Unit (RHU), call sign 841, guarding water-drilling equipment in the Mtetengwe TTL, came under small-arms, mortar and rocket attack by an estimated fifteen terrorists. The attack was repelled without injury. Information later gleaned from the locals suggested that two terrorists had been wounded in the attack.

On the night of 8 November, in the Mtetengwe TTL, elements of 2RR, while moving into a position to enable them to launch a first-light attack on a suspected terrorist base, were forced to open fire when some of the occupants of the base were disturbed. A first-light sweep through the suspect area revealed one dead African male. Although no fire was returned by the terrorists, it was assessed that the base had been occupied at the time of the attack.

On 9 November, a military vehicle detonated a landmine on the Tshiturapadzi road. The driver sustained severe injuries and was casevaced to Chiredzi hospital for treatment.

On 15 November, Patrol Officer Ian Perkins, recently transferred to my office, was deployed with elements of B Company 6RR, call sign 2 Golf, to the Mtetengwe TTL. While searching a kraal, Ian spotted a group of seven terrorists walking in their direction. He immediately opened fire – on the one and only time he was allowed to carry my RPD machine gun – and dropped one. A contact ensued and the remaining terrorists fled the scene. An air force helicopter with trackers on board was deployed to the scene and an unsuccessful follow-up operation was mounted. The terrorist Ian had shot was critically wounded and died while receiving treatment. His AK-47 was recovered. Ian was criticized by B Company which accused him of opening fire prematurely, allowing the terrorist gang to escape. The reason I mention that Ian was only allowed to carry my RPD on one occasion was because he was giving me a bad name! He was referred to as "the SB prick with the RPD" by B Company after they blamed him for the blotched contact. It was common knowledge in almost all Matabeleland that I was the only SB officer to carry an RPD, so everyone assumed that 'the SB prick with the RPD' was me. Even my boss in Bulawayo, Chief Superintendent Mike Reeves, had heard about the 'SB prick' and assumed, like everyone else, that it was me. I could barely keep a straight face when I told Ian of my decision regarding the RPD. At any rate, B Company had had little success on this deployement and, blaming Ian, I am sure, was an element of sour grapes.

On 23 November, a donkey-drawn scotch cart detonated a landmine on the Tshiturapadzi road. The occupants of the cart, an African male and female, were killed.

On 28 November, a Ministry of Works heavy vehicle detonated a landmine in the Mtetengwe TTL. The driver sustained minor injuries.

On 3 December, a Chibuku beer truck was stopped and the driver robbed by a group of approximately nine terrorists in the Mtetengwe TTL. During follow-up operations elements of B Company 6RR had a fleeting contact with approximately four terrorists. No casualties were inflicted by either side but a terrorist rifle grenade was recovered.

On 5 December, Ian Perkins with members of Scouter X-Ray made contact with an unknown number of terrorists in the Siyoka TTL. One terrorist was killed and his AK-47 assault rifle recovered. A wounded terrorist managed to make good his escape.

On 7 December, an Internal Affairs convoy came under small-arms and mortar attack in the Mtetengwe TTL. No casualties were inflicted on either side.

On 8 December, an Internal Affairs aircraft came under ground attack shortly after taking off from the Beitbridge airfield and while overlying the Mtetengwe TTL. Elements of A Company 6RR were deployed into the area but were unable to locate the firing positions. The aircraft was not hit.

On 8 December, a Guard Force vehicle detonated a landmine in the Mtetengwe TTL. No injuries were sustained.

On 9 December, elements of Guard Force guarding their vehicle which had been damaged in a mine explosion the previous day were attacked by six terrorists. They returned fire, forcing the terrorists to flee. No injuries inflicted on the Guard Force.

On 13 December, in the Diti TTL, elements of B Company 6RR, call sign 1 Foxtrot, while moving into a night ambush position, came under attack by a terrorist group estimated to number twelve. Fire was returned but no casualties were sustained by either side. At first light trackers were deployed to undertake a follow-up but tracks were eventually lost. It would appear from the expended cartridge cases recovered from the scene that at least one FN rifle had been used by the terrorists.

On 14 December, a security force member on leave reported that he had seen six terrorists cross the main Bulawayo road from east to west. Elements of A Company 6RR reacted. This was the last incident reported for the year 1977.

•••

In December 1977, I was contacted by Mac who advised me that a busload of Selous Scouts territorials would be crossing the border in the coming days and could I facilitate the securing of their weapons on arrival at Beitbridge as they would be travelling out of convoy. I readily agreed as I had a large strongroom at my office where their rifles could be stored until their return. I was not informed of the reason but simply told that the group would be posing as recently passed-out national serviceman who had hired the bus to holiday in South Africa to celebrate their brief freedom before their postings to the various Indep companies scattered throughout the country. I was never to establish the real reason for their trip, though possibly it was for nothing more hush-hush than parachute training in Bloemfontein. On the day in question Captain Rob Warraker, who commanded the territorial, or TA, element in the Selous Scouts, arrived in Beitbridge, having travelled that morning on the convoy from Fort Victoria. He met me at my office where he handed over his weapon for safe-keeping. We discussed the bus that was en route to arrive later that afternoon. He also advised that he could foresee no problems as all the 'lads' had valid travel documents and if asked would adhere to their cover story. With that he departed in his green Triumph sports car, a beaut of a car, with the roof down and his Andy Capp cap set at a jaunty angle on his southward journey.

As predicted, the luxury bus duly arrived with about twenty TA Scouts on board. I knew a few of them, in particular Pat Mavros whom I had first met as a sergeant with 2 Independent Company when based at Bindura in early 1973. The 'lads' were all in high spirits and were eager to cross the border. After they had packed their weapons in the safe, they boarded the bus and headed for the border.

Two hours later, I answered the telephone to hear Mavros on the other end. The disappointment in his voice was immediately apparent as he explained that he had been refused entry into South Africa. It transpired that he was travelling on a Greek passport and a visa was required to enter South Africa. His passport had been suitably stamped to reflect that he had been refused entry. I then drove down to the Rhodesian border post to collect a dejected Mavros and took him home. It was now after eight o'clock that night. At home, Pat mentioned that the bus would wait for him at the Messina Hotel until midnight.

Mavros was a first-class bloke and I could see that he was bitterly disappointed so I decided that after ten o'clock when the border posts closed down for the night, I would take him across in my Land Rover as I had 'freedom of the gate'; in other words, I could come and go as I pleased, without hindrance. So, just after ten we left for Messina. We passed through the Rhodesian border without problem but immediately on crossing into South Africa, I observed in my rear-view mirror vehicle lights being switched on and a car following us. As there was a real danger of game crossing the road – I had previously had a kudu bull try to jump the Land Rover when returning from Messina one night, only to have it land on the bonnet, causing some serious damage to the vehicle – I did not travel at any speed. The car behind also reduced speed and it was blatantly obvious that we were being followed. Messina at that time of night was a complete ghost town. I drove past the Messina Hotel and observed that the bus was waiting as arranged with a few of the 'lads' milling about but the majority asleep on the bus. After passing the bus without stopping, the 'tailing' car turned off and disappeared. I thought to myself, *Well, in for a penny, in for a pound* and returned to the bus where everyone was now awake as Mavros stepped out of the Land Rover to much cheering and whistling. I said my goodbyes and returned home to Rhodesia without incident. I went to bed thinking that if there were any repercussions Johan Taute of the Security Branch would iron them out.

The following morning, just after half past seven, the telephone directly connected to the SAP Security Branch rang. Nothing out of the normal, I thought, but, on answering, a worried Johan Taute asked if I had transported anyone across the border during the night. When I replied in the affirmative he whistled and said, "*Nou is daar groot kak in die land.*" (Now, there's big shit in the land.) He advised me that the Chief Immigration Officer was in an absolute rage and wanted to see me in his office immediately. Fifteen minutes later I was standing to attention in front of an enraged Chief Immigration Officer. Although his office was air-conditioned, he was very red in the face and was sweating profusely. Johan Taute, standing to attention next to me, was, for what reason, was also being yelled at. I quickly summed up our abuser. He was a typical South African civil servant, full of his own importance and with an over-inflated ego. It was abundantly clear that he was going to show Johan and me who was boss. At the end of his tirade he informed me that I had been declared a prohibited immigrant and was therefore banned from ever entering South Africa. Things had now turned serious.

After leaving the angry man, Johan and I walked across to his office where we had a much-needed cup of coffee while Johan filled me in on a few details. He had watched the arrival of the bus and the excited passengers who filed into the customs and immigration hall when it became apparent that one of them had been refused entry. The rest had then staged a bit of a protest with a sit-in on the entrance steps to the hall. They were then threatened by the border officials and so had all reluctantly filed onto the bus. Worse was to come. My name had been brandished about by the Scouts, openly defying the officials by shouting statements to the effect of: "Don't worry, Pat. Ed Bird will get you across," and "We'll wait for you at the Messina Hotel". Mavros had then crossed 'the Bridge' on foot back to the Rhodesian side where he had contacted me, with the South African officials lying in wait for my inevitable crossing.

I sat at my desk contemplating the next move. There was no way that I could report this to the Provincial Special Branch Officer or his deputy, Chief Superintendent Mike Reeves. Freedom of the border played a very important role in my posting and as the festive season was approaching, I would shortly have to smuggle bottles of Rémy Martin, Chivas Regal and the usual Johnny Walker and other such black-market whisky for the Bulawayo CID's Christmas party as I had done the previous year. After looking at various options, I decided that if I was to get out of this fix then the only person who could assist was Mr Mac in Bindura. I phoned him and gave him the whole story. Mac, in his typical way, brushed it off as trivial but confirmed that he would see what he could do. He then phoned the South African Chief Immigration Officer and sounding completely irate informed the officer that I was to be stripped of my rank and immediately transferred from Beitbridge. He apologized on behalf of the OC Special Branch to whom he had reported the matter to as soon as the incident had come to his attention. The immigration officer immediately changed his tune as he deemed the punishment excessive, remarking that he wanted to see me and Mavros punished but not to such a degree. Mac acceded on this point and told him that, in consultation with the OC SB, a lesser punishment might be imposed on me. As for Mavros, Mac informed him that he would face a military court martial as Special Branch had no jurisdiction over him.

Mac then managed to get hold of Rob Warraker who was still in South Africa and informed him of developments. Mac instructed Rob that on his return to the border he was to establish contact with the Chief Immigration Officer, making it known that he was Mavros's OC and that Mavros was to be tried by a military court. He should also make mention that I had received a severe reprimand which would be reflected on my service record and that, additionally, I had lost four years of seniority in the rank. In the meantime Mac had advised the immigration officer of my punishment which the officer agreed was suitable. However, I was still prohibited from entering South Africa. On Warraker's return to the border, with Mavros in tow, all part of Mac's plan, he made contact with Johan Taute and brought him up to date with developments. Johan then contacted me and I crossed the border and met them all in Johan's office. The plan was for Rob to march Pat and me into the immigration man's office where he would read the 'riot act' to us and then Rob would severely reprimand us both for our unacceptable and embarrassing actions. So, we were marched in and I could see this immigration officer with the over-inflated ego really enjoying the proceedings. Mavros and I had to play along but it was embarrassing having to stand to attention like two schoolboys before the headmaster. The official also made sure that his staff, as well as the transients clearing customs and immigration, also heard the ranting and raving. Before leaving his office, as a postscript, the immigration man informed me that he had lifted the order prohibiting me from entering South Africa and had reinstated my 'freedom of the border' concession.

So, all in all, a very successful outcome, acceptable to all parties, was achieved.

It was only once we had adjourned to Johan Taute's office that we were able to relax and laugh about it all.

Sadly this was the last time I was to see Rob Warraker as a few short weeks later he was killed when a Rhodesian Air Force Canberra bomber in which he had wangled a ride was lost on a night-reconnaissance operation in Mozambique. Recipient of the Silver Cross of Rhodesia, Rob was a good man if ever there was.

I phoned Mac and advised him of the very favourable outcome and thanked him. My bosses in Bulawayo were never to find out what had transpired and for the rest of my service in Beitbridge I was never again bothered at the South African border. I duly smuggled the consignment of expensive whisky and cognac into Rhodesia which was delivered to the CID offices in Bulawayo in time for their end-of-year bash where judges of the high court, regional magistrates and other leading dignitaries, including no doubt Detective Superintendent Dave Blacker, enjoyed the contraband without question.

Incidentally, Brian Perkins was to feel the same Chief Immigration Officer's wrath in 1979 when his 'freedom of the gate' concession was withdrawn over a very petty incident and Brian was to suffer similar anguish. The matter was eventually resolved without the knowledge of the bosses in Bulawayo, much to Brian's relief.

•••

During the year twenty terrorists had been killed by the Rhodesian security forces and four in interfaction fighting. Three had been captured. Eight members of the Rhodesian security forces had been killed, bringing the total to eleven since the start of terrorist incursions into the Beitbridge area. Seventeen landmines had been detonated by both Rhodesian forces and civilian vehicles with five being recovered. The majority of these mines were the TMH type, a tank mine fitted with an anti-handling device. It was understandable – a large amount of landmines could be portered into the area from nearby Mozambique.

It was assessed from captured documents and captured terrorist interrogations that by the end of 1977, approximately three hundred terrorists were active in the Beitbridge area. The terrorists were formed into eight- to ten-man sections with the capability of amalgamating one or more sections, on a temporary basis, for reinforced attacks against larger targets in the cases of base camps, vehicle ambushes and the like.

Their fighting ability was poor and they would generally flee from contacts or ambushes, firing wildly. However, they were the masters of the tribal trust lands, subjugating the local population by terror and brutality of the worst kind. The locals were, in the main, a peace-loving people, the majority being from the Venda tribe who really had no interest in a political war.

The Rhodesian government was not in a position to afford them constant protection, scattered as they were in their villages throughout the tribal trust lands. Based on the Malayan experience, it was therefore decided to remove the populace as a source of succour for the terrorists by relocating the people into a series of protected villages (PVs). District administrators and, in particular, the District Commissioner, Lew Watson, would be responsible for the construction of protected villages where the locals and their belongings would be moved. Lands would be prepared for these people to grow their crops and cattle kraals would be erected for their herds. Their movements outside the protected villages would be restricted from dusk till dawn but during the day they would be free to come and go as they pleased but were required to enter and exit via recognized checkpoints. The entire set-up would be under the protection of Guard Force who would, as part of their responsibilities, patrol the outside perimeter checking for holes in the fence and human spoor of locals or terrorists using this method to gain unlawful passage in and out. The Ministry of Internal Affairs would be responsible for the administration and welfare of the inhabitants as well as the issuing of rations until the locals became self-sufficient.

With the erection of these villages, it was anticipated that the terrorists' freedom of movement throughout the area would be dramatically curtailed and impact negatively on their operations. This, in theory, was the objective but in reality the concept failed. For the terrorists, it was to be pretty much business as usual, with little inconvenience.

CHAPTER SIX
Protected villages and the litany of terror continues
January–June 1978

On 1 January, Internal Affairs, supported by the army and police, began relocating locals into two protected villages at Penemene and Tongwe, both in the Mtetengwe TTL and within fifteen kilometres of Beitbridge. In spite of the locals being warned that the relocations would take place, the terrorists did not attempt to disrupt the operation. Gradually, those locals who had not fled into the bush to avoid the move were transported to their new homes and most were genuinely relieved, anticipating a more peaceful life.

Several more protected villages were being erected or would be erected in the coming months, culminating in the entire local population of the Beitbridge area being affected by the moves, whether willingly or not. Those who fled into the bush erected semi-permanent dwellings in camps in heavy bush which were sited by the terrorists and only detectable by the eye of a trained and experienced pilot from the air or a security force patrol stumbling into one. These dwellings became known as *povo* camps, *povo* being a Shona word for 'the people', originally from the Portuguese.

New Year's Day 1978 started with terrorists beating and bayoneting four locals in the Mtetengwe TTL, resulting in the death of one of them.

The 5th of January saw Les Mitchell of Lesanth Ranch come under attack at ten o'clock in the morning by seven terrorists. Mitchell's ranch manager was repairing the security fence surrounding the homestead and office buildings when he was fired upon by the group. He was on the wrong side of the fence and after firing a few shots at his attackers with a small pistol, clambered over the wire mesh to the relative safety of the farmyard with bullets whizzing around him. Mitchell and his Police Reserve protection rushed to the young man's aid and drove off the attack. No one was injured and an unsuccessful follow-up operation was undertaken.

On 7 January, a Coley Hall eighteen-ton vehicle detonated a landmine in the Chipisi TTL, severely injuring the driver and resulting in the loss of his right leg.

On 11 January, in the Diti TTL, a Coley Hall trailer which had been stuck in the mud for several days was burned out by a group of four terrorists who then booby-trapped with a stick grenade a wheel barrow which was part of the load. This was a very amateurish attempt and the grenade was discovered and destroyed on site.

On 17 January, at ten o'clock in the morning a civilian vehicle travelling alone on the main Bulawayo–Beitbridge road in the Mtetengwe TTL was fired on by an unknown number of terrorists. The vehicle was hit several times, slightly wounding a female occupant. Follow-up operations were undertaken.

On 2 February, the unoccupied homestead on Shobe Block, Liebigs Ranch was gutted by fire by an unknown number of terrorists who then went on to shoot several head of cattle.

On 3 February, an A Company 6RR heavy vehicle on loan to the Ministry of Works detonated a landmine in the Mtetengwe TTL. There were no casualties.

On 5 February, travelling alone en route to Fort Victoria, Basil Moss of the Selous Scouts was ambushed on the main Bulawayo–Beitbridge road by approximately twenty terrorists from the Mtetengwe TTL. Moss managed to escape injury although his vehicle was hit. Moss was in charge of a Selous Scouts deployment in the Beitbridge area, camping on the banks of the Mazunga River. Earlier that day, he had been informed that his son Kevin, a trooper in the Selous Scouts, had been seriously wounded in a terrorist ambush and had been admitted to the Fort Victoria General Hospital. Moss was making plans to travel to Fort Victoria by road to be with his son when he was informed that he had died. Nevertheless, Moss intended making the trip to escort the body to Salisbury. I spoke to him briefly when he reported the matter.

•••

About thirty minutes after Basil Moss had left, I received a very disturbing report from the driver of a Wards Transport vehicle. He had apparently been stopped by about twenty terrorists on the main Bulawayo road at the identical spot where Moss had been ambushed. He had given a lift to a young white man who had introduced himself as John Kennerley. Kennerley had been dragged from the cab by the terrorists and taken into the bush on the eastern, or the Mtetengwe, side of the road and that was the last the driver had seen of him. The remaining terrorists then relieved him and his crew of what cash and valuables they had and after warning them not to report the incident to the police, let the vehicle proceed.

John Kennerley was the son of Jim, a government vehicle and driving examiner at Beitbridge who lived in the village with his wife. John was seventeen years old, working as an apprentice for the daily *Bulawayo Chronicle* and was travelling to Beitbridge to visit his parents, who, incidentally, were standing outside the police station awaiting the arrival of their son while I was taking the report from the driver. Mobie van Wyk was also present and had the unenviable responsibility of breaking the news to Jim and his wife. My heart really went out to them. Night was fast approaching so a decision was taken to commence the follow-up at first light the following morning, as well as saturating the area with troops as the terrorists would possibly take John across the border into Mozambique. Over the next few days, a concerted effort was undertaken by all arms of the security forces available in the Beitbridge area.

One of the main problems facing the follow-up forces was John's security in the event of contact being made with the group escorting him: we did not wish to see him killed in the crossfire or being shot out of hand by his escorts in reprisal for being attacked. It was hoped that John would take cover and hide until rescued.

At first light the following morning, elements of D Company 1RAR and A Company 6RR located spoor of twenty terrorists at the abduction site and commenced follow-up. When the spoor split up the RAR followed one set and 6RR the other.

Late in the afternoon and after following the spoor from first light, elements of D Company 6RR made contact with an estimated eight terrorists in the Mtetengwe TTL. It was assessed by the troops on the ground and from blood spoor located after the contact that three terrorists had been wounded. Unfortunately, the spoor was lost in fading light. However one AK-47 assault rifle, one FN standard NATO-issue rifle, ammunition, mortar bombs and other equipment were recovered.

The search never stopped but John Kennerley's trail went cold and our fears that he had been taken across the border into Mozambique were ultimately proved right when information filtered through to this effect. John remained in captivity until early 1980 when Mugabe, under intesne pressure from the British government and the Red Cross, was forced to hand John over, together with several other abducted white Rhodesians, to the Red Cross authorities in Mozambique who eventually repatriated them.

•••

An incident that occurred at Beitbridge in early 1978 was the report of a BSAP mine-protected Land Rover, *sans* doors, seen driving around central Johannesburg. Fortunately the person who had observed the vehicle was unable to get the registration number but did manage to positively identify the letters, though, thankfully, nothing else.

One afternoon Inspector Winston Hart arrived in Beitbridge driving this big, baby-blue, gas-guzzling V8 American car, either a Chev or Plymouth, with very, very big tail wings. An early sixties model, it was obviously the car of the moment but was completely out of place in Rhodesia. When I started laughing at Winston behind the wheel he looked completely browned off and embarrassed as everyone seemed to be staring at the car. It was quite late in the afternoon and after greeting one another, he grunted, "Lock the office and let's go for a drink." He left the eye-catcher parked outside the police station, also causing quite a stir among the police personnel on duty, as we walked across to the Beitbridge Hotel. Winston was still with the Selous Scouts at the time and it transpired that the gas-guzzler, a donation from the SAP Security Branch, had been issued to him and as there was no other suitable vehicle available for his trip south. The one positive aspect about Special Branch was the need-to-know policy which was accepted by every member, so I never inquired as to the reason for the trip, and Winston never mentioned it. As far as I was concerned he was travelling to Johannesburg on business.

After a drink or two, Winston said that he had a brilliant idea: he would leave the vehicle with me and would borrow my official mine-protected vehicle to undertake the trip. Needless to say I nearly choked on my beer. I asked him if he was insane or words to that effect, but unfortunately he was dead serious. I put up a bit of a fight but I knew that I would accede sooner rather than later. Winston and I had developed a strong bond during the years I had worked with him in the Selous Scouts, a bond forged under extreme and very dangerous circumstances; I would do anything for this wonderful man. My argument ranged from, "What if you are involved in an accident or the vehicle is stolen?" to "CMED and the police authorities have only authorized the vehicle to travel as far as Messina," and, "What about fuel for that heap parked outside the police station?" Winston had an answer for everything and I eventually agreed but told him that I would have sleepless nights until he returned. He stayed with me that night and very early the next morning departed in my Land Rover, leaving me with the gas-guzzler and some petrol money as it would look out of place to drive up to the police pumps and tell the orderly to "Fill her up".

Over the next week I visited Bruce Cook, at Mazunga, almost on a daily basis as I was now restricted to tar roads. Although old, the car was very powerful and I covered the fifty or so kilometres to Mazunga in next to no time. On schedule, Winston returned to Rhodesia and I was extremely relieved to see my trusty Land Rover in one piece. As it was early we exchanged vehicles and Winston continued on his way to Salisbury.

About a week later I became aware of an internal police inquiry, emanating from Police General Head Quarters in Salisbury, into the sighting of a BSAP mine-protected Land Rover driving around the streets of Johannesburg. The inquiry was being handled by the Uniform Branch but I was never approached. Apparently the main suspects were members of the Police Reserve posted, on call-up, to Beitbridge. It was suspected that some had gone AWOL and had travelled to Johannesburg in one of the official Land Rovers but nothing ever came of it and the inquiry was filed. I have never mentioned this to anyone and I doubt that Winston has either, so if the Staff Officer (Transport) at PGHQ at the time ever reads this the puzzle has been answered.

•••

On 7 February, elements of A Company 6RR who were operating with trackers, contacted a group of eight terrorists in the Chipisi TTL and on following up after the contact, once again made contact with the enemy. No casualties were inflicted by either side but terrorist equipment was recovered by the attacking force.

On 9 February, a roving Police Reserve vehicle patrol was ambushed on the main Bulawayo road by an estimated fifteen terrorists from the Mtetengwe TTL. No casualties were sustained by the patrol. Elements of A Company 6RR reacted and located nineteen terrorist firing positions over a two-hundred-metre stretch of road. Due to fading light, no follow-up operation was undertaken.

On the same date, at approximately half past five, a Bubye farmer, Mr J.F. Wolvaardt, was reported missing after failing to return to the Lion and Elephant Motel after visiting his Swanscoe Ranch situated on the Bubye River road. Police from the Bubye police camp, reinforced by local farmers, mounted an immediate search and located Wolvaardt's ambushed vehicle twenty-five kilometres from the Bubye River Bridge on the Bubye River road. The body was soon located in the bush near the vehicle. Wolvaardt had been stripped of his clothing and relieved of his weapons, a 9mm pistol and a police-issue FN rifle. It was estimated that the ambush took place between two and three o'clock that afternoon when he was returning to the Lion and Elephant. For some time Wolvaardt had been commuting to his ranch on a regular basis and although warned of the dangers involved, took no heed of the warnings. On this day the terrorists were waiting for him. The security forces were so hard-pressed for manpower that it was impossible to afford him an escort and he therefore took his fate into his own hands: a brave man but, under the circumstances, foolish.

On 10 February, Guard Force located a landmine on the road between Tongwe and Penemene protected villages. Engineers were deployed and destroyed the landmine *in situ*.

On the same day, elements of A Company 6RR detonated a landmine in the same area, resulting in minor injuries being sustained by one of the vehicle occupants. During the sweep of the area trackers located a further landmine buried approximately three hundred metres away, a TMD-44 box-type which engineers managed to recover.

On 12 February, headman Tongwana Moyo was executed by a group of fifteen terrorists at his kraal in the Mtetengwe TTL after calling on his subjects not to aid the terrorists.

During the early hours of 15 February, the Tongwe protected village in the Mtetengwe TTL came under attack by a group of twenty terrorists. The attack lasted approximately thirty minutes. Guard Force retaliated with no injuries being inflicted on the opposing force; none of the occupants of the protected village were injured. At first light elements of A Company 6RR reacted but the terrorist spoor had been obliterated by cattle movement.

•••

On the same day, another avoidable incident occurred, one in which I was, to a large extent, personally involved. Toward the end of January 1978, I was approached by Mr. C. Thompson, the owner of Bubani Ranch which was situated on the Bubye River, south of the Lion and Elephant Motel. Thompson was accompanied by his brother-in-law Mr. P.J. Bezuidenhout. Thompson, an Afrikaner, was living in Messina at the time and informed me that he intended to return to Bubani Ranch and restart farming operations with his brother-in-law. I outlined the security situation, not only in the Bubye and Diti TTL areas, but gave him an overall briefing on the security situation in the entire Beitbridge district. He was adamant that he intended returning as was his brother-in-law. He explained that they would put up at the Lion and Elephant Motel and commute to Bubani Ranch on a daily basis. I warned them of the extreme dangers involved, informing them of the strong possibility of ambush and landmines. I also made it clear that we could offer no protection in the way of escorts and that they would be putting their own lives in their hands. I could see that they were steadfast in their decision and that my warnings were being disregarded.

On 29 January, a Sunday, Thompson, Bezuidenhout and a South African *Sunday Times* reporter pitched up at my office en route to the Lion and Elephant Motel. The latter was due to spend a day or two with the returning ranchers in preparation of a story for his newspaper. I again warned them of the extreme dangers they faced. At that stage, I was unaware that Wolvaardt, who was to die on 9 February, had returned under similar circumstances and I suspect that the three of them had planned their return together, as Wolvaardt also lived in Messina.

At six o'clock on the evening of 15 February, the alert was put out as Thompson and Bezuidenhout had failed to return to the Lion and Elephant from Bubani Ranch. (The reporter had returned to South Africa by this stage.) As the light was fading fast – there is very little twilight in the tropics – a security force patrol was quickly mustered. At great peril to themselves – ambushes, landmines and boobytraps were an ever-present danger as the terrorists always prepared for a security force reaction – they set off in the fading light to search for the missing ranchers. It did not take long to locate the ambushed vehicle and recover the bodies of Thompson and Bezuidenhout. Their weapons were missing but they had not been stripped of their clothing. It would appear that as the vehicle was entering the ambush, a terrorist with an RPG-7 stepped into the road as the vehicle passed him and fired a rocket into the rear of the vehicle, bringing it to a standstill in the killing zone.

These deaths, coupled with Wolvaardt's six days earlier, brought to an end any aspirations of absentee ranchers returning to their lands. The ranches on the Bubye River remained abandoned until after independence.

I had now been stationed at Beitbridge for close on two years and, as mentioned, had arrived prior to terrorist incursions into the area. During that time, from various sources, including captured documents, captured terrorists, informants, ballistic reports on weapons and weapon numbers, I had been able to compile a list, by name, of terrorists operating in the area, their sections, section commanders, detachment commanders and so on. This database was updated on a regular basis, so at any given time I was able give a detailed overview of the security situation. I was therefore extremely piqued when Thompson and Bezuidenhout decided not to heed my warnings and was angry at them for getting themselves killed.

Over the years I have found that the Afrikaans male is an obstinate customer who, once having decided upon a course of action, will not deviate from his course.

•••

On 17 February, the afternoon convoy from Bulawayo was ambushed, with the Express Motorways bus, a luxury bus operating between Bulawayo and Johannesburg, principally targeted, possibly because it was the largest vehicle in the convoy. The Police Reserve escorts in their Mazda pick-up trucks with mounted .30 Browning machine guns reacted valiantly and drew fire so as to enable the convoy to pass through safely. However, before the convoy commander finally managed to restore order, there was much stop-start activity among the civilian vehicles, with some civilians getting out of their cars to return fire with their private weapons. Eventually, the terrorists fled and convoy carried on its way.

About half an hour after the ambush had taken place, I, along with some army and police personnel, met the bus as it pulled up outside the Beitbridge Hotel. This was an unscheduled stop as the bus, under normal conditions, would proceed directly to the border post. However, this was not a normal occasion as the passengers, luckily all uninjured, were in desperate need of a drink. The attractive hostess was the first to alight and on stepping out, said calmly, "All I want to say is SHIT!"

With that, and to rousing applause from me and servicemen present, the excited passengers got off the bus and made their way to the pub for a celebratory drink before boarding the bus and continuing their journey. We could find only one bullet strike on the bus which had hit the rear toilet window, the pretty hostess confirming that the facility was vacant at the time.

•••

On 21 February, a Police Reserve Air Wing aircraft was subjected to ground fire from an unknown number of terrorists in the Mtetengwe TTL shortly after take-off from the Beitbridge airfield. Elements of D Company 6RR responded but were unable to locate the firing positions.

On 22 February, Shabwe protected village came under small-arms, rocket and mortar attack. No casualties were inflicted on any of the occupants of the PV. The following morning, elements of D Company 6RR located the twenty firing positions one kilometre from the PV. It had indeed been a very long-range attack: the effective range of an AK assault rifle in only four hundred metres. Due to rain and cattle movement, tracking was impossible.

On 23 February, elements of D Company 6RR made contact with ten terrorists in the Mtetengwe TTL. There were no casualties on either side. One AK-47 assault rifle and two 60mm mortar bombs were recovered.

On 27 February, Keith Knott's farm store on Nottingham Estates was broken into by twelve terrorists. The contents of the store were then loaded onto a trailer attached to a tractor and then driven by the terrorists into the Masera TTL where the loot was removed and the tractor gutted. Elements of D Company 6RR reacted but were unable to locate spoor. It was apparent that the tractor and trailer had offloaded in another area before being driven to the spot where the tractor was burned out.

On 1 March, Guard Force contacted six terrorists in the area of Penemene protected village. During the contact one of the Guard Force men went missing but reported back to the PV the following morning. Due to the fading light, elements of D Company 6RR were only able to react the following morning and found nothing to indicate that a contact had taken place except from the Guard Force side. The 'contact' was put down to jittery Guard Force members shooting at shadows.

On 4 March, Bruce Cook from Mazunga reported that the hunting camp belonging to the Rhodesia Meat Processing Company on the Mazunga River had been destroyed by fire by a group of seventeen terrorists earlier that day. The tracks led back to the Mtetengwe TTL where the group split up and spoor was lost in rocky terrain.

At approximately 9.30 p.m. on 5 March, the protected village at Shabwe in the Mtetengwe TTL came under intense attack from a large group of terrorists using small arms, RPG-7 rockets and 82mm and 60mm mortars. The attack lasted three quarters of an hour with three 82mm mortar bombs penetrating the perimeter fence, causing no injuries, but several tents were damaged by shrapnel. From the expended cartridge cases recovered from the terrorist firing positions, ballistics confirmed that twenty-nine different AK-47 assault rifles, sixteen SKS rifles, an RPD machine gun and one FN rifle had been used in the attack, indicating that at least fifty terrorists had participated. This was an extremely determined attack with the terrorists attacking from three hundred metres away. It was also an indication that the terrorists were feeling the squeeze of the locals being removed from the rural areas and placed in protected villages. The objective of this and subsequent attacks on protected villages was to drive the locals, through fear, back to their homes, but for the rest of the war they were unable to achieve this.

On 7 March, elements of D Company 2RR were guided by a police patrol from the Latumba base to a suspected terrorist camp in the Mtetengwe TTL. Just before three o'clock in the morning, terrorists in the camp opened fire on the patrol. Fire was returned and the terrorists fled. A first-light sweep of the contact area revealed the body of an African female who had been running with the terrorists. Recovery of an AK-47 assault rifle plus other terrorist equipment and valuable documents ensued. From blood spoor found in the camp, it was ascertained that two terrorists had been wounded.

On 7 March, the homestead on Bar G Ranch, owned by the absent Martin Grobler, was gutted by fire and completely destroyed by a gang of eight terrorists. The incident was only reported to the security forces on 9 March and no follow-up operation was undertaken.

On 10 March, elements of D Company 6RR, call sign 41 Bravo, had a fleeting contact with an estimated three terrorists in the Mtetengwe TTL. There were no casualties on either side but the patrol recovered the all-important documents plus other terrorist equipment. The patrol was unable to follow spoor because of rain.

On 16 March, a Police Reserve Air Wing aircraft, call sign Copper 82 and flown by Police Reservist Wesson, came under ground attack while assisting in the relocation of the locals to the Chaswingo protected village in the Diti TTL. The fuel tanks on the aircraft were hit, forcing Wesson to abandon the mission and make for Bulawayo, where he safely landed the aircraft for repairs. Elements of D Company 6RR reacted and located firing positions of approximately thirty terrorists. The body of an African juvenile was recovered, apparently beaten to death by the terrorists. The reason for this was never ascertained.

On 17 March, Police Reserve Air Wing aircraft, call sign Copper 182 and piloted by Robin Watson, came under ground attack while overflying the Diti TTL in support of ground forces assisting the locals in their move to the protected villages. The aircraft was not hit. Ground forces were unable to locate the terrorists' firing positions. Robin Watson was a great character who had flown Lancaster bombers with the Royal Air Force Bomber Command during the Second World War. After the attack, he spoke to some aircraft engineers who determined that his low-wing Cessna could be fitted with a machine gun on each wing. He duly made representation to both the air force and the police for permission to modify his aircraft so that the guns could be fitted. Both forces, in no uncertain terms, refused to grant permission and even his great friend, the Rhodesian prime minister, Ian Smith, could not override the decision. However, he did install a type of chute which enabled him to drop hand grenades from the aircraft onto selected targets. (During the ceasefire of early 1980, I was involved in this when grenades were dropped, with disastrous results. More on this later.)

On the same date, in the nearby Chipisi TTL, while undertaking the removal of the locals to the protected villages, an army patrol encountered an African male carrying a rolled-up reed mat which obviously contained something or other. On searching the mat, an FN rifle was found, determined, by the serial number to be a police weapon which had been issued to J.F. Wolvaardt and who had been in possession of the rifle at the time of his death on 9 February when he was ambushed by terrorists on the Bubye River road. The man was handed over to the police for prosecution.

On 17 March, the unoccupied homestead on Kayancee Ranch on the Bubye River was destroyed by fire by an unknown number of terrorists.

On 18 March, Robin Watson, while assisting in the protected village project and flying over the Chipisi TTL, once again came under ground attack. On this occasion, the aircraft was hit in the tail section.

Also on 18 March, elements of the army assisting with the protected village exercise in the Diti TTL were ambushed by approximately twenty terrorists using small arms and RPG-7 rockets. The security forces sustained four casualties, two critically wounded being airlifted to the Bulawayo General Hospital.

Again, on 18 March, the security force radio communication channel, channel 12, was jammed by the terrorists from nine o'clock in the morning until a quarter past eleven, making air-to-ground communication in the Diti and Chipisi TTLs impossible and hampering operations involving the movement of locals into the protected villages – a more sophisticated departure in terrorist tactics.

•••

During the morning of 19 March, Detective Section Officer Steve Acornley, from Special Branch Gwanda, and I happened upon a kraal in the Mtetengwe TTL which was situated near the Umzingwani River, about eight hundred metres south of the low-level bridge and about five kilometres from its junction with the Limpopo River. As we entered the complex, an African man dashed for the thick riverine vegetation. We both jumped out of the Land Rover and opened fire on him. In the meantime, our escort, consisting of five Special Branch officers who had been some way behind, caught up with us and wanted to know what was happening, as they had not heard the firing. We immediately set about questioning the few residents in the kraal who confirmed that, on our arrival, three terrorists had been present but had fled.

We were now in a predicament: there were an unknown number of terrorists in close proximity but in extremely heavy riverine vegetation. We decided to sweep the area where the terrorist had fled. Leaving behind vehicle guards, Steve, I and two officers entered the jungle but we did not have sufficient ammunition to sustain any type of prophylactic fire for too long. On breaking through to the Umzingwani River about fifty metres distant, we decided to return to the vehicles and discuss another plan of action. On the one hand, we all agreed that what we were doing was tantamount to a suicide mission; on the other, we convinced ourselves that the terrorists had long since fled the scene.

After hanging around for about another thirty minutes or so, we moved back to the kraal and spoke to the few residents still there. Farther on, we encountered a Guard Force roadblock/ambush site where we reported the developments to them. Later that afternoon, the Guard Force unit received reinforcements and proceeded to the scene of the morning's action. As they approached the same kraal, they came under attack by approximately six terrorists. The terrorists fled once again and the Guard Force withdrew to their ambush site as night was rapidly approaching. For several hours firing was heard emanating from the area. The following morning, when we returned, the kraals were deserted as the locals had fled, never to return. All their livestock was abandoned – over time, the cattle went completely wild. These locals should, in fact, have been moved into the protected villages in the Mtetengwe TTL but somehow seemed to have been overlooked. The cattle managed to survive and even thrived in that harsh environment, in the dry seasons obtaining water from the odd pool in the Umzingwani River. They were to stay in the bush for the duration of the war.

Steve Acornley and some of his men from the Special Branch station at Gwanda, during one of their quieter periods, had come down to Beitbridge to give me a hand, which was very much appreciated. Although not a roaring success, their visit had afforded me the opportunity to get around the area during the two weeks they were with me.

•••

On 20 March, elements of D Company 6RR travelling in convoy were ambushed by an estimated nine terrorists near the Tongwe protected village in the Mtetengwe TTL. No injuries were sustained by the security forces. Spoor was lost approximately five hundred metres from the scene of the action.

On 21 March, Scouter Yankee from the Latumba base moved onto a suspected terrorist base in the Mtetengwe TTL. Their presence was compromised by two African women who ran screaming through the bush and, consequently, all the terrorists occupying the base fled in panic. A large, well-kept camp was located. Spoor was soon lost due to anti-tracking tactics employed by the terrorists.

On 21 March, a Police Reserve Air Wing aircraft, call sign Copper 83 and piloted by Police Reservist Roberts, came under ground attack while assisting ground forces relocate locals in the Diti TTL to the protected villages. The aircraft was undamaged.

At 8.45 p.m. on 25 March, elements of the South African Defence Force initiated an ambush on the Beitbridge state land, wounding one curfew breaker and arresting two others. (The SADF liaison officer, André van Rooyen, who attended the daily Joint Operations Centre meetings, had proposed that elements of the SADF on border-control duties be authorized to patrol within the confines of the Beitbridge state land which covered a five-kilometre radius around Beitbridge. This was agreed to and the SADF commenced operations in the area, with André informing the JOC of SADF deployment intentions on a daily basis.)

On 29 March, a Coley Hall petrol tanker was stopped by four terrorists on the main Bulawayo road but was allowed to proceed after the driver informed the group that the fuel was destined for Zambia.

Also on 29 March, an unknown number of terrorists ambushed a fencing gang travelling to the Chaswingo protected village in the Diti TTL, ten kilometres distant from their destination. One Internal Affairs escort was slightly wounded.

On 30 March, a Cargo Carrier vehicle detonated a landmine in the Diti TTL. There were no casualties.

On 31 March, an Internal Affairs vehicle detonated a landmine in the Diti TTL. There were no casualties.

On 31 March, a Chibuku vehicle delivering beer to protected villages in the Mtetengwe TTL was stopped and the driver robbed of his takings for the day.

At approximately ten o'clock on the night of 31 March, Beitbridge village came under 82mm mortar and 75mm recoilless rifle attack by a large group of terrorists from Luchewe hill, a prominent feature approximately two kilometres east of Beitbridge. Fortunately, the terrorists aimed for the most prominently illuminated area – the Rhodesia Railways marshalling yards at the railway station. This area, for security reasons, was illuminated by scores of security lights as opposed to the dimly lit residential and business areas. The army was able to retaliate with an 81mm mortar and a 60mm mortar but not before the attackers had fired off a total of twenty-two rounds of 82mm mortar and 75mm recoilless. Minimal damage was caused with most rounds landing in the bush surrounding the station. Most of the locals were enjoying themselves at the club when the attack was launched and without a thought moved outside with their drinks to watch 'the show', a good excuse to continue the party. Unfortunately, being deployed, I missed out on all the fun and, by all accounts, a good party.

On 3 April, an Internal Affairs vehicle detonated a landmine in the Mtetengwe TTL. There were no casualties. Elements of C Company 1RAR conducted follow-up operations but were unable to locate tracks.

Also on 3 April, a C Company 1RAR vehicle detonated a landmine in the Mtetengwe TTL. There were no casualties. Troops from the same company located and followed spoor until it was lost on stony ground.

•••

On 8 April, an operation was mounted against a suspected terrorist base and *povo* camp thought to be occupied by twenty-plus terrorists and an unknown number of locals in the north of the Mtetengwe TTL near the Liebigs Ranch boundary. The Operation *Repulse* Fire Force was positioned at Beitbridge to spearhead the attack.

The exact position of the terrorist base, which had been located by a Police Reserve Air Wing pilot, could not be exactly determined, and a close-quarter reconnaissance patrol of the suspected area would therefore be necessary. Fortunately, Captain Martin Pearce of the SAS immediately got involved. He was the Brigade Intelligence Officer in Bulawayo and was visiting Beitbridge by chance. Never one to miss an opportunity for action, Pearce, himself an experienced close-quarter reconnaissance operator, arranged for me and a two-man 6RR section to deploy on foot and under cover of darkness to conduct the reconnaissance. In the event of the patrol locating the base, Pearce would direct the airborne force onto the target and my little patrol would join in the fray.

The walk-in was long and hard but we eventually arrived at the outskirts of the suspected base at around three o'clock the next morning. Although we had night-vision equipment, we had great difficulty in locating the actual base in spite of being in the immediate vicinity. For fear of compromising the attack, Pearce ordered us into cover shortly before first light where we were able to establish radio communications with the inbound Fire Force.

The results of the action were disappointing: no kills and a capture tally of one terrorist, armed with a 60mm mortar, four mortar bombs and a Tokarev pistol, and several locals who were running with the terrorists. The captured terrorist was airlifted to Mazunga Ranch headquarters where I joined him directly to carry out an immediate tactical interrogation so that relevant information could be fed back to the Fire Force commander who was still orbiting the base in the K-Car, the command helicopter.

The capture, who was to join the ranks of my turned terrorists, was extremely cooperative from the outset. He admitted that two terrorist sections had occupied the base but had left the day before the attack. He had been left behind as he was drunk and passed out under some bush where his comrades had failed to find him and so had left without him. This information was subsequently corroborated by the locals arrested in the base. By lunchtime, the exercise was over and the Fire Force returned to its base at Buffalo Range, Chiredzi.

Martin Pearce remained the Brigade Intelligence Officer for several months before returning to the SAS and operations. He was killed in a cross-border operation in Lusaka in mid-1979, being awarded a posthumous Silver Cross of Rhodesia.

The captured terrorist proved to be a hive of information and I was able to significantly update my appreciation of the area. He was extremely loyal but, like others, was to meet a gruesome death during the ceasefire period in early 1980.

•••

On 18 April, Scouter X-Ray, operating in the Siyoka TTL, made contact with ten terrorists. The terrorists fled without returning fire. There were no injuries.

Also on 18 April, at approximately 7.00 p.m., ten terrorists entered the Chaswingo protected village where they were fed by a kraal head. They then left, firing rifles and directing six 60mm mortar bombs at the Guard Force strongpoint inside the protected village. Guard Force returned fire with no casualties on either side. Later that night, the terrorists again attacked the PV with 60mm mortar and small-arms fire. Fire was returned and, again, there were no casualties on either side.

On 18 April, a Guard Force vehicle detonated a landmine in the Mtetengwe TTL. One Guard Force member was slightly wounded.

On the 18 April, a Railway Motor Service (RMS) cattle truck was stopped by five terrorists in the Mtetengwe TTL. The terrorists, after robbing the driver, attempted to set the vehicle alight. As this was taking place, another RMS vehicle drove onto the scene. Fired on by the terrorists, the driver did not stop and, although injured by flying glass, managed to escape and report the incident at Beitbridge.

On 22 April, an Internal Affairs heavy vehicle detonated a landmine on the main Tshiturapadzi road in the Diti TTL. There were no casualties. A Pookie, a Rhodesian-developed landmine-detection vehicle, was leading the convoy but had failed to detect the mine.

On 24 April, a Guard Force road-clearance patrol from the Shabwe protected village in the Mtetengwe TTL had a fleeting contact with five terrorists. There were no casualties on either side.

Also on 24 April, five terrorists gutted the farm store on Benfur Estates on the Mazunga River after robbing it of a large quantity of clothing and foodstuffs. They also shot and killed eight goats and four donkeys.

On 25 April, a police mine-protected vehicle detonated a landmine in the Siyoka TTL. There were no injuries.

On 25 April, the terrorist captured on 8 April indicated two 82mm mortar bombs cached in the Mtetengwe TTL to Scouter Yankee.

Also on 25 April, Scouter X-Ray was ambushed by an unknown number of terrorists in the Siyoka TTL. Fire was returned and the terrorists fled. There were no injuries on either side.

On 28 April, a large herd of cattle was stolen from River Ranch by approximately six terrorists and driven toward the Masera TTL. Elements of C Company 1RAR mounted a follow-up and all the cattle were recovered. No contact was made with the terrorists. However, the terrorists fled toward the main Bulawayo road. Thinking the road was clear, they attempted to cross over into the Mtetengwe TTL but a passing Internal Affairs convoy intercepted the gang and opened fire. The terrorists returned fire and managed to escape into the Mtetengwe TTL, with no casualties on either side.

During the early hours of 29 April, Penemene protected village in the Mtetengwe TTL came under attack by a large group of terrorists using small arms, an 82mm mortar and a 75mm recoilless rifle. The attack was ineffectual and caused no damage or injury to property or person. C Company 1RAR conducted a first-light follow-up but, due to anti-tracking methods employed by the terrorists, tracks were lost after about five kilometres.

On 2 May, elements of the South African Defence Force operating within the Beitbridge state land opened fire on three curfew breakers, killing one and seriously wounding another who was casevaced to the Messina hospital. The third was handed over uninjured to the Beitbridge police.

On 4 May, elements of C Company 1RAR had a long-range, fleeting contact with approximately five terrorists. Blood spoor was located during the follow-up, indicating that one terrorist had been wounded.

During the early hours of 5 May, a group of eight terrorists visited the homestead complex on River Ranch which was unoccupied at that stage as owners Piet and Leonie van der Merwe were away. The gun cabinet in the office block was forced and thirteen weapons, including a police-issue FN rifle, an Internal Affairs Sten sub-machine gun and a custom-made 9mm double-barrelled big-game rifle were stolen. The group attempted to set the complex on fire but was unable to do so. They then forced the ranch driver to drive them into the Mtetengwe TTL in van der Merwe's Land Rover where they destroyed it by fire before abandoning it. C Company 1RAR conducted the follow-up which was unsuccessful.

On 9 May, a Guard Force convoy travelling on the Tshiturapadzi road in the Diti TTL was ambushed by eight terrorists using small-arms and PRG-7 fire. There were no casualties on either side.

During the afternoon on 13 May, a group of ten terrorists stopped a Coley Hall lubricating oil tanker travelling to Bulawayo on the main road. The terrorists then drove the tanker off the road into the Mtetengwe TTL and, using RPG-7 rocket and small-arms fire, set the tanker ablaze. Due to the lateness of the report, elements of C Company 1RAR were only able to react at first light the following morning when the tanker was found to be completely destroyed. The driver was unharmed.

Early on the morning of 17 May, Scouter Yankee from the Latumba base in the Mtetengwe TTL made contact with approximately four terrorists and a running contact developed. A Police Reserve Air Wing aircraft, call sign Copper 84, was deployed to give assistance in any way it could. Elements of C Company 1RAR were deployed to the contact area to assist the police patrol. The PRAW pilot estimated that during the initial contact one terrorist had been killed that two had been wounded. The RAR patrol located blood spoor in the contact area and were in the process of following up when another more serious operation developed and all parties involved were recalled. The PRAW aircraft was holed twice from ground fire but the damage sustained was minor.

•••

At approximately noon on the same day, a northbound Wards Transport petrol tanker and a Coley Hall southbound petrol tanker were stopped on the main Bulawayo road by a group of at least ten terrorists. The drivers were forced out of their vehicles after parking them next to one another. The terrorists then opened fire on the two tankers, setting both alight before fleeing the area. Security forces reacted hastily and were soon on the scene. From those attending it was apparent that the Coley Hall tanker was empty of fuel but was in grave danger of exploding from the heat and flames of the Wards Transport tanker. It was decided to pre-empt any explosion by blowing a hole in the tanker to allow gas and fumes to escape. The intrepid Captain André van Rooyen, the SADF liaison officer, stepped forward with a 3.5-inch rocket launcher and, with his number two, fired the rocket which was followed by a tremendous explosion as the Coley Hall tanker received a direct hit. Much to his embarrassment, van Rooyen lost half his moustache to a flame that escaped from the rocket launcher on firing.

Section Officer Alistair Mommsen, the Ground Coverage coordinator at Beitbridge, was also at the scene, wearing normal office dress order that included leather shoes and khaki shorts. He explained to me later that, without thinking, he had followed some RAR troops into the bush on the side of the road. The troops started casting around for spoor, slowly moving farther and farther into the bush, away from the road. Eventually, Alistair inquired of the RAR platoon commander when they would be returning to the vehicles on the road. Alistair's heart dropped when he was informed that the patrol was on tracks and would stay on them for as long as possible, probably days, and that they would not be returning anytime soon. As night was approaching, Alistair had no choice but to stay with the patrol.

It was an unwritten law in the Rhodesian security forces, and I should imagine this law applies to most armies, that, when deployed, a soldier or policeman was expected to be self-sufficient in food, water, ammunition and bedding; in other words, what he carried had to last him without relying on his comrades. Poor Alistair, he only had the clothes he was wearing, his FN rifle with one spare magazine and leather-soled shoes to boot and no water, no food, no sleeping bag – the nights were chilly at that time of the year – and, worst of all, no cigarettes. Over the next three days, Alistair lost a lot of weight and when at last the follow-up came to an end, a very weary and dishevelled Alistair emerged from the bush.

•••

During the night of 19 May, two labourers on Nottingham Estates were beaten to death by a gang of terrorists who proceeded to set fire to the compound.

•••

On 22 May, Scouter Yankee from the Latumba base, accompanied by elements of C Company 1RAR, made contact with an estimated ten terrorists in the Mtetengwe TTL. One terrorist was wounded and subsequently captured and his AK-47 assault rifle and other equipment were recovered. He was casevaced to Fort Victoria where he was treated over several days for a gunshot wound to the ankle. I was flown to Fort Victoria to interrogate him in an attempt to extract immediate operational intelligence but this proved futile as he was heavily sedated at that time. I would have to wait until he was discharged from hospital before I could speak to him.

The captured terrorist was returned to Beitbridge about a week later and I immediately interrogated him. He had been out of circulation for over a week so the information he supplied was already history. However, when questioned about any arms caches that he was aware of, he immediately volunteered to indicate three in the Mtetengwe TTL. I scouted around and managed to raise a small escort and proceeded with the capture into the Mtetengwe. As was usual, the caches were located a long way from any type of road and after a long march, we arrived at the first one. We uncovered one weapon, a 9mm double-barrelled rifle and various other pieces of equipment which included, bizarrely, a slimming machine. The recovered goods were obviously the proceeds from the River Ranch robbery which had occurred on 5 May. I recognized the weapon as Piet van der Merwe's precious 9mm double rifle, as on a number of occasions he had proudly shown it to me. The wheel had indeed turned.

Shortly after I arrived at Beitbridge, I had bought a .3006 Parker Hale Safari Special rifle from Dave Ward, one of the patrol officers on the station. It was a beautiful rifle in excellent condition. I had only had it for a few weeks when my neighbour Monty van Vuuren asked if he could borrow it as he had purchased an impala licence from the District Commissioner's office but did not have a rifle. I reluctantly agreed and handed the rifle over on the Saturday of the hunt.

Later that afternoon, a forlorn Monty came to see me – without my rifle. He explained that he and his mate George had set off for the Masera TTL in his car, using the public road running through River Ranch. After driving for what seemed like hours, they eventually decided that they were now in the Masera TTL. They then shot their impala and, while they were loading it, along came an irate Piet van der Merwe who accused them of poaching on his land. They had, in fact, not arrived in the Masera TTL; it was still some miles off. Monty tried to explain what had happened and produced the impala hunting licence. After a while, Piet cooled down, and let them keep the impala but confiscated my rifle.

I immediately telephoned Piet to see what was going on and threatened to have him prosecuted for theft if he did not return my rifle. The conversation got a bit heated and I left the matter until the Monday morning when I went to see him. For a week he really messed me around in one way or another, by making one excuse after another, ranging from his wife being away in Messina with the gun-safe keys to them being mislaid or lost in the bush. Toward the end of the week, Piet could see that I was at the end of my patience and brought the rifle to my office where he handed it over to me. For a long time after that I had absolutely no time for Piet, but when the war stated in the Beitbridge area Piet would be the first to put his hand up when I called for volunteers to deploy with me.

So, now I had his precious double rifle in my hands. On my return to Beitbridge, I contacted Piet and informed him of our success in recovering some of the stolen items and asked him to come through and collect the goods. After handing over most of the recovered goods, including the slimming machine, I produced his double rifle with a tag tied to the trigger guard. Piet's immediate reaction was to reach out and take the rifle. However, I pulled it away from him, explaining that it was now a police exhibit and would be retained until such time as the persons responsible for the robbery were arrested and appeared in court. Piet looked absolutely devastated and left the police station like a broken man. After loading the recovered goods into his Land Rover, he climbed in to drive away. I sent one of my staff to call him before he drove off and when he entered my office, without a word, I handed the rifle to him. He gave me a puzzling look and I smiled and told him he could take it. I thought he was going to hug me and, before leaving, told me I could shoot an eland on his ranch anytime I wanted. This was a great honour as Piet would not, without exception, allow any shooting on his ranch. However, I never took him up on the offer.

The other caches the capture indicated had been removed prior to our arrival. As there was really nothing else to do with the capture, he joined the ranks of my turned terrorists and proved to be a loyal member.

•••

On 23 May, elements of C Company 1RAR located four *povo* camps in the Mtetengwe TTL. All were unoccupied when the RAR entered them but terrorist documents and packs were located.

Also on 23 May, elements of the Rhodesian Defence Regiment were ambushed by fifteen terrorists in the area of Madaula store in the Diti TTL. One of the troops was seriously wounded and another slightly injured. Both were casevaced to the Messina hospital. No casualties were sustained by the terrorists.

Again, on 23 May, an Internal Affairs convoy was ambushed by an unknown number of terrorists in the Mtetengwe TTL. Fire was returned with no casualties being inflicted on either side.

On 27 May, a Police Reserve Air Wing pilot detected four further *povo* camps in the Mtetengwe TTL. The following day, elements of C Company 1RAR conducted checks of these camps and found that they had been recently vacated.

On 4 June, elements of C Company 1RAR, call sign 31, engaged four to five terrorists at long range on Shobe Block, Liebigs Ranch. The patrol then located spoor and followed tracks in a southerly direction and entered the Masera TTL when they were ambushed. One soldier, Private M. Chihwayi, was fatally wounded and died while being casevaced to hospital.

On 6 June, an Internal Affairs vehicle detonated a landmine in the Diti TTL, without casualty.

On 8 June, elements of C Company 1RAR made contact with an estimated ten terrorists and an unknown number of locals in the Masera TTL. During the engagement two locals were killed, possibly by crossfire. Various items of terrorist equipment were recovered.

On 9 June, Scouter X-Ray, operating in the Siyoka TTL, made contact with a group of ten terrorists. One terrorist was wounded but managed to escape, discarding his AK-47 assault rifle in the process. This was later recovered, together with items of terrorist equipment. The police patrol sustained no injuries.

On 13 June, a police patrol traveling from Tshiturapadzi to Beitbridge was ambushed by an unknown number of terrorists in the Diti TTL. African Police Reservist Kenneth Kawadza was killed in the engagement and one Internal Affairs District Assistant was seriously injured, being casevaced to Messina hospital for treatment.

On 14 June, a police patrol located a recently vacated base camp in the Siyoka TTL.

Also on 14 June, elements of C Company 1RAR made contact with approximately seven terrorists in the Mtetengwe TTL. A number of locals who were running with the terrorists were caught in the crossfire and one was killed. There were no casualties on the RAR side.

Again, on 14 June, a lone Roads Department vehicle was ambushed in the area of the Chaswingo protected village, Diti TTL. The driver and passengers managed to escape unharmed.

On 16 June, Scouter X-Ray, while travelling from the Siyoka TTL to Beitbridge, was ambushed by seven terrorists. Fire was returned and the patrol managed to escape unharmed. No casualties were sustained by the terrorists.

On 17 June, two elderly locals were shot and killed by an unknown number of terrorists in the area of the Shabwe protected village in the Mtetengwe TTL. Both were shot for staying in the protected village against the orders of the terrorists and as a warning to other occupants to move back to the bush.

On 19 June, a civilian low-loader detonated a landmine in the Mtetengwe TTL. No injuries were sustained by driver or crew.

On 20 June, a Rhodesian Defence Regiment Protection Unit came under attack in the Chipisi TTL. The attack was ineffectual with no friendly casualties sustained.

Also on 20 June, elements of C Company 1RAR had a fleeting, long-range contact with approximately three terrorists. During follow-up operations the patrol located twenty locals, men and women, who had been abducted from various protected villages in the Diti TTL. They all willingly returned with the assistance of military transport to their respective PVs.

Again, on 20 June, a Rhodesian Defence Regiment change-over convoy was ambushed by an unknown number of terrorists in the Diti TTL. No casualties were inflicted on either side.

Yet again, on 20 June, a Bulawayo-bound vehicle owned by Katima Mulilo (Pvt) Ltd. was ambushed by an unknown number of terrorists on the main road. The driver and crew managed to escape unharmed.

On 21 June, elements of C Company 1RAR, while following spoor, contacted eight terrorists in the Mtetengwe TTL. There were no casualties on either side.

On 22 June, elements of C Company 1RAR made contact with a group of approximately fifteen terrorists in the Mtetengwe TTL. This contact was at long range and no injuries were sustained by either side.

On 25 June, a vehicle driven by locals in the Mtetengwe TTL was ambushed by six terrorists. One African female was killed and an African male was shot through the foot. The injured man was casevaced to the Messina hospital.

On 26 June, elements of C Company 1RAR made contact with a group of six terrorists while checking a possible *povo* base in the Mtetengwe TTL. There were no casualties on either side.

Also on 26 June, a security force patrol, consisting of police and elements of the Rhodesian Intelligence Corps (RIC) from the police Latumba base, was operating in the Mtetengwe TTL when the RIC vehicle detonated a landmine, killing one of the occupants, Corporal Kenneth Michael Michell of the RIC. Two RIC members were seriously injured and casevaced to the Messina hospital. Two others who were slightly wounded were treated locally. There is another version to the circumstances surrounding the death of Corporal Michell which differs entirely from the diary entry I have: that is, Michell was killed in action while clearing contour ridges, shot at close quarters by a terrorist who suddenly stood up out of cover.

On 27 June, elements of the Rhodesian Corps of Engineers travelling in a heavy vehicle detonated a landmine in the Mtetengwe TTL, without casualty.

•••

The first six months of 1978 proved to be very disappointing in terms of results. At the beginning of the year, a high-density-force operation had been mounted in the Beitbridge operational area. This force, commanded by Colonel Peter Rich, consisted of one RLI commando and several RAR companies. The operation lasted less than two weeks and achieved little. As soon as troops moved into an area, the terrorists simply melted into the bush. If the deployment had been longer and a Fire Force deployed in support of the operation, then results might have been more encouraging.

C Company 1RAR was another disappointment. The company was deployed under command of the eccentric Major Lionel Dyke. During a three-month deployment and after expending thousands upon thousands of rounds of ammunition in combat, the law of averages should dictate that a stray bullet or a ricochet would eventually find a target. This happened on 22 May when a C Company patrol wounded and captured a terrorist. This was their sole success in three months. Of course, Dyke put the blame squarely on the shoulders of Special Branch, and me in particular, for the lack of intelligence. The 'good old days' of Special Branch supplying accurate information on the exact whereabouts of the enemy was now but a distant dream. To be fair to Dyke, if he had had the luxury of a Fire Force at his disposal, he would have achieved more.

This was also a demoralizing period, as politically the country seemed to be heading for the abyss, with even the right-wing South African government exerting pressure on Prime Minister Ian Smith and his government to accept black majority rule. I was not opposed to this but was well aware that neither Robert Mugabe nor Joshua Nkomo would ever agree to negotiations of any kind unless the odds were heavily stacked in their favour. The days of moderation had long since passed and with the massive build-up of the ZANLA and ZIPRA armies externally, Mugabe and Nkomo were determined to take the country by force. Smith would therefore be forced to seek an internal political settlement with the moderate Black Nationalist parties, primarily Bishop Abel Muzorewa's United African National Council (UANC) and Ndabaningi Sithole's ZANU (not to be confused with Mugabe's militant ZANU, which had broken away in 1975).

In spite of alarming emigration statistics, the vast majority of white Rhodesians had complete confidence in Ian Smith who had led the country for the past fifteen years. He would continue to receive this unwavering support until the death.

Fortunately, or not, Beitbridge was isolated from the rest of the country, with no regular newspaper deliveries, apart from sporadic, sought-after copies of the *Bulawayo Chronicle* and the *Rhodesia Herald* getting dropped off by considerate travellers with the customs and immigration officials at the border post. Due to poor reception from the Rhodesian Broadcasting Corporation, the community tuned in to South African radio stations, particularly Springbok Radio. There was absolutely no television coverage. The white community of Beitbridge continued to enjoy the moment, living life to the full in a very sociable environment. But the days were ticking by; it was now a matter of months, not years.

CHAPTER SEVEN
Dirty tricks

In early April 1978 C Company 1RAR had just arrived on deployment at Beitbridge. One Saturday morning I was sitting in my Beitbridge office chatting to Sergeant Wally Insch of the Selous Scouts who was on a predeployment visit. We were intending to pop across the road to the Beitbridge Hotel for a beer when I knocked off at lunchtime. However, at about 10 a.m. the phone rang, unusual for a Saturday: it was Bruce Cook from Mazunga. Without saying too much, he requested that I travel, preferably alone, to Mazunga so he could speak with me on an extremely urgent matter. I agreed and, gathering my gear, explained to Wally that I had to dash off to Mazunga. Always a man of action, Wally asked if he could accompany me. Agreeing and glad of his company, as the possibility of being ambushed en route was great, we left Beitbridge, travelling north on the Bulawayo road to Mazunga.

After an uneventful trip, we arrived at Mazunga to be met by Bruce, Max Stockill, the Liebigs Lamulas section manager and Mike Gawler, the managing director of Liebigs Ranch who Bruce had also called to the meeting. I was to hear an amazing account, from Max Stockill, of what had transpired on Lamulas Section over the previous few days.

I had first met Max Stockill in late 1976 when he came and introduced himself at my Beitbridge office. He was a very secretive type of bloke who spoke in garbled sentences and was forever saying "throwing a red herring" and "blowing smoke screens". He was working for Union Carbide at the time, prospecting for diamonds on Nottingham Estates. He also inquired as to whether I had heard from my counterpart in Que Que to whom he used to pass information. I replied in the negative and I could see that he was a bit put out. My impression of him was that he had spent too much time in the sun and fancied himself as a super-spy. I gathered that when in the field he portrayed a left-wing attitude and made it known that he was anti-government and pro-liberation movements. This is what I suppose he meant when he spoke about "throwing red herrings" and "blowing smoke screens". He popped in to see me from time to time but I never really took him seriously. He left Union Carbide in 1977 and joined Liebigs Ranch as the Lamulas Section manager. Lamulas bordered onto the northern regions of the Mtetengwe TTL from where Stockhill drew the majority of his labour force.

About a week prior to the Saturday meeting, Stockhill had become aware of a strong terrorist presence on the ranch. He had decided not to report the matter but rather to try and establish contact with the terrorists. By now, his workers had accepted him as being pro-ZANLA as had Stockhill's African foreman who worked very closely with Stockhill. I have no doubt that in the past Stockill had actively assisted the terrorists, either by not reporting their presence or feeding them or both. When I pressed him on the subject he denied it and maintained that this was the first time he had become aware of a terrorist presence on the ranch. He discussed the possibility of meeting the terrorists with his foreman who assured him that he would broach the subject with the ZANLA group that evening.

I was aware that white farmers, particularly in the Chiredzi area, were supporting the terrorist cause by feeding them, seeing to their requirements and failing to report their presence to the authorities. It was not that they really supported the enemy as this aid was a form of protection which guaranteed them from being attacked. These farmers' actions were tantamount to treason of the highest order as the loyal farmers therefore bore the brunt of the intensified attacks with the disloyal farmers reaping the benefits of their dastardly deeds when Mugabe took over the country. I know of at least one Beitbridge farmer who was suspected of harbouring terrorists and which suspicions were confirmed after the war. So I was not really surprised when I Stockill related what had transpired.

The foreman had duly met with the terrorists that night and reported to Stockhill the next day that the terrorist commander was considering meeting him at the homestead security fence as Stockill had proposed. The meeting was tentatively arranged to take place after dark. That evening Stockill made the prearranged rendezvous at the fence but no one pitched up and so he returned to the house. The following day Stockill was informed by the foreman that the terrorists had in fact been present but, for security reasons, had only observed him. However, if he went to the fence at the same time that night they would speak to him. That night Stockhill made contact with three terrorists but the atmosphere was very tense and the conversation very stilted. However, they agreed to meet again the following night. This meeting was conducted in a more relaxed manner when Stockill handed over tins of food and other luxuries. He also told them that he would arrange for an ox to be slaughtered in their honour the next day. A further meeting was held on the following evening and another on Friday evening, by which time a rapport had developed between Stockill and the terrorists.

By this stage, Stockill had realized the enormity of situation and contacted Bruce Cook that evening and arranged a meeting with him at Mazunga the following day. When he met the terrorists on the Friday night he informed them of his intention of travelling to Gwanda the next day to purchase supplies. At the same time the terrorists informed him of their decision to leave the ranch on the Sunday. Prior to Stockhill's departure the following morning, the foreman arrived at the homestead with a note from the terrorists asking him to purchase medical supplies in the form of bandages, antiseptic cream, cottonwool, wound dressings and, wonders will never cease, Dr Strong 500 capsules and Eno's liver salts. On his arrival at Mazunga, he had informed Bruce Cook of what had transpired, which is how Gawler, Insch and I came to be there.

We sat around a table discussing the options. Bruce wanted an attack on the base carried out by the Buffalo Range Fire Force, although the exact location of the base was unclear. Wally Insch wanted to go in alone disguised as a labourer in the back of Stockhill's returning vehicle and carry out an attack single-handedly. Stockill wanted to return and carry out his clandestine operation with no action being taken by the security forces. Mike Gawler, who was in a state of shock, would support any action agreed upon. As I had just read the terrorists' medical wish list, I smiled inwardly: I knew what action would be taken.

While all this was going on I received an urgent radio message from Beitbridge advising me that a PRAW aircraft would shortly be landing at Mazunga and could I meet the plane as one of the passengers wanted to talk to me as a matter of top priority. Leaving the other four still debating, I drove across to the airfield. The aircraft landed and Captain Bob Warrington stepped out.

We went and sat under a tree; I was eager to hear what Bob had to say. He explained that he had been sent down to see me on behalf of ComOps who were investigating allegations by the Mozambican government that Rhodesian troops were infiltrating Mozambique from South Africa and, in particular, the Kruger National Park which forms part of the border with Mozambique. The Marxist Mozambican government had threatened retaliation against the South Africans with attacks against the tourist industry by carrying out raids on tourist camps, mining roads and ambushing vehicles in the Kruger. This was obviously of great concern to the South African government. The chief of the South African Defence Force, General Magnus Malan, had brought these allegations to the attention of his Rhodesian counterpart, General Peter Walls, who ordered an immediate investigation. There was some suggestion that Selous Scouts reconnaissance teams posing as tourists were using the Kruger to deploy across the border into Mozambique. As I had complete freedom of movement across both the Rhodesian and South African borders, I was in an ideal position to transport virtually anything or anyone, including weapons, across the border illegally and there was a suggestion that I may have assisted the Selous Scouts by transporting their teams across the Limpopo to the waiting back-up teams and vehicles in Messina.

I told Bob truthfully that I had never been involved in any such activity and had no knowledge of this. However, I did confirm that during 1977 I had transported a Selous Scout and his TR 48 radio 'illegally' across the border and handed him over to members of the SAP Security Branch at Pietersburg who had then transported him to the Pafuri border gate at Crooks' Corner within the Kruger National Park. The Scout had concealed himself on a hill overlooking the Mozambican town also known as Pafuri, his job being to direct fire onto predetermined targets in the town for the Selous Scout 81mm mortar crews positioned on the Rhodesian border under the command of Major Boet Swart. The mortar attack went in on schedule and from all accounts was very successful. I also added that as far as I was aware the hill was inside South Africa. That afternoon I had rendezvoused with the same Security Branch personnel and took charge of the Scout and transported him back to Rhodesia. I also made mention that on occasions elements of the security forces re-crossed the Limpopo River from South Africa – with the assistance of both the Security Branch and the SADF – into target areas in the Beitbridge area.

Bob appeared satisfied and I never heard anything further on the matter. Before he left, I discussed the matter of the terrorist group presently based on Lamulas Section and he agreed with me that poison was the answer. However, time was of the essence as the terrorists had stated their intention of leaving the area the following day. Bob was an old and trusted friend who had spent a considerable time as the JOC officer at Bindura and he knew Mac well, so I knew that I could count on his assistance. Bob, a past member of the SAS had lost all his fingers on his right hand – he always shook hands with his left – when freefalling into Mozambique at night as part of a pathfinder team. On deploying his parachute, his hand somehow got tangled in the rigging lines, resulting in his fingers being ripped from his hand, thus earning him a desk job. Between us it was agreed that I would telephone Mac to give him a veiled warning order, bearing in mind that the telephone I would be using was on a party line. On Bob's return to Salisbury later that afternoon, he would contact Mac and fully brief him on the developments, conveying the urgency of the matter. Although a coincidence, Bob's visit proved to be a blessing in disguise because without his assistance the outcome might have been different. Bob took off on his return to Salisbury and I returned to the council of war at the table.

I used Bruce's telephone to call Mac in Bindura. Knowing that the four at the table could hear what I said and after giving Mac as much information as I could,

I advised him that Bob would fill him in on all the details later that day, closing with a purposeful, "and don't forget the mealie meal" (mealie meal, or maize meal, is the national staple diet).

I now had to be very careful as Mike Gawler, the Liebigs general manager, would be present during my discussions and I needed his cooperation if the plan was to succeed. I must here digress as an incident had recently taken place affecting the Liebigs meat canning factory in West Nicholson. Although the factory did not fall under Gawler, the same British company employed him and he was a faithful company man. Gawler's loyalties to Rhodesia were unquestionable but he still retained his loyalties to his staff and his employer. In 1977, fourteen locals had died in the Shamva area after eating contaminated bully beef which had been canned at the Liebigs factory. Accusations were levelled that the bully beef had been intentionally contaminated by agents of the Rhodesian government, a fact that was vehemently denied. Tests were carried out by government scientists on the unopened tins and traces of bubonic plague bacteria were detected in some. The British management of Liebigs decided to send a team out from the UK to investigate. The team carried out tests and inspections at the canning factory which led to over one hundred employees being fired for unhygienic work practices as traces of bubonic plague were discovered at the factory. One case of bully beef had in fact been 'treated' by 'Mac's staff but, as the inspection finding indicated otherwise, the matter was dropped. However, a lot of people were convinced that the locals had been intentionally poisoned. As such, I asked Bob to ensure that Mac did not include any bully beef with the medical supplies.

Sitting down with the four men, I advised them that I had discussed the situation with Captain Warrington and that the various options up for discussion were not feasible. The Fire Force action would not work as the exact position of the terrorist base was unknown; for security reasons the terrorists used a day base and a night base and so the attacking force would be going in blind. I did not bother to comment on Wally's plan. Stockill's plan to carry on as normal was completely out of the question; in fact, I made it clear that Stockill's life would be in danger and I recommended to Mike Gawler that he be transferred to another part of the ranch for his own safety. Gawler heeded this recommendation and Stockill was never to return to Lamulas. Although I never mentioned the subject, it was now clear why Stockill had refused to have any form of ranch security on his section: it would have interfered with his 'intelligence operations'.

I then advised the war council that I had managed to secure the medical supplies that the terrorists had requested and that I would also be adding a 200-pound sack of mealie meal to the order. The maize meal would be perfectly harmless – in Stockill's terms I was 'blowing a smoke screen' – and I must say that the Liebigs staff swallowed the bait hook, line and sinker. (Recently I met up with John and Marie Barclay who mentioned the poisoned maize meal incident and when I tried to put the record straight John became quite irritable and told me that I had got the story wrong. I never pursued the matter and he is still convinced that the maize meal was poisoned. John and Marie had spent the war years on the southern sections of Liebigs Ranch, before eventually moving to Mazunga.)

As Stockill was not to return to Lamulas, Bruce Cook agreed to make arrangements for one of the Mazunga drivers to transport the supplies to Lamulas where he was to personally hand the consignment over to the foreman, together with a letter to be written by Stockill explaining his absence, that he had gone down with apparent malaria. As I had wanted to remain in control of the situation and bearing in mind that time was not on our side, Wally and I put up at Mazunga for the night where we were admirably entertained by my great friend Bruce Cook.

Around 8 p.m. Bob Warrington telephoned me at Bruce's house and confirmed that he had spoken to Mac who had organized my requirements and who had arranged for a PRAW aircraft to deliver the goods to the Mazunga airfield at 9.30 the following morning.

As arranged, the PRAW aircraft landed and the pilot handed over the carton of medical supplies together with the sack of maize meal. We took the supplies to Bruce's house where I inspected the carton, satisfied that the quantities I had asked for were there. Bruce then summoned the driver and from his storeroom assisted him in loading the sack of maize meal onto the back of the truck along with the re-sealed medical carton and the letter that Stockill had written the previous afternoon prior to his departure with Mike Gawler to the Liebigs Ranch headquarters at Towla. Bruce briefed the driver – Wally and I were not present – on his task and emphasized the fact that the goods and the letter had to be handed over to the Lamulas foreman personally and that immediately on his return to Mazunga, he was to report to Bruce.

Wally and I stayed at Mazunga until the driver returned and reported to Bruce that the Lumulas foreman had personally received the goods. He confirmed that a beer drink in the compound was now in progress. There was nothing much to do now but to sit back and wait for the results to start filtering in.

The following account was obtained from the interrogation of captured terrorists, from the questioning of locals and from documents recovered and, in particular, from a notebook recovered after a contact in the Sengwe TTL which found its way to the desk of Detective Section Officer John Davey, my good friend from Chiredzi.

The terrorists, still numbering thirty, had remained at the beer drink until early on the Monday morning when, as a group, they headed south into the Mtetengwe TTL. Presumably after the weekend beer drink, most were hungover and to remedy this they dug into the vitamin pills, the Dr Strong 500 capsules and the Eno's liver salts. The group stayed together for the next forty-eight hours when two of their number started complaining of severe toothache and headaches before being treated by the section medical officer. The condition of the two rapidly deteriorated with their vision becoming impaired (they were starting to go blind), their hair falling out in tufts and their feet developing suppurating sores which necessitated the two having to be carried. They both died during the night. The next morning, with other members of the group complaining of the same symptoms, it was decided to obtain the services of a witchdoctor in the Mtetengwe TTL. Several terrorists were dispatched for this purpose, duly returning that afternoon with a witchdoctor in tow. The witchdoctor carried out various cleansing rituals, after which he pronounced that the entire group had been cursed and his powers were not strong enough to lift the spell that had been placed on them. This diagnosis by the witchdoctor was in all probability concocted to save his own skin. The group was now under the impression that they had been bewitched and some terrible spell placed on them. Following a council of war, it was decided that the entire group would make for Mozambique where they knew they would find a powerful-enough witchdoctor to lift the spell.

Word soon spread to other terrorist groups in the area who wanted nothing to do with them for fear of being affected by the curse. Our target group was thus left to their fate. The situation must have been terrible for them because they knew that once they started suffering from toothache they would be dead within the next few days or so. Luckily, they still had medical supplies available in their desperate effort to stay alive. However, every day they were to leave more of their number dead in the African wilderness, all exacerbated by being treated as lepers by their own comrades.

Over a period of two weeks, the dwindling group continued on their southeastern journey to Mozambique and hopeful salvation. However, when the notebook was recovered after the contact in the Sengwe TTL, a list of twenty-three names had been recorded of those who had perished on that fateful march, with two other names appearing, indicating that they were dying from 'witchcraft'. The entries relating to the deaths of the terrorists had been penned by three different hands which would tend to indicate that two of the diarists were among those who had succumbed.

The medical supplies had been contaminated with a mercury-based poison which had caused a terrible and painful death, not to speak of the demoralizing affect it would have had on the others in the section, particularly when the first symptoms of toothache began.

All in all, it appeared to have been a very satisfactory operation for us. Recorded by ZANLA were twenty-three deaths and two dying. It is quite possible that all thirty may have ultimately died.

CHAPTER EIGHT
A busy two months
July–August 1978

The Special Branch station was upgraded to the rank of detective inspector, the post filled by Brian Perkins who as a detective section officer the previous year had been awarded a well-earned Commissioner's Special Commendation, the Silver Baton, for operations while stationed at the Plumtree Special Branch station. Brian would take over the bulk of the running of the office so as to release me for full-time operational work. Unfortunately, with the arrival of Brian, his young brother Ian 'Perkies', an excellent lad and a decided asset to the Beitbridge office, was transferred to Gwanda and I must say that I was extremely sorry when he left.

Prior to Brian's arrival, Chief Superintendent Mike Reeves, Deputy Provincial Special Branch Officer in Bulawayo, had offered me a transfer, initially to Bulawayo, as he considered my relegation to second-in-command an insult. I was not keen on a transfer to Bulawayo but gave the matter serious consideration, eventually declining the offer. I was enjoying the Beitbridge way of life, the danger and excitement, the isolation from reality and the live-for-today attitude of the remote border town. At any rate, Brian was a good friend and I knew the two of us would get on. Mike Reeves was quite relieved when I advised him of my decision.

The 6th Battalion the Rhodesian Regiment was once again deployed to Beitbridge and I looked forward to working with them again.

Mobie van Wyk was promoted to chief inspector with the upgrade of the police station.

•••

On 1 July, a contact took place in the Diti TTL when approximately ten terrorists fired on elements of No. 1 Psychological Operations Unit. The unit returned fire with no injuries inflicted by either side. No. 1 POU, or Psyops, was responsible for winning over the hearts and minds of the local population, an excellent idea but wholly negated by the terrorists who controlled the locals through pure terror or who were otherwise wholeheartedly supported by the local populace. Psyops had an impossible task but at that stage I supported any concept that might weaken the enemy.

Also on 1 July, approximately twenty terrorists visited the Gem Farm compound and seriously assaulted five labourers, accusing them of being government collaborators. All the injured were casevaced to Beitbridge for medical treatment.

On 2 July, a Springmaster removals van was ambushed on the main Bulawayo road by an unknown number of terrorists. The driver and crew were not hurt but the vehicle received several strikes.

Also on 2 July, ten terrorists visited the compound on Cawood's Mazunga Ranch where they bayoneted the foreman to death and severely beat a worker who was casevaced to Beitbridge for treatment. The terrorists abducted twenty other labourers, all of whom managed to escape during the security force follow-up operation the next morning.

On 3 July, an African Development Fund vehicle detonated a landmine in the Mtengwe TTL. Three Internal Affairs employees were slightly injured and were casevaced to Beitbridge.

Also on 3 July, the River Ranch compound was subjected to terrorist attack with RPG-7 rockets and small-arms fire. The farm watch returned fire. None of the compound occupants was injured. It was apparent from these attacks that the terrorist strategy was now to force the labour off the farms and ranches, thus rendering them unworkable. The farmers accordingly increased their protection forces to counter the threat.

On 6 July, a No. 1 Psyops Unit detonated a landmine on the Pande Mine road in the Mtetengwe TTL. One of the occupants received minor injuries and was casevaced to Beitbridge for treatment. I suspect this was the final straw for POU which ceased operations in the Beitbridge area, moving onto fresher pastures.

On 8 July, in the Diti TTL, elements of the Rhodesian Defence Regiment escorting a Roads Department vehicle were ambushed by approximately ten terrorists using RPG-7 rockets and small-arms fire. One of the soldiers received minor injuries and was later casevaced to the Messina hospital for treatment. There were no known casualties to the enemy.

Also on 8 July, elements of Guard Force travelling in a vehicle convoy were ambushed by between fifteen and twenty terrorists in the Diti TTL. The ambush was initiated with RPG-7 rockets, followed by AK-47 and RPD fire. One of the vehicles was disabled by a rocket. One Guard Force member was hit and killed and three others were wounded, all of whom were casevaced to the Messina hospital.

On 10 July, elements of B Company 6RR contacted a group of approximately nine terrorists in the Siyoka TTL. The terrorists did not return fire and simply fled the scene. Follow-up operations resulted in the recovery of one AKM assault rifle and one RPK rifle (similar to an AK but with a longer and heavier barrel and used as a light machine gun). The faction these terrorists belonged to was never determined but judging from the weapons numbers the weapons were of Soviet manufacture, indicating they were ZIPRA.

During the afternoon of 13 July, two Swift Transport vehicles travelling to Bulawayo on the main road were ambushed by an unknown number of terrorists in the Mtetengwe TTL. Both vehicles managed to pass through the ambush in spite of being hit several times by rifle fire. The drivers were unhurt.

On 14 July, elements of Bruce Cook's Liebigs Ranch security detail had a fleeting contact with fifteen terrorists on Shobe Section. There were no casualties on either side.

On 15 July, elements of B Company 6RR contacted eight terrorists who took up defensive positions in an abandoned village in the Mtetengwe TTL from where they continued to return fire. However, their nerve faltered and with a determined force advancing on them, they soon broke and ran. A search of the contact area resulted in the recovery of an FN rifle fitted with a telescopic sight and a 12-bore semi-automatic Winchester shotgun. Both these weapons were identified as belonging to Piet van der Merwe of River Ranch, stolen by the terrorists during the night of 5 May.

Also on 15 July, elements of the same company came under fire from a group of terrorists while investigating a suspected terrorist base in the Mtetengwe TTL. One of the terrorists was seen to fall to the ground before being assisted out of the contact area by two others; it was believed that he had been wounded. Two local males thought to be running with the terrorists were killed in the crossfire.

On 16 July, Scouter Yankee travelling to Tshiturapadzi from the Latumbo base was ambushed by an unknown number of terrorists. Fire was returned and the terrorists fled the scene. There were no casualties on either side.

Also on 16 July, three terrorists stopped a Wards Transport vehicle in the Mtetengwe TTL and forced the driver out of the vehicle. A terrorist then drove the vehicle off the road into the bush. The driver was taken into the bush where he observed a large terrorist group numbering between fifty and eighty. He was ordered to strip naked before being allowed to leave. The terrorists then gutted the vehicle. Elements of B Company 6RR conducted the follow-up without success.

•••

On 17 July, a local reported the presence of an occupied terrorist base in the Mtetengwe TTL about two kilometres north of the Limpopo River. After discussing the situation with the commander of B Company 6RR, we agreed that the most obvious and simplest way to attack the base was from the south. Arrangements were made with André van Rooyen, the South African Defence Force liaison officer for the SADF to assist in the deployment. The SADF had a squadron of Eland 60 armoured cars – or Panhards to the Rhodesians – in the area, constantly patrolling the border, so any movement along the border road south of the river would not raise suspicion, particularly at night when we intended to deploy.

That night a section of B Company 6RR under the command of a lieutenant, accompanied by me, Special Branch Reservist Geoff Blyth and the informer crossed the border and met up with the South Africans who then escorted us to our crossing point. Surprisingly, the Limpopo, about a hundred metres wide at that point, was still holding a lot of water at that time of the year and the crossing was fairly tricky with ice-cold water reaching our chests. The informer, dressed in camouflage with an extra-large floppy hat to conceal his identity, had to be coaxed across as he was absolutely terrified of crocodiles. We all made it safely to the other bank as the informer began guiding us toward the enemy camp. The South Africans were to stay in position on the southern bank until completion of the operation, primarily to assist with any casualties.

In spite of the section commander making use of a Starlite night scope, we could not detect the base; however, the informer remained steadfast in his knowledge and belief that the base was indeed there. As the night was breathless and extremely calm, we listened for any heavy breathing, coughing or snoring but also failed in this endeavour.

It was then that I realized our mistake. For security reasons terrorists always made use of two bases: a day base where they entertained and held council with the locals and a night base where they moved to at last light and where all locals, except for young girls, were banned.

We knew we were in close proximity to the terrorist bases but not knowing the exact location of the night base, decided to lie up until first light. We could not have spent a worse night; sleep was impossible as our clothes were soaking wet and being mid-winter, it was bitterly cold. I was extremely happy to see the first light of dawn.

At dawn we decided to head off north as spoor indicated movement in that direction. We had barely gone a few paces when three women carrying washing more or less bumped into the patrol. Their reaction was immediate: they screamed, tossed their baskets of washing in the air and disappeared into the bush. Almost simultaneously three 60mm mortar bombs came raining down on our position as the terrorists opened fire with everything they had from about fifty metres to our front. The bush was extremely thick and no terrorists were seen. Fire was returned and the terrorists fled.

About an hour later another B Company section manning an OP observed eight terrorists moving southwest from the contact scene. In all probability this was the same group we had made contact with earlier that morning. In the absence of any Fire Force or troops to react in real time, the B Company commander ordered an area mortar shoot to flush out the terrorists. We moved to higher ground and watched the 81mm and 60mm mortar display. It was never established whether the mortar barrage was successful or not but it is doubtful and in all likelihood the terrorists escaped unharmed.

After the attack, the section moved to a prearranged rendezvous from where we were uplifted by vehicle and transported back to Beitbridge. We were all in high spirits despite our lack of any clear success.

Although not normally superstitious, I think we were jinxed from the word go as I had included Geoff Blyth in the attacking force. Geoff, a good friend, was desperate to see action and would grab any opportunity to deploy in an endeavour to achieve this. I regarded him as something of a Jonah but nevertheless would take him along whenever appropriate. But with Geoff around, we never made contact with the enemy (although he did have a contact after I had left Beitbridge). Geoff's specialty was that of human landmine detector: he had been blown up no less than four times when the vehicle he was travelling in or on detonated a landmine. On one occasion his dog Jock was also blown up which resulted in both dog and master becoming hard of hearing.

•••

On 17 July, an SADF patrol operating in the Beitbridge state land area and within one kilometre of the town located an enemy 82mm mortar base plate and other equipment.

On 19 July, Scouter Yankee, which had been ambushed while travelling to the Tshiturapadzi base on 16 July, once again came under attack by an unknown number of terrorists when returning to the base at Latumba. On this occasion two members of their escort were slightly wounded, later being casevaced to Beitbridge for treatment.

On 23 July, elements of B Company 6RR fired on three terrorists whom they had observed in a village in the Diti TTL. The terrorists retaliated with 60mm mortar and small-arms fire before breaking off the contact. A second B

Company patrol was directed to assist and while checking for spoor came under RPG-7 and small-arms attack. There were no casualties on either side.

On 25 July, a B Company 2RR vehicle detonated a landmine in the Diti TTL. There were no casualties.

•••

On 28 July, I was undertaking a patrol accompanied by members of my staff including the turned terrorists. It was my intention of shooting a couple of impala or a kudu for the pot before returning to Beitbridge. That afternoon we encountered a local who explained that he was looking for his cattle. During his interrogation he gave out that he had come across fresh spoor which he suspected had been made by terrorists. He indicated the spoor which I decided to follow as it was assessed as being very fresh. Leaving the vehicles and cattle herder under guard, we took up the spoor of three people which was easy to follow. After two or three kilometres, the spoor led in the direction of a deserted village and it was apparent that the trio had entered the complex. While observing the kraal, an armed terrorist was seen to exit and then re-enter the same hut. As the shadows were lengthening, I decided to waste no time and resolved to open fire on the hut. When everyone was in position I initiated the engagement. Fire was returned from the hut but the volume of our tracer fire caused the hut to suddenly burst into flames. All firing ceased as we watched the thatched building blazing away. There was no movement or sound from within so I assumed that the terrorist or terrorists had been killed. There was no point in hanging around and as the blaze would continue for some time and with dusk falling fast, we went back to the vehicles and with our prisoner returned to Beitbridge.

Early the following morning, accompanied by 6RR, we returned to the scene of the contact. The fire, which was now out, had spread during the night and several other huts had been gutted. Six bodies, burned beyond recognition, were recovered from the target hut as well as an SKS 'Lancer' rifle, the remains of a stick grenade, one RPG-7 rocket projectile and a medical pack. At least one of the deceased was a confirmed terrorist with the remainder credited as being either recruits or locals running with the terrorists.

•••

On 28 July, ten terrorists cut through the security fence and gained entry into the Chikwarakwara protected village where they abducted sixteen locals whom they forced to march into the Chipisi TTL. Follow-up operations were immediately instituted but due to road-work operations and the movement of Roads Department heavy vehicles, all spoor had been obliterated.

On 29 July, a tractor on Jopempi Block, Liebigs Ranch was set on fire by and completely gutted by eighteen terrorists.

On 30 July, eighteen terrorists stopped a Timberlands truck and trailer in the Mtetengwe TTL. The vehicle was then driven off the road where the terrorists fired bursts of AK-47 fire into it before gutting it. The driver and crew were released unharmed.

Also on 30 July, a B Company 6RR vehicle detonated a landmine in the Diti TTL. There were no casualties.

Again, during the night of 30 July, a group of terrorists murdered an African female on Jopempi Block, Liebigs Ranch. The reason for the murder remains a mystery.

On 1 August, Scouter Yankee from the Latumba base was again ambushed, this time by an estimated twenty terrorists in the Mtetengwe TTL. One detective constable received minor wounds and was casevaced to Beitbridge. Elements of A Company 2RR responded and came under small-arms and mortar attack. There were no security force casualties and no known terrorist casualties during this attack.

On 3 August, a local civilian vehicle was ambushed in the Mtetengwe TTL. The occupants of the vehicle escaped injury. The exact position of the ambush could not be determined and therefore no follow-up took place.

Also during the night of 3 August, elements of A Company 6RR in ambush opened fire on an unknown number of people in the Mtetengwe TTL. A first-light sweep of the area revealed three dead African males who were assessed as being curfew breakers.

On 4 August, elements of A Company 6RR opened fire on a group of eight terrorists in the Mtetengwe TTL. Due to fading light, no immediate follow-up was undertaken but a first-light sweep of the area resulted in a suitcase full of maize meal being recovered. There were no casualties on either side.

On 6 August, a police patrol operating on Sentinal Ranch and which at the time was tracking eleven terrorists, came under mortar and small-arms fire. Fire was returned and the terrorists broke off the engagement. There were no police casualties and the terrorists escaped unharmed.

Also on 6 August, a Biddulphs removal vehicle travelling on the main Bulawayo road was stopped by three terrorists who then drove it off the road into the Mtetengwe TTL where twelve other terrorists were waiting. The driver and crew were robbed of any valuables after which the vehicle was set ablaze. The driver and crew were released unharmed.

Again, on 6 August, nineteen locals were abducted by a group of terrorists from the Chiswingo protected village in the Diti TTL. Two of the locals managed to escape. Guard Force reacted without success.

On 8 August, elements of A Company 6RR came under attack while patrolling in the Diti TTL. The terrorists assaulted in extended-line formation but their nerve soon crumbled when the patrol returned fire. The enemy then departed the field of battle. There were no casualties on either side.

On 9 August, the decomposed body of an African male was discovered in the Umzingwani farming area. It is believed that his death had been at the hands of terrorists.

On 10 August, an Internal Affairs convoy travelling in the Mtetengwe TTL was ambushed by an unknown number of terrorists. There were no casualties on either side.

Also on 10 August, elements of C Company 6RR engaged ten terrorists at long range in the Diti TTL with the now-common no casualties-on-either-side result.

Again, on 10 August, a ZIPRA group of terrorists clashed with a ZANLA group in the Masera TTL. From observations, indications and investigation it was apparent that both factions, on sighting one another, had opened fire simultaneously at a distance of two hundred metres. No evidence was found to indicate that any injuries had been inflicted. Ballistic examination of the recovered expended cartridge cases revealed that the one AK-47 and an RPD machine gun had been used in the contact between a police patrol and a group of eleven terrorists on Sentinel Ranch on 6 August.

On 11 August, a beer drink was in progress in the vicinity of Chaswingo PV. The villagers were permitted to maintain their properties during the day but were required to spend the hours of darkness inside the PV. Three members of Guard Force and a member of the African Police Reserve from the Chaswingo PV decided to ignore standing orders and were attending the beer drink. Details are sketchy due to the amount of alcohol involved but apparently at three o'clock that afternoon the four left together, whether to relieve themselves or not is unknown, but all were armed. They were then ambushed at close range by between ten and fifteen terrorists. The three Guard Force members managed to run off, abandoning their weapons with one guardsman shot through both arms. The African Police Reservist was mortally wounded but whether he was killed outright is unclear. The terrorists stripped him of his uniform and then beheaded him with an axe before departing the scene. During follow-up operations blood spoor of one terrorist was located, the amount of blood lost indicating that he had been critically wounded. It is likely that he had been accidentally shot by his own comrades during the ambush.

On 11 August, a group of six terrorists fired on and stopped an African bus on the main Fort Victoria road. After robbing the driver and passengers of their valuables, they attempted to drive the vehicle off the main road into the Mtetengwe TTL, possibly to burn it. However, they were unable to do so as the driver had applied the hand brake and had switched off the engine while it was engaged in fifth gear. After several failed attempts, the terrorists beat up the driver and departed into the Mtetengwe TTL, heading north. The driver and passengers then continued their journey. Of interest, four AK-47 assault rifles were identified by police ballistics as having been used in this incident. One AK-47 was identified as having been used in previous attacks, including the destruction of the Coley Hall petrol tanker on the main Bulawayo road on 13 May, the destruction of the Wards Transport and Coley Hall tankers on the main Bulawayo road on 17 May, the robbery of a Swift Transport vehicle and the ambush of another on the main Bulawayo road on 13 July and the destruction of the Timberlands vehicle and trailer in the Mtetengwe TTL on 30 July. As it was virtually unknown for terrorists to interchange weapons, as confirmed by interrogations and captured documents, one terrorist was proving to be a very busy highwayman on the two main roads out of Beitbridge.

On 16 August, elements of A Company 6RR, while moving into a night-ambush position in the Diti TTL, made contact with an unknown of terrorists, killing three and, from blood spoor located, wounding another who managed to escape. Three weapons, AK-47 webbing, three 82mm mortar bombs, an 82mm mortar sight and other terrorist paraphernalia were recovered from the scene.

On 19 August, terrorists ambushed a Roads Department vehicle in the Chipisi TTL using small-arms and rocket fire. The vehicle was hit by two RPG-7 rockets, seriously damaging the engine. The Roads Department employees were uninjured.

On 20 August, twenty terrorists stopped a Shu Shine bus on the main Fort Victoria road. The terrorists then led the driver, conductor and passengers into the Mtetengwe TTL for a distance of about three kilometres where they robbed them of their cash and valuables before releasing them and permitting them to return to the bus.

Also on 20 August, terrorists, using TNT explosive, blew up a section of the rail line to Rutenga approximately sixteen kilometres northwest of Beitbridge. A first-light check resulted in the recovery of six 200-gram and one 400-gram of Soviet-manufactured TNT slabs. A note left at the scene indicated that ZIPRA was responsible: the presence of Soviet explosives would support this claim.

On 21 August, six terrorists entered the farm compound on Benfur Estates in the Umzingwani farming area, robbing the foreman of cash before departing in the direction of the Masera TTL. While with the locals they gave out that they were members of ZIPRA and as all spoke Sindebele this would confirm their claim. At first light, elements of A Company 6RR followed spoor into the Masera TTL, where, on spotting two African males, called on them to halt. Both men then took off in an attempt to escape. One was shot and wounded and later casevaced to the Messina hospital and the other managed to escape. Both turned out to be local civilians.

On 21 August, an A Company 6RR vehicle detonated a landmine in the Mtetengwe TTL. No injuries were sustained and no spoor was located at the scene, indicating that the mine had been buried sometime beforehand.

On 22 August, elements of A Company 6RR came under terrorist attack in the Diti TTL, the terrorists using small-arms and rifle-grenade fire in the engagement. The patrol returned fire, causing the terrorists to run. There were no A Company casualties and no known terrorist casualties.

On 22 August, Scouter Yankee from Latumba base located a large *povo* camp estimated to be holding fifty-plus locals. It was apparent that the base had only been recently occupied. A search of the camp resulted in the recovery of terrorist documents, the ticket book of the Shu Shine bus that had been robbed on 20 August and documents belonging to the Timberlands vehicle which had been destroyed on 20 July. Terrorists under the command of Sam Svenyika appear to have been responsible for the main-road attacks.

Also on 22 August, an Internal Affairs mine-protected vehicle detonated a landmine in the Mtetengwe TTL without casualty.

On 23 August, elements of A Company 6RR came under attack by an unknown number of terrorists. Fire was returned and the terrorists departed the field of battle, with no casualties on either side.

On 24 August, elements of Guard Force, while driving into a kraal line, observed locals scattering in all directions. The Guard Force fired warning shots in an attempt to stop the locals and immediately came under terrorist attack. The terrorists were engaged, resulting in the capture of a wounded terrorist and the recovery of an AKM rifle. Guard Force sustained no injuries.

CHAPTER NINE
Deployment of 1 (Indep) Company Rhodesian African Rifles
September–December 1978

At the beginning of September 1 (Independent) Company the Rhodesian African Rifles, or simply 1 Indep, arrived in Beitbridge from Victoria Falls where they had been stationed for a number of years. 1 Indep was to relieve D Company 6RR and to remain in Beitbridge on a permanent basis.

The company was commanded by Major Don Price BCR with Captain Neill Jackson as the second-in-command. Both were regular officers on secondment from the Rhodesian Light Infantry. The company sergeant-major (CSM) was Roger Tyler and Chalkie van Schalkwyk was the company quartermaster sergeant (CQMS) and who later became the CSM when Roger left; both were also regular soldiers on secondment from the RLI. The rest of the company consisted of trained national servicemen who, on leaving school, had been conscripted for a period of two years. The platoon commanders, all second lieutenants, were a fine bunch of young Rhodesians, as were the NCOs and troops.

On the day of their arrival a PRAW aircraft had been organized for Price and me as part of his orientation of the area he was to be responsible for. We flew across as much of the area as was possible in the time allocated. We concentrated on the Mtetengwe TTL as I knew that this would be the centre of action, but also managed to overfly the Tuli Circle in the west and Chikwarakwara in the east, as well as the area in between. In my conversations with Don, he mentioned that he was lucky in deploying troops to the right places at the right times and had enjoyed considerable success in this way. I had also had one or two flukes and was confident that the tide would turn against the dastardly gangs of terrorists operating in the area, but to achieve this I knew that a Fire Force was essential.

In the meantime, the war paid little heed to our new arrivals.

•••

On 1 September, a police patrol operating on Sentinel Ranch attacked a terrorist base containing three terrorists. During the engagement, two terrorists were killed, with one managing to escape. An AKM folding-butt assault rifle, which would indicate a senior-ranking terrorist as its owner, and an AK-47 rifle, as well as ammunition, stick grenades and other equipment were recovered from the base. The police sustained no injuries.

Also on 1 September, a Coley Hall transport vehicle and trailer was stopped by an unknown number of terrorists on the main Bulawayo road. The driver was instructed to drive the vehicle into the Mtetengwe TTL where they set fire to the rig. The vehicle was completely destroyed, although the trailer was only slightly damaged. The driver and crew were released unharmed.

On 2 September, a Roads Department heavy vehicle detonated a landmine on the Tshiturapadzi road in the Chipisi TTL. No injuries were sustained.

On 2 September, elements of A Company 6RR came under fire from an estimated twenty terrorists as they were approaching a kraal in the Diti TTL. Fire was returned and the terrorists split up into two groups after abandoning their position. One group headed northeast and the other northwest. No injuries were sustained by the patrol.

Also on 2 September, elements of A Company 6RR, travelling by vehicle in the Diti TTL, detonated a landmine. The convoy then came under attack by an unknown number of terrorists who fled when they were fired upon. There were no casualties on either side.

Again, on 2 September, Scouter Zulu, on follow-up operations in the Siyoka TTL, entered the Dendele TTL after receiving clearance from JOC Gwanda to do so. After crossing into the Dendele, contact was made with nine terrorists. There were no casualties on either side.

On 3 September, an unarmed African male stopped a Shu Shine Bus in the Siyoka TTL and handed the driver a letter. The driver, without saying a word, exited the bus, departed with the man and was never seen again. No information was ever obtained regarding the driver's fate which, I believe, remains a mystery to this day. A relief driver had to take over the driving.

On 4 September, Scouter Zulu surprised three terrorists waiting on the side of the road in the Siyoka TTL. The terrorists immediately opened fire on the patrol and fled. It was assessed that the terrorists were awaiting the arrival of a Shu Shine bus which was scheduled to travel along that route. The patrol sustained no injuries.

Also on 4 September, a Roads Department tractor was fired upon and stopped by six terrorists in the Chipisi TTL. The driver was uninjured but the tractor was destroyed by fire.

On 5 September, a Wards Transport vehicle was stopped by six terrorists on the main Bulawayo road. The terrorists forced the driver to drive the vehicle into the Mtetengwe TTL where he and his crew were robbed of valuables before being released unharmed. The vehicle was then gutted by fire. Elements of 1 Indep deployed on follow-up, their first operational deployment.

Also on 5 September, a Shu Shine bus travelling in the Mtetengwe TTL was stopped by eighteen terrorists who forced the driver off the road into the bush where they proceeded to rob the crew and passengers of valuables, after which the terrorists departed.

Again, on 5 September, elements of 1 Indep contacted an unknown number of terrorists in the early evening. The contact lasted twenty minutes, during which time the terrorists fired seven RPG-7 rockets against the attacking force. No follow-up was undertaken that evening, but at first light a medical pack and documents were recovered.

On 6 September, Mr and Mrs Lubbe and their two children of Seller Farm, Hartley, were travelling alone and ahead of the Fort Victoria road convoy when they came under attack from an unknown number of terrorists from the Mtetengwe TTL. Mr Lubbe was critically wounded in the neck which necessitated his casevac, initially by helicopter to the Messina hospital where his condition was stabilized, and then by fixed-wing aircraft directly to New Sarum airbase in Salisbury before being rushed to Andrew Fleming hospital. His wife and children, unhurt but suffering from severe shock, accompanied him. Elements of 1 Indep deployed on follow-up operations.

Also on 6 September, an A Company 6RR convoy detonated a landmine in the Mtetengwe TTL. There were no casualties.

Again, on 6 September, elements of B Company 6RR made contact with between eight and ten terrorists in the Diti TTL. The terrorists fired four 60mm mortar bombs at the patrol before fleeing. There were no casualties on either side. One unexploded 60mm mortar bomb was recovered. The next morning, while following tracks, the patrol sighted four terrorists at a range of eight hundred metres, but the terrorists fled when they spotted the patrol. No contact was made.

Yet again, on 6 September, elements of 1 Indep had a fleeting contact with nine terrorists in the Mtetengwe TTL. Spoor was followed for an hour before eventually being lost. Two fully charged AK-47 magazines and a water bottle were recovered from the contact site. There were no casualties on either side.

On 7 September, elements of D Company 6RR were ambushed by an estimated twelve terrorists in the Mtetengwe TTL. One D Company rifleman was slightly wounded. Tracks were followed for a short distance before being lost.

•••

Late in the afternoon of 7 September, I was knocking off work for the day, planning on going for a nice cold beer. However, on passing the radio room,

Shortly after my arrival in Beitbridge with my newly-issued mine-protected Land Rover.

Tshiturapadzi police base, Christmas Eve 1976. Patrol Officer Dave Ward's mine-protected Land Rover which rear-ended a Hyena MPV that had been towing the Land Rover when the patrol was ambushed and the Hyena was hit by RPG-7 rocket fire, causing it stop abruptly.
Photo Dave Ward

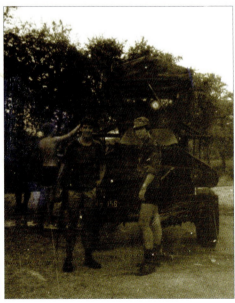

Tshiturapadzi police base, Christmas Eve 1976. Unidentified security force members who had been ambushed only hours earlier pose with the damaged Land Rover and Hyena MPV.
Photos Dave Ward

One of the dozens of fuel tankers ambushed and destroyed by terrorists on the main Bulawayo–Beitbridge road. This tanker was empty and stopped while travelling to South Africa to replenish stocks in 1977. The terrorists pulled the vehicle off the road – the Mtetengwe TTL, their escape route, is on that side of the road – before destroying it; smarter groups destroyed the vehicles on the road itself, causing damage to the tarmacadam and blocking the road for hours.
Photo Geoff Blyth

Geoff Blyth posing with the Hyena MPV shortly after being blown up on the Tshiturapadzi Road in 1977. His dog Jock was also in the vehicle.
Photo Geoff Blyth

Above: A policeman at the Tshiturapadzi police base in 1977. *Photo Dave Ward*

Below: Panhard armoured cars parked outside the Beitbridge police mess in 1977. *Photo Dave Ward*

A police patrol on the Tshiturapadzi road locates another landmine, the hard way, 1977. *Photo Geoff Blyth*

Scouter X-Ray, a temporary Police Ground Coverage patrol base on Robin Watson's Mikado Ranch in 1977 prior to the establishment of more permanent facilities. Dave Ward relaxes on his stretcher. *Photo Dave Ward*

Dave Ward's Scouter X-Ray team at the entrance to the more permanent base on Mikado Ranch. They are armed with an assortment of weapons including G3 and FN rifles, an MAG machine gun and a 60mm mortar, Dave with an AK-47. The mountain in the background is in the Siyoka TTL, the site where on the 13 October 1978 the Beitbridge Fire Force attacked a terrorist base and killed six ZANLA terrorists, the entire command structure of the Siyoka Detatchment. *Photo Dave Ward*

A Rhodesian Air Force DC-3 Dakota preparing to land at the Tshiturapadzi airstrip in 1977. The sparsely populated scrub-mopane terrain is typical of the Beitbridge area. *Photo Dave Ward*

A typical police Land Rover: open-doored, vulnerable and they went everywhere.

Two of the outstanding Shangaan trackers based at the Tshiturapadzi police base in 1977. Members of the African Field Reserve, the Shangaans were outstanding men of the bush, blessed with phenomenal bushcraft and tracking skills. *Photo Dave Ward*

Fire Force Delta prepares to deploy from the Mazunga airfield, October 1978. Stop 1 emplanes in the foreground. Second Lieutenant Arthur Kegel is standing at left, I am sitting in the door of the helicopter checking my RPD and Sergeant Theo Nel approaches on the right. Within the hour we were in action against a large ZANLA force in the Mtetengwe TTL. *Photo Theo Nel*

The inimitable Sergeant Theo Nel BCR (left) of 1 Indep Company en route to a Fire Force action. Nel, along with several 1 Indep officers, followed Major Price to the RLI on his transfer as OC 3 Commando. *Photo Theo Nel*

The Pookie landmine-detection vehicle, a marvel of Rhodesian engineering.
Photo Theo Nel

The Zulu Base camp guard.

At the Limpopo Gorge the day before I left Beitbridge on transfer to Gwanda, November 1979.

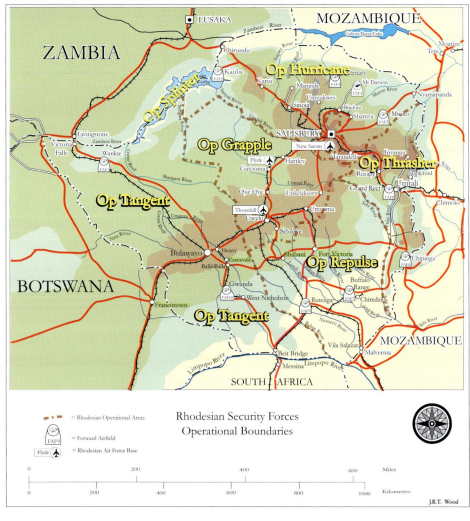

I heard Don Price transmitting over the radio. I was aware that one of his call signs had been tracking terrorist spoor for most of the day, but thought it odd that Don was still airborne. I went into the radio room and was brought up to date on the situation by Mimi Cawood, our renowned radio operator. Price's four-man call sign had walked into a trap, possibly not by enemy design, but the four troopers were now surrounded by a large number of terrorists. I decided to stay in the radio room until the matter was finalized. An armed air force Lynx aircraft was airborne in support of Price and his men. I felt utter frustration when Don failed to talk the air force pilot onto the terrorist positions before the pilot, due to failing light, was forced to abort the mission and return to base. The call sign reported the terrorist commanders blowing whistles and ordering their guerrillas to fix bayonets in preparation for an assault. However, this was all bravado on the terrorist side, we hoped, designed to terrify the 1 Indep soldiers who were surrounded.

Price continued to reassure the call sign in his confident, unwavering voice, urging them to "hang in there" and that he would get them out of danger. I thought to myself, *How the hell is he going to do that?* but the more I worked with Don Price the more I came to realize that he never made an idle promise and never once did he give his men false hope. He was a man of his word.

I think Price realized that time was running out for his men, so he made a last-ditch attempt to obtain assistance from the South African Air Force (SAAF) which had an unarmed Alouette helicopter positioned at the Messina airfield in support of SADF troops deployed on border-control operations and as a concession to assist the Rhodesian security forces in a humanitarian role confined to casualty evacuations only. The helicopter had assisted on two or three occasions of late, the last being the casevac of Mr. Lubbe to the Messina hospital after he was critically wounded in the vehicle ambush of 6 September.

The SAAF had previously been deployed in Rhodesia under the pretext of supporting the South African Police combating South African African National Congress (SAANC) guerrilla infiltrations from Zambia, but who were in reality attached to the Rhodesian Air Force. The South African pilots, particularly the helicopter pilots and their technicians, were fine, brave men who fitted seamlessly into the Rhodesian environment and who were a great asset to the war machine. Unfortunately, politics reared its ugly head when the South African government, in an effort to coerce the Rhodesian government into accepting majority rule, withdrew all military support in August 1976, resulting in the entire SAAF contingent being recalled.

Price, while still airborne, made an urgent appeal to the SAAF in Messina and explained the situation regarding his call sign on the ground, knowing full well that he was asking the pilot to disobey orders and face a court martial. Without hesitation, the Alouette pilot, Lieutenant Ola Grinaker, agreed to the request and, well aware of the consequences, took off and headed for the contact area, in his unarmed helicopter.

Price remained overhead and directed Grinaker onto his call sign still surrounded by a force in excess of sixty terrorists. Grinaker, without hesitation and under fire, dropped the helicopter onto the call sign's position. The four soldiers immediately scrambled into the aircraft as Grinaker lifted off. At the same time every terrorist in the immediate area, all sixty-plus, stood up and opened fire on the helicopter. Obviously Grinaker's immediate aim was to put as much distance between the enemy and him. The aircraft was hit time after time, the helicopter technician was hit five times and Pete Debarros of 1 Indep twice, but both survived to fight another day. (The Rhodesian army operated in four-man sticks and this is a prime example of why, the composition being directly linked to the carrying capacity of an Alouette helicopter which was four men with weapons and packs.)

The helicopter, by this time, was a flying colander, having been hit over eighty times. The hydraulics were gone and all the radio communications had been shot out, the aircraft literally flying on a wing and a prayer. Grinaker managed to coax the helicopter for a further three or four kilometres before having to crash-land on the old Beitbridge airfield. Elements of 1 Indep were quickly at the crash site as well as South African military personnel. The wounded were moved initially to the Messina hospital for treatment where the SADF military authorities were obliged to immediately report the incident to the chief of the defence force. Grinaker saw his career going up in flames. Not only had he disobeyed orders but he was also responsible for the total write-off of an expensive aircraft.

However, Don Price wrote an instant report on the gallant actions of Ola Grinaker who had most certainly saved the lives of four young Rhodesians: their chances of surviving the night had been very remote indeed; not only were they extremely short of ammunition but they faced odds of fifteen to one. The chances of a successful rescue mission being undertaken during the night were non-existent and at one stage I truly believed that there could only be one outcome: that the call sign would suffer the same fate as Major Allan Wilson and his men on the banks of the Shangani River when they were surrounded during the night by over five thousand Matabele warriors and killed to a man in December 1893. Price's report and recommendations were forwarded via army headquarters to the South African authorities who were surprisingly magnanimous. All thoughts of a court martial were immediately dropped, the pilot's bravery was recognized and Grinaker was awarded the Honoris Crux. Ola was a very brave man and went on to win a second Honoris Crux during operations in South West Africa.

With a change in political leadership in South Africa, the South African Air Force returned in full force to Rhodesia shortly after this incident and more Fire Forces became available. Beitbridge would benefit from the move. And after all the nail-biting excitement, I still managed to indulge in a few ice-cold beers.

•••

On 8 September, elements of D Company 6RR, call sign 42 Alpha, had a fleeting contact with an estimated sixteen terrorists in the Mtetengwe TTL. The terrorists, as normal, fled the scene and headed in a northeasterly direction where call sign 41 Delta contacted them, resulting in one of the terrorists being wounded and captured. One AK-47 assault rifle and a medical pack were recovered. The captured terrorist confirmed that he was the section's medical officer. The following morning, the two call signs plus 43 Alpha conducted a sweep of the contact area and located a terrorist base in close proximity. While checking the base, they observed nine terrorists moving south from their position. The terrorists were engaged and a fleeting firefight ensued. On this occasion, there were no injuries to either side.

•••

During the afternoon of 8 September, Second Lieutenant Alan Balson of 1 Indep Company was in charge of a section patrolling Bishopstone Estates in the Umzingwani farming area when he made long-range contact with approximately thirty terrorists who took up defensive positions in a heavily-wooded thicket. I was at 1 Indep HQ at that moment and, at Don Price's request, boarded a PRAW aircraft with him, after first removing the back door of the aircraft and mounting an MAG machine gun on sandbags in the doorway. Ian Ferguson, the pilot, then took off from the Beitbridge airfield and we made for the contact scene.

Ferguson was not too partial to flying low, especially over a contact scene. We were informed by Alan Balson that we were under extremely heavy fire from the ground; at normal flying altitude, ground fire could be heard in the aircraft, so we were obviously out of range. I was able to plot the approximate position of the terrorists. On our next orbit, I opened fire with the machine gun, as Balson confirmed that we were again taking ground fire. This continued for another three or four orbits until it was obvious that the terrorists and I were wasting ammunition. Price, in the meantime, had called up an 81mm mortar team from D Company 6RR who, once in position, commenced firing on the terrorist position. Price directed the mortar fire until nightfall when Ferguson was forced to return to Beitbridge. At first light, Balson and his patrol swept through the terrorist position but found only hundreds of expended cartridge cases, the large group of terrorists having made good their escape during the night. There were no casualties on either side.

As an aside, I was involved in many 'air gunner' actions prior to and after this occasion and must say that I thoroughly enjoyed the action, particularly when home-made 'bombs' were available and the pilot was a bit of a daredevil who attacked targets at low level. Generally, I wore *veldskoene*, or bush shoes, without socks: a very bad idea as the red-hot expended 7.62mm cartridge cases from the MAG machine gun would fall inside the shoes, resulting in bad blistering to my instep; but as the adrenaline was pumping, I never really felt discomfort until the action was over

•••

On 9 September, a Rhodesia Breweries truck was stopped by terrorists on the main Bulawayo road. The terrorists forced the driver to drive the vehicle approximately twelve kilometres into the Mtetengwe TTL where a further group was waiting. After robbing the driver and helping themselves to countless crates of beer, the terrorists destroyed the truck by fire. Elements of 1 Indep Company were deployed but could only commence the follow-up the next morning when tracks of fourteen terrorists were followed for a kilometre or two before being lost.

Also on 9 September, elements of B Company 2RR contacted an estimated twelve terrorists in the Diti TTL. One terrorist was killed and one SKS rifle, stick grenades, ammunition and one RPG-7 rocket were recovered. The patrol sustained no injuries.

Again, on 9 September, elements of B Company 2RR contacted nine terrorists in the Diti TTL. The terrorists fled in a northerly direction and were spotted by a PRAW pilot overflying the contact area. However, 2RR ground forces were unable to come to grips with the terrorists, and the follow-up petered out.

Yet again, on 9 September, elements of A Company 6RR, during a foot patrol in the Mtetengwe TTL, were ambushed by an estimated twelve terrorists. The terrorists were then engaged but departed the scene. The call sign, now reinforced, continued the follow-up but without success. There were no casualties on either side.

On 10 September, PRAW pilot, Ian Henderson, call sign Copper 84, came under ground attack from an unknown number of terrorists in the Siyoka TTL. Robin Watson took off in his armed aircraft – the aircraft with the grenade 'chute – from his airfield close by and went to help his friend, with the intention of 'bombing' the terrorists. Unfortunately, the terrorists had moved on and no contact was made. Henderson was uninjured and his aircraft received no strikes.

On 11 September, elements of 1 Indep Company, while tracking an estimated forty terrorists in the Mtetengwe TTL, made contact with the group's rearguard, resulting in one terrorist being killed and the capture of a local who was running with the gang. The follow-up continued but owing to fading light, the call sign was forced to abandon spoor and put up for the night close to the scene of the contact. During the night the call sign came under heavy mortar and small-arms attack from an estimated twenty terrorists. This was ineffectual and, at first light, the patrol continued the follow-up. No injuries were sustained by either side during the follow-up.

During the night of 11 September, the Beitbridge Rutenga railway line was sabotaged by terrorists in the vicinity of Lesanth Ranch. The line was blown in two places, with the terrorists using TNT explosive. The line was repaired and elements of 2RR from Rutenga conducted the follow-up.

Also on 11 September, call signs 41, 41 Alpha and 43 Alpha of D Company 6RR were again in action in the Mtetengwe TTL when they contacted an estimated twelve terrorists. The result was no casualties on either side, but an SKS rifle and one pack were recovered during a sweep of the contact area.

On 13 September, elements of D Company 2RR engaged eight terrorists at long range in the Diti TTL. One terrorist was wounded but managed to escape. There were no D Company injuries. The call sign continued the follow-up and, the next morning, discovered a resting place for approximately sixty terrorists where they had slaughtered and eaten an ox before heading in a northwesterly direction toward the Mtetengwe TTL.

Also on 13 September, elements of 1 Indep Company were ambushed by an estimated thirty terrorists in the Mtetengwe TTL. A firefight developed, during which two African males running with the terrorists were shot and killed. Don Price, while overflying the contact scene, came under heavy ground attack, indicating that a large number of terrorists had congregated in the area. A base camp was eventually located and various items of terrorist equipment recovered. 1 Indep Company suffered no casualties.

On 14 September, elements of D Company 6RR engaged six terrorists in the Mtetengwe TTL and a fleeting contact developed. The terrorists managed to escape; there were no casualties on either side.

On 15 September, elements of 1 Indep Company, operating on Jopempi Block, Liebigs Ranch, contacted five terrorists. The terrorists fled, resulting in no casualties on either side. A sweep of the contact area led to the recovery of three RPG-7 rockets, four packs and other equipment.

On 16 September, Scouter Zulu engaged nine terrorists after entering the Dendele TTL from the Siyoka TTL. There were no casualties on either side but one SKS rifle was recovered.

Also on 16 September, elements of D Company 2RR made contact with a group of seven terrorists in the Diti TTL. The action resulted in one terrorist being killed and the recovery of an SKS rifle. A PRAW aircraft was fired on while overflying the contact area in support of D Company. No casualties were inflicted by the terrorists.

On 17 September, a white hunter, operating in the Jopempi Block, Liebigs Ranch, was ambushed by several terrorists. The hunter was unhurt but his vehicle received several strikes.

Also on 17 September, a Shu Shine bus was stopped on the main Bulawayo road by two terrorists who then proceeded to rob everyone on board. The terrorists then let the bus proceed. No follow-up action was taken as the driver only reported the robbery to the Mzilikazi police station on his arrival in Bulawayo.

Shortly after dark on 19 September, the homestead on Bishopstone Estates in the Umzingwani farming area came under terrorist attack. The attack was repelled by two white security guards. Apart from automatic weapons, the terrorists made use of several stick grenades which exploded within the confines of the security fence but which caused no damage. During this action, another group of terrorists destroyed two tractors on the estate. Spoor, before being lost, headed in the direction of the Mtetengwe TTL.

On 20 September, twenty terrorists stopped a Premier Electric truck on the main Bulawayo road and forced the driver to drive into the Mtetengwe TTL. They set the vehicle on fire which was then completely destroyed.

On 21 September, while moving into a night ambush position, elements of B Company 6RR encountered seven African males carrying containers of water and who, after a quick interrogation, admitted that the water was for terrorists in a nearby base. The water party then led the call sign to the base where contact was made. There were no casualties on either side but a first-light sweep of the base revealed a dead African female who had been sleeping with the terrorists.

On 23 September, a police vehicle, in the process of recovering another damaged vehicle, detonated a landmine in the Mtetengwe TTL. The explosion damaged the broken-down vehicle as well. Fortunately, there were no casualties.

Also on 23 September, an armed air force Alouette helicopter came under ground attack while overflying the Siyoka TTL en route to Beitbridge from Gwanda. The pilot immediately attacked the firing positions, killing three of the terrorists. Scouter Zulu conducted the initial follow-up and recovered the bodies.

On 24 September, elements of B Company 6RR, while moving on a kraal line in the Mtetengwe TTL, shot and killed a local who attempted to run away when called upon to stop.

On 27 September, elements of A Company 2RR, while deploying by vehicle in the Siyoka TTL, spotted and engaged a lone terrorist at long range. The terrorist made good his escape.

•••

Toward the end of September, a Selous Scouts pseudo team was deployed in the Siyoka TTL, posing as ZIPRA terrorists. The coordinator for this operation was Captain Archie Moore; Fire Force Delta was deployed to Beitbridge in support of this operation, to be commanded by Don Price and manned by the men of 1 Indep Company.

On 30 September, Moore briefed Price on developments regarding the pseudo team operating in the Siyoka TTL and requested that Price position the Fire Force at Mazunga early the next morning so that reaction time to a brewing scene between his team and the terrorists would be minimal. It was decided that I would be included in the Fire Force and would be deployed with Stop 1. I had spoken to Don about being included as I had seen no action for some time and was itching to get to grips with the enemy once again.

The composition of the Fire Force consisted of a command Alouette helicopter flown by the senior pilot, accompanied by the army Fire Force commander who controlled the action and an air force gunner-technician who operated the Matra MG151 20mm cannon mounted on the aircraft. This helicopter was known as the K-Car. We believed the 'K' stood for a very definite 'kill' or 'killer' but technically it was simply alphabetical nomenclature.

I had flown with the Fire Force on one other occasion and that was in the Mount Darwin area when I was seconded to the Selous Scouts. I had seen at close range exactly what damage the 20mm cannon was capable of inflicting and was an extremely big fan of the weapon. I am convinced that if the Rhodesian Air Force had had more helicopters at their disposal and more fitted with the 20mm cannon, the terrorists would have been blasted to kingdom come.

Normally, three other Alouette helicopters – this number could be increased according to the size of the target and availability of helicopters – were used as troopers and ferried four-man sticks into the contact area to be deployed as the Fire Force commander dictated. These helicopters were fitted with either twin MAG machine guns or Browning .30 machine guns, which were deadly under the experienced control of the air force technicians, the Brownings being the preferred choice. These helicopters were known as G-Cars and referred to by the colour of their flight: so, Yellow 1 (which initially carried Stop 1), Yellow 2 (which carried Stop 2) and so on. Different Fire Forces used different colours for their flight identification, such as 'Red', 'Blue' and Green'.

In support of the Fire Force was the air force Lynx aircraft, a Cessna 337 fitted with two 250-pound frantan (napalm) bombs, SNEB rockets and mounted machine guns. These pilots were experts in dropping their bombs exactly on target.

Early on the morning of 1 October, the Fire Force repositioned at Mazunga, where we based up for the duration with good friends John and Marie Barclay who ranched the Mazunga Section of Liebigs Ranch. Two more generous people one would find hard to meet. With no call-out materializing by lunchtime, Marie produced a stew which fed the whole Fire Force and the support teams; there must have been over fifty of us, so how she managed to accomplish the feat is beyond me. Although we all protested her generosity, the meal really went down well and, unknown to us at the time, would fortify us for the coming action.

The Selous Scouts' scene fizzled out and by four that afternoon we were stood down and prepared to return to Beitbridge. During the course of the day, I had chatted to Don who had expressed concern over a certain area in the Mtetengwe TTL which he regarded as highly suspect; he wanted to check it out on our return to Beitbridge if the Siyoka scene did not pan out. Later, he told me that he had had a vivid dream the previous night about contacting a group of terrorists near the junction of two rivers. Studying the map the following morning, he was convinced he knew where to find the terrorists. As the Fire Force was in support of Selous Scouts operations, Price had to obtain authority from Brigade Headquarters in Bulawayo to make use of this asset. He duly obtained the necessary permission and we took to the air.

I was in Stop 1 with Second Lieutenant Arthur Kegel, Sergeant Theo Nel BCR and Colin Rhodes. We flew to the vicinity of the junction of the Tongwe and

Mtetengwe rivers, only twenty kilometres distant from Mazunga, where Price ordered Stop 3 to investigate what appeared to be a deserted terrorist base. The stop was deployed and the Fire Force commenced orbiting the suspected area.

All at once, the K-Car came under heavy ground attack from a large group of terrorists. Things happened very fast after that and I can only give an account of the action from my personal perspective. We were dropped on the periphery of the terrorist position and immediately went into action. The Lynx pilot did a successful bombing run on the enemy position but by the time of the strike, the terrorists had begun to 'snivel' out of the area, bombshelling in other words. I could hear the K-Car's 20mm cannon and the G-Cars' machine guns hammering away continuously. Stop 1 engaged targets as they appeared and achieved success, until no more targets were encountered, all the while moving in the direction of the airstrike.

It was very late in the afternoon and we were fast running out of daylight, and with little or no twilight in the tropics, darkness would soon be upon us. As darkness descended, with the Fire Force now en route to Beitbridge, we entered the smoldering bush where the frantan had exploded and shortly thereafter, we were joined by Stop 2, with whom we were to ambush the site. Stop 3 was ambushing an area several hundred metres away to our south. We then did a sweep through the area as best we could and found two smoking bodies of a male and female, assessed as locals running with the terrorists. We then went into our all-round ambush position.

Lieutenant Lionel Reynolds of the Rhodesian Intelligence Corps was part of Stop 2. He was an old friend, and so the two of us teamed up to lie in ambush together. As we were the oldest, we took the first watch. At about nine o'clock and halfway through our watch, we heard a distant cowbell which seemed to be getting closer. Neither of us had seen any sign of cattle, either from the air or from the ground, so we guessed that the bell was being tinkled by a terrorist. The ringing got louder and louder and was coming directly toward Lionel and me. There was no way that I was going to fire prematurely and told Lionel I would open up with my RPD machine gun on his cue. The terrorists, who were whispering at this time, seemed about to step on us when Lionel nudged me and we both opened fire. I remember seeing a bright flash and hearing an explosion only metres to our front, realizing that a terrorist had fired an RPG-7 rocket in retaliation and at point-blank range. Needless to say, the rocket went whizzing into the night and detonated in the area where Stop 3 was lying in ambush.

Everything then went quiet, all firing ceased. In the stillness of the night, I heard a long sigh emanate from close by and assessed that a terrorist had just died. I wondered if it was the bell-ringer. The night air was then rent by an eerie wail as a seriously wounded terrorist cried out for help. He was clearly calling out to his comrades, hoping they might return to assist their wounded. This wailing continued for hours and Lionel and I discussed the possibility of snivelling through the bush and capturing him; but after giving it some thought, we decided against it. The wounded terrorist was to our south, in the same direction as Stop 3, and as we did not know their position, did not want to take the chance of being hit by friendly fire.

At first light, we did a sweep of the area to the north of the camp and located the body of the dead terrorist literally metres from where Lionel and I had been lying. We searched the body and took possession of his AK-47 and webbing. His body was then dragged to a central point, before commencing a sweep of the area with Stop 3. It appeared that the wounded terrorist who had disturbed the stillness of the night with his wailing had been rescued by his comrades, but a set of AK chest webbing covered with congealed blood was recovered from his approximate position.

The final tally was thirteen terrorists killed and one captured-wounded. Seven AK-47 assault rifles, three AKM rifles, one SKS Chicom rifle, one SKS Lancer rifle and two SKS rifles, as well as thousands of rounds of ammunition, stick grenades, together with two grenades we were unable to identify, packs and documents were recovered. All in all, it had been a very successful action, and I recommended to Don that he eat plenty of cheese on a daily basis to induce dreams that would assist us operationally. The captured terrorist confirmed that in excess of forty terrorists were present in the base at the time of the attack.

•••

By mid-morning we were back in Beitbridge and by lunchtime the Fire Force was airborne again, heading toward the Diti TTL in response to a 1 Indep Company sighting of twenty terrorists advancing in extended line. Price commanded the Fire Force once again and dropped his stop groups in perfect positions to attack. Obviously, the 20mm cannon played a big part and by the end of the day, seven terrorists lay dead in the African bush. Four AK-47 assault rifles and three SKS rifles were recovered, together with webbing, stick grenades and hundreds of rounds of ammunition. During the contact, an African female was killed in the crossfire.

After the big contact on 1 October, an action that he took part in and from intelligence gleaned from captured terrorists and locals, Lieutenant Lionel

Reynolds of the Rhodesian Intelligence Corps prepared a report on the *povo* system in the Beitbridge area. Under signature of the Brigade Major, Roy Matkovich, this was released by the Brigade Commander for distribution to various desks.

Things were certainly looking up. Twenty-one terrorists had been accounted for in less than twenty-four hours. This did not include the wounded who had managed to escape and were now a burden to their comrades. The number of terrorists killed in these two contacts equalled the number of terrorists killed during the whole of 1977.

•••

On 3 October, a landmine was successfully recovered by a 1 Indep Company patrol in the Diti TTL.

On 4 October, a Shu Shine bus detonated a landmine in the Siyoka TTL, resulting in two passengers sustaining serious leg injuries. Both were casevaced to Beitbridge for treatment.

On 6 October, the Fire Force was again in action. On this occasion, it was in response to a B Company 6RR sighting of six terrorists moving in an easterly direction in the Diti TTL. At least two terrorists were killed in the engagement. Two AK-47 assault rifles and one SKS rifle were recovered, together with grenades, ammunition and documents. From BSAP ballistic reports on the weapons captured, one of the AKs recovered was linked to an ambush on a D Company 2RR convoy that had occurred in the Mtetengwe TTL on 7 September.

Also on 6 October, elements of B Company 6RR contacted a lone terrorist in the Diti TTL who, in spite of being heavily bandaged, made good his escape. He had clearly been wounded in a previous engagement with security forces.

On 7 October, the homesteads on Lamulas and Lutope sections of Liebigs Ranch came under simultaneous attack from a large group of terrorists, the homesteads being situated in close proximity to one another. The security personnel from both sections returned fire and the terrorists were driven off. No injuries were sustained by the Liebigs personnel. The following morning, two African males were found dead in the vicinity after being axed to death by the terrorists who had abducted two others. Elements of 1 Indep Company conducted the follow-up.

Also on 7 October, elements of D Company 2RR, while patrolling the Chipisi TTL, located spoor of a large group of terrorists moving east toward the Sengwe TTL. After obtaining clearance, the patrol followed the spoor across the

Bubye River into the Sengwe where soon after, an estimated thirty terrorists were sighted and fired upon. The terrorists, who were obviously heading for Mozambique and had no heart for a fight, broke ranks and ran. On sweeping through the contact area, fresh blood spoor was located, indicating that one of the terrorists had been wounded during the engagement. One SKS rifle, three stick grenades and eleven packs were recovered at the scene.

On 10 October, elements of 1 Indep Company were following tracks of an estimated twenty terrorists heading west in the Mtetengwe TTL. One terrorist was eventually seen and engaged but managed to escape. Tracks were followed onto Nottingham Estates and the Fire Force was deployed which engaged remnants of the group, killing one. Spoor was then followed to the dry Mutshilashokwe River on Nottingham Estates where unknown numbers of terrorists were taking refuge in a cave. It was impossible to take the cave from the ground without casualties being inflicted on the attacking force, and so Don Price requested the Lynx air force pilot, whom I am certain was Brick Bryson, to undertake an airstrike against the cave. Bryson then commenced his run-in and released a perfectly aimed 250-pound frantan bomb straight into the mouth of the cave which, on detonation, killed everyone inside. When the cave was checked sometime later the bodies of two terrorists were located. Two AK-47 assault rifles, one SKS rifle, three 82mm mortar bombs and over a thousand rounds of ammunition were recovered during the course of the follow-up. One member of the follow-up team was slightly wounded. Bryson later admitted that he had released the wrong bomb during his attack but, nevertheless, a more perfect strike could not have been wished for.

On 10 October, elements of C Company 2RR engaged eight terrorists in the Diti TTL, with no casualties on either side.

On 11 October, elements of A Company 2RR attacked a terrorist base in the Diti TTL. The base was occupied by fifteen terrorists at the time. The terrorists fled and heavy blood spoor was detected, indicating that one of the terrorists had been hard hit. Unfortunately, the blood spoor was lost after a short time. Two SKS rifles were recovered from the scene of the contact.

On 12 October, Scouter Yankee detonated a landmine with a mine-protected vehicle in the Mtetengwe TTL. No injuries were sustained.

Also on 12 October, Scouter Zulu contacted an estimated ten terrorists in the Siyoka TTL. There were no casualties, but one fully loaded RPD machine-gun ammunition belt and documents were recovered.

•••

Friday 13 October 1978 was extremely lucky for some. During the late afternoon of 12 October, Robin Watson flew from his airfield on Mikado Ranch to Beitbridge where, on arrival, he reported the presence of nine terrorists based on a prominent hill in the Siyoka TTL. A very excited Watson wanted Don Price to attack the base immediately. However, because of the lateness of the hour and the flying time to the target this option was out of the question and, so eventually, Watson saw the folly of this course of action. The base would be attacked at first light the next morning. Watson then returned to Mikado Ranch.

Once again, Don included me in Stop 1. The following morning, Friday the 13th, the Fire Force of one K-Car and three G-Cars departed Beitbridge before first light. The helicopters were refuelled approximately twenty kilometres from the target on the main Bulawayo road. Once this had been carried out, we again set off on the final leg to the target.

As mentioned, the terrorists were based on a prominent feature in the Siyoka TTL, the actual base being sited on the northern side of the hill. As we crossed the summit, the three G-Cars started to orbit the suspected area, while the K-Car gained altitude to 800 feet; we had been flying at low level in an attempt to reduce the noise as much as possible and retain the element of surprise during our approach.

All of a sudden, the base was spotted with the terrorists, all nine of them, fast asleep under their blankets. The attack went in and in next to no time, seven of the nine had been accounted for and the blood spoor of a wounded terrorist located. The spoor was followed but the wounded terrorist managed to escape.

After the action, the bodies of the terrorists were transported by air to the refuelling point on the main Bulawayo road before the stop groups were returned to base. The bodies of the terrorists were still stacked on the side of the main road when the morning convoy from Beitbridge to Bulawayo passed by, so the time must have been just after half past seven. Not a bad morning's work.

Three AKM and two AK-47 assault rifles, six hand grenades, hundreds of rounds of ammunition, backpacks and documents were recovered. A study of the documents revealed that the entire Siyoka Detachment command structure had been eliminated in one fell swoop, including the detachment commander, the detachment political commissar, the detachment security officer and the detachment medical officer. As I say, Friday 13 October 1978 was a lucky day for some, but not for others.

•••

Also during the early afternoon of 13 October, elements of C Company 6RR had a fleeting contact with five terrorists in the Diti TTL. There were no casualties on either side but one local thought to be running with the terrorists, was shot and wounded.

On 17 October, elements of C Company 6RR fired on locals who fled from a *povo* base in the Chipisi TTL. One juvenile was killed. Under interrogation, the captured locals gave out that seven terrorists had been in the base the previous evening, one of whom was heavily bandaged and walked with the aid of a stick.

Also on 17 October, elements of C Company 6RR detonated a landmine in a mine-protected vehicle. No injuries were sustained.

On 19 October, elements of 1 Indep Company, while conducting a patrol in Jopempi Block, Liebigs Ranch, observed five locals carrying water. The call sign followed the water party for a distance before coming across two terrorists who sighted the patrol simultaneously. A firefight ensued and one of the terrorists was killed. Owing to heavy rain, no further follow-up was undertaken. One AK-47 assault rifle, a set of webbing containing three rifle magazines and two RPG-2 rockets were recovered from the contact scene.

Also during the evening of 19 October, a ZANLA terrorist crossed the Limpopo River east of Beitbridge into South Africa. That night, he entered a farm homestead occupied by a farmer and his wife. The terrorist was armed with an SKS rifle with its butt sawn off. The farmer tackled the terrorist and managed to disarm him, causing him to flee the scene, disappearing into the night. Two days later, the terrorist was shot dead by South African farmers after refusing to surrender. This terrorist was regarded as a mental case and later captured terrorists identified his photograph and confirmed that he was *penga*, or 'off his rocker'.

On 22 October, elements of 1 Indep Company, while conducting a night ambush on Jopempi Block, Liebigs Ranch, opened fire on human movement during the night. At first light, they recovered the body of a curfew breaker.

Also on 22 October, elements of 1 Indep Company located the decomposed body of an African male estimated to have died three months beforehand. The body was recovered in close proximity to a *povo* camp which had been attacked in the past.

Again, on 22 October, elements of C Company 6RR engaged three terrorists in a fleeting engagement in the Diti TTL. One of the terrorists was seen to be wounded. There were no security force casualties.

On 26 October, a Roads Department heavy vehicle detonated a landmine in the Diti TTL. There were no injuries.

On 29 October, a Scouter Zulu vehicle detonated a landmine in the Siyoka TTL. There were no injuries and the destroyed vehicle was taken to Beitbridge.

On 1 November, elements of 1 Indep Company operating with Liebigs Ranch security fired on a group of eight terrorists in the Jopempi Block, Liebigs Ranch. Tracks were followed for over two kilometres before being lost as a result of cattle movement. There were no casualties on either side.

Also on 1 November, elements of A Company 6RR fired on four terrorists in the Siyoka TTL. One terrorist was thought to have been wounded; there were no C Company injuries. Tracks were followed but lost among local movement.

On 3 November, a 5RR vehicle detonated a landmine in the Chipisi TTL. One minor injury was sustained by a passenger who was casevaced to Beitbridge for treatment. 5RR were actually deployed in the adjacent Sengwe TTL but had crossed into the Diti TTL to follow up on intelligence received.

On 5 November, a Scouter Yankee Hyena mine-protected vehicle detonated a landmine in the Mtetengwe TTL. There were no casualties.

On 6 November, a Scouter Zulu mine-protected vehicle detonated a landmine in the Siyoka TTL. There were no casualties and the vehicle was recovered to Beitbridge.

On 8 November, a Roads Department driver located a landmine in the Mtetengwe TTL. Elements of 1 Indep Company and Engineers reacted, the latter lifting a TMH-46 landmine boosted by a TM-46 landmine and a stick grenade rigged as an anti-lifting device. The exercise proceeded without incident.

Also on 8 November, a Roads Department convoy in the Mtetengwe TTL was attacked by approximately ten terrorists who opened up with RPG-7 rockets, 60mm mortars and small arms. The convoy managed to escape undamaged, with no injuries being sustained by the personnel.

On 9 November, elements of B Company 2RR made contact with an estimated ten terrorists in the Masera TTL. During the engagement, two terrorists were killed and an AKM assault rifle, an SKS rifle, plus various other items of arms and equipment were recovered. There were no security force casualties.

Also on 9 November, elements of 1 Indep Company, call sign 11 Delta, followed spoor of eight terrorists into the Maramani TTL from Sentinel Ranch. 11 Delta made contact with the terrorists, killing one and wounding and capturing another. Various items of terrorist arms and kit were recovered from the contact scene.

On 10 November, a Roads Department convoy, protected by elements of the Rhodesian Defence Regiment, came under ambush attack by ten terrorists in the Mtetengwe TTL. Two minor civilian injuries were treated at the site.

On 13 November, the protected village at Chaswingo in the Diti TTL came under terrorist attack by a force estimated at fifty strong. The attack lasted two hours, during which time RPG-7 rockets, 82mm and 60mm mortars and automatic weapons were used. Four locals were seriously injured which necessitated their casevac to Messina hospital. The terrorists broke off their attack at 8.30 p.m. Elements of 1 Indep Company reacted at first light the next morning and located terrorist tracks heading in all directions from their attacking position. 1 Indep selected the best spoor and followed this for several kilometres until contact was made. There were no casualties on either side. However, thirteen locals abducted by the terrorists were rescued. The rescued locals confirmed that the terrorists were taking them to establish a *povo* base. One AKM assault rifle was recovered from the scene of the contact.

On 17 November, elements of B Company 2RR, acting on information from the locals, attacked a terrorist base in the Masera TTL occupied by an estimated twenty terrorists at the time. The terrorists returned fire and fled in a northwesterly direction. There were no casualties on either side. The terrorist spoor was followed for the remainder of the day with the Fire Force positioned at Mazunga for the purposes of quick reaction. However, the follow-up fizzled out.

Also on 17 November, a group of thirty African females from the Mapai protected village in the Diti TTL, who were out gathering wood at the time, were abducted by nine terrorists and forced to march in an easterly direction, apparently to the site of an extremely large base. Four of the females managed to abscond during the march and returned to the PV. The exact location of this large base was never identified.

On 18 November, elements of 1 Indep Company, conducting a night reconnaissance patrol in the Diti TTL, entered a *povo* camp, disturbing the sleeping occupants who immediately attempted to flee. The 1 Indep patrol opened fire. A first-light sweep of the base resulted in the discovery of four bodies killed during the night action: two male adults and two male juveniles. No terrorists were present in the camp at the time of the attack. One of the members of the patrol received slight injuries from a hand grenade which he had lobbed during the action. He was casevaced to Beitbridge for treatment.

Also on 18 November, Scouter Zulu was directed into a terrorist base by locals in the Siyoka TTL, reportedly occupied by twenty-two terrorists. The terrorists initiated the firefight before withdrawing from the base and bombshelling into the Siyoka TTL. There were no casualties either side.

On 22 November, Scouter Zulu, now reinforced with elements of the army and acting on information from a local, attacked a terrorist base in the Siyoka

TTL at first light. The base was occupied by nine terrorists at the time, three of whom were killed. There were no security force casualties. One Chicom SKS, two SKS rifles and an assortment of war matériel were recovered.

•••

During the night of the 21/22 November, terrorists made determined attempts to sabotage the Beitbridge–Rutenga railway line near the Bubye River. At Swanscoe Siding, twelve charges of TNT were laid over a three-hundred-metre length of railway line. Only one failed to detonate with the remainder cutting the line. The biggest break measured over thirty centimetres. Two railway telephone poles were also rigged with charges and although both were detonated, the charges failed to drop the poles.

At Lesanth Siding on Les Mitchell's Lesanth Ranch fifteen charges were set over a distance of four hundred metres. All charges fired, the line was cut in fifteen places and three railway telephone poles were dropped by explosive charges placed a metre off the ground.

At Basalt Siding six charges were set over a one-hundred-metre length of railway line. Five of the charges cut the line when fired, with the sixth failing to detonate. Recovered from this scene was a PMN anti-personnel mine complete with detonator.

During the check of the Lesanth Siding sabotage incident by railway security personnel, a boobytrap device was detonated, resulting in serious injury to four railway security staff. At Lesanth Siding, a landmine planted by the saboteurs was detonated by a large ox. Close to the siding three Electricity Supply Commission poles were destroyed by explosives, as well as a water drilling rig.

This was the most determined sabotage attack on the railway line so far, but the Rhodesia Railways repair teams had the line open within hours.

•••

During the early hours of 26 November, the protected village at Shabwe in the Mtetengwe TTL came under attack from a large group of terrorists estimated to number in excess of sixty. Their 75mm recoilless rifle was in action again, as well as 82mm and 60mm mortars. Fire was returned by Guard Force, which although mainly ineffectual, forced the attackers to stay where they were.

At first light the next morning, elements of 1 Indep Company commenced the follow-up and tracked the spoor of one group, coming upon two terrorists thought to be the rearguard. Both these terrorists were engaged and killed. A large number of abducted locals were also apprehended. The follow-up continued and at about noon, a further terrorist was sighted and killed. One AK-47 assault rifle and three SKS rifles were recovered from the scenes of these contacts.

A check of the protected village found that fifty metres of security fencing had been cut and that two hundred locals had been abducted before the attack was launched. During the course of the day, and subsequently, a number of the abducted locals returned to the PV, having managed to escape from their kidnappers. These abductions were always regarded with suspicion: it was suspected that the locals were warned of the impending attack and had fled the PV to escape the ordeal.

The attack was the most accurate up until then, with twenty-seven 82mm mortar fins and eight unexploded bombs being recovered from the confines of the PV, as well as seventeen 60mm mortar fins, M60 rifle grenade fins, and one RPG-2 rocket which had failed to detonate. Fourteen empty 75mm recoilless rifle cases were recovered from the attacking position. Several locals in the PV sustained injury but there were no fatalities.

•••

During the afternoon of 27 November, elements of 1 Indep Company observed an unarmed African male enter their ambush position. The man was called upon to halt but attempted to flee. He was immediately fired upon and wounded. Attempts to treat the injured man failed and he subsequently died. However, before dying, he gave out that he was an externally trained terrorist travelling with three others and that his weapon was being held by his companions. The call sign remained in ambush for the night but no further incident ensued.

On 30 November, elements of B Company 2RR came under 60mm mortar and small-arms fire in the Mtetengwe TTL. No injuries were sustained by the patrol. The terrorists' firing positions were located and spoor was back-tracked to where a resting place was found. Imprints in the sand indicated that the group was in possession of a landmine

On 1 December, the farm compound on Jopempi Block, Liebigs Ranch was subjected to a 60mm mortar attack. Five bombs were fired into the compound but only four detonated. The fifth was located by elements of 1 Indep Company during follow-up operations the next morning. Spoor of an estimated thirty terrorists was followed into the Siyoka TTL.

On 2 December, elements of B Company 2RR attacked an occupied terrorist base in Mtetengwe TTL. One terrorist was killed and one RPD machine gun and one SKS rifle were recovered. A large number of locals living in the base were apprehended and handed over to the administrative authorities for resettlement in protected villages. There were no security force casualties.

On 3 December, an Internal Affairs vehicle detonated a landmine in the Chipisi TTL. There were three casualties, one assessed as being extremely serious and who was casevaced to the Messina hospital by air force helicopter.

On 4 December, a large suspected terrorist base in the Diti TTL, previously undetected from aerial reconnaissance, was bombed by air force Hawker Hunter jets as a prelude to a ground attack by the security forces. The airstrike was perfect with all bombs hitting the target. However, although there was evidence of a terrorist occupation at the time of the strike, no terrorists were detected. Twenty-two locals were killed during the aerial attack. However, all had freely elected to run with and support the terrorists, ignoring repeated warnings to report to the protected villages. It could be said that the terrorists had forced the locals, on pain of death, to remain outside the protected villages, as the enemy could not survive without local support. In fact, the enemy was abducting locals from PVs for this very purpose. Most abductees who wanted to escape from their captors did so within hours, and even in the *povo* camps they were left unattended for days and had ample opportunity to escape and return to the PVs.

Also on 4 December, six locals collecting firewood outside the Shabwe protected village in the Mtetengwe TTL failed to return to the PV; it was suspected that they had been abducted by terrorists.

Again, on 4 December, elements of 1 Indep Company, following tracks of locals, four terrorists and a scotch cart, discovered a large terrorist/*povo* camp in the Mtetengwe TTL. Although unoccupied at the time, it was estimated that the camp had been vacated only the day before. The camp included bunkers and trenches, the first such defences to be encountered in the Beitbridge area.

Yet again, on 4 December, elements of 1 Indep Company fired on a lone terrorist in the Diti TTL but failed to account for him.

On 5 December, elements of 1 Indep Company engaged eight terrorists at long range in the Diti TTL but did not appear to inflict any injuries. The call sign continued following the tracks and just before noon sighted two terrorists whom they immediately fired on. One terrorist was killed and one RPG-2 rocket and a stick grenade were recovered. There were no security force casualties.

Also on 5 December, elements of B Company 2RR contacted five terrorists in the Diti TTL; one terrorist, later identified as Kataza Chimurenga, was killed, and his RPD machine gun recovered. There were no security force casualties.

Again, during the evening of 5 December, elements of B Company 2RR were in ambush positions on a suspected terrorist base. A small group of terrorists was heard to be calling out for "Joe". The call sign then opened fire in the direction of the noise. A first-light check of the area resulted in the recovery of three RPG-2 rockets complete with boosters, one stick grenade and one box mine identified as a British-made TM-44. There were no signs that any of the terrorists had received injuries during the ambush.

On 6 December, one of the vehicles in a 1 Indep Company convoy detonated a landmine in the Siyoka TTL. There were no casualties.

Also on 6 December, a group of thirty terrorists was reported to be on Jopempi Block, Liebigs Ranch. Elements of 1 Indep Company reacted and located spoor which was followed in a westerly direction toward the Siyoka TTL.

Again, on 6 December, elements of 1 Indep Company had a fleeting contact with three terrorists in the Mtetengwe TTL. There were no casualties on either side.

During the early hours of 7 December, an unknown number of terrorists cut the security fence of the Chikwarakwara protected village and abducted forty-seven locals. The following morning, elements of Guard Force followed spoor heading in a northerly direction for three kilometres when it was lost.

On 8 December, a terrorist surrendered to elements of Internal Affairs at the Tshiturapadzi protected village and handed over his AK-47 assault rifle and chest webbing containing four loaded magazines.

Also on 8 December, Mr Stockhill, the caretaker manager of Shobi Block, Liebigs Ranch, and his wife were ambushed by an estimated fifteen terrorists on their property. They were travelling in a mine-protected vehicle and managed to escape without injury. The vehicle was hit numerous times. The Fire Force from Beitbridge reacted but failed to make contact with the enemy.

On 9 December, Scouter Zulu, reinforced with elements of 1 Indep Company, had a contact with sixteen terrorists in the Siyoka TTL. There were no casualties either side.

On 10 December, elements of D Company 2RR, while conducting sweeps of *povo* camps in the Diti TTL, fired at movement within one of the base structures, resulting in the death of four male adults and the injuring of a male juvenile and a female juvenile, both of whom were casevaced to Beitbridge for treatment. During the sweep, numerous locals were apprehended and warned to report to the protected villages. A large quantity of foodstuffs was recovered and destroyed. From interrogations, it would appear that thirty terrorists were occupying the base until earlier that morning.

Also during the early evening of 10 December, elements of 1 Indep Company, in an ambush position in the Diti TTL, fired on human movement, killing two curfew breakers, an African male and female.

On 11 December, 1 Indep Company reported that an estimated eighty locals were moving from the bush in the direction of the Chaswingo protected village. Guard Force reported that, over the past two days, forty-four locals had reported to that PV and another fifty-four to the Chkwarawara PV, both PVs being located in the Chipisi TTL.

On 12 December, elements of C Company 2RR had a fleeting contact with three terrorists in the Mtetengwe TTL. There were no casualties on either side.

Also during the early evening of 12 December, elements of C Company 2RR made contact with an estimated fifteen terrorists in a *povo* camp in the Mtetengwe TTL. Nine locals, including three adult females, three female juveniles and three male juveniles were killed in the crossfire. One female juvenile was found to be wounded and was casevaced to Beitbridge where she was successfully treated. Large quantities of food, blankets and cooking utensil were recovered and destroyed. The locals killed had all opted to run with the terrorists as opposed to living in the relative safety of the protected villages.

On 13 December, two local men were abducted by a lone terrorist outside the confines of the Tokwe protected village in the Mtetengwe TTL. One managed to escape and reported the incident.

Also on 13 December, although not a terrorist incident and therefore not recorded in the Incident log, Bruce Cook, my brave friend and outstanding tracker, was killed in a vehicle accident during the morning. A very sad day.

On 14 December, Scouter Zulu detonated yet another landmine in the Siyoka TTL. There were no casualties and the badly damaged vehicle was recovered to Beitbridge.

Also on 14 December, The Fire Force was deployed to the Umzingwani farming area after twenty-five terrorists were sighted by a 1 Indep Company observation post. However, the Fire Force was unable to locate the group and returned to base.

Again, on 14 December, an Internal Affairs vehicle detonated a landmine while clearing the Chikwarakwara airfield in the Chipisi TTL. One of the occupants received minor wounds and was treated at the PV.

On 15 December, a Psychological Warfare Unit vehicle detonated a landmine in the Diti TTL. There were no casualties.

On 16 December, the Fire Force was deployed to the Mtetengwe TTL after elements of 1 Indep Company sighted fifteen terrorists advancing in extended-line formation. All the terrorists were dressed in blue denim. The Fire Force made contact, resulting in the death of four terrorists and the recovery of one AKM and three AK-47 assault rifles. During the contact, a total of fourteen civilians were killed. Three locals were captured and under interrogation gave out that they were moving with the terrorists to re-occupy a *povo* camp.

Also on 16 December, a Rhodesian Breweries delivery vehicle was stopped on the main Bulawayo road by four terrorists. The driver was forced to drive the vehicle into the Mtetengwe TTL where a large group of terrorists was waiting. The vehicle was then destroyed by fire. 1 Indep Company deployed and located spoor of thirty terrorists at the scene of destruction. Tracks were followed for some distance before being lost.

Again, on 16 December, elements of C Company 2RR in the Mtetengwe TTL shot and killed a female adult when she failed to heed their warnings and warning shots to stop.

On 17 December, elements of C Company 2RR engaged a group of eight terrorists in the Mtetengwe TTL. This engagement resulted in four terrorists being killed and the recovery of war matériel, including two SKS rifles and an AKM assault rifle.

Also on 17 December, a Shu Shine bus on the main Bulawayo road was stopped by nine terrorists who then relieved all on board of any valuables. The terrorists then departed into the Mtetengwe TTL.

On 18 December, an Internal Affairs vehicle detonated a landmine in the Mtetengwe TTL. There were no casualties.

Also on 18 December, elements of D Company 2RR shot and killed a male adult after he failed to stop when called upon to do so.

On 19 December, elements of D Company 2RR had a fleeting contact with five terrorists in the Mtetengwe TTL. There were no casualties on either side. A helicopter was dispatched with trackers who took up the spoor which led to an empty *povo* camp where all the contents were destroyed.

On 20 December, eight terrorists stopped a local storekeeper in his vehicle in the Umzingwani farming area, forcing him off the road into the bush for approximately six kilometres where the goods he was transporting, including footwear and foodstuffs, were stolen. His vehicle was then destroyed by fire.

On 21 December, twenty-eight locals were abducted by an unknown number of terrorists while collecting firewood from the Tshiturapadzi protected village in the Chipisi TTL. One female managed to escape and reported the incident to Guard Force who reacted and managed to follow the spoor for some considerable distance before losing the tracks.

Also on 21 December, a Shu Shine bus was stopped and all on board were relieved of their valuables by a group of terrorists estimated to number forty. The terrorists warned the driver not to report the incident to the police until the following day. However, he ignored the warning and reported it the same day.

On 22 December, a Bishopstone Estates (owned and occupied by Robbie Parks) tractor, escorted by two members of Guard Force, was fired on by an unknown number of terrorists. The tractor driver was killed but the two Guard Force members managed to make good their escape. Elements of 1 Indep Company deployed on follow-up and spoor was followed into the Jopempi Block, Liebigs Ranch.

On the night of 23 December, four large explosions were heard by the Bubye River bridge guard in the direction of Les Mitchell's Lesanth Ranch. At the same time Mitchell also reported the explosions and confirmed that he was not under attack. An air force Lynx aircraft was deployed to the approximate position of the explosions and dropped several flares but the cause could not be explained. At first light, elements of the security forces were deployed and located the site on the Rutenga–Beitbridge railway line. Terrorists had attempted to sabotage the line by detonating sixteen small explosive charges, resulting in two minor breaks to the line. Two nearby high-tension electricity poles were also sabotaged. A boobytrap comprising a stick grenade and an 82mm mortar bomb was also found and dismantled at the scene. Spoor of ten terrorists was followed into the Diti TTL where it was lost through high winds and rocky terrain.

Also on the evening of 23 December, the homestead on Lamulas Section, Liebigs Ranch, was attacked by an unknown number of terrorists. An air force Lynx was deployed from Beitbridge to drop flares over the homestead. Once the scene was illuminated, the terrorists broke off the attack. A Liebigs Ranch reaction force was deployed from Mazunga Ranch to secure the homestead and to commence follow-up operations the following morning when tracks were followed for five kilometres before being lost in hard ground. During this follow-up, the body of a ranch employee was found; he had been bayoneted to death.

Again, during the evening of 23 December, four explosions and automatic fire were heard from the Scouter Zulu base in the Siyoka TTL. At first light, Scouter Zulu located the scene of the action. Apparently, a group of extremely irate terrorists had arrived at a kraal and accused one of the males of being a 'sellout'. The group then went berserk and fired over one hundred and fifty rounds – confirmed by expended cartridges recovered from the scene – into the 'sellout' and let off four RPG-7 rockets before ending their shooting spree. A number of donkeys were also killed, whether intentionally or not was never ascertained. One seriously injured male was recovered and subsequently casevaced to Gwanda for treatment.

On 24 December, a railway-line-clearance vehicle patrol detonated a landmine on the tracks of the Rutenga line in the vicinity of Lesanth Ranch. The three occupants of the vehicle were all injured, one seriously. They were all casevaced to Messina hospital. Elements of the Engineers were deployed to check the area. One of the engineers detonated an anti-personnel mine which resulted in serious lower-body injuries; he was casevaced by air to Bulawayo General Hospital for treatment.

Also on 24 December, a Guard Force vehicle detonated a landmine in the Diti TTL. Two of the occupants of the vehicle received what appeared to be serious injuries and both were casevaced by air force helicopter to the Messina hospital. Approximately an hour later and ten kilometres farther on, a Psychological Warfare Unit vehicle detonated a second landmine but on this occasion there were no casualties.

On 25 December, a civilian vehicle travelling on the main Alko Towla road in the vicinity of the Bubye River detonated a landmine, killing two of the occupants and severely injuring two others, necessitating their casevac to the Gwanda hospital.

Also on 25 December, three hundred locals from the Siyoka TTL presented themselves to Robin Watson at his homestead on Mikado Ranch after being chased out of the TTL by an estimated twenty-five terrorists. The actual reason behind this was never ascertained, but the locals gave out that they were being used as human shields prior to an attack on Watson's homestead. A PRAW aircraft mounted with an MAG machine gun and an air force Lynx were deployed overhead. The PRAW sighted seven terrorists who were engaged with machine-gun fire, while the Lynx pilot completed a bomb run on the target. However, because of fading light, no follow-up was possible. At first light the following morning, elements of 1 Indep Company conducted a follow-up operation but nothing of interest was found.

Again, on 25 December, terrorists breached the security fence at Mapai protected village in the Mtetengwe TTL and abducted seventeen locals. However, all the abductees managed to escape and returned to the PV.

On 26 December, elements of C Company 2RR engaged an estimated six terrorists whom they located in a *povo* camp in the Diti TTL. One terrorist was killed and various items of war matériel were recovered, including an AK-47 assault rifle. The call sign was unable to locate tracks but they followed up as best they could. There were no security force casualties.

Also on 26 December, a 1 Indep Company vehicle detonated a landmine in the Mtetengwe TTL. There were no casualties.

Again, on 26 December, the northbound afternoon convoy was ambushed by an estimated seven terrorists on the main Bulawayo road. There were no casualties and the convoy managed to pass through unhindered. Elements of 1 Indep Company, with the Fire Force, were immediately deployed and an aerial and ground search commenced. Owing to thick vegetation, nothing was detected from the air and spoor was soon lost, with the terrorists adopting anti-tracking tactics.

Yet again, on 26 December, elements of A Company 2RR, while moving into an ambush position in the Diti TTL, shot and killed a male adult who failed to stop when challenged.

On 27 December, an operation was mounted against a recently discovered *povo* camp in the Chipisi TTL. The Fire Force, manned by 1 Indep Company, supported by ground troops from A Company 2RR, deployed onto the target. Two male adults were shot and killed after they refused to stop when challenged. Large quantities of foodstuffs, blankets and cooking utensils were recovered and destroyed. No terrorists were located but plenty of evidence was found to suggest they had been in recent occupation.

On 28 December, a 1 Indep Company vehicle detonated a landmine in the Mtetengwe TTL. There were no injuries.

On 29 December, a lone Rhodesian Intelligence Corps Unimog 2.5-ton vehicle transporting Lieutenant Lionel Reynolds and Sergeant Mervyn Sadler back to Bulawayo on completion of their call-up at Beitbridge was ambushed on the main Bulawayo road, in the vicinity of Mazunga, by an estimated seven terrorists. Only two of the terrorist bullets counted, one striking the bodywork of the vehicle and the other hitting the unfortunate Sadler in the head and killing him instantly. A further tragedy was to follow as Sadler's wife and two small children had arrived at the demob centre in Bulawayo to pick him up, not knowing that he had been killed a few hours beforehand; it was only with the arrival of Lionel Reynolds that she received the terrible news.

Also on 29 December, elements of A Company 2RR travelling in the Chipisi TTL came across a freshly-dug hole in the road and, on checking the area, located a box mine and spoor. It was apparent that the terrorists had been disturbed while burying the landmine.

On 30 December, a private vehicle travelling ahead of the southbound convoy on the main Bulawayo road was ambushed by an unknown number of terrorists. The passenger, Brian Mulhearn from Johannesburg, was seriously wounded in the arm and chest but, fortunately, the driver, also from Johannesburg, was uninjured and managed to drive Mulhearn as far as Beitbridge, from where he was taken to the Messina hospital, before being transferred by air to the better-equipped Pietersburg hospital.

Also on 30 December, a Guard Force convoy was ambushed by an estimated thirty terrorists in the Chipisi TTL. The convoy was attacked with RPG-7 rockets and automatic fire. Guard Force returned fire and eventually the terrorists broke off the attack. Blood spoor was located in the terrorist ambush position, indicating that one of the terrorists had been wounded by the return fire

On 31 December, army engineers located and lifted three landmines, one TMH-47 and two box mines, on the Tshiturapadzi Road in the Chipisi TTL.

•••

And so the year 1978 came to an end. During the past twelve months, ZANLA terrorists had extended their sphere of influence as far west as the Botswanan border, and had established themselves in the Maramani, Machuchuta and Dendele tribal trust lands, traditional ZAPU areas. Not only were ZANLA taking on the security forces but at every opportunity they were attacking ZIPRA, and vice versa. ZIPRA, because of their traditional support from one of their main recruitment regions, was reluctant to control the area through terror. However, these were the only means through which ZANLA could enjoy support, and they were not slow in murdering any suspected ZIPRA supporters or destroying their villages.

This benefited the security forces, with the old adage 'your enemy is my enemy' being applicable to a point. In the event of security forces deploying out of these areas, Special Branch sources would leak word to ZIPRA of this fact, with a view to fomenting inter-faction fighting. However, when security forces redeployed back into these areas, the perilous alliances fell away ZIPRA was treated in the same way as ZANLA, i.e. hunted down and eliminated.

With ZANLA infiltrating areas to the west, so the responsibility of the security forces based at Beitbridge increased to cover these areas, but without any matching increase in force levels; this was in direct contrast to ZANLA who were flooding the area with reinforcements.

The main responsibility of Beitbridge was to ensure that the two main roads remained open and that the railway line to Rutenga continued running. To this end, the main targets would remain the Mtetengwe and Diti TTLs from where the terrorists launched their attacks on these soft targets.

Unfortunately, during the year security forces lost seven members killed in action, with nine receiving serious injuries in either contacts or to landmines. On the plus side, sixty terrorists lost their lives to security force actions, with a further ten being either captured or surrendering. The number of terrorists wounded or who later died of their wounds and were buried in the Rhodesian bush was never established. The figure must have been quite considerable, taking into account that over one hundred contacts had taken place during the year, in spite of the fact that the vast majority failed to produce any sort of result and were reported as "no casualties on either side".

More and more locals were now being killed, unintentionally, by the security forces. With the implementation of the PV regime, those locals who refused to comply with the requirement to move into the PVs put their own lives at risk. Most of the locals were killed in attacks on *povo* bases, but others who failed to stop when called upon to do so were also fired on, normally with deadly consequences. However, this warning was not afforded to curfew breakers who were shot out of hand, for obvious reasons.

The arrival in Beitbridge of Major Don Price and the fine young men of 1 Indep Company during the latter part of the year was like a breath of fresh air. Within days rather than weeks of their arrival, the morale, not only of the security forces, but of the resident population, increased dramatically and, above all, we started producing results. A direct factor influencing this success was the positioning of the Fire Force at Beitbridge, although this was not on a permanent basis. On the occasions that it was *in situ*, Price took every advantage of its presence and ensured that it was used to its full potential.

I was, however, not so naïve to realize that the success we had recently enjoyed would last: ZANLA could replace their losses ten times over and feel little effect. The ZANLA high command had literally thousands upon thousands of newly-trained recruits to infiltrate Rhodesia as they saw fit. Nevertheless, after two years of frustration, I felt that at last, we, the security forces, were coming to grips with the situation and that we could only build on our success.

Mobie van Wyk was commissioned to the rank of superintendent and transferred to Bulawayo. He was replaced by Chief Inspector Tom Deacon.

On the personal front, I was really enjoying Beitbridge after the depressing period I had experienced earlier in the year and Maya and I were getting on really well.

I was also determined to pass the promotion examinations to detective inspector during the coming year.

I was really looking forward to 1979 and felt that it would be a good one. But, oh boy, how wrong I was.

CHAPTER TEN
Routine slaughter
January–June 1979

On 1 January, the store on Cawood Ranch in the Umzingwani farming area was robbed by three terrorists.

On 3 January, elements of C Company 2RR patrolling in the Diti TTL shot and killed four local men who failed to stop when challenged. This was part of an exercise conducted by C Company to check and clear *povo* camps in the area.

Also on 3 January, elements of C Company 2RR conducting a search of a *povo* comp in the Diti TTL shot and killed two women who broke cover and ran.

On 5 January, elements of C Company 2RR conducting a search of another *povo* base in the same area shot and killed a male adult who attempted to escape.

On 6 January, elements of 1 Indep Company, while deploying into the Mtengwe TTL from the main Bulawayo road, were approached by a lone armed terrorist who surrendered and handed over an AKM assault rifle, two AK-47 magazines, a stick grenade and a pack.

On 9 January, a Stutterfords removal van was stopped by eight terrorists on the Fort Victoria road. Three metal trunks were removed from the vehicle and carted off by the gang who, before leaving, relieved the driver and co-driver of all valuables. The crew was unharmed and permitted to proceed without incident.

On 10 January, the old warhorse, Les Mitchell, was ambushed on his Lesanth Ranch by what turned out to be four terrorists. Fire was returned and the terrorists vacated their position. Blood spoor of two of the terrorists was found, which was followed for some distance before being lost.

Also on 10 January, elements of C Company 2RR, while moving into a night ambush at last light, called on three local boys to halt. The warning was ignored which resulted in the call sign opening fire and killing one.

Again, on 10 January, elements of C Company 2RR, while manning a night ambush, shot and killed a local male curfew breaker.

On 11 January, a civilian vehicle detonated a landmine on the Alko Towla road, which resulted in two of the occupants sustaining serious injuries. Both were casevaced by road to the Gwanda hospital.

Also on 11 January, elements of C Company 2RR accidentally shot and killed a local who was guiding them into a suspected terrorist base in the Masera TTL.

Again, on 11 January, elements of C Company 2RR had a fleeting contact with two terrorists in the Masera TTL. One terrorist was killed and an SKS rifle was recovered.

Yet again, on 11 January, elements of C Company 2RR shot and killed two locals who attempted to escape after being detained by the call sign for interrogation.

On 12 January, elements of C Company 2RR had a fleeting contact with an estimated twelve terrorists in the Siyoka TTL, resulting in the proverbial 'no casualties either side'.

Also on 12 January, a Central Mechanical and Equipment Department (CMED) vehicle detonated a landmine in the Diti TTL, resulting in the death of one of the CMED staff and injuries to seven others who were all casevaced to Beitbridge for treatment. It was estimated by the engineers who attended the scene that the mine had been boosted by at least one other landmine. The detonation caused a massive crater in the road and the damage it caused to the mine-protected vehicle was extensive, to say the least.

Again, on 12 January, the second-in-command of the Beitbridge Prison, John Waters, accompanied by an African prison warder and returning to Beitbridge from Gwanda, was ambushed by an estimated five terrorists in the area of Mazunga Ranch. Both Waters and the warder were seriously wounded in the attack, but managed to drive through the killing zone until they encountered a security patrol from Mazunga Ranch. They were taken to Mazunga Ranch headquarters, where they were treated, before being casevaced to Bulawayo by air. Waters and his wife Jackie were popular members of the Beitbridge community and who hosted some excellent parties at their house. Waters eventually recovered but was transferred because of his injuries. I, like many others, was sorry to see them leave Beitbridge.

Yet again, on 12 January, the good old Shu Shine bus was stopped by eight terrorists on the main Fort Victoria road. The terrorists, after robbing the passengers and crew, permitted the driver to continue without incident.

Once more, on 12 January, the ranch manager of Jopempi Block, Liebigs Ranch opened fire on four terrorists who were washing clothes at one of the numerous cattle troughs on the ranch. He apparently wounded two. The Fire Force was deployed but owing to heavy rain no spoor could be found.

On 13 January, an Internal Affairs vehicle detonated a landmine in the Mtetengwe TTL. There were no injuries.

Also on 13 January, elements of B Company 2RR had a fleeting contact with four terrorists in the Siyoka TTL. The terrorists fled in an easterly direction. However, the Fire Force, under Don Price's command, arrived overhead and made contact with the group, killing four and recovering three SKS rifles, one AK-47 and one AKM assault rifle.

On 14 January, the Fire Force reacted to a contact involving B Company 6RR and ten terrorists in the Machuchuta TTL. The Fire Force was unable to make contact with the group, but one terrorist was killed during the initial contact. Two SKS rifles were recovered. There were no security force casualties.

On 15 January, a CMED convoy under Guard Force escort was ambushed in the Diti TTL. The only injury was to one terrorist who was wounded.

Also on 15 January, elements of Guard Force opened fire and killed a local man while following the spoor of six terrorists in the Diti TTL. The deceased was subsequently identified as a well-known, powerful witchdoctor from the area who had been running with the terrorists for some time.

On 17 January, elements of B Company 2RR had a contact with a large group of ZIPRA terrorists in the Siyoka TTL. A PRAW aircraft circling above then spotted twenty terrorists in olive-green and khaki uniforms break and run. The PRAW then came under attack from the ground as the observer took on the group with his FN rifle, possibly wounding two, as blood spoor was later found when the ground call sign swept the area. A Soviet high-frequency radio, an AKM folding-butt assault rifle, several RPG-7 rocket projectiles, thousands of rounds of AK-47 and RPK machine-gun ammunition and other war matériel were recovered.

On 19 January, elements of A Company 6RR in the Dendele TTL had a contact with three terrorists, who were later joined by a further five. Heavy blood spoor was located, indicating that one of the terrorists had been hit. One SKS rifle and a stick grenade were recovered during the follow-up. Spoor was eventually lost through local movement, but the persistence of the call sign paid off when one terrorist was sighted, fired on and killed. One AK-47 assault rifle was recovered. There were no C Company casualties.

Also on 19 January, elements of A Company 6RR, patrolling the Machuchuta TTL, had a fleeting contact with an estimated twenty terrorists, who broke and headed in a southwesterly direction. Blood spoor was located and followed until heavy rain obliterated the tracks. There were no C Company casualties.

On 20 January, elements of 1 Indep Company had a fleeting contact with ten terrorists in the Masera TTL. During the follow-up, two 82mm mortar bombs were recovered. There were no casualties on either side.

On 21 January, elements of 1 Indep Company attacked a *povo* base in the Mtengwe TTL reported to contain thirty terrorists and twenty locals. During the attack, two civilian men were killed while attempting to flee. Three Liebigs Ranch cattle were found slaughtered in the base. Blankets, clothing and foodstuff recovered from the base were destroyed.

Also, during the night of 21 January, forty terrorists breached the security fence of the Tshiturapadzi protected village and abducted three hundred locals. Three locals who refused to accompany the terrorists were badly beaten and were casevaced to Beitbridge the following morning. Spoor of the abductees was followed for several kilometres before being obliterated by cattle movement.

During the night of 22 January, an unknown number of terrorists breached the security fence at the Shabwe protected village in the Mtengwe TTL. Elements of Guard Force protecting the PV opened fire on the terrorists who then returned fire from supporting positions with automatic weapons, 60mm mortars and 3.5-inch 'bazooka' rockets. Two locals in the PV were killed in the crossfire. The terrorists managed to abduct an unknown number of locals who, over the course of the following day, returned to the PV. The follow-up was unsuccessful owing to the amount of human spoor in and out of the PV.

On 23 January, an Internal Affairs MPV detonated a landmine in the Maramani TTL. There were no injuries.

On 26 January, a combined Guard Force–Rhodesian Defence Regiment convoy was ambushed by fifteen terrorists in the Diti TTL. Fire was returned, while the terrorists retaliated with ineffectual 60mm mortar fire. The follow-up did not last long before spoor was lost. There were no security force casualties.

Also, at midnight on 26 January, a four-wheeled scotch cart detonated a landmine in the Machuchuta TTL. One local man was killed and another received minor injuries. No spoor was located because of cattle movement.

On 28 January, twenty ZIPRA terrorists entered a kraal in the Siyoka TTL and, after accusing one of the men of being a sellout for harbouring a female ZANLA contact person, executed him with AK-47 rifle fire. Two AK-47 assault rifles were identified by police ballistics as being used in the murder.

During the evening of 29 January, while ambushing a path, elements of the South African Defence Force shot and killed a curfew breaker on the Beitbridge state land.

On 30 January, Scouter Uniform, operating in the Masera TTL, had a fleeting contact with seven terrorists. There were no casualties on either side. After the contact, Scouter Uniform continued on its way and two and a half hours later, still in the Masera TTL, one of the vehicles detonated a landmine. On this occasion, there were three casualties who were all transferred to Beitbridge.

Also on 30 January, terrorists fired on a Shu Shine bus on the main Bulawayo road. The bullet strikes were only discovered on the arrival of the bus at Beitbridge. As no one could remember hearing shots being fired, the driver assumed that the ambush had taken place when the bus had passed through a severe thunderstorm.

On 31 January, a Swift Transport vehicle was ambushed on the main Bulawayo road. Although the vehicle sustained hits, the driver managed to drive through the killing zone unscathed. The ambush took place in the same area of the previous day's thunderstorm encountered by the Shu Shine bus when it was thought to have been ambushed.

During the night of 1 February, approximately fifty terrorists attacked the Tshiturapadzi protected village, using a 75mm recoilless rifle, 82mm mortars, machine guns – including an SG-43 Goryunov medium machine gun – and automatic weapons. Elements of Guard Force reacted to the attack which eventually drove off the attackers. However, prior to the attack, one group of terrorists breached the security fence around the PV and abducted one hundred and seventeen locals. One female was murdered by the terrorists for refusing to leave the PV. At first light the following morning, a check of the area revealed the attacking position where a wounded terrorist was captured. An SKS rifle, thirteen 82mm mortar bombs, grenades and other war matériel were recovered. An unsuccessful follow-up operation was undertaken.

During the evening of 2 February, a group of thirty terrorists robbed two men and a woman of all their possessions in the Beitbridge state land. The three were discovered completely naked the following morning by a police patrol.

At approximately eleven o'clock on the night of 4 February, the Internal Affairs Shashi base, positioned in the Maramani TTL in close proximity to the Botswanan border, came under attack by an estimated twenty-five terrorists using 82mm mortars, RPG-2 and -7 rockets, rifle grenades and automatic weapons. Internal Affairs reacted, forcing the terrorists to abandon their positions. There were no casualties on either side. The follow-up the next morning fizzled out after spoor was lost on rocky ground. From the examination of expended cartridge cases recovered from the firing position, police ballistics identified one of the RPD machine guns as having been previously used in the D Company 6RR ambush of 20 March 1978 and in the Shabwe PV attack of 5 March 1978. This was definite proof that ZANLA had extended their operational area westward to include the Botswanan border as their western boundary.

On 5 February, elements of Guard Force patrolling the Diti TTL located a wooden box mine of British manufacture. Army engineers reacted and destroyed the mine *in situ*.

Also on 5 February, a group of twenty terrorists set fire to, and destroyed, a tractor on Mavimba Section, Liebigs Ranch. Liebigs security reacted but was unable to locate spoor.

Again, on 5 February, an armoured PRAW aircraft overflying the Chipisi TTL fired on three terrorists. However, the fire was ineffective and the terrorists escaped.

On 6 February, a Roads Department MPV detonated a landmine in the Diti TTL causing serious injuries to one of the passengers and slight injuries to another. Both were casevaced to Beitbridge for treatment.

Also on 6 February, a police patrol located a TMD-44 landmine in the Maramani TTL. Army engineers reacted and destroyed the mine *in situ*.

Again, on 6 February, a Shu Shine bus was ambushed by an unknown number of terrorists on the main Bulawayo road. The driver managed to drive through the ambush and although the bus was hit by rifle fire, no injuries were sustained by the occupants.

On 7 February, a civilian vehicle driving out of convoy was ambushed on the main Bulawayo road. Fortunately, the driver was able to drive through the ambush unhurt and make good his escape.

Also on 7 February, a Roads Department vehicle, escorted by elements of Guard Force, was ambushed by four terrorists in the Mtetengwe TTL. The terrorists, apart from automatic weapons, used a 60mm mortar to attack the convoy. One Roads Department employee was slightly injured and casevaced to Beitbridge for treatment. An unexploded 60mm mortar bomb was located at the scene and which was later destroyed by army engineers.

On 8 February, a Roads Department gang reported hearing a large explosion close to where they were working in the Diti TTL. Elements of 1 Indep Company reacted and discovered the body of a dead terrorist lying next to a huge crater in the road. No weapon was recovered, but two forty-round AK magazines and ammunition were found near the body. It was assessed that the terrorist was rigging a landmine with some sort of anti-handling device when the whole lot went up in his face.

Also on 8 February, elements of A Company 2RR had a contact with thirty-plus terrorists in the Chipisi TTL. There were no casualties and no spoor located.

Again, on 8 February, elements of 1 Indep Company operating in the Siyoka TTL fired on five terrorists, killing two and wounding one other who managed to escape. The terrorists were identified as being ZIPRA. Two AK-47 assault rifles and various other items of war matériel were recovered. 1 Indep Company sustained no injuries.

On 9 February, elements of 1 Indep Company operating in the Siyoka TTL made contact with nine ZIPRA terrorists. During the engagement, seven terrorists were killed, with two managing to escape the ferocious firefight unharmed. This was an extremely successful contact as only ground forces were involved. Four AKM and two AK-47 assault rifles, as well as a Soviet PPSh submachine gun, were recovered, together with the seven bodies.

Also, during the night of 9 February, three terrorists abducted one of Les Mitchell's labourers from his compound on Lesanth Ranch and, the following evening, abducted two labourers from Sam Cawood's Kleinbegin Ranch compound, situated north of the main Fort Victoria road.

Again, on 9 February, elements of the Bubye farm reaction force, supported by an armed PRAW aircraft, made contact with an unknown number of terrorists on the vacant Bar G Ranch, owned by Martin Grobler. One terrorist was seen to be wounded but managed to escape. A local man who had been shot and wounded in the crossfire was casevaced to Beitbridge for treatment. A small amount of terrorist war matériel was recovered from the scene.

On 11 February, elements of Guard Force operating in the Mtetengwe TTL opened fire on a group of twelve terrorists. The terrorists did not return fire but fled from the area. Guard Force followed spoor for some distance before losing it through cattle movement.

Just before midnight on 12 February, an unknown number of terrorists entered the compound on Robbie Parks's Bishopstone Estates and began, for some unknown reason, to throw stick and hand grenades at a parked vehicle. The vehicle suddenly exploded in a ball of fire as the petrol tank exploded, setting fire to six nearby huts. After this, the terrorists lost interest and left the compound. One local boy was injured during this attack and was casevaced to Beitbridge for treatment.

At approximately eleven o'clock on the night of 13 February, an unfortunate incident occurred in the Masera TTL. Members of the SB office staff were accompanying elements of 1 Indep Company to conduct a reconnaissance of a known *povo* base in the Masera TTL. Visibility was good with a clear night and a full moon. The patrol commander positioned a machine-gunner on slightly higher ground overlooking the base so as to enable him to give supporting fire in the event of contact being made with the terrorists. Detective Constable Tshuma, for some unknown reason, did not stick to the plan and wandered out of the *povo* base, only to return from a different direction some minutes later. The machine-gunner, taking Tshuma for a terrorist, opened fire, killing him instantly. Tshuma's death was a shock to everyone, especially considering the circumstances as to how he met his death. He was a keen young policeman with an infectious sense of humour and the office felt his loss for some time. It turned out that the locals, as well as the terrorists, had vacated the base some days before the mission, so his death was in vain.

Also on 13 February, a civilian vehicle was ambushed by an estimated twelve terrorists on Jopempi Block, Liebigs Ranch. The driver managed to drive through the ambush and report the incident. Liebigs Ranch reaction force was deployed on follow-up operations. Fortunately, no one was injured during the attack.

On 14 February, the proverbial Shu Shine bus was stopped in the Siyoka TTL and the passengers and crew robbed of their valuables, after which the bus was allowed to proceed. Scouter Zulu responded to the incident.

Also on 14 February, terrorists ambushed a civilian vehicle travelling on the Jopempi Block of Liebigs. Unfortunately, on this occasion, one Perry Broomfield was wounded, which necessitated his casevac to Beitbridge for treatment.

At approximately noon on 15 February, a police patrol operating in the Machuchuta TTL near the Tuli Circle came under attack from a group of eight terrorists in a well-sited ambush position. During the engagement Constable George Makore Ncube was killed. Ncube had been stationed at Tuli and was part of a contingent of brave young men, black and white, who 'held the fort' at Tuli throughout the war. I made a point of visiting Tuli on every possible occasion that I could during the time I was stationed at Beitbridge, and later Gwanda, in a show of support. Additionally, Tuli and the Tuli Circle were of immense historical significance in the founding of Rhodesia, a subject that fascinated me and one that I took a deep interest in, so it was a pleasure to visit. I think it was one of the most sociable police stations in the country, in spite of the isolation experienced by the staff whose most important responsibility was to ensure that the ration and beer run got through from either Beitbridge or Gwanda, the two closest centres where essentials could be purchased.

Also on 15 February, the Liebigs Ranch reaction force on Jopempi Block encountered an unknown number of terrorists moving sacks of maize meal on donkeys, heading in the direction of the Mtetengwe TTL. The reaction force opened fire on the group who abandoned the donkeys and fled. Four donkeys were killed and a large amount of maize meal was recovered. Spoor was followed for some distance before being lost on hard ground.

During the early hours of 16 February, Piet van der Merwe's tractor and trailer were destroyed by fire on River Ranch by an estimated twenty terrorists. At first light, Scouter Uniform reacted to the incident, before managing to detonate a landmine on the same ranch, fortunately without suffering any casualties. At some stage, the terrorists attempted to knock out an electricity transformer by firing at it but in spite of hitting the transformer three times, no permanent damage was done.

Also on 16 February, elements of Guard Force located and successfully recovered an anti-tank box mine in the Diti TTL. On the same date but in a different area of the Diti TTL, Guard Force also located and successfully recovered another anti-tank box mine. Former army engineers who had joined the Guard Force were proving their worth and a damned fine job they were doing too.

Again, during the early afternoon of 16 February, a northbound Swift Transport vehicle was stopped by a large group of terrorists on the main Beitbridge–Fort Victoria road. After the driver was robbed of all valuables, he was allowed to proceed unharmed.

Yet again, during the late afternoon of 16 February and in the same area as the previous incident, a southbound Trek removal truck was stopped by twenty terrorists on the main Beitbridge–Fort Victoria road. The driver was robbed of all cash, including traveller's cheques, and was permitted to proceed unharmed.

On 17 February, four local women employed on Benfur Estates in the Umzingwani farming area inadvertently walked into a terrorist base established on the farm. The terrorists immediately opened fire on them, being under the impression they were being attacked. Fortunately, the women managed to escape uninjured. Elements of 1 Indep Company deployed on follow-up operations.

Also on 17 February, elements of 1 Indep Company detonated a landmine with one of their vehicles in the Siyoka TTL. No injuries were sustained by any of the occupants.

Again, during the afternoon of 17 February, a northbound train detonated an explosive device on the railway line in the area of Swanscoe Siding. The locomotive was slightly damaged and was recovered to Rutenga for repairs. Approximately forty centimetres of track was cut by the explosion. Elements of 1 Indep Company deployed on follow-up operations.

Yet again, on 17 February, an Internal Affairs convoy in the Diti TTL was ambushed by an unknown number of terrorists using automatic weapons and RPG-7 rockets. The convoy managed to escape without sustaining injury. Owing to the lack of troop availability, no follow-up was conducted.

On 18 February, terrorists ambushed a Wards Transport vehicle travelling north on the main Beitbridge–Bulawayo road. The vehicle managed to drive through the ambush but during the attack one of the crew was wounded. The driver reported the incident at Mazunga Ranch from where the injured was casevaced to Gwanda hospital. Elements of Liebigs security conducted the follow-up.

Also, during the night of 18 February, the homestead on Shobi Section, Liebigs Ranch was attacked by an estimated forty terrorists using automatic rifles, machine guns, 82mm mortars and RPG-7 rockets. The attack lasted approximately fifteen minutes before the enemy withdrew, the homestead being successfully defended by elements of Liebigs security. No casualties were inflicted by either side. Elements of Liebigs security conducted follow-up operations the following morning.

On 19 February, elements of Guard Force travelling in convoy detonated a landmine in the Diti TTL. Two guardsmen received minor injuries and were casevaced to Beitbridge for treatment.

Also on 19 February, five terrorists approached a gang of labourers working on fence lines on Jopempi Block, Liebigs Ranch. A tractor and trailer containing several sacks of maize meal which the labour gang was using was burned out after the maize meal had been removed. The labourers were then forced to carry the sacks of meal for several kilometres before being released. Later on the same day, terrorists destroyed a water pump engine not far from the earlier incident.

Again, during the evening of 19 February, Sam Cawood's Kleinbegin Ranch homestead came under attack by an estimated twenty terrorists using automatic and RPG-7 rocket fire. The occupants, including the farm security, managed to repel the attack and the enemy broke off their attack. No injuries were sustained by the defenders but damage to buildings and vehicles was caused. At first light, army engineers and elements of 1 Indep Company were deployed to the scene. The engineers detected and recovered an anti-tank mine on an access roads. There were no injuries during follow-up operations. Then, during the afternoon, while conducting follow-up operations, Liebigs security heard a very loud explosion on Jopempi and finally found the cause of the explosion: a smoking one-and-a-half-metre by one-metre crater in the road, indicating that a landmine had detonated. However, there was nothing found – animal, vehicle, human or anything – that could have caused the explosion and so it was put down to a premature detonation.

On 20 February, terrorists stopped a Shu Shine bus in the Siyoka TTL and were in the process of robbing it when elements of 1 Indep Company surprised the terrorists, and themselves, when coming across the scene. Both sides exchanged fire and the terrorists made off without injury. In spite of a concerted follow-up, no further contact was made with the terrorists.

On 21 February, the driver of a northbound train from Beitbridge to Rutenga observed explosions on the line shortly before arriving at Swanscoe Siding, which was followed by an ambush on the train by an unknown number of terrorists. The train continued, with the engine slightly damaged, to Rutenga. Army engineers and railway security conducted the follow-up and recovered the remains of a terrorist who had been killed, in error, by his comrades.

On 22 February, elements of Liebigs security fired on two terrorists on Jopempi

Block. The terrorists returned fire and managed to make good their escape.

On 23 February, a northbound Swift Transport vehicle was ambushed on the main Beitbridge–Fort Victoria road by an estimated fifteen terrorists. Fortunately, the driver managed to clear the ambush site without injury. Fifteen minutes later, a southbound civilian vehicle came under attack from the same group and, although the vehicle was hit nine times, the driver and occupants escaped without injury.

Also on 23 February, Scouter Zulu located and successfully disarmed a wooden anti-tank box mine on a road in the Siyoka TTL.

Again, on 23 February, elements of the Rhodesian Defence Regiment operating in the Diti TTL located a wooden box mine, which was later disarmed by army engineers. On the same day, elements of the same regiment located a further anti-tank box mine in the Mtetengwe TTL which was also successfully disarmed.

Yet again, on 23 February, elements of Guard Force operating in the Diti TTL detected and successfully lifted a wooden box mine without incident, thanks again to their engineers.

Once more, on 23 February, two local civilian vehicles were stopped in the Mtetengwe TTL and the occupants robbed of valuables. There were no injuries and the vehicles were allowed to proceed.

On 24 February, an employee on Sentinal Ranch was murdered by eight terrorists who slit his throat. The reason for his death was never established but he had obviously been fingered. Because of terrorist warnings, this incident was only reported late in the day and no follow-up operation was undertaken.

On 25 February, army engineers attempting to defuse a boobytrapped stick grenade in the Diti TTL accidentally detonated the device, resulting in serious facial and body injuries to one of them. The casualty was initially casevaced to Beitbridge but, because of the gravity of his wounds, was airlifted to Bulawayo Central Hospital.

On 28 February, elements of 1 Indep Company engaged four terrorists on the Jopempi Block of Liebigs Ranch. The contact resulted in one terrorist killed and possibly another wounded. In addition, there was recovery of an AKM assault rifle, an RPD machine gun and three RPG-7 rockets, complete with boosters. No Indep Company members were injured.

•••

During mid-February, Don Price was tasked with planning an operation in the Chipise TTL, scheduled to commence at the beginning of March and to run for a ten-day period. The operation would include troops from his company, as well as elements of 6RR. I would accompany the HQ element which was to be based at the Tshiturapadzi airfield, so as to take charge of, and interrogate, any captured terrorists. Apart from the operational planning, Don and I discussed the possibility of getting in some elephant hunting while in the area, provided, of course, that this did not interfere with the operation.

I had first shot elephant in the Tshiturapadzi–Chikwarakwara area shortly after my arrival in Beitbridge in 1976. The standard arrangement with the District Commissioner, Lew Watson, was that a permit would be issued once the elephant had been shot and the tusks presented to his office for registration. This was because game permits were only issued for a maximum of forty-eight hours, after which time they would expire, with the licence fee being non-refundable. On this occasion in 1976, in the company of Mobie van Wyk and four members of the District Commissioner's staff, we proceeded to Chikwarakwara where we based up to hunt for elephant. Only three elephant were shot: one by me, one by Mobie and one by the Assistant District Commissioner. The other three DC staff members failed to get a shot in.

On our return to Beitbridge, we all registered our ivory after paying for the permits. This policy was adhered to by the DC for the duration of my posting at Beitbridge. I only mention this instance, as the accommodating approach adopted by Lew Watson on the issue of permits would have serious repercussions in the not-too-distant future.

We approached Lew Watson and informed him of our plans with regard to the possibility of shooting elephants in the Tshiturapadzi area during our deployment in March. He authorized the hunt on the usual condition that we would only pay for a permit in the event of an animal being shot. Therefore, on deployment, we had authority to shoot four elephant bulls, one each for me, Don Price and Neill Jackson, the second-in-command of 1 Indep Company. The fourth was allocated to the Assistant District Commissioner at Beitbridge who had asked Don, provided the opportunity present itself, to shoot an elephant for him, to which Don agreed.

The deployment followed and we established our headquarters on the Tshiturapadzi airstrip. The police base at Tshiturapadzi had closed down with the introduction of the protected villages at the beginning of 1978. The troops were subsequently deployed between Tshiturapadzi and Chikwarakwara. Due to the difficult terrain, radio communication between the ground troops and the HQ was virtually non-existent, and so Price was obliged to make use of a PRAW aircraft on a twice-daily basis to ensure that radio communication was maintained. A radio relay station had been positioned in the area but because of the flat terrain proved useless.

After the troops had been deployed for four days, it was obvious that, with the increase of security force activity in the area, the terrorists had gone to ground. Only one incident took place, which occurred on 5 March when four terrorists attempted to abduct five adults who were working outside the Tshiturapadzi protected village. The terrorists failed in their mission and all five returned safely to the PV.

On 5 March, Price was airborne early to carry out his morning radio schedules with the ground forces, before returning to the airstrip at around ten o'clock on completion of the exercise. On his way back, while overflying a fairly mountainous region known as the Dyke, he spotted a herd of bull elephants feeding in thick bush. As nothing was happening, Don and I decided to take a drive to the Dyke and see if we could spot the beasts. After sorting out our heavy guns, we departed with a small escort of volunteers keen to take part in an elephant hunt. The PRAW aircraft was due to return to Beitbridge for standby duties, so Don asked the pilot to overfly the Dyke on his way back to confirm that the herd was still there. Needless to say, it was. On getting up to them, Don and I shot our elephants. Neill Jackson had not arrived as yet.

The following day, and under similar circumstances, Don shot a further elephant for the Assistant District Commissioner at Beitbridge. That night, due to increased terrorist activity in the Mtetengwe TTL, I decided to return to Beitbridge early the following day which I did without incident.

On the conclusion of the operation, my ivory, together with the others, was transported back to Beitbridge by the returning troops. Immediately on receiving mine, I paid for my permit, had the ivory registered and was issued with a permit to possess ivory, so, as far as I was concerned, everything was above board and legal. Not once did I ever imagine that I had committed an offence under the Wild Life Act.

•••

On 1 March, terrorists placed an explosive device on the Rutenga railway line in the vicinity of Swanscoe Siding. An early-morning inspection trolley detonated the device, causing it to derail. There were no known injuries, and the railway security team was deployed.

On 2 March, elements of Guard Force in convoy in the Chipise TTL detonated a landmine assessed as being a box type. Three Guard Force members were slightly injured and were casevaced to Beitbridge by road for treatment. Shortly after noon, elements of Guard Force guarding the damaged vehicle spotted three terrorists, two of whom were carrying AK-47 rifles and the other a yellow box. The guardsmen opened fire on the group, causing them to flee. There were no casualties on either side. The three terrorists were deemed as being a mine-laying team and that the yellow box was the landmine.

Shortly before first light on 3 March, elements of the Rhodesian Artillery Regiment manning a battery of 25-pounder guns in the area of Lesanth Ranch fired eighteen shells on known *povo* base positions located on the deserted Bubye farms. Elements of 1 Indep Company then conducted a search of the bases and recovered the bodies of nine civilians killed during the bombardment. The terrorists had occupied the base until 1 March when they had left.

Also on 3 March, a landmine detonated in the Mtetengwe TTL. The site of the explosion was located and the corpses of two mangled donkeys were found next to the crater. It was assessed that they had been the cause of the detonation.

On 6 March, as a result of aerial reconnaissance, the Fire Force from Buffalo Range, manned by elements of Support Commando 1 Rhodesian Light Infantry, as well as elements of 1 Indep Company, attacked a *povo* base in the Mtetengwe TTL. The attack resulted in the death of four terrorists and eight women and the capture of two local women. From interrogation of the women, it was established that seven terrorists and eleven women had been in the camp at the start of the attack. Three AK-47 assault rifles, one SKS rifle and other war matériel were recovered during a search of the base.

Also, during the night of 6 March, two Land Rovers were destroyed by fire on Safari Ranch on the Bubye River by an unknown number of terrorists.

On 7 March, a mixed convoy of army and local militia was ambushed by an estimated twelve terrorists in the Diti TTL. The ambush was ineffective, with only one of the vehicles receiving four strikes. No casualties were inflicted on the militia who valiantly fought off the group with their First World War-issue Lee Enfield .303 rifles.

On 8 March, an RMS bus was ambushed by approximately three terrorists on the main Bulawayo–Beitbridge road. The driver returned fire and drove through the ambush, without injury, although the vehicle was hit several times.

On 9 March, a civilian vehicle travelling south on the main Bulawayo–Beitbridge road was ambushed by an unknown number of terrorists. Some three hours later, the same vehicle was being driven north on the same road and was again ambushed in the same vicinity of the first attack. No occupants of the vehicle were injured on either occasion.

Also on 9 March, elements of Internal Affairs were involved in a highly suspect contact with two groups of terrorists in the Mtetengwe TTL. Travelling in convoy, one member of the group fired three rounds at a stray dog seen running on the road when all hell broke loose. The convoy came under instant terrorist attack from two positions. The engagement carried on for nearly an hour and a half before Internal Affairs were obliged to retire as they were running low on ammunition. The contact lasted so long that a battery of artillery was able to position their 25-pounder guns, calculate their target acquisition and fire six shells into the ambush area as soon as the Intaf convoy was out of the immediate danger zone. Elements of 1 Indep Company conducted follow-up operations at first light the following morning. No spoor, no AK-47 or any other type of expended enemy cartridge case were found at the site, or anything else for that matter to indicate that even one round had been fired at the convoy. No member of Intaf was injured during the sustained 'attack'.

During the night 10 March, the Chaswingo protected village in the Diti TTL came under terrorist mortar and small-arms attack, lasting fifteen minutes. Elements of Guard Force protecting the PV returned fire. During the attack, another group of terrorists entered the PV and abducted forty-eight locals. Three locals in the PV were slightly injured during the attack.

•••

Also during the night of 10 March, Keith Knott's homestead and compound on Nottingham Estates came under terrorist attack. The terrorists attacked both targets with mortar and small-arms fire but, fortunately, elements of Guard Force and Knott's farm security were present and managed to repel the attack. Knott was spending the weekend with his wife Wendy and their children in Beitbridge at the time of the attack, and I actually informed him of the situation while the attack was still in progress.

Keith and his manager, Clive Ambler-Smith, who was also spending the weekend in Beitbridge, wanted to rush back to the ranch to render what assistance they could, and they most certainly would have had I not been able to talk some sense into them. It was the terrorists' strategy to mine or boobytrap access roads to their targets in the hope of causing further casualties, or to actually ambushing access roads, with the same intent.

The security forces, except in extreme cases, would only react to homestead attacks at first light for this very reason. So, reluctantly, Keith and Clive were forced to delay their departure until they could join the 1 Indep reaction force which left at first light. During the attack on the compound, one young African female was killed and fourteen men, women and children were wounded to various degrees. All were casevaced to the Gwanda hospital which was the closest facility able to accommodate that many patients. The security forces suffered no casualties.

•••

On 11 March, a Shu Shine bus was stopped on the main Bulawayo–Beitbridge road by an estimated twenty terrorists who commenced to rob the passengers and bus crew of valuables. They had just relieved the conductor of Rh$40 and the passengers of three pairs of shoes and a wristwatch when a civilian vehicle approached the scene. The occupants of the vehicle were members of the security forces who, on seeing what was unfolding before them, opened fire on the terrorists who immediately returned fire and fled into the nearby bush. The soldiers in the car instructed the bus driver to load his passengers and to evacuate the area without delay. The area was then secured until reinforcements arrived in the form of 1 Indep Company who immediately took up the spoor. No one was injured during this incident.

On 12 March, a Roads Department vehicle detonated a landmine on the boundary of Sentinel Ranch with the Maramani TTL. There were no injuries.

Also, during the late afternoon of 12 March, a Black Cat removal van was robbed by a group of terrorists on the main Bulawayo–Beitbridge road. Owing to the lateness of the report, no follow-up action was taken.

Again, during the night of 12 March, my old friend Les Mitchell's homestead on Lesanth Ranch came under terrorist attack once again. The homestead complex, which sustained slight damage, was subjected to mortar and small-arms fire. The terrorists were repelled by Mitchell and his farm security. There were no casualties. Elements of 1 Indep Company conducted the follow-up at first light the following morning.

On 13 March, the bodies of three African males were located by elements of 1 Indep Company in a terrorist base in the Mtetengwe TTL. All three had been savagely beaten to death during the past day or so; all were thought to be employed on Section 1, Liebigs Ranch.

On 14 March, the body of an African male was located in the Mtetengwe TTL, the cause of death appearing to be a gunshot wound to the chest. It was estimated that he had been dead for two months. The body was dressed in two sets of clothing, indicating that, in all probability, he was a terrorist. Dressing in two completely different sets of clothing was standard operating procedure among the terrorists and was done in an attempt to fool the security forces. The reasoning was that they could remove a green set of clothing and reappear in khaki or denim and thus fool the enemy into believing they were after the wrong people. This never happened in reality, of course.

Also on 14 March, elements of Guard Force located a wooden box mine on a road in the Diti TTL and the army engineers were called in. Because of the poor condition of the mine, the engineers destroyed it *in situ*.

On 15 March, Max Stockhill of Liebigs Ranch was ambushed by an unknown number of terrorists on Jopempi Block. One round struck his vehicle but Stockhill and his escorts were unharmed. Elements of 1 Indep Company conducted the follow-up.

Also on 15 March, elements of Internal Affairs operating in the Mtetengwe TTL were ambushed by approximately twenty terrorists. Intaf returned fire, sustaining no casualties. On this occasion, scores of expended cartridge cases were recovered from the scene, with ballistic results showing that eleven AK-47 assault rifles and four SKS rifles were used during the attack.

Again, on 15 March, an empty Oxyco gas tanker travelling south on the main Bulawayo–Beitbridge road was ambushed by an unknown number of terrorists. The tanker was hit five times but the driver managed to drive through the killing zone and escape unharmed.

On 16 March, elements of an Internal Affairs convoy detonated a landmine in the Diti TTL, resulting in two minor casualties who were casevaced by road to Beitbridge for treatment.

On 17 March, a PRAW pilot located two *povo* bases in the Mtetengwe TTL. Both appeared to be occupied at the time. Again the artillery went into action with their trusty 25-pounders firing on both camps. After the shelling, the PRAW pilot once again overflew the targets but observed no movement. Elements of 1 Indep Company were deployed to investigate.

Also, during the evening of 17 March, terrorists blew up two of Les Mitchell's water pumps on Lesanth Ranch. Local farm security conducted the follow-up.

On 19 March, Liebigs security were patrolling the Mavimba Section and, while arresting a local who had in his possession a stick grenade, came under attack from the surrounding bush. Fire was returned and the terrorists decamped. The security stick conducted the follow-up but failed to make contact again.

On 20 March, elements of 1 Indep Company made contact with three terrorists on Joko Ranch. Two terrorists were seen to be wounded, with one being assessed as serious from the amount of blood found. The blood spoor was

The wedding of Alice Cook and John Bryan at Beitbridge in mid-1977. Alice, Bruce's daughter, ran the police communication centre before resigning to get married. Others in the photo are from left: Don Munroe, the Liebigs Ranch Mazunga Section HQ manager, District Commissioner's wife Phyllis Watson obscuring her husband Lew, Mrs Roth and my neighbour Monty van Vuuren of the Parker Hale .30/06 rifle saga.

Another wedding shot of Alice and John. In the foreground is Tom Crawford, the Liebigs Ranch Shobi Section manager and ex-member of the BSAP. Mimi Cawood is at the back (with spectacles) with her sister Norma on her left. Mimi took over the communication centre from Alice and played an anchor role at the station where she stayed until after the end of the 1979 ceasefire.

Cleaning up at the Beitbridge foot and mouth quarantine camp after the Shu Shine bus was commandeered for the round trip to Tshiturapadzi in early 1977. We had dressed as locals in an attempt to lure the terrorists into contact. I am smiling on the left, with Bruce Cook directly behind me.

Another shot of the clean-up. Piet van der Merwe of River Ranch is washing his hands in the centre.

Pete Burgoyne's bachelor party in the Bulawayo SB mess, 1978. Standing are Ken Bird and Hamish Scott-Barnes; in front Les Milne, Pete Burgoyne and Willie van der Merwe.

Major Don Price BCR.

Captain André van Rooyen, the SADF Liaison Officer and his wife Carmen on their wedding day in November 1979. Gail White and Brian Perkins look on.

'Les Girls' – Patsy Smith, Sharron Bailey and Gail White – prepare to strut their stuff at the Beitbridge Club, late 1979. Due to the town's isolation the local community had to band together to provide their own entertainment.

Above left: 'Beauty and the Beast' – Sharron Bailey briefs Keith Lowe of the BSAP on his duties as a bunny boy at the Beitbridge Club, late 1979.

Above right: Patsy posing on my 3.5 Chevrolet, November 1979. This was an ex-SAP vehicle that had been issued to Lieutenant Johan Taute of the Security Branch and which I purchased at an SAP auction held at the Messina police station in 1977 after it had been boarded. The auctioneer was under strict instruction to ensure that I purchased the car for precisely R100. To this end all the tyres were deflated, the spare tyre and battery were removed and tatty electrical wiring placed strategically in the engine and dashboard. After the auction the tyres were inflated, the battery and spare wheel replaced and the wiring removed and I drove happily out of the Messina police station.

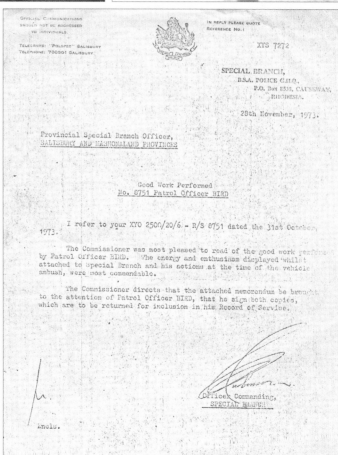

Notification that the BSAP Commissioner had instructed that a 'Note of Good Work' be brought to my attention. This was awarded for my work while attached to Special Branch in 1972–73 and for my actions during the vehicle ambush of 1973.

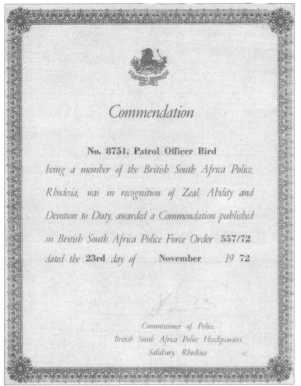

The Commissioner's Commendation (Bronze Baton) was awarded for leading a successful rescue operation to save the lives of four African children who were stranded on a fast-disappearing island in the middle of the flooded crocodile-infested Lundi River. Patrol Officer Jim Higham and Constable Gwala were also awarded the Bronze Baton for their brave efforts in the rescue, undertaken in 1972 when I was stationed at Chibi.

The Commissioner's Special Commendation (Silver Baton) was awarded to me during September 1977 in recognition of actions against the enemy in the Beitbridge area.

BSAP Gwanda District OC, Officers in Charge and Members in Charge, December 1979. Standing from left: Ed Bird, P.J. Cloete, G.J. Oberholzer, C.T. Crage, R.A. Munro, P. Frankleyne; seated: R.G. Francis, T.A. Deacon, D.W. Kerr, H.G. Marshall, D.C. Waddon, D.C. Blake, Brian Perkins.

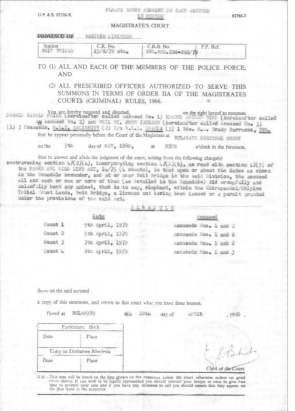

The court summons for Don Price, Neill Jackson and me to appear in the Bulawayo Regional Court on 5 May 1980. Detective Chief Superintendent Dave Blacker was really going for the jugular by splitting the charges against the three of us.

The Limpopo River in full flood, looking south and upstream from the Limpopo Gorge and Beitbridge, late 1976.

The Beitbridge PATU stick at the Tshiturapadzi police base, 1977. Standing from left: the late Tom Crawford, stick leader Doug Dugmore, Eddie King and Herman Neimeyer; Aleck Croik is sitting. *Photo Ian Perkins*

Steve Acornley guides a typical SB vehicle patrol across a swollen stream in the Gwanda TTL sometime during 1978. Due to the shortage of troops, we were forced to operate without escorts in the operational areas.

Fire Force Delta positioned at Mazunga airfield, October 1978. The four helicopters are identified from left as Stop 1, Stop 2, Stop 3 and, next to the armoured Crocodile troop-carriers at the back, the command K-Car with the 20mm Matra cannon. In the foreground is the air force Lynx strike aircraft armed underwing with 250-pound frantan bombs and SNEB rocket pods, with the machine guns mounted centrally on top of the wing. *Photo Theo Nel*

Elephant hunting —judgment today

Chronicle Reporter

JUDGMENT is expected today in a case in which three members of the security forces are appearing at the Regional Court, Bulawayo, on charges of hunting elephant in the Beitbridge area without hunting permits.

Maj. Donald Harold Price, D/S/O Edmund Arther Bird, a member of the CID, and Capt. Neil St. John Jackson, have pleaded not guilty.

They are alleged to have hunted four elephant in the Chiturapadzi-Chipisa TTL on April 5, 7 and 8.

At yesterday's hearing, Jackson claimed that authority to hunt the elephant had been given by the district commissioner of Beitbridge, Mr. Lewis Watson, and he thought that the verbal authority was sufficient.

He said he had also been asked by the assistant district commissioner at the time, a Mr. Hancock, to shoot an elephant for him if Price was unable to do so.

He admitted shooting an elephant and said he thought Mr. Hancock's request was his authority to hunt.

Sensationalized coverage of the fourth day of the trial as reported in the *Bulawayo Chronicle*.

Prospecting in the Gwanda area, May 1980.

The final outcome of the trial as reported in the *Bulawayo Chronicle*. Blacker must have fumed when he had to report the not-guilty verdict to the Commissioner of Police.

Court finds SF elephant hunters not guilty

Chronicle Reporter

THREE members of the security forces were yesterday found not guilty at the Regional Court, Bulawayo, of hunting elephant without permits.

Maj. Donald Harold Price, D/S/O Edmund Arthur Bird, a member of the CID, and Capt. Neil St. John Jackson, had pleaded not guilty to hunting four elephant without permits in the Chiturapadzi-Chipisa TTL, Beitbridge, on April 5, 7 and 8.

The magistrate, Mr. J. H. Wallace, in judgment said neither uniform nor correct procedure was carried out by the District Commissioner at Beitbridge, Mr. Lewis Watson.

He said the men were open in what they did and it was common knowledge in Beitbridge that they were going to hunt elephant. They were acting with the authority of the District Commissioner.

Price and Bird were experienced hunters, but they had previously hunted with verbal authority, although the Wild Life Act stipulated that a written permit had to be obtained.

Mr. Wallace said he accepted their reasons for hunting without first getting written permits.

Adv. Chris Jordaan, instructed by Mr. L. Konson, appeared for Price and Bird and Mr. M. McGoey defended Jackson.

Construction of the 30-ton leaching tanks at the Emerald Isle Mine in Gwanda, June 1980.

Assisting in the filling of the leaching tanks on the Emerald Isle, June 1980.

Emerald Isle, June 1980.

The first 'button' of gold recovered from the Emerald Isle, July 1980. The button weighed seventeen ounces. After refining by the Bullion Department, ten ounces of 99.9% of pure gold was realized – not bad for a beginner. The price of gold at that time was US$650 per fine ounce, a fortune in those days.

Patsy, Diane and Tracey, Durban, October 2011.

The Bird family – Ed, Diane Tracey and Patsy – October 2011.

followed for approximately five minutes when an explosion was heard to the patrol's front; it was assessed that one of the wounded terrorists had committed suicide. However, keeping to the spoor, the patrol continued until it got dark before going into a defensive ambush position. At approximately nine o'clock that evening, an estimated seven terrorists walked into the ambush and were fired on. The following morning, one dead terrorist was found, together with his AK-47 assault rifle and other items of war matériel. 1 Indep Company sustained no injuries. It was never determined if the wounded terrorist had committed suicide or not.

Also on 20 March, Max Stockhill of Liebigs Ranch was again ambushed by terrorists but this time on Mavimba Ranch. The vehicle was not hit and Stockhill and the other occupants of the vehicle were uninjured. Liebigs security conducted follow-up operations but without success.

On 21 March, elements of Internal Affairs travelling in convoy in the Mtetengwe TTL detonated a landmine, resulting in minor injuries being sustained by one of the members who was casevaced by road to Beitbridge for treatment.

On 22 March, a Veterinary Department convoy was ambushed by three terrorists in the Siyoka TTL. The convoy was not hit and no injuries were sustained. Elements of 1 Indep Company reacted.

Also on 22 March, a Selection Cartage haulage vehicle was stopped by three terrorists on the main Bulawayo–Beitbridge road. The terrorists forced the driver to drive the vehicle into the bush where they destroyed it by fire. The driver was released unharmed.

Again, on 22 March, elements of Guard Force, supported by the local militia – now known as the Venda Militia and still armed with their trusty bolt-action .303 Lee Enfield rifles – attacked a *povo* base in the Chipise TTL. The base was occupied by an estimated twenty terrorists who met the attack with mortar, RPG-7 rocket and automatic fire. The attacking force managed to capture the base after forcing the terrorists to flee. They did, however, apprehend a mixed bag of thirty-four local *povo* and over five hundred head of cattle stolen from the locals living in the Chaswingo and Tshiturapadzi protected villages, which were duly returned to their rightful owners. An excellent job executed by poorly trained men. The Venda Militia fell under the control of Internal Affairs and, for command purposes, the District Commissioner and his staff at Beitbridge. They assisted mainly in the guarding of the protected villages, in conjunction with Guard Force, in the Beitbridge area.

On 23 March, a 1 Indep Company convoy travelling in the Mtetengwe TTL was ambushed by approximately thirty terrorists. Once fire was returned, the terrorists broke off the engagement and made off into the bush. Spoor was then followed for over five kilometres before being lost. One security force member was slightly injured during the ambush and was subsequently casevaced to Beitbridge for treatment.

On 24 March, a local travelling by vehicle on River Ranch was ambushed by an estimated fifteen terrorists. The ambush was ineffectual and the driver and occupants of the vehicle escaped unscathed, with the terrorists missing their target completely. Scouter Uniform reacted to the attack and during the follow-up, sighted two terrorists whom they then engaged, killing one of them. One SKS Chicom rifle and various other items of war matériel were recovered from the contact scene.

Also on 24 March, elements of Liebigs security made contact with an unknown number of terrorists on Section 1, Liebigs Ranch. In the initial contact one terrorist was killed and an AK-47 assault rifle and two SKS rifles were recovered. Blood spoor was located and followed for some distance before being lost.

Again, on 24 March, a local travelling by vehicle on Lesanth Ranch detonated a landmine which killed the driver and badly injured two female passengers who were casevaced by road to Beitbridge for treatment. When the reaction force arrived and on checking the road, a further landmine was located and recovered one hundred and fifty paces from the one that had detonated.

Yet again, on 24 March, elements of Guard Force in convoy were ambushed by terrorists in the Chipise TTL. Fire was returned, forcing the terrorists to break off the engagement. The convoy escaped unscathed.

During the early hours of 25 March, a battery of artillery opened fire with their 25-pounders on three known *povo* bases situated in the Bubye farming area. Elements of 1 Indep Company conducted sweeps of all three bases and found them deserted, although, from signs detected in the camps they had not been vacated for very long.

Also on 25 March, elements of B Company 2RR made contact with a group of terrorists in the Chipise TTL, killing one and recovering an AK-47 assault rifle. One D Company member was slightly wounded and casevaced to Tshiturapadzi.

Again, on 25 March, a terrorist attempted to obtain treatment for gunshot wounds at the Penemene protected village in the Mtetengwe TTL. Guard Force immediately apprehended him. Under interrogation, the terrorist confirmed that he had been involved in the contact on Section 1, Liebigs Ranch the previous day where he had received his wounds. He also confirmed that he had discarded his SKS rifle after being shot. This information was passed onto Liebigs security with the congratulations they deserved.

of the Northern Transvaal. He owned and piloted a light aircraft and on the rare occasion he visited his Sentinel Ranch property, he always arrived by aircraft. He would also meet Soda in Beitbridge to sort out problems on the ranch. He had no loyalty to Rhodesia. Across Rhodesia a small minority of white farmers was strongly suspected of paying the terrorists protection in the form of food, clothing and medicine and permitting them to base on their farms without reporting their presence to the authorities, in return for not being attacked or molested in any way. Bristow fell into this category. In addition to supplying large quantities of rations from South Africa, he had Soda purchase large quantities in Beitbridge, far in excess of normal requirements. Although Bristow's name was never mentioned in any captured document, it was obvious that he was financing this appeasement programme, as Soda would never have been in a position to bankroll the operation. Soda also had the use of a ranch pick-up truck to travel around the area. Locally, he was well known to the permanent authorities but was never questioned.

Through captured documents, I was able to follow Soda's exploits over a period of three or four months. On a visit to Beitbridge by the District Special Branch Officer, I expressed my concern and recommended that Soda be permanently removed from society, in other words assassinated. The DSBO listened to me but refused to sanction my recommendation.

One day, I happened to be involved in the interrogation of a terrorist who had surrendered to Scouter Zulu in early May. He was extremely cooperative so it was a more of a question-and-answer interview. He had been operating in the Mtetengwe and Diti TTLs for some time and was a font of knowledge. I mentioned the name Johannes Soda; his response was that Soda was *the* most important enemy collaborator in the whole of the sector. He had actually met Soda once when his terrorist group had unloaded supplies off the back of Soda's vehicle in the Bubye River area. More disturbing was his revelation that the terrorist leaders were receiving large amounts of cash from Soda. However, we were unable to corroborate this allegation.

This was all without any prompting from me: as the interrogated terrorist had voluntarily surrendered, there was no doubt in my mind that Soda was a collaborator of the first order. I also suspect that Bristow was more involved in treasonable acts by assisting the terrorist cause than we will ever know. However, the extent of his involvement was taken to his grave when he was killed in a light aircraft crash during the early 1980s.

Bristow lived in another country, with no allegiance to Rhodesia, but someone had to 'pay the piper': that person would be Soda. On the DSBO's next visit to Beitbridge I informed him of developments and apprised him of the latest facts regarding Johannes Soda's involvement with the enemy. This time the DSBO sanctioned his assassination. I took full responsibility for undertaking the unsavoury task and the DSBO never broached the subject again.

My first task in the planning stage was to obtain a terrorist weapon that had not been captured and subjected to ballistic examination, as was standard procedure when weapons were captured or recovered. There were plenty of these weapons available but were of no use to me as they were all on the ballistic record. I then contacted Mr Mac who was still in Bindura and, without giving too much away, asked for a terrorist weapon that was not traceable, preferably one that had been captured during external operations in Mozambique or Zambia. Mac agreed to assist and to this end, my old friend George Mitchell dropped off an SKS rifle on his way through to South Africa shortly thereafter.

The terrorists did not normally use SKS rifles when carrying out executions of so-called sellouts. Without exception, the AK-47 assault rifle was used. However, all that concerned me was that the weapon was untraceable as I would be destroying it anyway after I had carried out the assassination. I would also take the precaution of carrying my RPD machine gun on the mission to avoid having to use the SKS in any possible action either before or after the killing

I now needed some back-up as the terrorists were very active in the neighbouring Dendele TTL, as well as on Sentinel Ranch for that matter. I intended using two of my most trustworthy turned terrorists but felt I needed something more substantial in the event of bumping into a terrorist group. Over a few beers one evening, I put my dilemma to Don Price who immediately volunteered to accompany me, adding that he would bring along two of his most trusted troops.

I then made arrangements with Johan Taute of the SAP Security Branch to transport my team to a secure area over the Limpopo opposite the Dendele TTL which borders Sentinel Ranch to the east.

During the evening of 11 June, we crossed the South African border where Johan Taute and Dirk Venter were waiting for us. I left my Land Rover at the border. The team – Don Price, his two troops, my two turned terrorists and me – were then transported by Johan and Dirk almost to a point where the South African, Rhodesian and Botswan borders meet, some considerable distance from our target. Dirk and Johan were under the impression that our target was in the Dendele TTL. Once we arrived at our start point, we changed into terrorist clothing, the whites among us blackening any exposed skin and crossed the dry Limpopo riverbed into the Dendele TTL. Once across, we anti-tracked for some time before heading east. After walking for some hours, we reached the target:

the homestead of the Sentinel Ranch manager Johannes Soda.

It was around midnight, so without any dilly-dallying I sent the two turned terrorists to call Soda out from the house under the pretext that an important terrorist commander wanted to meet him. We positioned ourselves about thirty metres from the house which we kept under observation the whole time. With a full moon it was virtually daylight.

The two turned terrorists duly returned with Soda in tow and sat him down under a pre-selected tree. Not wanting to delay the inevitable, I approached Soda and without a word fired several rounds into his chest, killing him instantly.

We then left in the direction of the Dendele TTL, using anti-tracking methods for some time before crossing the Limpopo River again and meeting up with Dirk and Johan. After cleaning up and changing into normal clothes, we were transported back to Beitbridge. We collected the Land Rover and were back in Rhodesia by seven o'clock that morning. The incident had obviously just been reported as a police patrol was being mobilized to attend the scene.

The first priority was the destruction of the SKS rifle. I achieved this by detonating a hand grenade under the breechblock, rendering the weapon useless.

Johannes Soda's wife applied for financial assistance from the state-sponsored Terrorist Victims' Relief Fund and was awarded a monthly stipend.

•••

On 12 June, elements of 1 Indep Company patrolling the Maramani TTL discovered the shallow grave of a terrorist estimated to have been killed two months prior.

Also on 12 June, elements of a 2RR company made contact with six terrorists in the Machuchuta TTL. Three terrorists were killed in the engagement and two AK-47 assault rifles, an SKS rifle and a quantity of war matériel were recovered. There were no security force casualties.

Again, on 12 June, elements of a 2RR company manning an OP in the Machuchuta TTL observed thirty terrorists moving into an ambush position. Elements of the OP engaged the terrorists, causing them to flee. There were no casualties on either side.

Yet again, on 12 June, elements of a 2RR company operating in the Machuchuta TTL made contact with eight terrorists. There were no casualties either side.

Once more, on 12 June, terrorists destroyed a water pump engine on Jopempi Block, Liebigs Ranch.

On 14 June, two of Les Mitchell's labourers were abducted by forty terrorists on Lesanth Ranch. The two managed to escape. Elements of 1 Indep Company reacted and followed spoor in an easterly direction until tracks were lost in rocky terrain.

On 15 June, an Internal Affairs vehicle detonated a landmine in the Mtetengwe TTL. There were no casualties.

On 18 June, an Internal Affairs vehicle detonated a landmine in the Diti TTL. There were no casualties. Army engineers who were travelling in the convoy conducted a sweep of the road and detected a wooden box mine which they successfully lifted.

On 21 June, elements of 1 Indep Company made contact with three terrorists in the Siyoka TTL. During follow-up operations, a group of six terrorists was sighted and fired upon. There were no casualties in either of the engagements.

During the night of 22, a southbound train detonated an explosive device on the line in the Mtetengwe TTL. The two diesel locomotives and ten wagons derailed. One hundred and fifty metres of track were destroyed. Elements of 1 Indep Company reacted at first light. Any casualties are not recorded in the Incident log.

On 24 June, the good old Shu Shine bus was stopped on the main Bulawayo–Beitbridge road and the driver, conductor and passengers were relieved of their valuables. After carrying out their well-oiled drill, the terrorists permitted the bus and passengers to go on their way.

On 25 June, elements of Guard Force surprised five terrorists preparing to bury a landmine in a road in the Mtetengwe TTL. The terrorists were fired on but managed to escape with their mine. There were no casualties on either side.

Also on 25 June, elements of 1 Indep Company operating on Kayansee Ranch on the Bubye River made contact with six terrorists at long range. The terrorists fled but during follow-up operations one SKS rifle was recovered. No casualties were incurred by the patrol.

Again, on 25 June, elements of 1 Indep Company had a long-range contact with two terrorists on Kyalami Ranch on the Bubye River. The terrorists fled. During the follow-up, an African man who failed to halt when challenged was shot and killed. The ranch had been abandoned so no one should have been there.

• • •

The 26th of June turned out to be another life-changing day. Maya was going to the UK on six weeks' leave to visit her family. She had organized a lift to

Salisbury, departing with the seven o'clock convoy. About half an hour prior to the convoy departure, her lift collected her at our house in Beitbridge and, after helping her with her luggage, I kissed her goodbye, waving her off as the car went down the driveway. I did not know it at the time but I was never to see her again: she never returned to Rhodesia or Zimbabwe–Rhodesia as it was then known. When I did eventually hear from her, she made it clear that she was not prepared to return to Beitbridge and suggested that I travel to the UK to discuss our situation. I never did and we divorced a year later. To this day, when my mind wanders back to 'those days' I think of Maya with fondness and wonder how she is getting on. I understand why she left but maybe, someday, by chance, she will read this book and understand the pressure I was under during our time at Beitbridge, because we never really discussed my work.

•••

On the same day, 26 June, a *povo* base in the Mtengwe TTL was attacked by the Rhodesian Air Force, including Hawker Hunters ground-attack aircraft. This was a massive base covering a large area, with fourteen well-camouflaged and -constructed defensive bunkers. Elements of 1 Indep Company conducted the follow-up and recovered the body of one dead terrorist, as well as the remains of eight locals. One SKS rifle was recovered. There were no security force casualties.

Also on 26 June, Scouter Zulu located a TMH-57 landmine in the Siyoka TTL. Elements of army engineers were called in and successfully lifted the mine.

Again, on 26 June, elements of 1 Indep Company contacted twenty-five terrorists in the Masera TTL. The terrorists broke and ran and the 1 Indep patrol was unable to locate spoor. There were no casualties on either side. However, during follow-up operations, the patrol bumped into another nine terrorists. On this occasion, blood spoor of a wounded terrorist was located but after a short follow-up, this spoor was also lost.

On 27 June, no names no pack drill, the jolly old Shu Shine bus was stopped by an estimated thirty-five terrorists on the main Bulawayo–Beitbridge road. However, on this occasion, the terrorists were surprised by the morning convoy and fled into the Mtengwe TTL. 1 Indep Company reacted and followed spoor for some distance before losing it.

Also on 27 June, elements of 1 Indep Company located a buried TM-57 landmine on a road in the Mtengwe TTL. Army engineers attended and decided to destroy the mine *in situ*.

On 29 June, elements of 1 Indep Company contacted three terrorists in the

Masera TTL, killing one of them and recovering an SKS rifle. There were no security force casualties.

Also on 29 June, an Internal Affairs vehicle detonated a landmine in the Machuchuta TTL. There were no casualties.

Again, on 29 June, elements of 1 Company in the Diti TTL located a box mine boosted with two slabs of TNT. Assessed as unsafe, it was destroyed *in situ*.

CHAPTER ELEVEN
Sweet Banana and a Q bus
July–November 1979

On 1 July, elements of Scouter Yankee operating in the Masera TTL made contact with an estimated eight terrorists. One terrorist was killed and an AK Lancer – adapted to fire rifle grenades – was recovered, with other war matériel.

On 2 July, elements of Guard Force fired on a suspected terrorist moving near the railway line in the Mtetengwe TTL. The suspect fled and on following up, the Guard Force located one stick grenade.

On 3 July, elements of 1 Indep Company were following tracks of an estimated fourteen terrorists in the Mtetengwe TTL when they heard talking ahead of them. Don Price decided that as an armed air force Lynx aircraft was available, he would put in an airstrike on the terrorist position. The Lynx duly attacked with two frantan bombs, while an armed helicopter and an armed PRAW aircraft orbited the target. After the air force pilot had completed his strikes, the ground troops moved into the *povo* base covering an area of approximately four square kilometres. The bodies of eleven locals killed during the airstrike were recovered and plenty of blood spoor located. It was estimated that six terrorists had been wounded but an intensive air search detected no signs of life. There were no security force casualties.

On 9 July, elements of Guard Force located and recovered a TM-57 landmine on Lesanth Ranch. Another TM-57 landmine was then located and recovered by the same patrol in the Bubye River farming area.

On 12 July, a vehicle in an Internal Affairs convoy detonated a landmine in the Maramani TTL. There were no casualties.

Also on 12 July, Scouter Uniform attacked a terrorist base camp in the Masera TTL, occupied by six terrorists at the time. One terrorist was killed and blood spoor indicated that two others had been wounded. Three SKS rifles and a quantity of war matériel were recovered. There were no security force casualties.

Again, on 12 July, elements of Guard Force attacked an estimated ten terrorists in the Diti TTL. One terrorist was killed. Two Guard Force members were wounded, one seriously and who was casevaced by air to Bulawayo for treatment. One SKS rifle was recovered.

During the night of 17 July, a group of ten terrorists abducted seven locals from the compound on Safari Ranch near the Mtetengwe TTL.

On 18 July, a Scouter Uniform vehicle detonated a landmine in the Masera TTL. There were no injuries.

Also on 18 July, Scouter Yankee, operating on Lesanth Ranch, made contact with an unknown number of terrorists. The action resulted in two terrorists being killed and one wounded who was taken prisoner; however, he died of his wounds shortly thereafter. One AKM and two SKS rifles were recovered.

On 21 July, an Internal Affairs vehicle detonated a landmine in the Diti TTL. On this occasion, there were several minor injuries necessitating casevac to Beitbridge for treatment.

On 22 July, elements of 1 Indep Company operating in the Siyoka TTL were attacked by terrorist mortar and rocket fire while checking out a terrorist base. The patrol suffered no casualties.

On 24 July, a battery of 25-pounders fired six shells into a known *povo* base. There was no follow-up owing to lack of troops, so the results of the bombardment are unknown.

Also on 24 July, a police convoy operating in the Machuchuta TTL came under ambush attack when one of the vehicles in the convoy detonated a landmine. The patrol returned fire and the terrorists broke off the engagement. There were no police casualties.

Again, on 24 July, army engineers located and recovered two landmines, a TMA-3 and a TM-57, in the Diti TTL.

On 27 July, a Liebigs civilian mine-protected Land Rover detonated a landmine on the Shobi Section. Fortunately, this was a front-wheel detonation as there were passengers in the unprotected back of the vehicle. Four slightly injured were casevaced to Beitbridge for treatment.

Also on 27 July, elements of the artillery opened fire with rifles on an unknown number of terrorists preparing to attack their position on the old Beitbridge airfield. The terrorists returned fire as they fled. The artillery had positioned their 25-pounders on the old airfield from where they could protect Beitbridge and deploy into the area as required. Not to be outdone, they fired one 25-pound shell in the direction of the fleeing terrorists.

On 28 July, elements of Guard Force located a landmine in the Diti TTL. Engineers, finding the box mine to be unstable, destroyed it *in situ*.

On 31 July, elements of the engineers clearing a road in the Mtetengwe TTL located a box mine and, on checking, found that it had been boosted with an 82mm mortar bomb. Deciding that the device was unstable, they destroyed the mine and bomb *in situ*. The terrorists had given away the presence of the mine by pegging two sticks on either side of the road.

Also on 31 July, an artillery vehicle detonated a landmine in the Mtetengwe TTL, with no casualties sustained.

Again, on 31 July, in the Diti TTL, an air force Lynx aircraft bombed a terrorist position discovered by elements of Guard Force, who had observed an estimated thirteen terrorists in the position. When the camp was later checked nothing was found.

On 1 August, elements of Guard Force patrolling the railway line in the Mtetengwe TTL observed a group of terrorists digging under the tracks. The Guard Force then opened fire with rifles and a 60mm mortar and the saboteurs fled. The patrol was unable to locate spoor because of the rocky terrain.

On 2 August, elements of 1 Indep Company made contact with an estimated thirty terrorists in the Siyoka TTL. There were no casualties on either side.

Also on 2 August, elements of D Company 2RR made contact with two terrorists in the Siyoka TTL. The pair fled. Follow-up operations resulted in one of the terrorists being sighted and again fired upon. However, it was his lucky day as he once more managed to escape injury. There were no D Company casualties.

Again, on 2 August, elements of B Company 2RR made contact with approximately twelve terrorists in the Siyoka TTL. There were no casualties to either side but an SKS rifle, a rifle grenade and documents were recovered.

Yet again, on 2 August, elements of D Company 2RR operating in the Siyoka TTL were fired on by one terrorist. The reason is not given in the Incident log but no fire was returned. There were no D Company casualties.

O 3 August, elements of D Company 2RR opened fire on an estimated fifteen terrorists in the Siyoka TTL. There were no casualties on either side. An SKS rifle was recovered.

On 10 August, a northbound train detonated an explosive on the line in the Mtetengwe TTL. Both diesel locomotives and twelve wagons were derailed. There were no casualties. Later that night, a railway trolley reacting to the derailment struck a large boulder placed on the tracks in the area of Chapfuche Siding and derailed. The trolley was quickly placed back on the rails and continued to the site of the train derailment. Fortunately, no railway men were injured. The damaged one hundred and fifty metres of track were soon replaced, with the line fully operational by first light. Engineers who attended the scene determined that an electrically-detonated metallic mine boosted with ammonium nitrate fertilizer had been used.

On 12 August, my old friend Les Mitchell accepted the surrender of a terrorist on Lesanth Ranch. Mitchell was presented with an AK-47 assault rifle, chest webbing, three fully charged magazines and two stick grenades.

Also on 12 August, a Liebigs mine-protected Land Rover detonated a landmine on Mavimba Section of the ranch. The mine had been boosted with an 82mm mortar bomb. The driver and passengers sitting in the cab were uninjured. There were no passengers sitting in the back.

Again, on 12 August, just after ten o'clock that night, the Chaswingo protected village in the Diti TTL came under attack from a large group of terrorists. The attack was repelled by the Guard Force defenders and the terrorists abandoned their positions. At first light, elements of 1 Indep Company commenced follow-up operations but failed to make much ground before losing the spoor. However, the shock was still to come when police ballistic reports confirmed that two 75mm recoilless rifles and one DShK 12.7mm heavy machine gun had been used in the attack. The DShK 12.7mm HMG is a fearful weapon often used in an anti-aircraft role; in the right hands it can be deadly against helicopters. Apart from these formidable weapons, forty-five AK-47 assault rifles, twenty-five SKS rifles, one RPD machine gun, one RPK heavy-barrelled AK-47 and one Goryunov MMG were identified as having been used during the attack.

On 14 August, thirty-one head of cattle were stolen on Jopempi Block, Liebigs Ranch and driven toward the Mtetengwe TTL. Elements of Liebigs security conducted a follow-up and located and arrested five African men busy slaughtering five head of the stolen cattle near the border fence with the Mtetengwe TTL.

On 15 August, elements of Guard Force located a landmine in the Diti TTL. Engineers were deployed and recovered a TM-57 landmine.

Also on 15 August, a Guard Force patrol operating in the area of Chaswingo protected village in the Diti TTL located the body of a terrorist thought to have been killed during the attack on the PV of 12 August. No weapon was recovered.

On 21 August, elements of 1 Indep Company located the spoor of a lone terrorist in the Diti TTL. Tracks were followed for some distance before the terrorist was sighted and killed when the patrol opened fire on him. One SKS rifle was recovered.

Also on 21 August, elements of C Company 2RR sighted fifteen terrorists in the Diti TTL. Spoor was followed for approximately three kilometres before the patrol entered a large *povo* base. Human movement was detected directly in front of the patrol which immediately opened fire, killing three women who were living in the camp. A search of the complex resulted in the discovery of eight underground bunkers containing a large stash of food and blankets. The bunkers were obviously constructed to counter air and artillery attack. The *povo* base and everything in it was destroyed.

On 22 August, elements of 1 Indep Company operating in the Diti TTL sighted two terrorists, opened fire and killed both of them. Two SKS rifles were recovered. Continuing the patrol, and about two hours later, the same call sign fired on a lone terrorist. The terrorist managed to escape but four locals with him were killed.

Also on 22 August, elements of 1 Indep Company following terrorist spoor in the Diti TTL came across four PRG-2 rockets and two slabs of TNT. After checking around, they realized the reason for the find was that the terrorists knew they were being followed and had split up into two-man groups to confuse their pursuers. The rockets and TNT left lying around was possibly a delaying tactic.

Again, during the evening of 22 August, Guard Force reported heavy automatic fire in the Mtetengwe TTL. Artillery reacted by firing three 25-pound shells into the suspect area. Three illuminating flares were then seen by Guard Force who reported this and so the artillery fired a further three shells into the area. At first light, elements of 1 Indep Company reacted but were unable to find anything of interest.

On 23 August, elements of 1 Indep Company shot and killed four local men in the Diti TTL who refused to surrender when called upon to do so.

Also on 23 August, elements of A Company 2RR patrolling in the Diti TTL located two stick grenades while checking an unoccupied terrorist base.

On 24 August, elements of D Company 2RR travelling by vehicle in the Diti TTL detonated a wooden box mine, resulting in the injury to one soldier who was casevaced by helicopter to Beitbridge for treatment.

Also on 24 August, a D Company 2RR vehicle detonated a landmine in the Chipise TTL. One of the troops was slightly injured and casevaced to Beitbridge for treatment. It was assessed that the mine had been buried for some time.

On 25 August, a Liebigs security mine-protected Land Rover detonated a landmine on the Shobi Block of Liebigs. The vehicle rolled and caught fire, the end result being that four members of the security staff died in the blast or in the subsequent inferno. Those killed were José Riveiro de Pinho, Stephan Sibanda, Boy Dube and Moses Vengani. A wounded survivor was casevaced to Beitbridge for treatment.

Also on 25 August, elements of C Company 2RR made contact with three terrorists in the Chipise TTL, killing two of them and recovering a PPSh sub-machine gun and an SKS rifle. The SKS rifle did not fire the normal 7.62mm intermediate round but the more powerful 7.62mm long round and was later identified as a Soviet-manufactured long-rimmed Karabin obr 1944 carbine, the first to be captured in the sector.

On 26 August, elements of A Company 2RR operating in the Diti TTL located spoor of ten terrorists which they began following. Shortly, human movement was detected and the call sign opened fire, killing one local and capturing two others whom they detained for interrogation.

Also on 26 August, elements of D Company 2RR on the spoor of twenty terrorists in the Diti TTL sighted and opened fire on six terrorists. Two terrorists were killed and a third, who escaped, was wounded. Two SKS rifles were recovered.

Again, on 26 August, elements of D Company 2RR sighted and opened fire on a lone terrorist, killing him and recovering his SKS rifle.

Yet again, on 26 August, elements of Guard Force sighted twenty terrorists with pack donkeys on Lesanth Ranch. Elements of 1 Indep Company reacted but because of heavy rain no spoor was found.

Once more, on 26 August, ten head of cattle were stolen from the Shobi Block, Liebigs Ranch and driven toward the Mtetengwe TTL. Elements of Liebigs security reacted.

On 27 August, a labourer working on Lutope Section of Liebigs Ranch found an AK-47 assault rifle which he handed in. The weapon was in a terrible state and had obviously been abandoned months before.

On 29 August, elements of D Company 2RR operating in the Siyoka fired on and killed three curfew breakers travelling in a scotch cart.

On 30 August, elements of 1 Indep Company made contact with an estimated fifteen terrorists in the Siyoka TTL. By the end of the engagement, four terrorists were dead. From blood spoor located in the terrorists' firing positions, one terrorist had been wounded but had managed to escape. Two AK-47 assault rifles, one SKS rifle and an RPD machine gun were recovered.

Also on 30 August, elements of A Company 2RR were attacked by an estimated six terrorists in the Siyoka TTL. Fire was returned and the terrorists broke off the engagement. There were no casualties on either side.

Again, during the afternoon of 30 August, an Internal Affairs convoy travelling in the Diti TTL was ambushed by a large group of terrorists. The terrorists put down heavy fire, using rockets, rifle grenades and heavy machine guns, as well as the usual small arms. The convoy managed to pass through the killing zone unscathed. However, half an hour's drive from the ambush site one of the Intaf vehicles detonated a landmine. While sorting out the damaged vehicle, the convoy again came under attack by terrorists using 60mm mortars, rockets and small arms. Intaf returned fire and the terrorists broke off the engagement. Elements of 2RR en route to assist with the landmine-damaged vehicle then detonated a landmine at about midnight, several kilometres from the Intaf landmine incident. A further 2RR rescue-and-recovery convoy was deployed and at two o'clock in the morning, one of the convoy vehicles detonated a landmine. No follow-up operation was undertaken and, at first light, the job of extracting the damaged vehicles began. During all these incidents, the security forces suffered only two minor injuries from one of the landmine detonations. Nevertheless, three landmines in so many hours was an impressive enemy tally.

Yet again, on 30 August, elements of D Company 2RR operating in the Siyoka TTL contacted eight terrorists, killing one and recovering an AK-47 assault rifle and items of war matériel.

On 1 September, Corporal Brian Kenneth Tucker, a member of an A Company 2RR patrol operating in the Siyoka TTL, stood on and detonated a wooded box mine while walking down a road. He was killed instantly. Another member of the patrol was slightly injured and casevaced, initially to Beitbridge and then to Bulawayo. It was assessed that the landmine had been buried for some considerable time and had become unstable.

On 3 September, another 'first' occurred in the Beitbridge operational area. While climbing a hill to a previously-used army OP in the Diti TTL, a member of C Company 2RR detonated an anti-personal mine and sustained serious injuries which necessitated his immediate evacuation by helicopter to the Messina hospital. Fortunately, he survived. A second AP mine was later detonated by a cow.

Also on 3 September, elements of C Company 2RR inadvertently followed terrorist spoor into a terrorist camp and were fired on by the terrorists occupying the base. Fire was returned and the terrorists fled. A search of the camp resulted in the recovery of thirteen back packs and various other items of war matériel.

On 4 September, elements of A Company 2RR operating in the Siyoka TTL shot and killed a local who failed to stop when called upon to do so.

Also on 4 September, elements of 1 Indep Company moving into an OP position in the Diti TTL heard an explosion which they assessed as being an AP mine detonation, possibly set off by an animal.

Again, on 4 September, elements of A Company 2RR operating in the Diti TTL followed spoor into a *povo* camp and fired on and killed two locals hiding in thick bush. An hour later and still searching the base, the patrol was attacked by an estimated eight terrorists. Fire was returned and one terrorist was killed. One AK-47 assault rifle and a quantity of war matériel were recovered. Also recovered from the base were large quantities of clothing and food. From the price tags and the unavailability of these particular goods in Rhodesia, it was blatantly apparent that all the goods had been purchased in South Africa. There were only two possibilities as to how the goods had been obtained: the terrorists had sent locals to South Africa to purchase the goods from farm stores, but as Rhodesian currency was not legal tender, the South African rand would have had to have been the currency used; or a South African collaborator was supplying the terrorists with South African goods. My mind went back to the activities of John Bristow and his late farm manager, Johannes Soda, and I cursed them both.

Again, on 4 September, elements of 1 Indep Company operating in the Diti TTL shot and killed six locals who failed to stop when called upon to do so.

On 6 September, a northbound heavy-vehicle convoy was ambushed by an estimated six terrorists on the main Beitbridge–Bulawayo road. Several vehicles were hit, including the Police Reserve escort vehicle. One horsebox was hit three times, wounding the very expensive racehorse inside, which then had to be put down. The horse was returning from South Africa after competing in that country. Elements of 1 Indep Company deployed to follow up.

On 8 September, a different group of terrorists and estimated to be twelve strong, stopped an African-driven civilian vehicle on the same road. The driver and his five passengers were then robbed of all valuables, including their clothes. Before departing the scene, the terrorists set the vehicle alight, completely gutting it. The six occupants left standing in their underpants were unharmed. Owing to lack of troops, the police had to react.

Also on 8 September, elements of Liebigs security conducting stock-theft follow-up operations on Lamulas Section sighted five suspects whom they called on to halt. They refused to stop and were fired on. Three were killed and two escaped.

On 9 September, a heavy vehicle and trailer belonging to Mr K.S. Henry of Gwanda was stopped on the Bulawayo–Beitbridge road. The driver was forced by an estimated twelve terrorists to drive a kilometre into the bush where the vehicle was set on fire and completely gutted. The burning vehicle also caused a huge bushfire. No follow-up was undertaken because of the fire. The driver was unharmed.

On 11 September, a northbound train detonated three explosive devices on the line in the Mtetengwe TTL, resulting in ten wagons being derailed and forty metres of track being destroyed. There were no casualties and 1 Indep Company conducted the follow-up.

Also on 11 September, elements of 1 Indep Company contacted and killed a lone terrorist in the Diti TTL. One PPSh sub-machine gun was recovered.

Again, on 11 September, elements of the Venda Militia escorting locals in

On 29 September, a cargo-carrying vehicle and trailer detonated a wooden box mine on the main Bulawayo–Beitbridge road and overturned, resulting in both lanes of the road being blocked. Army engineers arrived to sweep the road for further mines and reopen the road, while 1 Indep Company undertook the follow-up. Tracks of six terrorists were located by 1 Indep and followed into the Mtetengwe TTL but were lost through anti-tracking tactics used by the terrorists.

Also on 29 September, elements of E Company 1 Guard Force based at the Bubye River near the Lion and Elephant Motel on the Beitbridge–Fort Victoria road came under terrorist attack from the southwestern side of the Bubye River. The terrorists used mortars, rockets and small arms during the attack but broke off the contact when the Guard Force returned fire. At first light, elements of 1 Indep Company conducted the follow-up, during which four 3.5-inch rockets were located and destroyed by army engineers. There were no security force casualties.

On 30 September, elements of Guard Force fired on two terrorists in the Mtetengwe TTL. The terrorists returned fire and managed to escape. Elements of 1 Indep Company reacted but were unable to locate tracks.

•••

Several developments took place during September which were to affect me personally. On the political front, the Lancaster House conference, hosted by the British government, was attended by the Zimbabwe–Rhodesian government headed by Bishop Abel Muzorewa, ZAPU's Joshua Nkomo, ZANU's Robert Mugabe and all their respective military commanders, lawyers and other hangers-on. An agreement was reached which would see the introduction of a ceasefire on 1 January 1980 as a prelude to a general election taking place in March of that year. Everyone knew that this was the end of the road for Rhodesia, but the war would rage on for another three months and many young Rhodesian lives would be needlessly sacrificed.

I had made a concerted effort to pass the written examinations for promotion to detective inspector, which paid off when I passed with ease. The next barrier was an interview before a board of officers who determined a candidate's suitability for promotion. Successful candidates would then be published in order of seniority in Force Orders. Listed sixth in order of seniority, I was advised that my promotion was imminent and that I would be among the first to be promoted. Mike Reeves, the deputy Provincial Special Branch Officer in Matabeleland, mentioned a possible transfer to Victoria Falls and, quite naturally, I was pleased.

However, shortly after this, I was contacted by a good friend of mine from CID Bulawayo who advised me that the CID, under the supervision of Detective Chief Superintendent Dave Blacker, was investigating an elephant-poaching charge against Don Price, Neill Jackson and me. At first I thought it was a joke and my friend had to convince me that he was telling the truth. Blacker was one of the foremost criminal investigators in Rhodesia, so I wondered why the CID, let alone Dave Blacker, was involved in a case which needed no investigation at all. The charge stemmed from the fact that when we had shot the elephant in March – over five months before the investigation started – we had not technically been in possession of a licence: as mentioned, licences were issued on registration of the ivory. I found this quite impossible to believe and when I heard that Commissioner of Police P.K. Allum was taking a personal interest in the case, I was utterly flabbergasted.

The initial outcome was that my promotion was suspended pending the outcome of the trial, although I was never officially informed of this. My CID friend kept me abreast of developments as best he could: apparently, Blacker was trying to justify the charges by claiming that we had endangered the lives of security force personnel when we had embarked on our hunt and that we had also made unofficial use of a PRAW aircraft, but these allegations were never looked into by Blacker or his investigation team. However, there was a more sinister reason for the CID investigation, which I suspected at the time and which was confirmed some years later. It is a pity that both people who confirmed my suspicions have since died but I have no reason to disbelieve them; when I later cover this subject in more detail, I make mention of this fact.

Meanwhile, my good friend and fellow 'criminal' Don Price was advised of his transfer to 3 Commando 1RLI to take over command under somewhat tragic circumstances: he was to replace Major Bruce Snelgar who had been killed in a helicopter crash on 22 September. Not only was Don leaving but his best officers, Lieutenants Alan Balson, Arthur Kegel and Andy Barrett, along with the remarkable Sergeant Theo Nel, had elected to follow him to the RLI. This would be a big blow and 1 Indep Company would never quite be the same again.

In the meantime, the Beitbridge Rural Council, supported by the Beitbridge residents and farming community, had agreed to confer the Freedom of Entry to the Town of Beitbridge on the officer commanding, officers and men of 1 Indep Company. A colourful ceremony took place one Saturday morning; during the official march-past, the company sang *Sweet Banana*, the regimental song of the Rhodesian African Rifles That night, Don, his officers and NCOs were entertained to a formal dance at the Beitbridge Sports Club. It was a very enjoyable day indeed.

I was then advised that I was to be transferred as the member-in-charge of the Special Branch station at Gwanda. This transfer had no appeal for me. I would be regarded by some as an outcast because of my pending poaching case and I would surely see myself as a little red devil holding a trident with a big black cloud over my head.

Apart from 1 Indep's Freedom of the Town, the only other positive aspect to occur in Beitbridge during this period was the arrival, on transfer, of a very pretty customs officer by the name of Patsy Smith.

•••

After Don Price left Beitbridge, I only visited the 1 Indep Company base on one or two occasions and never got to know any of the new arrivals. I now regret this, as they were all good, solid men who kept up the good work and good name of the unit.

On 1 October, elements of Guard Force patrolling the line of rail near Lesanth Siding located an explosive device consisting of twenty kilograms of TNT primed for electrical detonation. Elements of 4 Engineers were deployed, dismantled the device and reopened the line at eleven o'clock that morning.

On 3 October, elements of 1 Indep Company were attacked by an estimated forty terrorists in the Diti TTL. Two 1 Indep Company troops were wounded, one fatally and the other seriously. They were moved by road to the Chaswingo PV airstrip, then by fixed-wing aircraft to Beitbridge and then onto the Messina hospital. On 12 October, Private Robert Pasino of the Rhodesian African Rifles succumbed to his wounds. Pasino was the only member of 1 Indep Company to lose his life to terrorist action in the Beitbridge area.

On 4 October, terrorists again used the conductors on the telephone lines on the main Beitbridge–Bulawayo road as target practice. Post office technicians soon had the line up and running.

On 6 October, a civilian vehicle travelling south on the Bulawayo–Beitbridge road was stopped by thirteen terrorists. Three African men and three women were beaten up by the group who then departed with three boys press-ganged into their ranks. Because of the lateness of the incident, no follow-up action was taken.

Also on 6 October, the Scouter Zulu base and the homestead on Robin Watson's Mikado Ranch came under attack from an estimated forty terrorists.

The attack lasted for over half an hour. The terrorists fired four 75mm recoilless rifle rounds, thirty 82mm mortar bombs, four 3.5-inch rockets, several RPG-7 rockets and over four thousand rounds of AK, RPD and SKS ammunition. Three policemen received minor injuries, necessitating two of them being casevaced to the Gwanda hospital. One building and three vehicles were damaged during the attack. At first light, elements of 1 Indep Company were deployed on follow-up and made contact with six terrorists on the ranch. There were no casualties on either side.

On 7 October, an Internal Affairs vehicle detonated a landmine in the Maramani TTL. There were no casualties.

On 9 October, elements of 1 Indep Company operating in the Siyoka TTL had a long-range contact with three terrorists. There were no casualties.

On 11 October, one hundred and eighty-one head of cattle were stolen from the Shobi Block, Liebigs Ranch, and driven into the Siyoka TTL. Elements of Liebigs security investigated.

On 12 October, elements of D Company 2RR had a fleeting contact with four terrorists in the Siyoka TTL. There were no casualties to either side

Also on 12 October, the Guard Force at the Shabwe protected village in the Mtetengwe TTL reported that they were under attack. At first light, elements of 1 Indep Company deployed on follow-up but could find no evidence of an attack.

On14 October, elements of the Venda Militia located a boosted landmine in the Mtetengwe TTL. Army engineers who attended the scene decided to destroy the landmine *in situ*. On the following day, a cow detonated an anti-personnel mine in the vicinity of the landmine; it was assessed that the AP mine had been laid at the same time.

On 15 October, a further six head of cattle were stolen from the Shobi Block of Liebigs Ranch and herded into the Siyoka TTL. Liebigs security investigated.

During the late evening of 17 October, elements of 1 Indep Company attempted to capture seven locals in the Diti TTL. In spite of repeated calls for them to surrender, they refused to do so and, eventually, the patrol opened fire, killing four.

On 18 October, elements of 1 Indep Company operating in the Diti TTL observed eight terrorists at a distance of one hundred paces, advancing toward their position in an extended-line formation. The 1 Indep patrol opened fire, causing the enemy to flee without firing a shot.

On 19 October, elements of Guard Force operating in the Diti TTL located a buried landmine and called for the army engineers to deal with it. The engineers successfully lifted the mine which they identified as a P2 Mk3.

During the early hours of 20 October, three explosions were heard from the railway line in the Mtetengwe TTL. At first light, elements of Guard Force, army engineers and railway security reacted. The line had been blown in three separate places. The engineers assessed the explosive as being TNT but were unable to determine the mechanism used to detonate the device.

Also on 20 October, a cow detonated a landmine on Mavinga Section, Liebigs Ranch. This incident was only discovered some days later and no follow-up was undertaken.

On 22 October, elements of the Venda Militia located a landmine in the Diti TTL. Engineers reacted and recovered it.

During the early hours of 24 October, the homestead on Shobi was attacked by a group of twenty-five terrorists who fired 3.5-inch and RPG-7 rockets and small arms. The ineffectual attack lasted for approximately fifteen minutes before the terrorists broke off the engagement and returned to the Machuchuta TTL. Elements of 1 Indep Company reacted at first light and followed tracks of eight into the Machuchuta TTL.

On 25 October, elements of the Venda Militia operating in the Diti TTL found a landmine which was lifted by army engineers who identified it as being a P2 Mk3.

On 26 October, a southbound Beitbridge train detonated some sort of explosive device on the line in the Mtetengwe TTL. The train and wagons were unaffected by the detonation and no damage could be found to the tracks, so the line was declared safe four hours later.

Also on 26 October, elements of the Venda Militia operating in the Mtetengwe TTL located a freshly-buried landmine, which was subsequently lifted by engineers who identified it as a P2 Mk3. Elements of 1 Indep Company were deployed and located spoor of fifteen terrorists which they followed for three kilometres before losing it to the enemy's anti-tracking skills.

On 28 October, elements of Internal Affairs travelling by road in the Maramani TTL detonated a landmine, resulting in two passengers receiving minor injuries. Both the injured were casevaced by road to Beitbridge for treatment.

On 29 October, a Coley Hall vehicle detonated a landmine on Shamba Yetu farm. The explosion killed passenger Joseph Sibanda and injured two boys who were casevaced to Beitbridge for treatment.

On 1 November, surrendered terrorists indicated three buried landmines to elements of 1 Indep and police, one in the Mtetengwe TTL and two in the Diti TTL. The mines were either destroyed *in situ* or recovered.

During the night of 2 November, a group of terrorists ambushed a southbound train in the area of Lesanth Siding with RPG-7 rocket and small-arms fire. The guard, Dave Briggs, who was travelling in the same locomotive as the driver, was killed outright and the driver sustained serious wounds. Fortunately, there were other railway men in the locomotive to assist. On arrival at Beitbridge, the driver was rushed across the border to the Messina hospital. David John Peter Briggs, a tall, unassuming, good-natured man, lived in Beitbridge with his wife and small children. I had got to know him rather well as he occasionally frequented the Beitbridge Hotel. His death was felt by most of the Beitbridge community.

On 3 November, elements of Internal Affairs made contact with an estimated twenty terrorists in the Diti TTL. The enemy fired off several mortar bombs which proved ineffective and soon broke off the engagement and fled.

On 4 November, elements of 1 Indep Company operating in the Chipise TTL fired on a lone terrorist who managed to escape under a hail of bullets.

Also on 4 November, elements of 1 Indep Company operating in the Chipise TTL located an occupied *povo* base and, on further investigation, shot and killed three locals who failed to stop. On conducting a search of the base, a large quantity of terrorist ammunition was recovered.

Again, on 4 November, elements of 1 Indep Company contacted two terrorists in the Chipise TTL, killing one and wounding the other, who managed to escape. During the engagement, one local male running with the terrorists was shot and killed. Two AK-47 assault rifles were recovered.

• • •

Yet again, on 4 November, a Shu Shine bus was stopped by thirty terrorists on the main Bulawayo–Beitbridge road and the normal procedure followed: passengers out, line up against the bus, get searched, valuables removed, conductor relieved of ticket-and-money bag, passengers board bus, terrorists wave them goodbye. This routine must have taken place on scores of occasions and I can hear the Special Forces operator, or the aspiring operative, thinking, *Why didn't we exploit the situation and use the Shu Shine bus to our advantage?*

The answer is simple – we did. At the beginning of 1977, a Shu Shine bus, the only bus service licensed to operate in the Beitbridge area, was being harassed by terrorists on the Tshiturapadzi road on a fairly regular basis. So, I commandeered the Shu Shine bus and, with about a dozen suitably attired and blackened-up police regulars and reservists, undertook the trip to Tshiturapadzi and back. After this exercise, I realized that if a large group of terrorists had stopped us, we would have had to fight from inside the bus as there was only one door and an emergency exit at the rear window. Had we attempted to de-bus from these exits we would have been picked off one by one. Fighting from inside the bus would have proved fatal, as the only thing between the passengers and the outside was a thin sheeting of aluminum. This was a once-off exercise for when the terrorists realized what the bus was being used for then it would have been attacked at every opportunity until it was forced to stop running. The owners of the Shu Shine Bus Service would have brought a massive legal action against the government.

The Selous Scouts operated a 'Q bus' – named after the Q boats of the First and Second World Wars which were freighters with concealed guns – and I did a trip with one when Sergeant-Major Pete McNeilage and Colour Sergeant Cecil van den Berg commanded one on a trip from Beitbridge to the Tuli Circle area, and then into the Machuchuta TTL. This bus had been armour-plated throughout, carried mounted machine guns disguised as luggage on the roof and with mounted machine guns covering the emergency exits. This was a fighting vehicle if there ever was.

However, there were a number of flaws. The first obstacle we hit was a security force roadblock. Pete and I had to get out of the bus without our shirts to prove that we were white, as we had blackened our faces and hands so as to be taken for locals. We then approached the troops shouting out that we were Special Branch, before explaining what we were up to. This immediately compromised the whole operation but we carried on regardless. The second stumbling block was the type of bus we were using: our bus had been captured in Mozambique and was one of those fancy, luxury types never seen on dirt roads. The third was that we were travelling on no known bus routes and some of the local kids had never seen a bus in their lives before.

All in all, it was a complete disaster and it was never tried again. The bus would have been ideally suited for the main Bulawayo road but, again, it was easily identifiable and therefore could only have been utilized once against the terrorists. From time to time, Q cars were used on the main Bulawayo road in the area between Beitbridge and the Siyoka TTL. I cannot recall these vehicles having any success.

This was the last occasion that a Shu Shine bus was stopped and robbed by terrorists in the Beitbridge area. The reason for this would soon become abundantly clear as the ZANLA high command changed their strategy. With the ceasefire due to take effect at midnight on 31 December 1979, the terrorists were ordered to maintain as low a profile as possible while the Matabeleland area – stretching as far north as Plumtree on the Botswanan border – could be reinforced with thousands of ZANLA terrorists flooding southern Matabeleland from Mozambique. The reasons were threefold: firstly, it was to intimidate the locals who would witness first-hand the overwhelming numbers of ZANLA occupying their areas, outweighing ZIPRA and the security forces combined; secondly, that on the ceasefire coming into effect, ZANLA could claim complete military dominance of southern Matabeleland; and thirdly, if the Zimbabwe–Rhodesian government reneged on the Lancaster House agreement and decided to attack the assembly points where all the terrorists were expected to assemble, it would not be too difficult for ZANLA to recover their vast arms caches and resume the war in vastly superior numbers, and with the additional benefit of not having to run the gauntlet of infiltrating the country. As well as their beefed-up forces within the country, ZANLA would retain tens of thousands of cadres in Mozambique until after Mugabe had taken over the country. ZANLA was also to leave substantial forces on the ground in the operational detachment areas during the ceasefire to ensure 'cooperation' from the locals: hundreds of acts of intimidation, including murder, were carried out in the Gwanda area alone during the ceasefire. From captured documents recovered in the Sengwe TTL, it was revealed that in excess of eight thousand ZANLA terrorists had entered Matabeleland alone, with tens of thousands saturating the rest of the country. Even after the ceasefire had come into effect, fresh ZANLA troops continued to stream unhindered into the country and it is for this reason that a military coup d'état very nearly took place, which I will expand on later.

•••

On 5 November, elements of 1 Indep Company operating in the Chipise TTL came under mortar attack. The attack was ineffectual and no injuries were sustained.

During the evening of 6 November, thirteen terrorists destroyed a water pump on River Ranch. The following morning, elements of 1 Indep Company and Scouter Uniform reacted. One of the 1 Indep vehicles detonated a landmine, causing injuries to two members. Both were casevaced to Beitbridge where it was decided to casevac the one critically wounded soldier to the Messina hospital.

Also on 5 November, elements of 1 Indep Company operating in the Diti TTL shot and killed a local who failed to stop when ordered to do so.

On 7 November, elements of 1 Indep Company ambushed two terrorists accompanied by four locals on Bubani Ranch in the Bubye River farming area.

One terrorist was wounded and blood spoor was followed until lost in rocky terrain.

On 8 November, elements of 1 Indep Company travelling by road in the Chipise TTL detonated a landmine. There were no injuries.

Also on 8 November, elements of 1 Indep Company operating in the Chipise TTL sighted a lone terrorist collecting water from a small stream and opened fire, but he managed to escape.

On 10 November, elements of 1 Indep Company operating on Bishopstone Estates made contact with six terrorists. The terrorists returned fire and fled. There were no casualties to either side.

On 11 November, elements of 1 Indep Company captured a terrorist armed with a PPSh sub-machine gun on Lesanth Ranch.

Also on 11 November, elements of the Venda Militia operating in the Diti TTL engaged a group of about ten terrorists. During the action, no injuries were sustained by either side.

On 12 November, a fuel-tanker convoy was attacked by an estimated twenty-two terrorists on the main Beitbridge–Bulawayo road. As this was a northbound convoy, all the tankers were full. The terrorists launched their attack with RPG-7 rockets and 60mm mortars, followed by automatic fire. A North Eastern Transport tanker was hit by an RPG-7 rocket and exploded in flames and was completely gutted. Two Coley Hall tankers were damaged by rifle fire but did not ignite and, once through the ambush position, the drivers were able to plug the holes without too much loss of fuel. The driver of a Swift Transport removal vehicle who had joined the convoy was wounded in the leg and was casevaced to the Gwanda hospital. The Fire Force reacted to the attack but arrived too late to be of any use.

Also, during the night of 12 November, a southbound train detonated an explosive device on the railway line in the vicinity of Lesanth Siding. Nine wagons derailed but, fortunately, no one was injured.

On 13 November, Scouter Zulu, operating with elements of 2RR, made contact with two terrorists in the Siyoka TTL. One terrorist and a woman running with the terrorists were killed. An AKM assault rifle was recovered.

On 14 November, Scouter Zulu operating by vehicle on the Jopempi Block of Liebigs Ranch detonated a landmine which was assessed as being a TM-57. There were no casualties to the occupants of the vehicle.

Also, during the evening of 14 November, elements of Scouter Yankee and 1 Indep Company ambushed an estimated seven terrorists on Lesanth Ranch. Two terrorists were killed and, unfortunately, a farm employee was wounded in the crossfire. An AKM assault rifle and an SKS rifle were recovered.

On 15 November, elements of 1 Indep Company sighted an estimated fifteen terrorists accompanied by a group of locals in the Diti TTL. With the assistance of an armed PRAW aircraft, the patrol attacked the terrorists. One terrorist and two locals running with them were killed. An AK-47 assault rifle was recovered.

On 16 November, elements of the Venda militia located and successfully lifted a TM-57 landmine.

On 18 November, a Rhodesia Railways security trolley detonated an explosive device on the railway line in the vicinity of Lesanth Siding. The trolley derailed without injuring any of the occupants.

CHAPTER TWELVE

Transfer to Gwanda
November 1979

The 19th of November, the day I was dreading, finally dawned bright and sunny. In a few hours I would leave Beitbridge for good and retrace my route back over the Umzingwani River Bridge at West Nicholson, the same bridge I had crossed three and a half years earlier on my southward journey to my new home. I had stayed at Beitbridge for as long as I possibly could; my replacement, John Phillpot, had already arrived and was staying at Peter's Motel with his wife, Darlene, so I was obliged to head north. I had made a lot of good friends and I had become better acquainted with the pretty customs officer, Patsy Smith. The thought of moving did not appeal to me. I suppose the adage 'All good things must come to an end' really applies here.

However, inside, I was bitter. Professionally, I was completely demoralized and despondent. A CID team, as part of their poaching investigation, had interviewed me. I never denied shooting the elephant and, in fact, assisted them as much as possible by pointing out, from the air, where the elephant had been shot. I still could not understand why the Commissioner of Police was taking such an interest in the case which I regarded as petty, but my CID friend in Bulawayo kept me informed, reporting that Chief Superintendent Dave Blacker, still heading the investigation, was keeping the commissioner updated on a regular basis. Although I freely admitted to shooting the elephant, I refused to admit that I was in the wrong and had merely taken advantage of an arrangement that the District Commissioner, Lew Watson, had extended to every previous elephant hunter over the years. As mentioned, there was a more sinister motive behind the investigation.

I had worked hard to pass the promotion examinations, coming sixth in the country, only to be denied my promotion. I did not want a transfer to Gwanda and could not motivate myself, no matter how much I tried, to accept it. As I crossed the Umzingwani, my thoughts were in complete contrast to those of my southward crossing back in March 1976: all I could think of was getting out of the police force as soon as possible.

I had been posted to Gwanda as member in charge of the Special Branch station. However, this only worked in theory: in reality, the District Special Branch Officer ran this side of things and called all the shots, so everyone bypassed me and reported to him. I was to serve under two different DSBOs during the relatively short time I was there.

In terms of the Lancaster House agreement, a ceasefire was to be implemented on 1 January 1980, with all ZANLA and ZIPRA combatants being required to enter designated 'assembly points' from that date. A contingent of New Zealand troops, part of the Commonwealth Monitoring Force, pitched up in Gwanda during December. They were all excellent chaps and I made good friends with them.

Meanwhile, the war went on.

•••

The 22nd of November saw the last member of the security forces being killed in action in the Beitbridge area when elements of C Company 2RR contacted an estimated ten terrorists in the Machachuta TTL. Rifleman James Stewart Kerr of C Company 2RR was killed in this action.

On 13 December, the vehicle Max Stockill was driving detonated a landmine on Liebigs Ranch. His injuries were initially assessed as being minor, but as a precaution he was casevaced to the Bulawayo General Hospital where he died later that day from internal injuries. He was the last white man to die before the ceasefire.

On 28 December, the last local to be killed before the ceasefire came into effect was Muzwibziwa Dube, a tractor driver who detonated a landmine on Shamba Yetu farm.

My last action, as recorded on the continuing Beitbridge log, occurred on 21 February 1980. I had been deployed from Gwanda for a period of about a week in an attempt to obtain intelligence on the Juliet Assembly Point established in the Siyoka TTL for ZANLA terrorists returning from the bush, and was staying with my old friends John and Marie Barclay at Mazunga.

On the 21st, I was visiting Robin Watson at his Mikado Ranch. As mentioned, Robin was a wealth of information and had well-placed sources within the Siyoka community. While we were discussing the situation, one of his informers reported that six terrorists were attending a beer drink in the Siyoka TTL, in clear violation of the ceasefire. Robin, a pilot with the Police Reserve Air Wing, invited me to accompany him on a flight over the kraal. I readily agreed and we took off in Copper 128.

While overflying the kraal in question, at low level, we came under heavy ground attack from an estimated thirty to forty terrorists. Robin requested assistance from Support Unit's Delta Company which was based nearby. Call sign Delta 3 responded, while we remained airborne and just out of range of the enemy's guns until the section was nearing the kraal. I am not too sure what happened next but we banked and came screaming in at treetop level toward the kraal. Robin then gave the order to release the 'bombs'. I pulled on the lanyard which released the 'bombs' – one shrapnel grenade and one white phosphorus grenade – that Robin had loaded into 'bomb chute' made of PVC piping. The bombs went whistling straight onto the Support Unit patrol, resulting in three of them being injured and one, a sergeant, received serious phosphorus burns. This was really a most unfortunate accident. However, undaunted, Delta 3 continued with its objective and engaged the enemy, causing them to flee and recovering one AK-47 assault rifle, one SKS rifle and other war matériel. On landing and after carrying out an inspection of the aircraft, it was discovered that the one wing flap had been hit by ground fire.

Poor old Robin was ordered to remove his 'bomb chute' and was never again called upon to perform PRAW duties. It was ironic, but fitting, that my last action during the Rhodesian war was with a distinguished ex-617 'Dambuster' Squadron pilot who had seen extensive operational service in the Second World War; ironic, as my father Arthur had served with 44 (Rhodesia) Squadron. When later I related the story to my father he had a good laugh as, unbeknown to me, he knew Robin well.

•••

During February, I submitted my application for discharge – BSAP form 71 – requesting that it be effective from 1 May 1980. In terms of the Lancaster House agreement, this was the earliest date that members of the security forces and civil service could resign with extra benefits.

CHAPTER THIRTEEN
A case of political expedience

I heard nothing of the court case until the end of April when I was served with a summons to appear in the Bulawayo regional court on 5 May 1980 to face three charges under the Parks and Wild Life Act: three counts of shooting elephant without a permit. Don Price was charged with four counts and Neill Jackson with one. Blacker was really going for the jugular by splitting charges; the commissioner must have been very pleased with him.

It is appropriate here to outline certain developments which took place over a lunch date I had with Mr Mac in Johannesburg during the mid-1980s. We were chatting about old times when he suddenly changed the subject and stated that I had been the sacrificial lamb in the commissioner's plan to retain his position in the police force after independence. I asked Mac to explain. He revealed the gist of a conversation he had had with Ken Flower, the Director-General of the Central Intelligence Organization, shortly after independence. Flower had said, "That man of yours, Bird, and the two army fellows were investigated on the specific instructions of Allum, you know." Mac expanded and went on to tell me that, according to Flower, Allum needed some dirt, preferably on regular white members of the security forces which he could use to his advantage to reinforce his stance that the police was apolitical and served without fear of favour – something Allum banged on about *ad nauseum*. As Allum had at one time been the officer commanding the Criminal Investigation Department, he had loyal and trusted officers within the ranks. He must have thought he had hit the jackpot when the CID in Bulawayo told him that they could bring charges against one white policeman and two white regular army officers. When he attended the Lancaster House talks in London, he reinforced his apolitical speech by mentioning the fact that three white members of the security forces had court cases pending against them.

It all made sense.

An incident, reported in the Beitbridge Incident log and one in which I became personally involved, was to make make a mockery of Allum's credibility and his 'apolitical and fear or favour' nonsense. This was a terrible episode but, because it was political, the CID wouldn't touch it with a barge pole.

On 12 March 1980, Brian Perkins at Beitbridge was instructed to issue the five trusted turned terrorists, who had served us loyally over the years but who had now become an embarrassment, with bus warrants to any destination in Rhodesia of their choice. Four opted for Bulawayo and one Salisbury. The four

Afterword

During the course of the war in the Beitbridge area over two hundred and thirty terrorists were accounted for, either killed or captured, as opposed to the deaths of twenty-one members of the security forces. The real losers – the civilians – suffered enormous casualties, but remain either untallied or unrecorded. Over one hundred and forty anti-tank mines were detonated by vehicles, bicycles, humans and animals.

In spite of overwhelming odds, the terrorists never succeeded in achieving their main objectives: the closure of the two main roads and the railway line servicing the entire country from our only lifeline, South Africa. It is a credit to everyone – man and woman, black and white, who served in the Beitbridge area and who risked their lives, and who died – that the enemy failed.

I think I have used the saying already that 'the wheel turns' but this will be the last time. P.K. Allum became the Commissioner of the Zimbabwe Republic Police and served in that capacity until one fateful Monday morning in February 1982 when he was summarily discharged from the ZRP – that is, ordered to clear his desk of personal items and immediately vacate his office at Police General Head Quarters – by none other than President Robert Mugabe himself. He was discharged, on political grounds, as a result of a serving CID detective inspector with previous service in the BSAP, assisted by former BSAP and army members, in the successful springing from the Salisbury Central Prison of an ex-Rhodesian Army officer the previous day. This officer had been responsible for a major sabotage attack which had destroyed one of the main Zimbabwe National Army magazines in the country. Allum, now a bitter old man, moved to South Africa where he still lives.

As for Dave Blacker: well, my old friend, George Mitchell, had immigrated to South Africa in 1980 before returning to Salisbury in 1981 to finalize his affairs. Blacker, by then an assistant commissioner in the ZRP, had George arrested under the emergency regulations of the Law and Order Maintenance Act and detained in the notorious Chikurubi Maximum Security Prison, without charge – for a month in solitary confinement, the maximum permitted under law – before having him released with a warning not to return to Zimbabwe, under threat of further arrest. Blacker's new masters must have been delighted with him. The CID, during the days of the BSA Police, would never have used the emergency regulations to detain a criminal suspect, as this was a law that had been passed to assist the Special Branch and CID in the field of security and, in particular, in dealing with terrorist incursions. The arrest had something to do with Special Branch funds suspected to have disappeared across the border into South Africa during late 1979. Blacker retired from the ZRP in 1982 and settled in South Africa where he still lives. George married the lovely Jane Kirk, widow of Dr Sandy Kirk of Selous Scouts fame. They live near Durban.

Steve Acornley left the BSAP in 1980 and initially settled in South Africa before moving to the Far East where he worked for a number of years. He now lives in Scotland. John and Marie Barclay left Zimbabwe in 1980 and settled in South Africa. They now live in retirement on the KwaZulu-Natal South Coast. Hamish Barnes left the BSAP in mid-1980 and returned to the family farm in Zululand where he still works. Geoff Blyth initially left Zimbabwe shortly after independence and settled in South Africa. However, he returned to Zimbabwe and settled in Kariba where he still lives. Gray Branfield resigned from the BSAP in May 1980 and moved to South Africa. Involved in security work, he was killed in Iraq in 2004.

I last saw Roger Britland in early 1978. In late 1979, Roger, an active member of the BSAP sub-aqua club, was part of a team which was to dive the Sinoia Caves one weekend. Being an avid diver, he arrived a day earlier than the others and ignored the diver's cardinal rule of diving alone. His body was recovered two days later trapped in one of the smaller caves. His parents must have been devastated as their only other son, Peter, had been killed in action in August 1976 serving with the BSAP. Mimi Cawood left Beitbridge in early 1980 and moved to Gwanda with her first husband, before the family migrated to Pietersburg in the Northern Tansvaal. Her parents, Benji and Mavaunie, remained on their farm on the Mazunga River, both passing on some years ago. Mimi remarried an old friend, Beaver Shaw (author of *Choppertech*), and is presently living in East Africa where Beaver flies helicopters. Keith Cloete continued working for Mac until the Selous Scouts disbanded shortly before independence when he moved to Durban. He was an extremely fit, strong man but succumbed to a heart attack a good number of years ago. John Davey retired from the BSAP during mid-1980 and now lives in the USA after running a successful photographic safari company in Zambia and Botswana.

After handing over the Special Branch station to me, Pete Gatland moved to South Africa where he worked in the transport industry, making a success of it before starting his own business. By some miraculous form of fate he was nearly killed when several armed robbers entered his business premises outside Durban and made a determined effort to kill him, shooting him several times with 9mm pistols. Although the wounds proved almost fatal, he hung in there and after a considerable length of time in hospital made a full recovery. He still lives in the Durban area. Pete Dewe left the BSAP in mid-1980 and tried his luck at Kariba but subsequently moved to Natal where he started a business with Steve Acornley. In the late 1980s, he joined Ron Reid-Daly's team involved in the retraining of the Transkei Defence Force; however, he had not been there very long before the government was ousted in a military coup. He then started his own business which entailed working in the rural areas on the South Coast of Natal and where he was shot several times by black youths and left for dead. As in Pete Gatland's case, he recovered from his near-fatal injuries. He was then forced to work in the UK for a number of years but has recently returned to South Africa and now works in Central Africa. Lionel Dyke transferred to the Zimbabwe National Army, rising to the rank of colonel and commanding the Parachute Brigade. He was awarded the Silver Cross of Zimbabwe for action against ZIPRA dissidents. On his resignation from the ZNA, he formed a de-mining company operating in Africa and Europe. He is now retired and lives in the Cape, where his most onerous duty is as commodore of the local yacht club.

Keith Knott stayed on on his ranch on the banks of the Limpopo River but lost most of his land in the land invasions of 2000; however, he managed to negotiate the retention of his citrus orchard which remains productive. Keith and his wife moved to South Africa where he lives in semi-retirement but still keeps an interest in his farming operations on Nottingham Estates. Bruce Fitzsimmons was killed in a road accident in South Africa a number of years ago. Winston Hart retired from the BSAP in mid-1980 and settled in South Africa where he became a very successful sculptor producing some fine work. Several years ago he moved to New Zealand where he still lives. Wally Insch also lives in New Zealand, having spent a number of years in South Africa following the disbandment of the Selous Scouts. Charlie Krause left the Rhodesian Army on the disbandment of the Selous Scouts and moved to South Africa where he became a very successful businessman. Pete McNeilage moved to South Africa during mid-1980. He was also involved in the retraining of the Transkei Defence Force until the government was ousted in a military coup. He recently returned to South Africa after living in the UK for several years. Mac McGuinness retired from the BSAP in mid-1980 and moved to South Africa. He was murdered in his home in Pretoria in 2011. Les Mitchell stayed on on his farm after independence, also experiencing problems during the farm invasions of 2000. I was extremely sorry to hear that his wife Fran passed away some years ago. Alistair Mommsen retired from the BSAP in mid-1980 and moved to South Africa where he died several years ago.

Robbie Parks continued farming in the Beirbridge area after independence, becoming personal friends with Robert Mugabe to whom he has unlimited access. His farm was not subjected to any form of land invasion.

Brian Perkins retired from the BSAP in May 1980 and moved to South Africa where he became involved in the security business. He now lives near Durban. Ian 'Perkie' Perkins resigned from the BSAP at the end of 1979 and ran a successful business in Bulawayo before moving to Australia where he still lives. Don Price resigned his commission on the disbandment of the Rhodesian Light Infantry but stayed in Zimbabwe. He realized his ambition and became a very successful professional hunter, his safari company operating in Central and East Africa. A number of years ago he moved to the Eastern Cape where he lives in semi-retirement.

Mike Reeves retired from the CIO in the early 1980s and moved to the Cape where he succumbed to cancer in 1984. Raymond Roth continued running his store at Beitbridge until he was arrested in 1982 by the Zimbabwean CIO, for what reason I was never able to ascertain. He was detained without trial for thirty days in the notorious Stops Hostel situated within the ZRP camp in Bulawayo and, if my memory serves me correctly, his detention was extended by a further thirty days. The only possible reason was that Roth openly supported Joshua Nkomo's ZAPU party and was therefore suspected of disloyalty during Mugabe's reign of terror in Matabeleland. I never heard of him again. Pete Stanton retired from the BSAP in 1978 and joined the Selous Scouts before moving to South Africa on the unit's disbandment in 1980. Still a wealth of knowledge on the Rhodesian bush war, he now lives in Johannesburg.

The last I heard of Sarel Strydom him was in 1989 when he commanded the Security Branch in South West Africa/Namibia, having attained the rank of brigadier. Johan Taute resigned from the SAP Security Branch in the early 1990s and now owns a game farm in the Northern Transvaal. Piet van der Merwe moved out of the Beitbridge area in 1979 after selling River Ranch and purchasing another in central Matabeleland, when I lost all contact with him. André van Rooyen resigned from the SADF with the rank of kommandant in the early 1990s while serving in the Eastern Transvaal. After that I lost contact with him but if he ever reads this book it would be a real pleasure to hear from him again. 'Fires' van Vuuren left the SAP and took over the running of a game farm in the Northern Transvaal bordering Botswana. I was sad to hear that he took his own life a number of years ago. The last time I had contact with Johann Viktor was in 1982 when he was still serving in the SAP with the rank of general.

Dave Ward left the BSAP in 1980 and decided to see a bit of the world, eventually settling in Canada. He is a staunch BSAP Association member and represents the BSAP on Canada's Remembrance Day parades. Lew Watson stayed on as the DC in Beitbridge until the Ministry of Internal Affairs became redundant. I last saw him in May 1980 when he gave evidence against me in the regional court in Bulawayo. I have no idea what happened to him after that. Robin Watson stayed on on his Mikado Ranch after independence and resumed normal farming operations. He died in Zimbabwe a number of years ago. Ant White left the Rhodesian Army on the disbandment of the Selous Scouts before moving to Mozambique where he established himself as a very successful businessman in Beira. Henry Wolhuter retired from the BSAP in May 1980 and moved to South Africa where he served with the SAP's Brixton Murder and Robbery Squad for several years. Toward the end of the 1980s, both Henry and his wife Beryl were diagnosed with cancer. Beryl died at the end of 1986, followed by Henry six months later. Henry was convinced, till the day he died, that the handling of the contaminated clothing was responsible for causing the cancer. On numerous occasions, Beryl also had cause to come into contact with the contaminated clothing.

And what happened to me? I stayed on in the Gwanda area for the next eighteen months, working several profitable old gold dumps by treating the sand with cyanide to extract the gold. Patsy left her job with the customs department, also on 1 May, and joined me in my mining venture. We were married at the end of September 1980 once my divorce from Maya was finalized and we have been together ever since. We have two wonderful daughters, Tracey and Diane, who gave us extreme pleasure as they grew into the wonderful women that they are today. Both now live in the United Kingdom, but Patsy and I still manage to see them on a fairly regular basis.

Incidentally, the gold-mining venture proved very lucrative and I was sorry to have to pack it in. I felt that Zimbabwe was not a suitable place to raise my children and the decision to leave had to be made. We moved on and ended up in South West Africa, spending seven wonderful years on the banks of the Zambezi River in the sleepy little border town of Katima Mulilo on the Zambian border.

I suppose the question remains: was it worth it? I am still adamant that we Rhodesians could have achieved an acceptable settlement had the world, in particular the British, not interfered in our internal policies.

And would I do it all over again?

… Hell, yes.

APPENDIX I
The *Povo* system: Beitbridge area

SB BEIT BRIDGE

SECRET

Copy No 13 of 30

G(Int)/1/4

Telephone : 75921
Extension : 112

JOC Tangent,
Brady Barracks,
P.O. Box 698,
Bulawayo,
10 October 1978.

POVO SYSTEM : BEIT BRIDGE AREA

Appendix A : Intrep : POVO System Beit Bridge

1. 'POVO' is the ZANLA CT term for the masses or locals. In the Beit Bridge area those locals that have not moved into the PVs have been forced by the CTs to live in "POVO camps" in the bush.

2. The CTs are very dependent on the POVO for intelligence, food and supplies.

3. Attached at Appendix A is an Intrep of the POVO System as it is known. The Intrep was compiled by Lt L. Reynolds (RIC) and the primary source was CCT Dicks Masone, supplemented by on the ground investigations and interrogation of other CCTs. Although it is too early to predict definite patterns the intrep has valuable information for troops operating in the area.

(R.M. Matkovich) Maj,
for Brig,
Comd.

RMM/LAS

DISTRIBUTION   Copy No

For action:

    Sub JOC Gwanda   1 - 2
    1 (Indep) Coy RAR   3
    2RR   4 - 6
    6RR   7 - 9
    Air HQ Ops - For Recce   10
    PGHQ - For PRAW Recce   11
    Police Beit Bridge   12
    SB Beit Bridge   13

For information:

    Com Ops   14
    JOC Repulse   15
    Army HQ   16
    RIC   17

SECRET

2

Internal:	Copy No
Comd	18
Air Rep	19
RIC	20
File Tangent D/F	21
G(Int)/1/4	22
Spare	23 - 30

SECRET

SECRET

3

APPENDIX A TO
G(INT)/1/4
DATED OCTOBER 1978

INTREP : POVO SYSTEM BEITBRIDGE AREA

1. **CT Organisation of POVO System**

    a. ZANLA CTs have established a structured and purposeful system whereby the indigenous populace not yet in PVs are used to aid the CTs in the pursuit of their objectives.

    b. Locals in the POVOs have precise instructions and their entire move= ments and activities are controlled by the CTs.

    c. POVOs have conformity of layout and a pattern of movement which is predictable and hence potentially vulnerable. (See Annexure 1).

    d. The POVOs are used for the feeding of CTs, for counter-intelligence and monitoring of SF activity, as well as sexual gratification and normal domestic needs.

2. **Physical Description of POVOs**

    a. POVOs are simple bush habitation complexes where the locals are made to camouflage and carefully conceal their occupancy away from general SF movement and presence.

    b. POVOs very in sophistication from neatly built but small thatch shelters which are hidden in thick vegetation and under tree or bush canopy, to very simplistic arrangement where small sleeping positions are cleared under brush or suitable vegetation cover.

    c. The POVO layout normally consists of several cell like centres where individual families or groups will ensconce themselves. Sleeping places are in evidence in each cell and a fire-place for communal cooking exists in each cell.

    d. The CTs place their sleeping places in 'battle formation' approximately 100 to 200 metres from the POVO complex. (See Annexure 1). The CT sleeping points are in an extended line of normally three groups (at section level) and the siting of the CT situation is always placed advantageously; for example use of heaviest cover or on high ground.

    e. No fires are made in the CT base, except occasionally in winter in extremely cold conditions.

    f. A network of paths links up the POVO cells and also the adjacent CT base.

    g. Fires are made in pits for concealment purposes.

    h. Meat is often hanging in strips in trees in the POVO area. Blankets, personal effects, and cooking utensils will be in evidence hidden under trees and bushes and camouflaged where possible.

/j. Use is.....

SECRET

4

j. Use is made of antbear holes and shallow scrapes where personal effects, CT medical kit, and small quantities of ammunition are hidden in the ground and covered with earth and leaves to disguise the positions.

k. No heavy arms caches are ever established within the POVO complex however.

l. Sometimes scotch carts and one or two large 44 gallon water drums are present in a POVO area which is sited at some distance from surface water.

m. Branches are cut in some POVOs and used to wall in sleeping areas to provide further concealment. This is not common however.

3. CT Modus Operandi Related to the POVO System

a. When CTs arrive at a POVO complex they make a cautious approach and ensure that the area is safe for them before entering. This is done by moving carefully into the vicinity, apprehending one of the POVO inhabitants, and questioning the individual on relevant security matters.

b. CTs never stay for long periods in one particular POVO. This practice varies from section to section, however two or three nights is a normal period of time for basing up at a particular POVO. Less security conscious sections do however sometimes stay in a POVO for several days.

c. The CTs never inform the POVO inhabitants of future intentions and will move out of an area without giving either departure times nor destination.

d. Movement of the locals is very strictly controlled and they are threatened under point of death if they attempt to leave the POVO complex.

e. Trusted locals in the POVOs are used for messenger purposes and for purchasing of food or personal effects needed by the CTs.

f. Some CT sections make the male occupants of a POVO patrol the general area in order to alert CTs of SF movement in the area. This is not always the case however.

g. When SF are in the vicinity of a POVO both CTs and the locals adopt a highly vigilant profile. OPs are posted and should the POVO be discovered both CTs and locals will flee and re-group at an RV.

h. If a POVO is 'compromised' by either SF or recce aircraft the CTs make the locals move to a new site selected by the CTs.

j. 'Compromise' by aircraft is assessed if the aircraft persistently circles the POVO complex. In this situation the CTs and locals adopt a 'hide alternate run' tactic depending on the proximity of the aircraft and the amount of canopy cover available.

/k. CTs frequently.....

SECRET

5

k. CTs frequently use the nearest POVO as an RV and will re-group at the relevant POVO complex should they be surprised by SF.

l. After an attack on a POVO/CT base camp by SF the CTs will return at night to collect the wounded, personal effects, and medical kit left behind.

m. CTs returning to a compromised POVO/CT Camp will approach cautiously at night and either lay down prophylactic fire before entering the POVO area, or in some circumstances tinkle a cowbell and await the return signal from colleagues who have already re-grouped in the POVO.

n. Feeding takes place twice a day in a POVO. In the morning and late afternoon. Cooking fires are extinguished before dark.

o. In some POVOs only selected locals can frequent the adjacent CT base. However other sections allow free movement by locals in and out of the CT positions in daylight hours. At night the CTs do not allow POVO occupants into their base. Girlfriends are the exception to this rule.

p. When CTs move from POVO to POVO in normal operations they do not take any locals along with them.

4. Comments on the POVO System

a. In the Beitbridge area the ZANLA CTs are heavily reliant on the POVO system.

b. If it were possible to remove POVOs or seriously reduce the number of POVOs in the Beitbridge area CT efficacy in the area would be considerably undermined.

c. Troops on the ground must patrol with discipline and aggression. Thick cover must be investigated thoroughly for possible POVO presence.

d. In the event of capture of a locals he or she should be interrogated immediately reference CT presence or movement.

e. Capture of a local in a 'no go' area is preferable to shooting of the individual for two reasons:

   i. Immediate intelligence of CT presence may be available.

   ii. Compromise would be inevitable with negligible achievement and possible ambush retaliation by CTs.

f. All troops should be briefed on what to anticipate on the ground regarding POVOs, i.e.,

   i. Smell of meat could indicate a POVO.

   ii. Numerous footpaths leading to a particular area could indicate a POVO complex.

/iii. Scotch cart......

iii. Scotch cart tracks leading through bush should be investigated.

iv. Rifle shots (not automatic fire) could indicate killing of livestock by CTs.

v. Any voices or noises atypical of the bush should be investigated.

vi. All watering points should be carefully examined for spoor and/or ambushed.

vii. Dead foliage placed about a thicket could indicate POVO camouflage efforts.

viii. In a POVO complex a very careful search should be conducted with a view to looking for personal effects hidden in bags under trees; the prodding and investigation of soft earth and antbear holes; the seeking out of food and water receptacles and the destruction thereof.

ix. The identification of the CT sleeping positions and a very close scrutiny for hidden ammunition and kit in this area.

APPENDIX I: THE *POVO* SYSTEM: BEITBRIDGE AREA | 257

SECRET

7

ANNEXURE 1 TO
APPENDIX A TO
G(INT)/1/4
DATED OCTOBER **1978**

LAYOUT OF A POVO CAMP

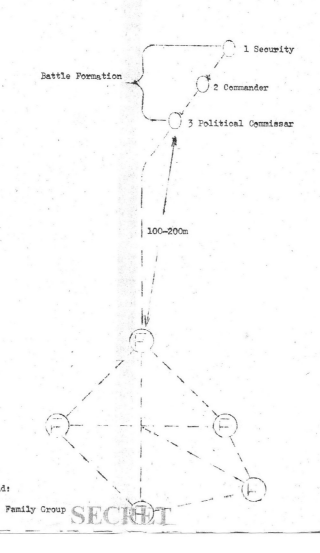

Legend:
F = Family Group

APPENDIX II

Samples of the incident log

CONFIDENTIAL

INCIDENT LOG : BEITBRIDGE

FORM S.B. 10.
B.S.A.P.—20M—24-3-76.

SPECIAL BRANCH
B.S.A. POLICE

DIARY

Page No.: 2

Date	No.	Entry	Cross References and Index:
19/12/76	11 INTIM	A group of between 12 and 20 terrs visited the kraal of Headman TSETANA and ordered the locals to feed them. Terrs then went to the kraal of PHILLIP (INTAFDA) and burned his kraal to the ground. Terrs then assaulted PHILLIP's wife and one other local.	TL 603512
15/12/76	12 S	DONDOLO DIP filled in by terrs causing minimal damage. Usual note left at the scene where the terrs remained until 19/12/76.	TL 476687
24/12/76	13 C	Crusader c/s 55 shot and killed two AMA who failed to stop when called upon to do so.	TL 556613
24/12/76	14 A	Scouter Romeo Base and elements of Crusader whilst returning from the above incident were ambushed by an estimated 8 terrs. Hyena was hit by RPG and small arms fire. Fire returned by c/s and the terrs made good their escape. Minor injuries received by P/O WARD, NSPO WEAKES, NSPO FOLKS and CST MUDAU.	TL 704466 armsxfixe
29/12/76	15 M	Internal Affairs Dip Attendant and Water Carrier murdered by terrs on 28/12/76. Terrs gave out that dipping was to cease in the area.	TL 278598
29/12/76	16 IN	Two groups of terrs with 12 terrs in each group held two day meetings and would appear also to have interchanged within their groups.	TL 292510
31/12/76	17 O	Information to hand suggests that there is a new group of 8 terrs operating in the DITI area and they had as a guide a member of one of the already resident groups.	TL 325467
1/1/77	18 LM	Scouter Pappa Base located a TMB3A landmine on the main road between Pappa Base and DITI. Landmine lifted by crusader. No tracks found.	TL 295307
2/1/77	19 P	A group of terrs were being fed at a kraal in the DITI area and absconded prior to the arrival of a patrol from Pappa Base. Fresh food was found at the feeding place by the patrol.	TL 352342
4/1/77	20 LM	Pappa Scouter located landmine (TMB3A) on the main road to DITI approx half a Kilometer from the mine mentioned in entry 18. Mine lifted and assessed as having been laid within the past 3 days. No tracks.	TL 297387
5/1/77	21 M	Owner of CHIBI Store beaten to death by a group of 9 terrs. Terrs gave out that he was a sell out. Deceased attempted to abscond and terrs opened fire with small arms and an RPG. deceased was recaptured and subsequently beaten. Terrs collected most of the expended cartridge cases and hid them in an antbear hole.	TL 281545

CONFIDENTIAL

CONFIDENTIAL

INCIDENT LOG : BEITBRIDGE

**SPECIAL BRANCH
B.S.A. POLICE**

DIARY

Page No.: 4

Date	No.	Entry	Cross References and Index:
15/1/77	28 C	Crusader made contact with an unknown number of terrs. One terr killed and 1 AK, 1 RPG projectile, 1 Stick grenade and other equipment recovered.	TL 264324
17/1/77	29 AC.	AMA captured by Crusader, who later turned out to be a terr gave out that he knew the whereabouts of four arms caches in the area. Arms caches were indicated at the following places. (1) Two RPG 7 projectiles, One box ammunition. (2) Nine 60mm Mortar Bombs and detonators and two boxes of 7.62 intermediate ammo. (3) Two landmines and two boxes 7.62 int ammo. (4) Cache appeared to have been lifted by terrs prior to the arrival of Bailiff Acorn.	TL 334489 TL 804501 TL 770532
21/1/77	30 C	At approx 1205 Acorn Romeo Base shot and killed an AFA who attempted to abscond whilst making indications.	TL 630474
17/1/77	31 C	Crusader callsign shot and killed 2 AMA s who absconded when called upon to halt.	TL 831498
18/1/77	32 C	Crusader callsign shot and killed 1 AMA when he refused to stop when called upon to do so. A further AMA was arrested	TL 674515
21/1/77	33 C	Crusader callsign had contact with 8 terrs. No casualties either side. Tracks followed for a short distance where lost.	TL 943385
22/1/77	34 LM	Crusader vehicle detonated a landmine. No cas. Assessed that landmine laid same day.	TL 640488
26/1/77	35 LM	Crusader vehicle detonated a landmine. No cas. Mine probably laid same day as entry above.	TL 641488
30/1/77	36 A	LESANTH RANCH came under small arms and Rocket fire. House damaged but no casualties.	TL 363845
29/1/77	37 C	D/S/O BIRD and F/R BALDWIN had fleeting contact with 2 terrs and approx 8 locals. No cas.	UL 018205

CONFIDENTIAL

CONFIDENTIAL

INCIDENT LOG : BEITBRIDGE.

SPECIAL BRANCH
B.S.A. POLICE

DIARY

Page No.: 32/78

FORM S.B. 10.
B.S.A.P.—20M—24-3-76.

Date	No.	Entry	Cross References and Index:
3/9/78.	194.	ABDUCTION. At 1600 this date at QG 724189 (Siyoka TTL) Shu Shine Bus boarded by A/M/A who handed letter to driver purporting to originate from ZANLA sources. Driver accompanied A/M/A into bush and not seen again, Relief driver drove bus into Beitbridge. Name of driver abducted - CHIPINGE.	T 4/9 para A1(4)
4/9/78.	195.	AMBUSH. At QG 756209 (Siyoka TTL) elements of Scouter ZULU ambushed by estimated 3 CTs - ineffectual - thought that CTs were waiting to rob the bus. Assessed as ZANLA.	T 4/9 para A1(5)
4/9/78. istics - 4 AKs, S', 1 AK tied ,52,29/78.)	196.	AMBUSH. At 1700 at TL 620430 (Chipise TTL) Roads Department tractor ambushed by an u/k number of CTs. No injuries but tractor destroyed.	T 5/9n para A1(1)
5/9/78.	197.	ARSON occurred at RF 054585 (Mtetengwe TTL) when Wards Transport vehicle (open back) was stopped on the Main Byo. - Beitbridge Road, by 6 ZANLA CTs. CTs forced driver to drive vehicle off the road, where same was set fire to. Dvr and assistant robbed of total of $30, jacket, and shoes.	T 5/9 para A1(2)
5/9/78. stics - Two ms, 2 SKS', 1 covered weapons o previous trace.	198.	CONTACT. At 1510 hours this date Fire Force contacted 8 CTs at TL 885506 (Sengwe TTL) 6 CTs killed and 2 believed wounded. Not known what type of weapons, but 6 were recovered. FF remaining in the area to carry out sweeps.	R 5/9 para A2(2)
5/9/78.	199.	ROBBERY - occurred at RF 074535 (Mtetengwe TTL) at 1700 hours this date. Shu shine bus stopped by 10 CTs who are assessed as being ZANLA and forced driver to drive 2 Kms into bush where they robbed crew and passengers.	T 6/9 para A1(3)
5/9/78.	200.	CONTACT. at SL 091582 (Mtetengwe TTL) elements of 1 Indep Coy. RAR had contact at 1845 hours this date with u/k number of CTs. Initial contact from 100 metres and firing continued for 20 mins. 7 x RPG 7 fired at callsign, no cas. Sweep of area at first light revealed medic pack and docs.	T 6/9 para A1(4)
6/9/78. stics - 1 AK to entries (73) Tongwe Keep on 21/12/77)	201.	AMBUSH - occurred at RF 013710 (Mtetengwe TTL), at 1335 hours, when lone civilian vehicle travelling ahead of convoy ambushed by an unknwon number of Cts. Driver E.M.A. LUBBE of Seller Farm, Hartley wounded in the neck - condition critical.	T 6/9 para A1A(2)

CONFIDENTIAL

CONFIDENTIAL

INCIDENT LOG : S.B. BEITBRIDGE.

SPECIAL BRANCH
B.S.A. POLICE

DIARY

Page No.: 37/78

FORM S.B. 10.
B.S.A.P.—20M—24-3-76.

Date	No.	Entry	Cross References and Index
13/9/78.	230.	MIP entry 224. - further established that 2 borehole engines destroyed in the same vicinity as the tractor that was burnt out. Int. from locals indicates that 4 well used base camps exist in the areas :- TM 042160, TM 134058 and TM 237088 (all Liebig's Ranch).	T 13/9 para B1(1)
13/9/78.	231.	CONTACT - at TL 594334 (Diti TTL) elements of D Coy 2 RR had contact with 8 CTs - one CCT wounded. No SF Cas.	T 13/9 para A1A(1)
13/9/78.	232.	CONTACT - Occurred 1540 hrs at RF980620 (Mtetengwe TTL) when elements 1 (Indep) Coy reacting to indications by AMA were ambushed by approx 30 CTs. During ensuing fire fight, 1 AMA running with CTs killed and 1 AMA wounded who has subsequently died. Callsign on follow-up located base camp containing medical kit and documents. PRAW Copper 32 with Sunray 1 Indep Coy subjected to heavy small arms fire whilst overflying contact area. No SF cas.	T. 14/9 para A1(1).
13/9/78.	233.	SIGHTING/AIRSTRIKE - Occurred 1700 hrs at RF090670 (Mtetengwe TTL) when two CTs were observed entering cover. Lynx deployed and fired on position. No known CT cas.	T. 14/9 para A1(2).
14/9/78.	234.	FOLLOWUP - At 1130 hrs at TL545297 (Diti TTL) Elements D Coy 2RR located resting place for approx 60 CTs. CTs had slaughtered and eaten one ox during night. Spoor located heading northwest, c/s remains on followup.	T. 14/9 para A1A(1).
14/9/78.	235.	CONTACT - Occurred at 1120 hrs at TL068369 (Mtetengwe TTL) when elements 6RR had fleeting contact with 9CTs. No cas to either side.	T. 14/9 para A1A(3).
15/9/78.	236.	CONTACT - Occurred at 1100 hrs at TM025123 (Jopempi Block Leibigs Ranch) when c/s 11A of (1 Indep Coy) had contact with 4-5 CTs, no cas to either side. Sweep of area resulted in recovery of 3 x RPG 2 rockets, 4 kit bags and misc items clothing.	T. 16/9 para A1(2).
16/9/78. istics - 5 AKs, S (captured),all revious traces.	237.	CONTACT - Occurred at 1125 hrs at QG538022 (Dendele TTL) when elements Scouter ZULU had contact with estimated 9 ZANLA CTs in base camp area. No SF cas. Blood spoor located but lost after short distance. One SKS rifle and one AK mag recovered. SKS No 1511340.	T. 16/9 para A1(3). IV 19/78

CONFIDENTIAL

CONFIDENTIAL

INCIDENT LOG : BEITBRIDGE

SPECIAL BRANCH
B.S.A. POLICE

DIARY

Page No.: 41/78

FORM S.B. 10.
B.S.A.P.—20M—24-3-76.

Date / Ref	Incident	Cross References and Index
7/10/78. 258. listics – 1 AK, previous traces.	HOMESTEAD ATTACK/MURDERS – Occurred at 2230 hrs at TM 087014 (Lamulas Section One Liebigs) and TM 087012 (Lutope Section One Liebigs) when both homesteads came under attack by approx 20 CTs from approx 500 metres. Fire returned, one homestead usustained a number of small arms strikes. Two AMA's from nearby compound were axed to death and three abducted. Elements 1 Indep Coy RAR followed tracks to TM140078 and continue followup.	T. 8/10 para A1(1).
7/10/78. 259. listics – No evious traces on tured weapon.)	CONTACT – Occured 1515 hrs at TL994487 (Sengwe TTL) after sighting and followup by D Coy 2 RR from TL873476 (Chipise TTL). Contact made with approx 30 CTs, no SF cas, poss one CT wounded as blood spoor located. One SKS 1702984, 3 stick grenades and 11 packs (destroyed at site) recovered from scene of contact.	T. 8/10 para A1(2). IV 19/78
10/10/78. 260. listics – Test es from recovered 18079974 – no ious traces.)	CONTACTS – At 1245 hrs at RF053623 (Mtetengwe TTL) elements 1 Indep Coy RAR whilst following tracks of estimated 20 CTs had fleeting contact with 1 CT. No cas either side. FF Delta deployed and c/s continued followup resulting in further contact at QF838551 (Beitbridge farming area – Nottingham Estates) killing one CT. One ES received minor shrapnel wounds. CTs bombshelled with unknown number fleeing into a cave. Lynx trike resulted in further two CTs being killed. Following equipment recovered, 3 X 82mm mortar bombs, 1000 rounds 7,62 intermediate, AK18079974, AKM 967279 and SKS1516552 .	T. 10/10 para A1(1). IV 21/78
10/10/78. 261.	CONTACT – Occured 1930 hrs at TL525640 (Diti TTL) when elements C Coy 2RR contacted 6-10 CTs, no cas to either side. 1 AK mag recovered.	T. 11/10 para A1(3).
11/10/78. 262. llsitics – No evious traces of recovered SKS'.)	CONTACT – Occurred 1130 hrs at TL603453 (Diti TTL) when elements A Coy 2RR had contact with approx 15 CTs in base camp. NO SF cas, CTs fled in N.W. direction and heavy blood spoor located and followed to area TL5746 (Diti TTL) where lost. Wounded CT appears to have been picked up by others and carried away. SKS 1506850 and SKS 22017398 / EKB1524449 recovered. c/s remains in area.	T. 11/10 para A1(4). IV 21/78
11/10/78. 263.	ROBBERY – Occurred approx 0900 hrs at QF978768 (Blshopstone Estates Umzingwani) when 10 CTs with 3 AFAs arrived at hunting camp forcing caretaker to open camp and took 8 blankets and various items of bedding.	T. 12/10 para A1(1)

CONFIDENTIAL

CONFIDENTIAL

INCIDENT LOG : BEITBRIDGE

Page No.: 44

SPECIAL BRANCH

B.S.A. POLICE

DIARY

FORM S.B. 10.
B.S.A.P.—20M—24-3-76.

Date	No.	Entry	Cross Reference and Index:
26/10/78.	280.	LANDMINE - Occurred at QF413559 (Maramani TTL) when Intaf MPV LMA 219 detonated a landmine with the left rear wheel. No casualties.	T. 27/10 para A1(1).
26/10/78.	281.	HOMESTEAD ATTACK - Occurred at 1640 hrs at RG109506 (Mjingwe Section Liebigs) when wife opened back door of house to check fence alarm and saw lone CT standing in yard. Ct fired two shots and EFA retired to house. CT followed but when EFA brandished rifle CT fled, firing around homestead killing dogs and wounding one AMA (not serious). CT absconded through hole cut in fence. Tracks followed for short distance before being lost on hard ground.	T. 27/10 para A1(2).
29/10/78.	282.	PRESENCE - Tracks of 16 CTs followed to QG945168 (Jopempi block Liebigs Ranch) then east to TM070198 (Dyers ranch lessee Liebigs Ranch Nuanetsi) where they were joined by a further 16 CTs. CTs gave out intentions to attack consolidated village at TM 085055 (Lamulas section Liebigs ranch).	T. 29/10 para A1(1).
29/10/78.	283.	LANDMINE - Occurred at 0930 hrs at QG605062 (Siyoka TTL) when scouter Zulu detonated a landmine in MPV LMC 27 with right rear wheel. No casualties and vehicle recovered to Beitbridge.	T. 29/10 para A1(2).
29/10/78.	284.	ARSON - At 1305 hrs at TL461929 (Bothasrust - Minnie - Bubye Farming area) unconfirmed report received that vacant homestead destroyed by fire.	T. 29/10 para B(1)(1
1/11/78.	285.	CONTACT - Occurred at 1000 hrs at TL281987 (Liebigs Jopempi Block) when elements of 1 Indep Coy and Liebigs Security had fleeting contact with estimated 8 CTs. No cas to either side. Tracks followed 2 Klms south west and lost due to cattle movement. Old huts in area of contact containing food, clothing and cooking utensils destroyed. Two AK mags recovered.	T. 1/11 para A1(2)
1/11/78.	286.	CONTACT - Occurred at 1730 hrs at QG772101 (Siyoka TTL) when elements A Coy 6RR had contact with 4 CTs. One CT escaped wounded. No SF Cas. Tracks followed to QG775108 where lost due to local movement.	T. 2/11 para A1(4)
3/11/78.	287.	LANDMINE - Occurred at TL940335 (Chipise TTL) when RM belonging to 5RR (operating Sengwe TTL) detonated landmine with right rear wheel. One minor cas recovered to Beitbridge.	

CONFIDENTIAL

FORM S.B. 10.
B.S.A.P.—20M—24-3-76.

CONFIDENTIAL

INCIDENT LOG : BEITBRIDGE

SPECIAL BRANCH
B.S.A. POLICE

DIARY

Page No.: 48

Date	No.	Entry	Cross References and Index
22/11/78.	308.	RAIL LINE SABOTAGE - occurred at the following sidings/locstats during the night of the 21-22/11/78 :- TL 386912 (Swanscoe Siding) - 12 charges over 300 metres of railway line, 11 of which cut line; longest break being 12 inches, 1 remaining charge failed to detonate as safety fuse only half burnt. In same area 2 railway poles set up for demolition, but charges failed to cut poles: TL 360880 Lesanth Siding, 400 metres railway line prepared with 15 charges, all charges cut the line. 3 railway telephone lines cut with charges about 3 feet from the ground: TL 307826 BASALT SIDING - 6 charges laid on railway line, 5 detonated, remaining 1 lifted by engineers. Also lifted in this area 1 PMN anti personnel mine and 1 PMN detonator regarded as dangerous. Knife also located assessed as having been used in preparation of demolition charges.	T. 22/11 para A1(4) Stop press 23/ para A1(1)
22/11/78.	309.	BOOBY TRAP - occurred at 1300 hours, at TL 326847 (near Lesanth Siding) when Railways Security Personnel set off booby trap device, resulting in serious injury to 1 EMA and 3 AMA. Device set up on the railway line in conjunction with demolition charges mention in entry 308 above.	T. 22/11/78 para A1(5)
22/11/78.	310.	EXPLOSIONS - heard by Guard Force details at SHABWE PV between 2103 and 2213 hours this date. 5 explosions heard from the area of TL 2146 (Mtetengwe TTL)	T. 22/11 para A1(6)
22/11/78.	311.	SABOTAGE - Occurred at TL 287810 (Lesanth Ranch) Bubye River Ranches - owner Mitchell, when drilling rig (water) and 3 E.S.C. poles destroyed by explosions. Occurred near Basalt Siding mentioned in entry 308 above. Drilling machine assessed as having been destroyed by TNT and evidence that TMN mine detonated by initial blast on machine.	T. 22/11 para A1(7)
22/11/78.	312.	LANDMINE - Occurred at TL 367837 (area of Lesanth Siding) when Ox detonated Landmine assessed as being TM 46.	T. Stop press 23/11 para A1(1)
26/11/78.	313.	P.V. ATTACK/CONTACT -Occurred at 0230 hrs at Shabwe PV Mtetengwe TTL (TL136534) when PV came under heavy mortar, 75 rec, rocket and small arms attack by estimated 60 CTs. Fire returned, no SF cas. First light check revealed approx 50 metres of PV fence cut and approx 200 locals abducted. Elements 1 Indep Coy followed spoor to TL115408 where contact took place with	T. 26/11 para A1(1).

CONFIDENTIAL

INCIDENT LOG : BEITBRIDGE

SPECIAL BRANCH
B.S.A. POLICE

DIARY

Page No.: 52/

FORM S.B. 10.
B.S.A.P.—20M—24-3-76.

Date	No.	Entry	Cross References and Index
8/12/78.	332.	SURRENDER - Occurred at 0745 hrs at TL720440 (Tshiturapadsi PV) when lone CT surrendered himself to elements of Intaf. Ct armed with AK 17112109, four magazines and chest webbing. Dressed in Khaki uniform.	T. 8/12 IV para A1(4).
8/12/78. llistics - 3 AKs, SKS. One AK tched to entry	333.	AMBUSH - Occurred at 0745 hrs at QF732866 (Shobi Block Liebigs ranch) when EMA STOCKHILL and wife travelling in mine protected landrover were ambushed by an estimated 10-15 CTs. No cas, numerous strikes on vehicle. FF Delta deployed. No contact made.	T. 8/12 para A1(5),
9/12/78.	334.	CONTACT - Occurred at 1430 hrs at QG6512 (Siyoka TTL) when elements of Scouter ZULU and 1 Indep Coy had contact with 16 ZANLA CTs at site of large base camp. No cas either side. One note book and 50 x 7,62 inter cartridge cases recovered.	T. 10/12 para A1(2).
10/12/78.	335.	GT CAMP ATTACK - Occurred 1000 hrs in area TL 4534 (Diti TTL) when elements D Coy 2 RR carried out sweep of suspected Povo bases. CT base camps located at TL433328, TL473339, TL470362 and TL480355. Numerous occupied Povo's containing food located in area. Elements D Coy 2RR opened fire on movement in Povo area, 4 AMA killed, 1 AMJ and I AFJ wounded and casevaced to Beitbridge. All Povos destroyed and locals instructed to move into P.V.'s. Interrogation of locals reveals approx 30 CTs were in area earlier that morning.	T. 10/12 para A1(1).
10/12/78.	336.	ATTACK - Occurred 0930 hrs at QG534254 (Doddiburn Ranch West Nicholson) when estimated 5 CTs attacked stationary National Parks and Wild Life vehicle. Vehicle left with 2 guards whilst foot patrol deployed. Guards absconded, no cas. No damage to vehicle. Tracks lost in thick bush. Copper 87 (Darlow) deployed.	T. 10/12 para A1(4).
10/12/78.	337.	BASE CAMP ATTACK - occurred at 1600 hours, at TL 705563 (Nuanetsi Farming Area) when combined Air and Ground attack carried out on CT base. Camp located by Air Recce - 6 locals killed. Contact made with unknown number of CTs at TL 702569 no cas. Elms A Coy 2RR and 1 Indep RAR remained in area in ambush. Ambush initiated 0100 hrs 11/12 killing 1 AMA and 3 AMJ. Sweep of area at first light revealed no tracks due to cattle movement. Grass huts, grain huts, civ kit and equipment destroyed. No CT equipment recovered.	T. 11/12/78 para A1(2)

CONFIDENTIAL

CONFIDENTIAL

INCIDENT LOG : BEITBRIDGE

SPECIAL BRANCH
B.S.A. POLICE

DIARY

FORM S.B. 10.
B.S.A.P.—20M—24-3-76.

Page No.: 57/78

Date	No.	Entry	Cross References and Index
25/12/78.	369.	SHOOTING - Occurred at 1855 at TL323740 (Lesanth Ranch Bubye Farming area) when elements C Coy 2RR shot and killed 1 AMA who attempted to escape during interrogation. Body identified and handed to relatives on farm.	T. 26/12 para A1(1).
25/12/78.	370.	PRESENCE/PRAW SHOT AT - Occurred 1840hrs at QG833248 (Makado ranch) when approx 300 locals appeared at farm homestead having apparently been chased by approx 25 CTs. Int from locals was that CTs intended attacking Makado ranch. Lynx and Praw deployed. Praw fired upon by approx 7 CTs. Lynx put in last light strike. No known CT cas.	T. 26/12 para A1(4).
25/12/78.	371.	ABDUCTION - Occurred 2200 hrs at SL975355 (Mapai P.V. Mtetengwe TTL) when fence was breached by unknown number of CTs and 17 locals abducted. Abductees made good their escape and returned to PV. Note handed to Guard Force at PV from CTs.	T. 26/12 para A1(6).
26/12/78.	372.	CONTACT - Occurred at 0925 hrs at TL 515687 (Diti TTL) when elements C Coy 2RR had contact with estimated 5-6 CTs in Povo base. 1 CT killed, No SF cas. 1 AK no 815610, 5 AK mags, 1 stick grenade, 1 set chest webbing and items of clothing recovered. No tracks located.	T. 26/12 para A1(2). IV 1/79
26/12/78.	373.	LANDMINE - Occurred at 1310 hrs at 1310 hrs at SL978389 (Mtetengwe TTL) when 1 Indep vehicle no 29DB77 reacting to abduction at Mapai PV with SB detonated a landmine with front right wheel. No SF cas.	T. 26/12 para A1(7). C.R. 4/1/79.
26/12/78.	374.	CONVOY AMBUSH - Occurred at 1335 hrs at QF985795 (Beitbridge-Byo road - Mtetengwe TTL) when north bound convoy ambushed by approx 7 CTs. No cas. Fire Force Delta deployed, tracks located and followed to vicinity RF073810.	T. 26/12 para A1(8). C.R. 1/2/79.
26/12/78.	375.	SHOOTING - Occurred 1755 hrs at TL 866450 (Chipise TTL) when elements A Coy 2RR whilst moving into stop position shot and killed an AMA who ran when challenged.	T. 27/12
27/12/78.	376.	POVO CAMP/FF DEPLOYMENT - Occurred 0700 hrs at TL865468, TL857473 and TL850480 (Chipise TTL) when FF Dela in conjunction with ground troops deployed to investigate povo complex located by air recce. No CTs located, 2 AMA killed, food stuffs, blankets etc destroyed.	T. 27/12 para A1(9).

CONFIDENTIAL

CONFIDENTIAL
INCIDENT LOG : BEITBRIDGE

Page No.: 2/79

SPECIAL BRANCH
B.S.A. POLICE

DIARY

FORM S.B. 10.
B.S.A.P.—20M—24-3-76.

Date	No.	Incident	Cross References and Index
8/1/79. listics - 4 AKs, KS, all no vious traces.)	6.	AIRCRAFT SHOOTING - Occurred 0615 hrs at RG 052385 (Ripple Creek Ranch - Darlow) when PRAW aircraft c/s 87 off duty fired on with small arms fire after take off. Fired on by approx 20 CTs from area RG053373 (Ripple Creek Ranch Liebigs).	T. 8/1 para A1(3).
9/1/79.	7.	VEHICLE ROBBERY - Occurred 1300 hrs at TL280805 (Main Beitbridge/Fort Victoria road) when 8 CTs robbed Stuttafords van travelling between Fort Victroia and Beitbridge. CTs stole 3 metal trunks, watches, valuables and documents. Left in North westerly direction.	T. 9/1 para A1(3). C.R. 59-61/1/79
10/1/79.	8.	AMBUSH - Occurred 1120 hrs at TL382799 (Lesanth Ranch) when owner MITCHELL ambushed by u/k no of CTs. Fire returned and spoor of 4 CTs two of whom apparently wounded located.	T. 10/1 para A1(6).
10/1/79.	9.	SHOOTING - Occurred 1800 hrs at QG747014 (Siyoka TTL) when elements 2RR whilst moving into night location were observed by 3 AMJ who bombshelled and failed to halt when challenged. c/s opened fire killing one AMJ.	T. 11/1 para A1(4).
10/1/79.	10.	SHOOTING - Occurred 1930 hrs at QG740014 (Siyoka TTL) when elements 2RR in Ambush shot and killed one AMA.	T. 11/1 para A1(5).
11/1/79.	11.	LANDMINE - Occurred 1530 hrs at QG9526 (Alka-Towla road) when a civilian vehicle detonated a landmine. 2 AMA's injured casevaced to Gwanda.	T. 11/1 para A1(6). C.R. 28/4/79.
11/1/79.	12.	SHOOTING - Occurred 0110 in area QF6876 (Masera TTL) when elements Recce Plt 2RR accidently shot and killed AMA guide leading callsign to suspect CT base. Informer identified as Michael SHAVA X24806 Belingwe.	T. 11/1 para A1(10).
11/1/79. listics - No vious trace of overed weapon.)	13.	CONTACT - Occurred 0630 hrs at QF674764 (Masera TTL) when elements Recce Plt 2RR had fleeting contact with two CTs. One CT killed, One CT escaped wounded. SKS 1511329 recovered.	T. 11/1 para A1(11). IV 1/79
11/1/79.	14.	SHOOTING - Occurred 1400 hrs at QG722045 (Siyoka TTL) when elements C Coy 2RR whilst interrogating locals shot and killed 2 AMA who attempted to abscond.	T. 13/1 para A1(2).
12/1/79.	15.	CONTACT - Occurred 0808 hrs at QG6712 (Siyoka TTL when elements B Coy 2RR had fleeting contact with 10-12 CTs. No cas either side. PRAW AC deployed to recce ahead located 5 AMA's	T. 13/1 para A1(10),

CONFIDENTIAL

CONFIDENTIAL

INCIDENT LOG : BEITBRIDGE

SPECIAL BRANCH
B.S.A. POLICE

DIARY

Page No.: 6/79

FORM S.B. 10.
B.S.A.P.—20M—24-3-76.

Date	No.	Incident	Cross References and Index
22/1/79. listics - 4 AKs, of which tied entry 190/78. All ers no previous ces.)	36.	**PV ABDUCTION** - Occurred 2200 hrs at TL 141536 (Shabwe Protected Village) when an unknown of CTs breached the fence. Elements of Guard Force opened fire resulting in CTs returning small arms fire, mortar and 3,5 rocket fire. Two AMA's killed in cross fire and unknown number of locals abducted the vast majority of whom have since returned to the PV.	T. 23/1 para A1(1). C.R. 4-5/2/79.
23/1/79.	37.	**LANDMINE** - Occurred 0930 hrs at QF 425564 (Maramani TTL) when Intaf MPV no LMC209 detonated landmine with left front wheel. No SF cas.	T. 23/1 para A1(2).
23/1/79. listics - 4 AKs, no previous ces.)	38.	**MURDER** - Occurred 1600 hrs at TM 076183 (Montana Ranch Wanezi Block) when Farm manager James SOUTER murdered by unknown number of CTs using RPG 2 and small arms fire. Deceased was riding motor cycle and was captured by CTs prior to being murdered.	R. 24/1 para A3(1).
26/1/79. listics - 3 AKs, KS, all no vious traces.)	39.	**AMBUSH** - Occurred 0830 hrs at TL316564 (Diti TTL) when elements Guard Force and 2 RDR ambushed by estimated 10-15 CTs using small arms fire, rockets and mortars. No SF cas, spoor lost in immeadiate vicinity.	T. 26/1 para A1(2). C.R. 98/1/79.
26/1/79.	40.	**LANDMINE** - Occurred 2300 hrs at QF367748 (Machuchuta TTL) when four wheeled scotch cart detonated landmine killing one AMA and 1 AMA sustaining minor injuries. No spoor located due to cattle and local movement.	T. 28/1 para A1(1).
28/1/79. listics - 2 AKS. matched to entry 8.)	41.	**MURDER** - Occurred 1600 hrs at QG688165 (Siyoka TTL) when 20 CTs shot and killed AMA for allegedly harbouring AFA who was ZANLA informant/runner. 27 expended 7,62 intermediate cartridge cases recovered at scene of murder. Deceased buried by relatives.	T. 30/1 para A1(5). C.R. 6/2/79.
29/1/79.	42.	**SHOOTING** - Occurred 1930 hrs at RF067417 (Beit-Bridge state land) when elements Sparkplug shot and killed AMA curfew breaker. Body handed to Police.	T. 30/1 para A1(1).
30/1/79. listics - 1 AK, S, both no ous traces.)	43.	**CONTACT** - Occurred 1230 hrs at QF772782 (Masera TTL) when elements Scouter Uniform investigating base camp had fleeting contact with 7 CTs. No cas to either side.	T. 30/1 para A1(2).
30/1/79.	44.	**LANDMINE** - Occurred 1457 hrs at QF790670 (Masera TTL) when elements Scouter Uniform in Map Hyena H21 detonated landmine with front wheel. 3 cas casevaced to Beitbridge.	T. 30/1 para A1(6). C.R. 2/2/79.

CONFIDENTIAL

CONFIDENTIAL

INCIDENT LOG : BEITBRIDGE

SPECIAL BRANCH
B.S.A. POLICE

DIARY

Page No.: 8/79

FORM S.B. 10.
B.S.A.P.—8M—19-8-75.

Date	No.	Incident	Cross References and Index
6/2/79	54	LANDMINE - Occurred 1145 hours at TL 285543 (Diti TTL) when roads department MP 7 ton lorry No TL790 detonated landmine with right front wheel. One AMA pax received serious injuries and one EMA pax slight injuries, casevaced to Beitbridge.	T. 6/2 para A1(2). C.R. 29/2/79.
6/2/79	55	LANDMINE - Occurred 1500 hrs at QF 378674 (Maramani TTL) when elements Police located a TMD 44 landmine. Elements engineers out to investigate.	T. 6/2 para A1(4).
6/2/79	56	AMBUSH occurred main Byo Rd. QG 914090 when Shu Shine bus ambushed by u/k no. of ters, no casualties.	C.R. 20/2/79. T7/2 para A(1)
7/2/79	57	Ambush Occurred main Byo Rd. QF 978812 when civ. vehicle ambushed by u/k no. ters, no injuries.	C.R. 18/3/79. T 7/2 para A(2)
7/2/79. istics - 7 AKs , 1 RPD. 1 AK ed to entry 8.)	58	AMBUSH - Occurred at 0600 hrs at TL108541 (Mtetengwe TTL) when roads department vehicle ambushed by four CTs using small arms and mortars Fire returned by army escort resulting in CTs fleeing. One AMA driver sustained slight injury. Spoor lost to hard ground. One 60mm mortar bomb recovered, destroyed in situ.	T. 8/2 para A1(1). C.R. 15/2/79.
8/2/79.	59	LANDMINE DETONATION - Occurred 0905 hrs at TL 297555 (Diti TTL) following report of explosion roads department located large crater in road and remnants of body of one CT, one note book, 2 x 40 rounds mags (damaged) and two clips 7,62 ammo.	T. 8/2 para A1(2).
8/2/79.	60	CONTACT - Occurred 1415 hrs at TL 920385 (Chipise TTL) when elements A Coy 2RR had contact with approx 30 CTs. No cas either side and no spoor located.	R. 8/2 para A2(6).
8/2/79. istics - No ious traces.)	61	CONTACT - Occurred 2000 hrs at QG617237 (Siyoka TTL) when elements 1 Indep Coy had contact with 5 ZIPRA CTs. One CT wounded, 2 CTs killed. AK HW4233P and AK KT17-0874 recovered. (0871)	T. 9/2 para A1(2). IV 3/79
9/2/79. istics - No ious traces.)	62	CONTACT - Occurred 1250 hrs at QG6123 (Siyoka TTL) when elements 1 Indep Coy had contact with nine CTs. 7 ZIPRA CTs killed, no SF cas. Following weapons recovered : a) PPSH no 7594 b) AKM 1977-117053 c) AK KT17-4528 d) AK 17-1260 e) AKM 1976-150724 f) AKM 1976-995374 (450724)	T. 9/2 para A1(3). IV 3/79

CONFIDENTIAL

FORM S.B. 10.
B.S.A.P.—8M—19-8-75.

CONFIDENTIAL
INCIDENT LOG : BEITBRIDGE

SPECIAL BRANCH
B.S.A. POLICE

DIARY

Page No.: 11/79

Date	No.	Incident	Cross References and Index
16/2/79.	82.	ROBBERY - Occurred 1725 hrs at TL 385928 (Swanscoe B/Bridge to Fort Victoria rd) when south bound Trek transport vehicle robbed by 20 CTs of 850 rand (travellers cheques) and $80. 9 CTs of group spent night at TL325937 where gave out intention to kill owner of Safari ranch McDonald.	T. 17/2 para A1(3). C.R. 15/4/79.
16/2/79.	83.	ROBBERY - Occurred 1430 hrs at TL345875 (Safari Ranch - Fort Vic - B/Bridge road) when north bound Swift Transport vehicle was robbed by an unknown number of CTs.	T. 17/2 para A1(4). C.R. 7/5/79.
17/2/79.	84.	BASE CAMP/ATT MURDER - Occurred 0730 hrs at QF903634 (Befar Estate) when 4 AFA's walked into CT base camp. CTs opened fire. AFA managed to escape without injury.	T. 17/2 para A1(5).
17/2/79.	85.	LANDMINE - Occurred 0800 hrs at QG 705176 (Siyoka TTL) when elements 1 Indep Coy detonated landmine in vehicle 288HC75 with right rear wheel. No SF cas.	T. 17/2 para A1(6). C.R. 31/2/79.
17/2/79.	86.	AMBUSH - Occurred 1145 hrs at TL335573 (Diti TTL) when INTAF vehicle ambushed by unknown number of CTs using small arms and rocket fire. No cas, no damage to vehicle. No follow-up due to lack of troops.	T. 17/2 para A1(7). C.R. 16/4/79.
17/2/79. 87. listics - 2 AKs previous traces, no previous e.)		RAIL EXPLOSION - Occurred 0745 hrs at TL393920 (Swanscoe Siding) when North Bound train detonated explosive device resulting in 18 inches of line being blown. Loco damaged and recovered to Rutenga.	T. 17/2 para A1(8).
18/2/79.	88.	AMBUSH - Occurred 1430 hrs at QG808269 (B/Bridge to Bulawayo road) when Wards Transport vehicle ambushed by unknown number of CTs. AMA injured casevaced to Gwanda by road. 2 strikes to vehicle.	T. 18/2 para A1(6).
18/2/79. 89. listics - 12 AKs KS, 1 MG 34/42 hinegun. All previous traces)		HOMESTEAD ATTACK - Occurred 1945 hrs at TL602881 (Shobi Block homestead, Liebigs) when approx 40 CTs attacked homestead with small arms, rocket and 82mm mortar fire. Fire returned by occupants and attack ceased after 15 minutes. No cas. 1 Liebigs security guard sufferred self inflicted gunshot wound to stomach, cas to Bulawayo.	T. 19/2 para A1(2). C.R. 49/7/79.
18/2/79.	90.	ROBBERY - Occurred 1745 hrs at QG866673 (Shamba Yetu Farm, Umzingwane) when 5 CTs robbed AMA employee of radio and yellow overalls. No spoor located.	T. 19/2 para A1(3). C.R. 5/5/79.

CONFIDENTIAL

CONFIDENTIAL

INCIDENT LOG : BEITBRIDGE

Page No.: 13/79

SPECIAL BRANCH
B.S.A. POLICE

DIARY

FORM S.B. 10.
B.S.A.P.—8M—19-8-75.

Date	No.	Incident	Cross References and Index
22/2/79.	101.	CONTACT - Occurred 1700 hrs at QF881906 (Jopempi Block - Liebigs) when elements Liebigs had contact with 2 CTs. No cas either side, spoor followed to QF935835 (Jopempi block) where lost.	T. 23/2 para A1(7).
23/2/79.	102.	AMBUSH - Occurred 1000 hrs at TL376915 (Main B/Bridge - Fort Vic rd) when Swift Vehicle was ambushed by 15 CTs. No injuries, damage to vehicle from rifle grenade. At 1015 hrs at same location, civilian vehicle ambushed by same no of CTs. Nine strikes to vehicle, no cas.	T. 23/2 para A1(9). C.R. 32-33/2/79
23/2/79.	103.	ATTEMMPTED MURDER - Occurred 1000 hrs at TL375900 (Lesanth Ranch - Mitchell) when AMA was fired upon by unknown number of CTs. No injuries.	T. 23/2 para A1(10).
23/2/79.	104.	LANDMINE (RECOVERED) - Occurred 0900 hrs at QG827178 (Siyoka TTL) when elements Scouter ZULU located and lifted wooden box mine.	T. 23/2 para A1(11).
23/2/79.	105.	LANDMINE (RECOVERED) - Occurred at 0920 hrs at TL283527 (Diti TTL) when elements RDR located wooden box mine which was lifted by engineers.	T. 23/2 para A1(12).
23/2/79.	106.	LANDMINE (RECOVERED) - Occurred at 1015 hrs at TL 220518 (Mtetetengwe TTL) when elements RDR located wooden box mine which was lifted by engineers.	T. 23/2 para A1(13).
23/2/79.	107.	LANDMINE (RECOVERED) - Occurred 1412 hrs at TL250576 (Diti TTL) when elements Guardforce located and lifted a wooden box mine.	T. 24/2 para A1(1).
23/2/79.	108.	ROBBERY - Occurred 1730 hrs at SL966395 (Mtetengwe TTL) when approx 10 CTs robbed two civilian vehicles of $65. watches and clothing.	T. 24/2 para A1(4).
25/2/79.	109.	GRENADE EXPLOSION - Ocurred 1115 at TL 280523 (Diti TTL) when member of holdfast detonated a stick grenade receiving in facial and arm injuries. Cas to Beitbridge and then Bulawayo.	T. 25/2 para A1(5).
25/2/79.	110.	CONTACT - Occurred 1215 hrs at TL280523 (Diti TTL) when Intaf detail at scene of grenade explosion mentioned above saw 1 CT crossing road approx 300 metres east of loc, opened fire, no fire returned. Investigations of road located 12 CT firing positions.	T. 25/2 para A1(6).
2/2/79.	111.	MURDER (Late Report) - Occurred at QF603496 (Sentinal Ranch) when AMA murdered by 8 CTs who cut his throat. Police investigating.	T. 26/2 para A1(1).

CONFIDENTIAL

CONFIDENTIAL

INCIDENT LOG : BEITBRIDGE

SPECIAL BRANCH
B.S.A. POLICE

DIARY

Page No.: 19/79

FORM S.B. 10.
B.S.A.P.—20M—24-3-76.

Date	No.	Entry	Cross References and Index
24/3/79. listics - 1 AK ned to entry 79.)	155.	AMBUSH - Occurred 0800 hrs at QF912590 (River Ranch Umzingwane) when African civilian vehicle was ambushed by 10-15 CTs, no cas or strikes to vehicle.	C.R. 24/4/79. T. 24/3 para A1(4).
24/3/79. listics - No vious trace of vered weapon.)	156.	CONTACT - Occurred 1020 hrs at QF914578 (River Ranch) when elements Scouter Uniform following spoor from ambush mentioned entry (155) had contact with 2 CTs. No SF cas, 1 CT killed, 1 Chicom no 90200617, 1 set webbing, 2 x 20 round mags, 2 x 30 round mags, 120 rounds and two note books recovered.	T. 24/3 para A1(2). 9029067 IV 4/7
24/3/79. listics - No vious traces of overed weapons.)	157.	CONTACT - Occurred at 1200 hrs at TM 046020 (Section One Liebigs) when elements Liebigs had contact with unknown number of CTs. 1 CT killed c/s following blood spoor of wounded CT. AK no 20071617 , SKS no 1516578 , SKS no 22016001 recovered.	T. 24/3 para A1(1). IV 4/79
24/3/79.	158.	LANDMINE DETONATION/RECOVERED - Occurred at 1320 at TL344862 (Lesanth Ranch) when AMA in civilian vehicle detonated landmine. 1 AMA killed, 2 AFAs injured cas to Beitbridge. Further landmine located 150 metres from first incident uplifted.	T. 25/3 para A1(1). C.R. 9/4/79.
24/3/79. listics - 12 AKs S. 1 AK matched try 47/79.)	159.	AMBUSH - Occurred 1445 hrs at TL685440 (Chipisi TTL) when Guardforce convoy ambushed by unknown number of CTs. Fire returned, no SF cas, no tracks located.	T. 25/3 para A1(2). C.R. 39/4/79.
25/3/79.	160.	CT/POVO CAMP ATTACK - Occurred 0600 at TL586869 TL583897, TL588844 and TL537912 (Bubye Farming) when elements 1 Indep and Arty attacked CT/Povo bases, no cas, camps believed evacuated that am.	T. 25/3 para A1(3).
25/3/79. istics - No vious trace of overed weapon.)	161.	CONTACT - Occurred 1445 hrs at TL625517 (Chipisi TTL) when elements B Coy 2RR had contact with u/k of CTs. 1 CT killed, AKM 146419 recovered, 1 minor SF cas casevaced to Tshiturapadzi.	T. 26/3 para A1(3). IV 4/79
25/3/79.	162.	CAPTURE - Occurred 1600 hrs at TL065744 (Tshemene PV) when locally trained unarmed CT captured by elements Guardforce whilst attempting to obtain medical treatment for wounds received during contact mentioned entry 157/79 above.	T. 26/3 para A1(2).
26/3/79. istics - 1 AK revious trace.)	163.	AMBUSH - Occurred 0925 hrs at QF878719 (Bishopstone Estate) when EMA JOUBERT in Map vehicle ambushed by u/k no of CTs using small arms and rockets. No cas, several strikes to vehicle.	T. 26/3 para A1(1). C.R. 24/4/79.

CONFIDENTIAL

CONFIDENTIAL
INCIDENT LOG : BEITBRIDGE

Page No.: 23/79

FORM S.B. 10.
B.S.A.P.—20M—24-3-76.

SPECIAL BRANCH
B.S.A. POLICE

DIARY

Date	No.	Entry	Cross References and Index
11/4/79.	189.	LANDMINE - Occurred 1000 hrs at TL 523778 (Bea Ranch Bubye farming area) when elements 2RR vehicle no 494 HC75 detonated unidentified landmine. No cas.	T. 11/4 para A1(11). C.R. 29/4/79.
13/4/79. (isites - No ous trace of ered weapon.)	190.	SHOOTING - Occurred 0100 at QG824211 (Siyoka TTL) when Makado ranch Militia checking kraal for suspected wounded ZIPRA CT shot and killed AMA who absconded while being questioned. Elements 1 Indep Coy investigating located AKM 969342 in hut in vicinity of shooting.	T. 13/4 para A1(7). IV 8/79
13/4/79.	191.	SHOOTING - Occurred at 1000 hrs at TL665334 (Chipise TTL) when elements C Coy 2RR ambushed 6 locals carrying bundles of dried meat. 1 AMA killed and 1 AFA wounded.	T. 13/4 para A1(8).
13/4/79. (listics - No vious traces of overed weapons.)	192.	CONTACT -Occurred at TL480360 (Chipise TTL) when elements A Coy 2RR made contact with 10-15 CTs who were tracking callsign. Two CTs killed, AK 20060366* and AK 1975-714053** recovered, two notebooks. One minor SF cas wound to foot cas to Tshiturapadzi. 14/4 Para B1(1).	T. 13/4 para A1(9). * IV 6/79 ** Gda IV 25/78
13/4/79.	193.	CONTACT - Occurred 2105 hrs at QG 995275 (Towla Ranch) established that no contact took place, fire fight between two Liebigs callsigns. No cas, no CT presence.	T. 14/4 para A1(2).
13/4/79.	194.	CONTACT - Occurred 2100 hrs at QG861303 (Drie Hoek ranch) when the presence of CTs in the farm compound was investigated by BOTHA and guardforce who had contact with a group of 8 CTs. 2 AFA killed in crossfire. Cts absconded.	T. 14/4 para A1(3).
13/4/79.	195.	M.I.P. - Occurred night 13-14/4 at QG725285 (Makado Ranch) when African civilian vehicle burned out by 6 ZANLA CTs. Owner a known ZPRA supporter.	T. 14/4 para A1(8).
13/4/79.	196.	M.I.P. - Occurred night 13-14/4 at QG 712314 (Highway Ranch) when 6 CTs burned main Water Pump and cut water pipe line three times.	T. 14/4 para A1(10).
13/4/79.	197.	SHOOTING - Occurred 1225 hrs at TL545462 (Diti TTL) when elements 1 Indep Coy shot and killed 1 AMA.	T. 14/4 para A1(14).
13/4/79.	198.	SHOOTING - Occurred 1520 hrs at TL 784336 (Chipise TTL) when elements C Coy 2RR shot and killed AMA.	T. 14/4 para A1(15).
13/4/79.	199.	CONTACTb- Occurred 1740 hrs at TL525464 (Diti TTL) when elements 1 Indep Coy had contact with 4 CTs. 1 CT killed wearing chest webbing, no weapon recovered.	T. 14/4 para A1(17).

CONFIDENTIAL

Rhodesian Security Forces

FN, SMLE .303 AND .303 MK 4

Calibre: 7.62mm
Length: 1,090mm
Barrel length: 533mm
Rate of fire: 650–700rpm
Range: 400–600m
Weight: 4.3kg
Ammunition: 7.62×51mm

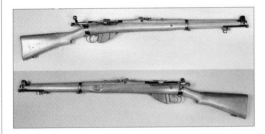

Calibre: .303 / 7.7mm
Length: 1,118mm
Barrel length: 767mm
Rate of fire: 20rpm
Range: 503m
Weight: 4kg
Ammunition: 7.7×56mm

MAG AND .30 BROWNING MMGS

Calibre: 7.62mm
Length: 1,263mm
Barrel length: 630mm
Rate of fire: 650–1,000rpm
Range: 800m
Weight: 11,79kg
Ammunition: 7.62x51mm

Calibre: 7.62mm
Length: 964mm
Barrel length: 610mm
Rate of fire: 400–600rpm
Range: 1,400m
Weight: 14kg
Ammunition: 7.62x51mm

81mm MORTAR AND BOMBS

Type: 81mm mortar
Weight (combat): 35.3kg
Barrel length: 1,280mm
Rate of fire: 15rpm
Range: 5,650m9
Ammunition: 2.4kg, 81mm shell
Crew: 3

25 POUNDER PLUS ROUNDS

Type: 25 pounder fieldgun/howitzer
Weight: 1,633kg
Length: 4.6m
Barrel length: 2.47m
Width: 2.13m
Rate of gunfire: 6–8rpm
Range: 12,253m
Ammunition: 87.6mm HE
Crew: 6

1.5 TON UNIMOG

Type: Mine-protected infantry fighting vehicle
Weight: 7.2 tonnes
Length: 4.95m
Width: 2.4m
Height: 2.8m
Crew: 2+11
Armament: 2 x 7.62mm MAGs
Engine: Daimler-Benz OM352 turbo diesel 120 hp
Power/weight: hp/ton hp/tonne
Suspension: wheels, 4x4
Operational range; 700 km
Speed: 60–80km/h

APPENDIX IV
Letter from Lt-Gen. G.P. Walls to Margaret Thatcher

SECRET

cc Mr Powell FCO
PM has seen
2.3.80

Reply sent.

L^ /Rnd - 3/3

Salisbury
1 March 1980

The Right Honourable Margaret Thatcher, MP
Prime Minister
10 Downing Street
LONDON SW1

Dear Prime Minister

I am exercising the right conferred upon me by you personally that I have direct access to you when the situation warrants it. I believe it is my solemn duty and responsibility to now report to you directly and make an appeal on behalf of all freedom-loving and law-abiding Zimbabwe Rhodesians. Many of these have trusted you and your Government because of my colleagues and my own example, assurance and encouragement, and in the case of the security forces, our command. We have now completed three days of voting as part of the electoral process agreed at Lancaster House and await announcement of the results on next Tuesday morning. I therefore judge this to be the right moment for me to take this action. I must first explain the background. Despite your assurance to me that Lord Soames would measure up to the grave responsibility delegated to him, I must confirm reports sent to you, through intermediaries, that he has proved to be inadequate, lacking in moral courage, lacking in ability to listen and learn, and above all incapable of implementing the solemn promise, given by yourself and Lord Carrington, that he would rely on us for advice on military and other situations, and act in accordance with the interests of survival of a moderate, freedom-loving and anti-marxist society. I will not accuse him of being unwilling to do so, although many in their bitterness think this to be the case. He has often treated us as if we had no special status in your eyes and certainly not as people who, at great political sacrifice, had agreed to go to the conference table after militarily forcing the other parties to agree to do so. It is true his task has not

-2-/...

SECRET

SECRET

- 2 -

been made easier by your Government insisting on unrestricted entry of hundreds of observers and journalists, many of whom are avowedly left wing orientated and definitely anti-Muzorewa. Many of them, and some junior monitors, have been arrogant enough to set themselves up as instant experts on this country, and Africa generally, and have made pronouncements accordingly, contributing greatly to the emotional and hysterical wave of hostile propaganda levelled against us. Had the Governor acted resolutely and effectively in the early days of the pre-election period, his task would have been much easier, and our survival as a democratic nation would not now be so seriously imperilled.

Although it is possible the moderate parties may achieve acceptable results in the election, I must say to you in all sincerity and gravity that it will be a miracle if it happens and in spite of intimidation, breaches of the ceasefire, and sheer terror accepted pathetically by your representatives. Although I have sufficient faith in God to hope that the true wishes of the people in this country will be manifested some day in some way and may be even now, I must take the precaution of making contingency plans for the worst case on this occasion, especially as reports from all around the country indicate that massive intimidation makes a victory by Mugabe the most likely if not inevitable result of the election.

I should add that many of the affidavits about intimidation, in the hundreds being forwarded to us today, have been sworn by your British policemen and other visitors. I wish you could see the sullen hurt and misery in the eyes and faces of our black people, who are normally so cheerful, good-natured, and full of goodwill.

My appeal to you must be on the following basis :

    (a) If Mugabe succeeds in gaining a simple majority by winning 51 seats or more, or if he is able to attract sufficient defectors from other parties, it is vital to our survival as a free nation that you declare the election nul and void on the grounds of official reports of massive intimidation frustrating the free choice of the bulk of the people

SECRET

SECRET

- 3 -

(b) If Mugabe gets less than 50 seats but has more than any other party, our present efforts to form a coalition based on the tripod of Muzorewa, Nkomo and Smith must be given every opportunity and help, however overt or devious as may be necessary, to succeed in governing the country and resisting the efforts to overthrow them of Mugabe, and anybody who supports him

(c) In the event of the election being declared nul and void, or the moderate parties failing to form a viable coalition with a working majority in the House of Assembly, it is essential from my considered point of view that you maintain a British presence in ZR to run the country with a Council of Ministers, thus allowing us to provide, if necessary, the military conditions for an orderly and safe withdrawal of those people of all races who wish to take refuge in South Africa or elsewhere. This will be preferable to my taking unconstitutional action which would be fraught with snags and dangers, apart from being loathsome to me as a professional soldier, and almost certain to result in much bloodshed and damage to property, and embarrassment to your Government. However, if you are unable to see your way to honouring the bond between us I must reserve the right to take whatever action is necessary in the interests of the majority of people whom I am pledged to serve.

It must be without precedent or at least abnormal, for a person like myself to address such a message as this to no less than the Prime Minister of Britain, but I wish to assure you I do so only in the extremity of our possible emergency, with goodwill, and in the sincere and honest belief that it is my duty in terms of the privileged conversations I had with you and Lord Carrington. I don't know how to sign myself, but I hope to remain your obedient servant,

PETER WALLS

SECRET

APPENDIX V
Foreign and Commonwealth Office responds

```
                         OUT TELEGRAM

        Classification and Caveats          Precedence/Deskby
        SECRET                              FLASH
```

1 ZCZC
2 GRS
3 SECRET
4
5
6 FM FCO 031400Z
7 TO FLASH SALISBURY
8 TELEGRAM NUMBER
9
10 MY TELNO   : RHODESIA: MESSAGE FROM GENERAL WALLS
11 1. The Prime Minister does not intend to reply to Walls'
12 message in writing, but would be grateful if you or Sir A Duff
13 could speak to Walls on the following lines, making clear that
14 you are doing so on her personal instructions. (In the light
15 of some of the comments in Walls' message, you may prefer to
16 ask Sir A Duff to do so).
17 2. The Prime Minister was glad that Walls felt able to get in
18 touch with her personally to explain his concerns. She fully
19 understands what a difficult time this is and in particular
20 the uncertainty and tension which inevitably exists between
21 the elections and the declaration of results. She has greatly
22 admired the lead taken by Walls in bringing together the forces
23 of the two sides and in encouraging co-operation between Nkomo,
24 Muzorewa and the Whites, and these efforts have her full support.
25

Catchword
/The prospects

File number   Dept   Distribution
               Rhodesia Dept   Files
                                    PS
Drafted by (Block capitals)   PS/LPS
        C D POWELL   PS/Mr Luce
                                    PS/PUS
Telephone number   Mr Day
        3466   Head, Rhodesia Dept
```
```

OUT TELEGRAM (CONT)

Classification and Caveats: SECRET
Page: 2

<<<<

The prospects for a peaceful and stable outcome will depend upon others being willing to show the same spirit of reconciliation. The Prime Minister is very grateful to Walls for his outstanding contribution, and hopes that he will continue to do his best to keep all the parties calm during the difficult period ahead.

3. It should be made clear to Walls that the Prime Minister regards his criticisms of you as entirely unjustified. The RSF have been deployed fully throughout the interim period and in a way which has enabled them to maintain full control over the military situation. No attempt has been made to interfere with the NJOC's military judgment. The admission of observers to the elections was agreed at Lancaster House. It is also vital to securing international acceptance for Rhodesia.

4. You should leave Walls in no doubt that, in the light of the reports from our own supervisors and observers (as well as international groups, the Prime Minister does not share his view that massive intimidation has frustrated the free choice of the people (although she realises that there has been some intimidation). There are no grounds, in the Prime Minister's view, on which the election could be declared null and void. The task now is to make the best of the outcome to ensure a stable government.

5. The composition of the future government must, in the Prime Minister's view, reflect the need for unity and reconciliation. It remains her objective, as explained to Walls during the Lancaster House conference, to see Rhodesia brought to independence with as stable and moderate a government as possible which fairly reflects the wishes of the people. The Prime Minister has heard with interest and approval of the discussions which have been taking place between Bishop Muzorewa, Mr Nkomo and the Rhodesian Front, with the

---

NNNN ends telegram | BLANK | Catchword /encouragement

XY 48 A

OUT TELEGRAM (CONT)

Classification and Caveats: **SECRET** Page 3

<<<<
encouragement of the NJOC, and hopes that these can establish the foundations for successful collaboration in the post-election period. Depending on the election results, it may also be necessary to accommodate other parties who are equally prepared to commit themselves to the goals of unity and reconciliation. The Prime Minister has asked the Governor to keep her closely informed of his discussions with the political leaders following the announcement of the election results and [will be in touch further with Walls] to consider how our common objective of a stable future for Rhodesia can best be achieved. We intend to assist in any way we can with the problems involved in the transition to independence. In the meantime the Prime Minister urges Walls, in the strongest terms, to counsel his colleagues to show calm and restraint; it is only on that basis that we can work successfully together for a government with broad support under which all the people of Rhodesia will continue to feel secure in their future.

CARRINGTON
NNNN

SECRET

Foreign and Commonwealth Office

London SW1A 2AH

3 March 1980

Dear Michael,

Rhodesia: Message from General Walls

The Foreign and Commonwealth Secretary discussed with the Prime Minister yesterday evening the message from General Walls. Lord Carrington recommends that instructions should be sent as soon as possible today for the Governor or Sir A Duff to reply to Walls on the Prime Minister's behalf. The purpose will be to calm and reassure Walls, without giving hostages to fortune about the precise composition of the government, or our own role after the election results are known.

The implied threats in Walls' letter are worrying and no doubt reflect the strong pressure which Walls is under from within the armed forces. But he has played a helpful role over the past week or so both in bringing together the forces of the two sides and in establishing the foundation for a coalition between Mr Nkomo, Bishop Muzorewa and the Whites. He will be aware of the grave consequences of any action to overturn the election results; and it is unlikely that he has any firm assurances of South African support. While the risk of hasty action in the event of a Mugabe landslide undoubtedly exists and there is evidence of contingency plans in the Rhodesian forces to deal with the PF in the assembly places, we have no grounds to think that any action is imminent.

Lord Carrington considers that the Prime Minister's reply should so far as possible seek to reassure Walls and to recognise the vital part he has played in recent days. Clearly he cannot be given any specific commitment about the formation of a government. But provided Mugabe gets less than 40 seats (ie short of a majority of the African seats), the sort of coalition between Nkomo, Muzorewa and the Whites which Walls is seeking to promote would be a perfectly legitimate objective, though it might be possible to take some elements of ZANU(PF) into it. Walls should therefore be reassured that we share the goal of a broad, moderate and stable government which contributes to national unity and reconciliation.

/If Mugabe

M O'D B Alexander Esq
10 Downing Street

SECRET

SECRET

If Mugabe gets more than 40 seats, the situation will be much more difficult; and it will be hard to avoid a situation in which he does not have a leading role in the government. Walls and the Whites could probably be brought to accept some form of national government, though their suspicion of Mugabe is such that we should have to approach it carefully, emphasising the need for unity and reconciliation after the elections and for a broadly based government which reflected all viewpoints in the country.

If Mugabe wins an absolute majority, then our aim will again have to be a national government in which all parties are represented, and Mugabe's influence thus diluted. It will be very difficult to bring the Whites to accept such a government in which Mugabe would inevitably have a very prominent role, and the risks of a White reaction would be strongest in these circumstances. But it is probably the best outcome we could hope for. Our role in such a case would be difficult. But to reassure the Whites we would have to indicate that we stood ready to help with the problems involved in the transition to independence (though we would not envisage extending the Governor's stay by more than a matter of days and certainly not beyond independence).

I enclose a draft telegram of instructions for the Prime Minister's approval.

Yours ever

Roderic Lyne

(R M J Lyne)
Private Secretary

SECRET

Ed Bird grew up on his parents' farm in Bembesi in Matabeleland, Rhodesia in the 1950s. He joined the British South Africa Police (BSAP) in 1964. After a year's overseas sabbatical in 1971, he rejoined 'The Force', still in uniform with the District Branch stationed in the Victoria Province. In October 1972, he was attached to Special Branch (SB) and deployed, with only a constable as company, to the Zambezi Valley in the Centenary/Sipolilo area, where he soon established that the area had been heavily infiltrated and subverted by ZANLA. Phase II of the 'bush war' began in earnest in December that year with the opening of Operation *Hurricane*. Bird was then posted to Dotito in the Mount Darwin area, again on his own, where he worked closely with the embryonic Selous Scouts in the new 'pseudo' concept. After a brief CID probation, he was posted to the Prime Minister's Office at SB HQ as the SB liaison officer to the Selous Scouts in March 1974. In 1976, he was posted to SB Beitbridge, where he stayed until his transfer to Gwanda in late 1979. He resigned from the BSAP in May 1980 and after a spell of gold mining, moved to South Africa. Married to Patsy, with two daughters, Tracey and Diane, he lives on the South Coast of KwaZulu-Natal.

On 26 March, a Mr Joubert was ambushed by terrorists on Bishopstone Estates. Although the vehicle was hit several times, Joubert and his party managed to escape unharmed.

On 27 March, elements of the Rhodesian Defence Regiment located a landmine in the Diti TTL. Army engineers were called in and successfully lifted a wooden box mine of British manufacture.

On 28 March, two full Wards Transport petrol tankers travelling north on the Beitbridge–Bulawayo road were stopped by approximately twenty terrorists. After being robbed of valuables, the two drivers were ordered to leave the area. The terrorists then either fired rifle grenades or RPG rockets, followed by bursts of automatic fire into the tankers. Both tankers caught fire and were completely destroyed. Approximately fifty metres of tar on the main road sustained substantial damage but was confined to half the road only, ensuring that the road could stay open. Elements of 1 Indep Company conducted follow-up operations.

On 29 March, a Roads Department vehicle detonated a landmine in the Maramani TTL, resulting in two employees receiving serious injuries, necessitating their casevac to hospital in Bulawayo by air.

Later that day, on 29 March, an Internal Affairs convoy detonated a further landmine in the same area which resulted in two locals receiving minor wounds. Both were casevaced to Beitbridge for treatment.

On 30 March, a military vehicle detonated a landmine in the Diti TTL. Four members of D Company 2RR received minor injuries and were casevaced to Beitbridge for treatment.

On 2 April, elements of D Company 2RR made contact with an unknown number of terrorists in the Diti TTL. During the engagement one terrorist was killed and one D Company soldier sustained serious injuries which necessitated his casevac, firstly by helicopter to Beitbridge and then by fixed-wing aircraft to Bulawayo. During a sweep of the area after the contact, one RPG-7 rocket launcher plus six rockets, one AKM and two AK-47 assault rifles, plus a substantial quantity of war matériel were recovered. Sadly, the wounded D Company member, Corporal Richard Lionel Sanderson-Smith, died on 18 April from wounds received in this action.

On 3 April, Francis Zindoga, the co-minister of justice, law and order in the transitional government of Bishop Abel Muzorewa, was travelling in a combined army, police and Internal Affairs convoy when the convoy came under ambush attack. The minister had been visiting the Mapai protected village in the Mtetengwe TTL. Shortly after leaving the PV, the lead vehicle in the convoy stopped in order to inspect a suspicious hole in the road when the convoy came under immediate attack by six terrorists in ambush position on the side of the road. Apart from the normal automatic weapons, the terrorists made use of a 60mm mortar. The fire was ineffective and, on being engaged by members in the convoy, the terrorists broke off the engagement. Minister Zindoga and his escort escaped unscathed.

Also on 3 April, a northbound Stuttafords removal van was ambushed by an unknown number of terrorists on the main Beitbridge–Bulawayo road. The vehicle received several strikes and two of the occupants were wounded. The driver continued to Mazunga where he sought assistance with the two wounded passengers being casevaced by road to Gwanda hospital.

Again, on 3 April, an Internal Affairs convoy was ambushed by an unknown number of terrorists in the Diti TTL. While under attack, one of the Intaf vehicles detonated a landmine which added to the confusion. The occupants of the mine-damaged vehicle, two of whom had received minor injuries, managed to scramble to safety and the rest of the convoy was able to drive through the killing ground. Fire was returned and the terrorists broke off the engagement. The two minor casualties were casevaced by road to Beitbridge.

On 4 April, an Internal Affairs patrol discovered the body of two local teenagers in the Mtetengwe TTL. Both were bound with wire, one had been shot through the head and the other through the chest. It was assessed that the murders had been committed during the night. Notes written by the terrorists and left at the scene accused the two boys of being members of the Venda Militia who were conducting reconnaissance patrols at the time of their capture. 1 Indep Company deployed on follow-up operations.

Also, during the late afternoon of 4 April, a lone terrorist stopped a tractor and trailer on Lesanth Ranch and, after destroying both tractor and trailer by fire, handed the farm workers a letter to present to owner Les Mitchell in which his life was threatened. Elements of C Company 2RR, who were in close proximity to the scene, reacted immediately. Spoor of several terrorists was located, which was followed for some distance before the terrorists were sighted and fired upon. Night was rapidly approaching and the terrorists escaped unscathed. One German-made 7.62 NATO G3 rifle plus two fully-loaded magazines were located after the contact.

On 5 April, Scouter Uniform, while operating in the Maramani TTL and supported by elements of 1 Indep Company, opened fire on two terrorists. The pair was obviously part of a much larger group which then opened up on the security force position. On being engaged, the terrorists broke off contact and absconded. A search of the area resulted in the discovery of the body of one local woman who had been running with the terrorists, as well as an AK-47 assault rifle and other war matériel. Spoor was followed for over three kilometres before being lost because of anti-tracking methods adopted by the terrorists.

Also on 5 April, elements of B Company 2RR located a wooden box mine planted in a road in the Siyoka TTL. Army engineers were called in and, on examination, discovered that the mine had been boosted by ten kilograms of TNT. It was assessed as being too dangerous to move and was detonated *in situ*.

Again, on 5 April, elements of Liebigs security travelling in convoy on the Shobi Block of Liebigs Ranch were ambushed by an estimated six terrorists. One white and one black member of the unit were seriously wounded, necessitating casevac to Bulawayo. Two other less seriously wounded were casevaced to Beitbridge for treatment. The follow-up was conducted by Liebigs security staff.

Yet again, on 5 April, elements of Liebigs security travelling in convoy on the Jopempi Block of Liebigs Ranch were ambushed by an estimated six terrorists. Fire was returned and the terrorists broke off the engagement. No one was injured during this engagement although one of the vehicles was hit. Follow-up operations were conducted by 1 Indep Company.

Once more, on 5 April, in the Siyoka TTL, elements of B Company 2RR shot and killed a local boy who was spotted hiding in thick bush, while the B Company section was following fresh spoor of four terrorists.

Again, on the same day, elements of 1 Indep Company operating in the Chipise TTL shot and killed seven local men who attempted to flee when challenged. Numerous suspected terrorist tracks were located in the immediate vicinity and followed until lost on hard ground.

Yet again, on the same day, elements of D Company 2RR operating in the Diti TTL shot and killed a local man who failed to stop when called upon to do so near the site of a known terrorist base camp.

On 6 April, the southbound Shu Shine bus was stopped by six terrorists on the Bulawayo–Beitbridge road. After relieving the conductor of the collected fare money and robbing the passengers of all their valuables, the terrorist gang permitted the driver to proceed. No follow-up action was taken owing to the lack of available troops.

Also on 6 April, an armed PRAW aircraft, call sign Copper 72, while overflying the Mtetengwe TTL, observed five scotch carts and numerous locals in the area of a known *povo* base. The PRAW aircraft opened fire, killing one of the men. Elements of 1 Indep Company reacted and apprehended eleven locals, three scotch carts and thirty donkeys in the vicinity of the *povo* base. All the donkeys were shot and the three scotch carts destroyed. The eleven locals were taken to protected villages where they were handed over to Internal Affairs administrators.

Again, on 6 April, elements of C Company 2RR, while mounting an ambush in the area of the Bubye farms, opened fire on two terrorists, killing one and wounding the other who managed to escape. One AK-47 assault rifle and an SKS rifle were recovered from the scene. There were no C Company casualties.

On 10 April, an attack was launched on a terrorist base situated on Kayansee Ranch in the Bubye farming area. The attack was spearheaded by the Fire Force, supported by elements of C Company 2RR and 1 Indep Company. Unfortunately, the Fire Force failed to make contact with the terrorists, but elements of C Company in a stop position shot and killed two terrorists fleeing from the base. One AK-47 assault rifle and one SKS Chicom rifle were recovered. That night, C Company ambushed the base and fired on people moving into the base. At first light, the bodies of four local men killed in the ambush were recovered and a boy captured.

Also on 10 April, a battery of artillery 25-pounders fired eight rounds into an occupied *povo* base in the Mtetengwe TTL. Because of the unavailability of troops, the artillery was due to undertake the follow-up on the target the following morning. Unfortunately, the artillery follow-up troops failed to report on the results of their attack, so no results were recorded.

On 11 April, elements of C Company 2RR travelling by vehicle in the Bubye farming area detonated a landmine. There were no casualties.

During the early hours of 13 April, Robin Watson's militia from Mikado Ranch were conducting an inquiry in the Siyoka TTL as to the whereabouts of a wounded terrorist known to have received assistance in a certain kraal. During questioning by the militia, a man from that particular kraal suddenly made a bid for freedom and was shot and killed during his attempt. Elements of 1 Indep Company reacted the following morning and located an AKM assault rifle which was believed to have belonged to the wounded terrorist.

Also on 13 April, elements of C Company 2RR in ambush in the Chipise TTL fired on six locals carrying what appeared to be bundles of wood but what was in reality dried meat. One woman was killed and one wounded and captured. The meat had been obtained by slaughtering cattle stolen from locals living in the PVs and sun-dried in the bush before being transported to the *povo* camps.

Again, on 13 April, elements of A Company 2RR surprised a group of approximately fifteen terrorists who were tracking them in the Chipise TTL. Two terrorists were killed and two AK-47 assault rifles were recovered. One A Company member was slightly wounded in the foot and was casevaced to the clinic in the Tshiturapadzi PV for treatment.

Yet again, on 13 April, a civilian vehicle was stopped by six terrorists and destroyed by fire on Robin Watson's Mikado Ranch.

Once more, on 13 April, elements of 1 Indep Company operating in the Diti TTL shot and killed a local male who failed to stop when called upon to do so.

On the same day, elements of C Company 2RR in the Diti TTL shot and killed a local male who failed to stop when called upon to do so.

Again, on the same day, elements of 1 Indep Company engaged four terrorists sighted in the Diti TTL. Owing to thick bush, only one was accounted for, with the patrol unable to locate his weapon.

Yet again, on the same day, elements of D Company 2RR shot and killed one local male and two local females when they ignored calls to stop.

On 14 April, elements of C Company 2RR operating in the Chipise TTL made contact with three terrorists, killing one and recovering an AK-47 assault rifle and an SKS rifle, as well as other war matériel.

Also on 14 April, as a result of an air reconnaissance conducted by a PRAW aircraft in the Mtetengwe TTL, the Fire Force, manned by 1 Indep Company, attacked a suspected occupied terrorist base. During the attack, four terrorists were killed and two women, one of whom was wearing camouflage and carrying a back pack, were killed. As well as an assortment of war matériel, three SKS rifles and an AK-47 assault rifle were recovered. There were no security force casualties.

Again, on 14 April, elements of 1 Indep Company operating in the Diti TTL made contact with six terrorists. There were no known terrorist casualties and none inflicted on the 1 Indep Company patrol. During the afternoon and after following the terrorist spoor for most of the day, the 1 Indep patrol again came upon the terrorist group, now numbering four, and opened fire on them. One terrorist was killed and one SKS rifle was recovered.

On 15 April, elements of C Company 2RR operating in the Chipise TTL shot and killed a local man and a boy who failed to halt when called upon to do so.

On 18 April, a mobile police patrol operating in the Machuchutu TTL was ambushed by an estimated twenty terrorists using automatic weapons and RPG-2 rockets. The patrol managed to drive through the ambush position without sustaining any injuries.

Also on 18 April, a tractor travelling on Jopempi Block, Liebigs Ranch detonated a landmine, resulting in three labourers being killed. Two others were seriously injured and casevaced by air to Bulawayo, while two with minor injuries were treated locally.

Again, on 18 April, elements of C Company 2RR, operating in the Diti TTL shot and killed a local man who failed to stop when called upon to do so.

Yet again, on 18 April, the 1 Indep Fire Force was deployed to investigate a large *povo* base in the Diti TTL. The base was occupied by terrorists and civilians and in the ensuing contact two men, a woman and a boy were killed in the crossfire. No terrorists were killed and there were no injuries to the security forces.

On 19 April, a lone, unarmed terrorist stopped a Rhodesian Defence Regiment vehicle on the main Beitbridge–Bulawayo main road and surrendered. He then handed over an AKM assault rifle, four magazines, a stick grenade and a medical pack which he had stashed in the bush on the roadside.

Also on 19 April, elements of Liebigs security fired on seven terrorists sighted on Jopempi Block. All the terrorists managed to escape.

Again, on 19 April, a cow detonated a landmine in the Maramani TTL.

On 20 April, elements of C Company 2RR operating in the Diti TTL shot and killed a local man who refused to stop when called upon to do so.

Also on 20 April, a police patrol, travelling in a National Parks vehicle, detonated a landmine near Tuli in the Machuchuta TTL. The mine was assessed as being a wooden box type. There were no injuries.

Again, on 20 April, elements of C Company 2RR manning an OP in the Chipise TTL sighted fourteen terrorists moving west. Apart from the OP personnel, the only other asset readily available was an air force Lynx, armed with two 250-pound bombs and machine guns. Supported by the Lynx, the members of the OP then attacked the terrorist group, with the end result being six terrorists killed and three AK-47 assault rifles and three SKS rifles recovered. A fine result for C Company.

Yet again, on 20 April, elements of 1 Indep Company were following the spoor of forty terrorists on River Ranch heading in a westerly direction toward Nottingham Estates. Around mid-afternoon, the 1 Indep patrol made contact with a group of terrorists and, after a brief firefight, the terrorists broke off the engagement. Spoor was located and followed toward Nottingham. Major Don Price decided to deploy the Fire Force with the intention of cutting off and engaging the terrorists. This worked perfectly and soon 1 Indep Company was engaging a splinter group of five terrorists on Nottingham Estates. After a short contact, all five were dead. One AK-47 and four AKM assault rifles, as well a quantity of war materiel and documents were recovered. There were no security force casualties.

Once more, on 20 April, elements of 1 Indep Company travelling by vehicle in the area of the Masera TTL and River Ranch boundary detonated a landmine assessed as being a wooden box type. There were no casualties.

During the night of 20 April, Liebigs Ranch headquarters at Towla was attacked by an estimated eighteen terrorists using small-arms and rocket fire. The attack was ineffectual as none of the buildings or property was damaged and no casualties were inflicted. The terrorist group broke off their attack when fire was returned. The follow-up was conducted by Liebigs security the following morning but spoor was lost after a kilometre because of anti-tracking methods employed by the terrorists.

On the morning of 21 April, a local man was instantly killed when the bicycle he was riding detonated a landmine at Towla HQ, Liebigs Ranch. On examining the crater, another damaged bicycle was discovered but the rider, if there had been one, was never located. The mine was assessed as being a wooden box type.

Also on 21 April, a mobile police patrol was ambushed by an estimated fifteen terrorists near the Shashi River in the Machuchuta TTL. The vehicle was hit by RPG-2 rockets and small-arms fire but the driver safely managed to clear the killing zone. A patrol officer and a constable were injured in the attack and were subsequently casevaced by air to Bulawayo for treatment.

On 22 April, elements of 1 Indep Company tracked six terrorists into a terrorist base on Wanezi Section, Liebigs Ranch and opened fire. Only one terrorist was killed. During a search of the base, one AK-47 assault rifle, two SKS rifles and a quantity of war matériel, including three RPG-7 rocket projectiles, were recovered.

On 23 April, elements of 1 Indep Company observed fifteen terrorists in the Maramani TTL. Without a minute to lose because of the distance involved, Don Price deployed the Fire Force and was directed by the ground troops onto the terrorist position. In the ensuing contact, eleven terrorists were killed and one was captured. Three AKM and three AK-47 assault rifles, six SKS rifles and one RPG-7 rocket launcher were recovered. There were no security force casualties. Another successful contact with outstanding results.

Also on 23 April, elements of C Company 2RR had a fleeting contact with an unknown number of terrorists in the Machuchuta TTL. There were no casualties on either side. However, later that day, another C Company 2RR patrol made contact with a different terrorist group in the same TTL. During the ensuing contact, the C Company patrol accounted for eight terrorists killed and the recovery of one AKM and seven AK-47 assault rifles, one SKS rifle and a quantity of war matériel. There were no security force casualties. The troops involved in this action did a first-rate job, considering they were without air support.

On 24 April, elements of Liebigs security made contact with an unknown number of terrorists on Wanezi Block, Liebigs Ranch. There were no casualties on either side.

On 25 April, elements of 1 Indep Company sighted and attacked two terrorists in the Machuchuta TTL. One terrorist was killed and an AK-47 assault rifle and various items of war matériel were recovered.

Also on 25 April, a Swift Transport vehicle on the Beitbridge–Bulawayo road was ambushed by terrorists who attacked the vehicle with automatic and rocket fire. One of the RPG-7 rockets struck the engine, bringing it to an immediate stand still. The terrorists then vacated the scene. The driver and crew were uninjured.

During the early hours of 26 April, a northbound train detonated a boosted landmine in the area of Lesanth Siding and came under immediate attack by an unknown number of terrorists. The explosion ripped up forty metres of track, causing a section of the train to derail: five sugar wagons and three empty carriages were derailed and extensively damaged. Luckily, only one of the train's crew was slightly injured. Elements of 1 Indep Company reacted at first light.

Also on 26 April, acting on information, elements of Liebigs security made contact with a lone terrorist on Mazunga Ranch, killing him and recovering his AK-47 assault rifle, magazines and ammunition.

Again, on 26 April, a water pump on Robin Watson's Mikado Ranch was destroyed by thirteen terrorists, who afterwards returned to the Siyoka TTL.

On 27 April, elements of the police and C Company 2RR travelling in convoy were ambushed by a large group of terrorists in the Machuchuta TTL. One of the mine-protected vehicles was hit in the gearbox by a rocket, immobilizing it immediately. Enemy fire was returned at close quarters, causing the terrorists to break off the engagement and head for safer pastures. One C Company member was hit in the leg and arm by shrapnel and was casevaced by air to the Gwanda hospital for treatment.

On 28 April, elements of 1 Indep Company operating in the Siyoka TTL shot and killed a local man hiding in thick bush. He had refused to surrender when called upon to do so.

Also on 28 April, elements of 1 Indep Company operating in the Siyoka TTL had a fleeting contact with two terrorists who managed to escape unhurt. There were no 1 Indep Company casualties.

Again, on 28 April, elements of C Company 2RR made contact with an estimated ten terrorists in the Siyoka TTL. During the engagement, two terrorists were killed. With foresight, Don Price headed for the action in the K-Car. Once overhead, he directed the ground forces who again made contact with the terrorists, killing another one. Two AK-47 assault rifles, one SKS rifle and a quantity of war matériel were recovered.

Yet again, during the late afternoon of 28 April, elements of C Company 2RR were attacked by an unknown number of terrorists in the Siyoka TTL. Fire was returned and the Fire Force, now positioned on Robin Watson's Mikado Ranch, reacted. However, by the time the Fire Force arrived overhead, the terrorists had broken off the engagement and scattered. Owing to fading light, the follow-up petered out, and after replenishing the ground forces with ammunition, the Fire Force returned to base. There were no security force casualties.

The next morning, 29 April, elements of C Company 2RR were once more in action when they were again attacked by an estimated twenty terrorists in the Siyoka TTL. The terrorists' fire was returned, causing them to break off the engagement and scatter. The Fire Force was deployed to assist but by the time it arrived overhead, the terrorists were long gone. Two local men were killed during the initial stage of the engagement when they appeared to be leading the enemy onto the C Company position. There were no security force casualties.

During the night of 30 April, an estimated twenty terrorists attacked the homestead on Lutope Section, Liebigs Ranch. The attack lasted approximately twenty minutes, during which time a PRAW aircraft was deployed to overfly the scene of the attack: more of a morale-boosting exercise than anything else. At the same time, elements of Liebigs security proceeded by vehicle to the scene to assist. On their approach, one of the vehicles detonated a landmine, fortunately only slightly injuring one of the reaction team. None of the homestead defenders was injured.

On 1 May, terrorists destroyed a water pump and engine in the Mtetengwe TTL with PRG-7 rocket fire.

On 2 May, elements of Guard Force opened fire on a group of approximately thirty terrorists whom they observed crossing the main Beitbridge–Bulawayo road. Elements of 1 Indep Company were deployed to undertake follow-up operations, which resulted in the recovery of a TMH-57 landmine and various other items of war matériel. There were no casualties on either side during the initial engagement.

On 4 May, a PRAW aircraft overflying the Mtetengwe TTL sighted six terrorists and kept them under observation until an air force Lynx aircraft arrived on the scene. The PRAW pilot directed the Lynx pilot onto the terrorist position and, once fixed, the Lynx then dropped a frantan bomb. Owing to a lack of troops, the strike was never checked so results are unknown.

On 6 May, elements of Internal Affairs located and lifted a wooden box mine in the Mtetengwe TTL. No injuries were sustained.

On 7 May, twenty terrorists broke into the farm store on Nottingham Estates and stole a large quantity of foodstuffs and clothing, before heading off in the direction of the Masera TTL. Elements of 1 Indep Company conducted the follow-up without success.

On 10 May, two diesel locomotives and several carriages were derailed near Lesanth Siding after detonating an explosive device placed on the line. Three railway employees were slightly injured. Elements of army engineers reacted and located several anti-personnel mines scattered at the scene. Obviously, the terrorists were hoping that the AP mines would be activated by security force personnel walking around at night; had they buried them, they themselves would have been at risk when further sabotage attacks were carried out.

On 11 May, a Veterinary Department vehicle was ambushed by an estimated fifteen terrorists on Bishopstone Estates. Fortunately, the driver was able to drive through the killing ground unscathed, as were the other occupants. The vehicle only received one strike.

At midday on 14 May, a lone terrorist stopped the Chibuku beer truck on the main Beitbridge–Bulawayo road. He asked the driver to transport him to the West Nicholson police station where he intended surrendering. The Chibuku driver refused to accommodate him, explaining that he was not permitted to carry passengers. The terrorist then requested that the driver report his presence to the police at West Nicholson and that he would stay where he was until one o'clock when he would leave. The report was duly made at West Nicholson but by the time a reaction force arrived at the rendezvous, the terrorist was no longer there. At half past two that afternoon, the terrorist pitched up at the Scouter Zulu police base on Mikado Ranch where he surrendered and handed over his SKS rifle, a stick grenade, webbing and ammunition.

Also on 14 May, a cow detonated a landmine in the Masera TTL.

Just before nine o'clock on the night of 14 May, Shabwe protected village in the Mtetengwe TTL was attacked by a large group of terrorists using 75mm recoilless rifles, 82mm mortars, 60mm mortars, medium and light machine guns and small arms. The attack was ineffective, causing only minor damage to a few huts. A battery of artillery reacted with their 25-pounders, breaking the spirit of the terrorists and causing them to break off the engagement. Ballistic results of expended cartridge cases recovered at the scene showed that eighteen AK-47/AKM assault rifles, fifteen SKS rifles, one RPD machine gun and one trailed Goryunov medium machine gun had been used in the attack. Because of its intensity, the attack could be heard from Beitbridge. No one was injured.

On 18 May, two Swift Transport removal vehicles were stopped by fourteen terrorists on the main Bulawayo–Beitbridge road. Both vehicles and contents were completely destroyed by fire. The drivers were released unharmed.

On 19 May, an unknown number of terrorists fired on a Roads Department grader repairing roads in the Mtetengwe TTL. No injuries were sustained by the Roads Department employees and no damage was caused to the grader.

Also on 19 May, the second-in-command of the Guard Force, who had been off duty and was returning to his post on Nottingham Estates in his private car, was ambushed by an unknown number of terrorists on the estate. He managed to drive through the ambush position unscathed and reported for duty. Elements of 1 Indep Company reacted.

On 21 May, elements of Guard Force located a buried landmine in the Diti TTL. Army engineers reacted and destroyed the mine *in situ*.

On 22 May, a Scouter Zulu vehicle detonated a boosted landmine in the Siyoka TTL, injuring one patrol officer and three constables. The patrol officer and two of the constables were casevaced to Bulawayo for treatment and the one constable with minor injuries was casevaced by road to Gwanda.

Also on 22 May, the Fire Force was fired on in the Siyoka TTL as it was returning to Beitbridge at last light. No action could be taken as it was too dark.

On 28 May, a Liebigs Ranch Land Cruiser detonated a landmine on Shobi Section, resulting in three occupants receiving injuries; they were casevaced to Gwanda for treatment.

On 29 May, a scotch cart being pulled by donkeys detonated a landmine in the Siyoka TTL. The explosion killed two young boys who were the sole occupants of the cart.

On 30 May, a Rhodesia Railways train detonated an explosive device on the Beitbridge–Rutenga line, approximately twenty kilometres from Beitbridge. The two locomotives and ten wagons were derailed, with the tracks extensively damaged. The number of casualties was not recorded.

On 1 June, elements of Liebigs security were following terrorist spoor from the Jopempi Block into the Siyoka TTL where they sighted and fired on three terrorists. A firefight developed and the commander of the Liebigs unit, Jerry Gaze, was killed and one of his men wounded. This was a big blow to all who knew Jerry, who was really the salt-of-the-earth type and a very likeable man.

On 1 June, in what was known as the 'Internal Settlement', Rhodesia officially became Zimbabwe–Rhodesia, with the new prime minister, Bishop Abel Muzorewa, leading the African National Council government. Muzorewa had won a landslide victory during the general election held in 1978. His government had worked alongside the outgoing Rhodesian Front government ministers for a period of time before assuming complete control. The only problem with the 1978 election was that the two crucial parties – ZAPU under Joshua Nkoma and ZANU under Robert Mugabe – had refused to take part, vowing to continue the fight until total capitulation. If anything, the war was to intensify during the coming months while the world refused to recognize the newly elected government.

Shortly before midnight on 1 June, the District Commissioner's rest camp on the Shashi River in the Maramani TTL was attacked by an estimated twenty terrorists using 82mm mortars, 60mm mortars, RPG-2 rockets, 3.5-inch 'bazooka' rockets and small arms. Fire was returned and after approximately twenty minutes, the terrorists broke off their attack. There were no security force casualties, but one labourer was killed and two women received minor injuries. From ballistics of the expended cartridge cases recovered from the terrorist positions, it was established that twenty-eight AK-47 assault rifles, six SKS rifles, one RPD machine gun and one Tokarev pistol had been used in the attack: a substantial armoury.

On 2 June, a Scouter Zulu vehicle detonated a landmine in the Siyoka TTL. There were no casualties.

Also on 2 June, a civilian mine-protected vehicle detonated a landmine on Bishopstone Estates, resulting in minor injuries to three of the occupants. That night, a group of fifteen terrorists entered the compound and instructed the work force to leave the estate and to emphasize their point they fired off a 60mm mortar bomb, with some firing their rifles. They then left the compound. No one was injured during this incident.

On 3 June, a Shu Shine bus was stopped by an estimated twenty terrorists on the main Bulawayo–Beitbridge road. The driver, conductor and passengers were then robbed of all valuables, after which they were permitted to proceed unmolested. The incident occurred during the late afternoon and by the time the report was made at Beitbridge, it was dark so no follow-up operation was undertaken.

On 5 June, a scotch cart detonated a landmine in the Siyoka TTL, killing the driver.

Also on 5 June, elements of Liebigs security travelling by vehicle on Jopempi Block sighted and engaged ten terrorists. The terrorists returned fire before fleeing the contact area. None of the Liebigs staff was injured. That night, a diesel water pump was destroyed by terrorists operating on Jopempi Block.

On 7 June, elements of a 2RR company made contact with nine terrorists in the Siyoka TTL. During the initial contact, five terrorists were killed and, on arrival of the Fire Force, the remaining four were eliminated. Eight AK-47 assault rifles, one SKS rifle and a quantity of war matériel were recovered. There were no security force casualties but two African women running with the terrorists were wounded and casevaced by air to Beitbridge for treatment.

On 8 June, a Roads Department vehicle operating in the Diti TTL detonated a landmine, fortunately with no casualties.

Also on 8 June, terrorists burned one hundred and twenty bales of cotton on Bishopstone Estates. Owing to the delay in the reporting of this incident, no follow-up action was taken.

On 9 June, a Rhodesia Railways security trolley detonated an explosive device on the line in the area of Lesanth Siding. The trolley derailed but no serious injuries were sustained by the occupants. Two metres of track and three sleepers were damaged. Army engineers, on scene at first light, assessed the explosive device as being two landmines.

On 10 June, elements of Guard Force engaged in the recovery of the Roads Department vehicle damaged by a mine on 8 June in the Diti TTL detonated a landmine, slightly injuring one of the occupants who was subsequently casevaced to Beitbridge for treatment.

•••

I will quote the following entry directly from the Incident log, as reported by the police investigation team to the Joint Operations Centre Beitbridge on 12 June: "11/6/79 entry 277/79 MURDER – Occurred 1210 hrs at QF616495 (Sentinel Ranch) when African manager, Johannes SODA, was shot and killed by two CTs. Several intermediate cartridge cases were recovered at scene. Ballistics – 1 SKS no previous traces."

Johannes Soda first came to my attention at the beginning of the year when his name was mentioned in a captured terrorist's notebook. Thereafter, it began cropping up more and more, especially in documents recovered from contacts in the Diti and Chipse TTLs. In one captured document, mention was made of a food delivery made by Soda near the Bubye River, consisting of six hundred pounds of maize meal and cigarettes. I was aware that Soda was the Sentinel Ranch manager and, after investigating further, I discovered that the owner, John Bristow, had farming concerns in the Nuanetsi area as well, and that Soda delivered rations to Bristow's labourers there on a weekly basis, by vehicle.

Bristow was a wealthy absentee landlord who lived in the Louis Trichardt area the Mtetengwe TTL were ambushed by approximately ten terrorists. Fire was returned, causing the terrorists to flee. There were no militia or civilian casualties and elements of Guard Force undertook the follow-up.

Yet again, on 11 September, while patrolling on Kayalami Ranch in the Bubye River farming area, elements of 1 Indep Company were attacked by a large group of terrorists using small arms and rockets. Fire was returned and the terrorists broke off the engagement. A check of the area revealed that four local men running with the terrorists had been killed. There were no 1 Indep Company casualties.

Once more, on 11 September, elements of 1 Indep Company travelling by vehicle detonated a wooden box mine in the Diti TTL. There were no casualties.

On 12 September, elements of Guard Force and the Venda Militia travelling by vehicle in the Diti TTL detonated an unidentified landmine. There was one minor casualty who was casevaced by road to Beitbridge for treatment.

Also on 12 September, late reports received for 9 and 11 September indicated that terrorists had destroyed a borehole and water pumps in the Mtetengwe and Diti TTLs.

On 15 September, Scouter Yankee travelling by vehicle in the Diti TTL detonated a landmine, resulting in two minor casualties who were casevaced to Beitbridge for treatment.

Also, just after dark 15 September, Guard Force reported that the protected village at Chaswingo in the Diti TTL was under small-arms and mortar attack and that seven mortar bombs had detonated inside the strongpoint of the PV. Elements of 1 Indep Company reacted at first light but could find no evidence of an attack or any indication that mortar bombs had detonated in the strongpoint.

On 16 September, elements of 1 Indep Company operating in the Diti TTL located and followed the spoor of two terrorists. The tracks were followed for some distance when the patrol was attacked by an estimated twenty terrorists. Fire was returned before the terrorists eventually broke off the engagement and fled. The 1 Indep Company patrol was resupplied with ammunition before last light. There were no injuries on either side.

On 17 September, nine head of cattle were slaughtered on Shobi Block of Liebigs Ranch and the meat carried into the Mtetengwe TTL.

Also on 17 September, while undertaking a river-line sweep in the Diti TTL, elements of 1 Indep Company were ambushed by an estimated twenty terrorists from a distance of fifty metres. The terrorists broke off the engagement when fire was returned. There were no casualties.

Again, on 17 September, elements of 1 Indep Company operating an OP in the Diti TTL observed three African men running in a northerly direction. An airstrike was called for and the target attacked. A follow-up patrol discovered the bodies of two women and a boy who had been killed in the airstrike.

On 18 September, elements of 1 Indep Company fired on locals who refused to stop when called upon to do so. Three men and two women were killed.

On 19 September, elements of Liebigs security located a terrorist base on Jopempi Block of Liebigs Ranch. Robin Watson's armed PRAW aircraft attacked the suspected base and came under ground attack before the terrorists fled. The aircraft was hit three times by small-arms fire. No one was injured during the engagement.

Also on 19 September, eleven terrorists destroyed a water pump on Sentinal Ranch and then instructed the labourers to leave the ranch. A total of nine left and returned to their rural homes.

On 20 September, elements of Guard Force travelling in Chipise TTL located a buried landmine. Army engineers were deployed and recovered the mine.

Also on 20 September, a police patrol operating in the Siyoka TTL engaged a group of four terrorists in a running firefight, but without casualties on either side. The patrol then followed tracks for approximately three kilometres before losing them. While attempting to relocate the spoor, the patrol was ambushed by the terrorists. Fire was returned before the terrorists broke off the engagement and withdrew, again with no casualties on either side.

On 21 September, a Veterinary Department vehicle detonated a landmine on Towla Section, Liebigs Ranch, while driving slowly past a herd of cattle. The cattle herdsman was killed in the explosion and minor injuries were inflicted on three of the vehicle passengers.

Also on 21 September, elements of Guard Force sighted eight terrorists in the Chipise TTL and moved into a position to attack them. The terrorists were then engaged at a distance of approximately sixty metres. The contact was unsuccessful, with no casualties on either side.

On 23 September, a terrorist surrendered to labourers on Sentinal Ranch, requesting that the authorities be contacted. Elements of the police responded and accepted the surrender of the terrorist who handed over an SKS rifle and other equipment.

Also on 23 September, elements of Guard Force located a wooden box mine in the Chipise TTL. Army engineers reacted and destroyed the mine *in situ* as it was suspected to have been boosted.

On 24 September, elements of 1 Indep Company located and followed the spoor of fourteen terrorists in the Diti TTL. After following the tracks for over six hours, the patrol made contact. One terrorist was killed and an AK-47 assault rifle was recovered. The patrol, now reinforced, continued on spoor and located a large recently-deserted terrorist base which was assessed as being occupied at the time of the initial contact.

Also on 24 September, elements of 1 Indep Company made contact with terrorists in the Diti TTL. There were no casualties either side.

On 25 September, terrorists used the telephone-line insulators on the line running from Beitbridge to Bulawayo for target practice and managed to sever the line in several places.

Also on 25 September, elements of 1 Indep Company made contact with seven terrorists in the Diti TTL. Two terrorists were killed in this engagement and two AK-47 assault rifles were recovered. 1 Indep Company suffered no casualties.

Again, during the night of 25 September, a group of ten terrorists entered the compound on Benfur Estates in the Umzingwani farming area. Three men, five women and four young girls were singled out for special treatment: firstly, they were beaten and then their private parts were sadistically burned with open flames in a most barbaric manner. When the terrorists had had enough, they abducted forty farm workers but released thirty-eight of them after making them all strip naked. Two young girls were retained by the group for their pleasure. The twelve tortured souls suffered serious injuries and were casevaced, initially to Beitbridge for immediate treatment and then to the bigger hospitals. Not all of them survived.

On 26 September, elements of 1 Indep Company fired on and killed a lone terrorist in the Diti TTL, recovering an AK-47 assault rifle and a substantial quantity of medicine. There were no security force casualties.

Also on 26 September, elements of 1 Indep Company located the shallow grave of a terrorist who was estimated to have died the week before. He was dressed in denim and wore empty chest webbing. The cause of death was undetermined.

Again, during the night of 26 September, the homestead on Sentinal Ranch came under attack for half an hour by an estimated twenty-five terrorists using rocket and small-arms fire. Elements of Guard Force protecting the homestead suffered two seriously wounded casualties who were casevaced to Bulawayo by air for treatment. Both subsequently recovered after specialized treatment. Interestingly, after Johannes Soda, the Sentinel Ranch manager, had been killed, John Bristow sought farm protection from the DC Lew Watson; in view of the 'murder' of the farm manager, the DC afforded Bristow this protection with a continginent of the Guard Force. It is curious that prior to Soda's elimination Bristow did not require any security.

travelling to Bulawayo boarded an RMS bus at Beitbridge. For some unknown reason, and completely contrary to policy, a joint security force–ZANLA patrol consisting of three SF and eight ZANLA members had established a roadblock on the main Bulawayo road, with all traffic travelling out of convoy being stopped and searched. The guerrillas were from the Juliet Assembly Point in the Siyoka TTL which catered for ZANLA operating in southern Matabeleland and the Beitbridge area, in particular. When the bus was searched, the four turned terrorists were recognized by their former comrades who removed them from the bus. All this took place without interference from the security force element manning the roadblock. The four were taken to the assembly point where they were forced, after severe beatings, to dig a trench which was to become their prison. The hole – described to me by one of Robin Watson's female sources, who visited the AP for sexual purposes – was approximately fifteen feet deep and only accessible by rope ladder. The only time they were pulled out of their hole was for savage beatings. Food was tossed down to them because they were "pigs" and should eat like them. There was no shelter from the elements. The female source claimed that there were at least seven prisoners being held there.

I reported all this to the CID but no one showed any interest. When the assembly points closed down ZANLA simply covered in the trench, burying the prisoners alive. They met their deaths in the most barbaric way possible. This was now a multiple murder case. Was the CID interested? Not a chance. They had more important cases to investigate and prepare for court, like the case against Don, Neill and me, and a case like this could be a political hot potato.

When Mugabe became president of Zimbabwe he granted a general amnesty for atrocities, or war crimes, committed by all protagonists during the war years, which extended up until 31 December 1979. The amnesty did not include the ceasefire period, so criminal acts during this period should have been punishable under the law. It is a funny old world: there I was receiving a pardon for the assassination of Johannes Soda, but having to face a court of law for not paying Rh$100 before I shot an elephant.

My discharge from the police force took effect on 1 May and I must admit that I was a very bitter man indeed. I reflected over the years, to the night that Steve Acornley and I were sleeping on the Centenary police mess lounge carpet when we were wakened to be informed of the first terrorist attack on a white farm in that area. The date was 21 December 1972 and from that date until the ceasefire I had been more or less continuously involved in the war.

The trial started on Monday, 5 May 1980, before regional magistrate Mr J.H. Wallace in Bulawayo. I had not seen Don Price since he left Beitbridge. He was still serving and still commanded 3 Commando 1RLI. It was good to see him again. He had the big guns with him in the form of advocate Chris Jordaan, who after the trial would be appointed a state council. I was confident that no court could convict us, in view of the procedure adopted by Lew Watson over the years. In my opinion, technically, Lew should have been reprimanded for permitting the hunting practice of 'shoot now, pay later', a facility, which I might add, was much appreciated at the time.

However, in spite of my confidence, I engaged Mike Mcgoey to defend me. Mike was a major with 6th Battalion the Rhodesian Regiment. I had worked with him on many an occasion when he was deployed with his company in the Beitbridge area. I was supported by my brother Ken, and Don and Neill by an RLI sergeant-major. Allum, through Blacker, was represented by Detective Inspector Paul May. Other than the police court orderly, they all attended the trial on a daily basis. May's job was to report on the day's proceedings to Blacker, who would then pass the information onto the commissioner.

Thanks to Dave Blacker and his contacts at the *Bulawayo Chronicle*, the court case was sensationalized. We were the lead story the following day up until the Friday edition. My uncle, Martin Boyd, worked at the *Chronicle* and he too was convinced that we would be found guilty. He even asked if I had sufficient funds to pay the anticipated fine on a guilty verdict.

On Friday afternoon, 9 May, Mr Wallace found all three of us not guilty and dismissed the case. The elderly police court orderly who had sat through the proceedings began to clap, which was taken up by everyone else, except the public prosecutor, and Mr Wallace who left the court with a wry smile.

Paul May left the court in a hurry. I did not envy his job of notifying Blacker of the verdict; the old saying 'Don't shoot the messenger' sprang to mind. The *Bulawayo Chronicle* published an article on the outcome of the trial, not much bigger than a domestic notice, in the Saturday edition which was in complete contrast to the Friday edition coverage.

Although I had expected the not-guilty verdict, I was relieved that the ordeal was over. It had been very taxing sitting in the dock, day after day for five stressful days. Before I left court, I gave Mike Mcgoey one further instruction: to write to "that prick" the commissioner and inform him that if my promotion to detective inspector was not forthcoming, he would face my wrath in civil court.

In due course I was issued with a new certificate of service which indicated that I had left the BSAP as a detective inspector and received back pay from the time I was eligible for promotion to that rank. P.K. Allum, in his spite, refused to amend my conduct rating and I remained classified with the worst option. I suppose I could have taken legal action against him but decided he just was not worth the effort. Another omission I discovered years later was that Allum had petulantly instructed that the records not be amended to indicate that I had left the force with the rank of detective inspector. So my rank remains, on record, as having been discharged as a detective section officer.

It was a sour end to my police career.

CONFIDENTIAL

INCIDENT LOG : BEIT BRIDGE.

SPECIAL BRANCH
B.S.A. POLICE

DIARY

Page No.: 13/77

FORM S.B. 10.
B.S.A.P.—20M—24-3-76.

Date	No.	Details	Cross References and Index
13/8/77	114 C	Crusader c/s 83 C had contact with estimated 5 C.T.'s at QF 909667 Mtetengwe TTL. One terr killed and AK recovered from the scene. (See details from S.B. Diary)	SITHOLE
	M	Btw 1200-1400 Hrs on this date a civilian vehicle was stopped on the Pande Mine road. The vehicle was taken some distance into the bush by the C.T's where the occupants of the truck were taken into the bush and were bayoneted and shot. One of the AMA recovered from the scene made the report to SF that were reacting to the scene. Same brought into Beit Bridge where he recieved medical treatment.	CHINANA
	LM	c/s Mantle India located Landmine at TL 271428. Holdfast deployed to the scene and the LM was lifted and brought through to Beit Bridge.	CHINANA
14/8/77	115 R	Report recieved from Driver of Super Express Bus Service to the effect that at approx 17.50 at QF 956 488. The bus was en route to Beit Bridge when he was stopped by a lone terr. The terr asked if there were any CID details on the bus and them releived the conductor of the money that was held for the bus takings. The terr claimed that he was ZAPU and showed the driver a photo of Nkomo, he then departed.	SITHOLE
15/8/77	116 VA	This date at approx 13.50 Hrs Lighthouse escort were ambushed on the Tshuturipasi Road by an estimated 15 terrs at TL 151535. Mtetengwe ttl. Fire initiated by three terrs who stepped into the road and then fire was directed at the vehicles from both sides of the road, one D.A. was injured in the leg not serious cas to Beit Bridge.	CHINANA
18/8/77	S	Report recieved this date to the effect that terrs had filled in the Dip at Malala RF 068 567. Two propaganda notes were left at the scene Unknown how many terrs involved.	SITHOLE

CONFIDENTIAL

CONFIDENTIAL

Page No.: 19/7

INCIDENT LOG : BEIT BRIDGE.

SPECIAL BRANCH

B.S.A. POLICE

DIARY

Date	No.	Entry	Cross References and Index
5/12/77	152	Acorn Minor with Scouter Zulu had contact with an unknown number of terrs at QG 015 177 (SIYOKA TTL) One terr was killed and another was wounded but made good his escape. There were no SF casualties.	
7/12/77	153 VA	At 1450 this date Lighthouse vehicles were ambushed at RF 063 495 (MTETENGWE TTL) by an unknown number of terrs using small-arms and motar fire. There were no casualtiess on either side, C/S 1F, 1 G and 1D (A COY 6RR) deployed to scene.	
8/12/77	154 AIR ATTCK	At 1000hrs this date a lighthouse aircraft was fired upon in the vicinity of SL 975 455 (MTETENGWE TTL) shortly after takeoff from the Beit Bridge airstrip. Elms of A COY 6RR deployed to area.	
8/12/77	155 LM	At 2210 hours at TL 130548 (Mtetengwe TTL) Guard Force vehicle struck landmine with right front wheel. Vehicle number LM 1107.	
9/12/77	156 C	At 1700 hours at TL 124539 (Mtetengwe TTL) Guard Force details guarding vehicle damaged by L/M above, had contact with group of 6 CTs. No follow up carried out as area was frozen at the time.	
13/12/77	157 C	At 1745 hrs. at TL 133 322 (DITI TTL) c/s 1F (B Coy 6RR) whilst moving into night position came under fire from 12 CTs. Fire returned and no casualties on either side. Sparrows Deployed this am and tracks followed to TL 124 327 where lost. Possible that FNs were used by terrs. Investigations continue.	
14/12/77	158 Sighting	At 1500 hrs. at RF 084474 (Main Beitbridge to Byo Road) Security Force Member on leave sighted 6 CTs crossing the road from East to West. c/s 1 (A Coy 6RR) deployed.	
14/12/77	159 R.	Late report received that at 0715hrs. this date at QF 8962 (Beitbridge Farming Area) SHU SHINE Bus 116 stopped by lone terr carrying AK and dressed in dirty tatterred green uniform, and robbed of $3,00. Conductor handed 3 x 7,62 inter rounds. No follow up due to delay of report.	

CONFIDENTIAL

CONFIDENTIAL

Page No.: 9/78

INCIDENT LOG : BEITBRIDGE.

SPECIAL BRANCH
B.S.A. POLICE

DIARY

FORM S.B. 10.
B.S.A.P.—20M—9-6-76.

Cross References and Index:

1973·EA 2484 (?)

Date	No.	Entry
7/3/78	31	At 0250 hrs. this a.m. at TL 138582 (Mtetengwe TTL) C/S 41 (D Coy 6RR) were guided into a terr base, by local supplied to them by Scouter Yankee. Contact was initiated by terrs. and fire returned. Sweep of area at first light revealed that 1 A/F/A running (sleeping) with terrs killed and 1 AK recovered with 6 mags, together with large amount of clothing blankets, pots and documents. It is thought that 2 terrs may have been wounded. (listics on the overed AK - does match previous es.)
9/3/78	32	Report received from Crusdaer 5, at Bueye that the Bar G Ranch, at TL 565900 (Bubeye Farming Area) homestead has been gutted by terrorists. Interrogations revela that homestead gutted on the night of the 7/3/78 by approximately 8 CTs.
10/3/78	33	Crusader callsign 41B (D Coy 6RR) had fleeting contact with 3 C/Ts at TL 195567 (Mtetengwe TTL) no casualties on either side. Tracks followed but later lost due to rain. Notebooks, haversacks and waterbottles recovered, together with 1 AK mag fully charged.
10/3/78	34	Late report from C.W. Kleynhans of JOCO RANCH that one of his herd boys, heard heavy automatic fire coming from the direction of Gongwe Peak at TL 074877.
14/3/78	35	Report received from an A/M/A that he had been beaten by terrs in the Chinavazwime Area, earlier this date, whilst collecting mealie cobs from his lands. He also had word ZANU carved into his forearm with a knife (injury not serious). The terr responsible is named JESUS. Area is RF075575 (Mtetengwe TTL) see diary for further int.
16/3/78	36	At 0700 hours this date, PRAW 82 (Pilot WESSON) fired on in the vicinity of TL504726 (Diti TTL). This occurred whilst he was acting as telstar for Crusader details moving persons into CHASWINGO KEEP. Starboard tanks holed and fuel lost. PRAW landed safely and then flew to Byo. for repairs. Elms of D Coy 6RR deployed into the area, and found base for 30, with body of A/M/A who had been beaten to death. Further enquiries being made.

APPENDIX III
Weapons used in the Beitbridge area of conflict

ZANLA and ZIPRA

AK-47 and AKM

Calibre: 7.62mm
Operation: Gas, selective
Length: 870mm
Barrel length: 410mm
Magazine capacity: 30 rounds
Rate of fire: 600rpm
Range: up to 800m
Weight: 5kg
Ammunition: 7.62x39mm

SKS – SKS 'LANCER' – SKS CHICOM

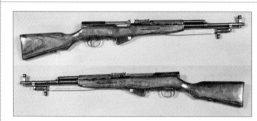

Calibre: 7.62mm
Length: 1021mm
Barrel length: 500mm
Weight: 4kg
Magazine capacity: 10 rounds
Effective range: 400m
Operation: Gas, semi-automatic
Ammunition 7.62x39mm

RPD, PKM AND RPK

Calibre: 7.62mm
Operation: Gas, automatic, air cooled
Weight loaded: 8.8kg
Length: 1053mm
Sight: front: hooded post; rear: adjustable v-notch
Feeding device: 100-round metallic belt carried in drum
Effective range: 800m
Rate of fire: 150rpm
Ammunition: 7.624x39mm

GORYUNOV MMG (ON WHEELS)

Calibre: 7.62mm
Length: 1,150mm
Barrel length: 720mm
Weight: 41kg on wheeled mount
Rate of fire: 500–700rpm
Effective range: 1,100m
Operation: Gas operated
Ammunition: 7.62x54mm

60mm MORTAR WITH BOMBS

Type: 60mm mortar (M2)
Calibre: 60mm
Length of tube: 726mm
Total Weight: 19.5kg
Rate of fire: 18rpm
Maximum range: 1,815m

82mm MORTAR WITH BASE PLATE AND BOMBS

Type: 82mm mortar
Calibre: 82mm
Length of tube: 1,2m
Total Weight: 56kg
Rate of fire: 15–25rpm
Maximum range: 3,040m
Crew: 4

RPG-2 AND RPG-7 WITH ROCKETS AND BOOSTERS

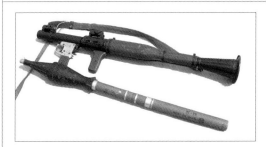

Calibre: 40mm (tube), 85mm (projectile)
Weight: 5.5kg
Length: 95m
Effective range: 300–500m
MV: 120m/sec
Rate of fire: 4–6rpm
Ammunition: Rocket-assisted HEAT grenade
Armour-piercing capability: 3h-37cm/0°

3.5 INCH ROCKET LAUNCHER

Type: 3.5in rocket launcher
Calibre: 3.5in
Length (assembled): 1,524mm
Total Weight: 6.5kg (unloaded)
Rate of fire: 12–18rpm
Maximum range: 823m
Operation: electrical
Crew: 2

12.7mm HMG SINGLE BARREL MOUNTED ON BIPOD

Type: 12.7mm heavy machine gun
Calibre: 12.7mm
Length: 1,656mm
Weight (gun only): 38.15kg
Rate of fire: 485–635rpm
Maximum range: 2,000m

75mm RECOILLESS RIFLE PLUS ROUNDS

Type: M20 75mm recoilless rifle
Calibre: 75mm
Cartridge: 75×408mm
Length: 2,080mm
Total Weight: 52kg
Maximum range: 6,400m

Landmines: TM - TMH - BOX MINES ETC AND AP MINES

Type: TM-38 anti-tank landmine
Length: 220mm
Width: 220mm
Height: 80mm
Weight: 47.5kg
Explosive weight: 2.8kg
Frag range: 400m
Casement: Steel
Explosive: TNT